ESSENTIALS OF TESTING AND ASSESSMENT

A Practical Guide for Counselors,
Social Workers, and Psychologists

SECOND EDITION

Edward S. Neukrug
Old Dominion University

R. Charles Fawcett
University of Virginia

BROOKS/COLE
CENGAGE Learning

Australia • Brazil • Japan • Korea • Mexico • Singapore • Spain • United Kingdom • United States

BROOKS/COLE
CENGAGE Learning™

Essentials of Testing and Assessment, Second Edition

Edward S. Neukrug and
R. Charles Fawcett

Publisher/Executive Editor: Marcus Boggs

Acquisitions Editor: Seth Dobrin

Assistant Editor: Allison Bowie

Editorial Assistant: Rachel McDonald

Marketing Manager: Trent Whatcott

Marketing Assistant: Darlene Macanan

Marketing Communications Manager: Tami Strang

Project Manager, Editorial Production: Jared Sterzer

Creative Director: Rob Hugel

Art Director: Caryl Gorska

Print Buyer: Karen Hunt

Permissions Editor: Bob Kauser

Production Service: Pre-Press PMG

Copy Editor: Pre-Press PMG

Cover Designer: Laurie Anderson

Cover Image: © Stephen Marksen

Compositor: Pre-Press PMG

For product information and technology assistance, contact us at **Cengage Learning Academic Resource Center, 1-800-423-0563**

For permission to use material from this text or product, submit all requests online at **www.cengage.com/permissions**. Further permissions questions can be e-mailed to **permissionrequest@cengage.com**.

Library of Congress Control Number: 2008942957

Student Edition
ISBN-13: 978-0-495-60458-7

ISBN-10: 0-495-60458-5

Brooks/Cole, Cengage Learning
10 Davis Drive
Belmont, CA 94002-3098
USA

Cengage Learning products are represented in Canada by Nelson Education, Ltd.

For your course and learning solutions, visit **academic.cengage.com**.

Purchase any of our products at your local college store or at our preferred online store **www.ichapters.com**.

Printed in Canada
2 3 4 5 6 7 8 9 12 11 10 09

To my father and my brother, the real math experts in the family.
—Ed Neukrug

To my loving wife Laura, who makes my life richer.
—Charlie Fawcett

BRIEF CONTENTS

CONTENTS

CHAPTER 10

Informal Assessment: Observation, Rating Scales, Classification Methods, Environmental Assessment, Records and Personal Documents, and Performance-Based Assessment 217

PREFACE

There's a little secret in the publishing world that they don't like to tell you: The second edition of a book is almost always better than the first. And thus it is with this book—we hope and we think! Why better? Well, first we eliminated a few awkward sentences and dare we say "mistakes" here and there. And, by getting some good input from reviewers, we found out what we were missing and added it. The list of additions was longer than we thought it would be, and included the following:

- A section on forensic evaluation to Chapter 2
- A discussion regarding false positives and false negatives to Chapter 3
- A section on Item Response Theory to Chapter 3
- An expanded discussion on cumulative distributions in Chapter 4
- The addition of Standard Error of the Estimate to Chapter 5
- A piece about the National Assessment of Educational Progress (NAEP) to Chapter 6
- Expanded discussion on high stakes testing in Chapters 2, 5, and 6.
- A section on non-verbal intelligence testing that includes a discussion of the CTONI and UNIT to Chapter 7
- A section on neuropsychological assessment in Chapter 7 including a discussion on the Halsted-Reitan and Boston Process Approach.
- New clinical assessments to Chapter 9: The 16 PF, The NEO PI-R and NEO-FFI, The PAI, and The SASSI
- A section on performance-based assessment to Chapter 10

We also "tweaked" a number of other aspects of the book. For instance, we updated ACAs ethical code to its latest version and we expanded the sections on the ADA and FERPA. We also presented a summary of seven standards of testing in table form to make it easier for the reader to examine and moved the ethical codes to Appendix B. We added some information to the historical figures and events section. We added a bit more information on the use of computers in assessment. We beefed up the sections on No Child Left Behind and high stakes testing. We removed the CPI from Chapter 7. We moved environmental assessment to Chapter 10: Informal Assessment. And of course, we updated all the versions of assessment instruments that were revised since the last edition.

Despite its additions and changes, we still believe the text covers all you can learn in a one semester course on testing and assessment and not more than that—the essentials of testing and assessment. But don't let that fool you. The Essentials includes quite a bit of information! We believe the book is written in a down-to-earth fashion that you will hopefully find interesting. In addition, we offer stories and vignettes that highlight the learning. We are confident the text will offer you all that is needed in an overview course on testing and assessment.

The text is divided into four sections: Section One, History and Current Professional Issues; Section Two, Test Worthiness and Test Statistics; Section Three, Commonly Used Assessment Techniques; and Section Four, Diagnosis and Writing the Assessment Report. Brief definitions of major concepts are provided in the margins, and a glossary highlighting major terms and concepts is included at the end of the book. The following provides a brief overview of the four sections of the text and the appendices.

Section One includes two chapters: Chapter 1, History of Testing and Assessment and Chapter 2, Ethical, Legal, and Professional Issues in Assessment. These chapters offer an overview of the field of testing and assessment and provide a link between the history of assessment and issues that affect us today. Chapter 1 begins by discussing the differences between testing and assessment and points out how their current definitions are directly related to their history. We then trace the history of assessment from ancient history to the development of modern-day assessment instruments. Along the way, we highlight some of the people who were critical to the development of assessment measures and discuss some of the many controversial issues that arose. The chapter nears its conclusion by examining the current categories of assessment instruments, including ability testing (achievement and aptitude testing), personality assessment, and informal assessment. We finish by raising a number of concerns that continue to face us today as we administer assessment instruments.

Chapter 2 is about the complex ethical, legal, and professional issues that are faced frequently by individuals who are assessing others. We begin by recognizing the complexity of ethical decision-making and then identify some important ethical issues, including identifying codes and standards critical to testing and assessment. We go on to discuss the importance of wise and ethical decision-making, and we identify a number of laws that have been passed and lawsuits resolved that impinge on the use of tests and the assessment process. The chapter concludes with a discussion of some important professional issues, including professional associations that address assessment, accreditation standards of professional associations, the relatively new and growing field of forensic evaluation, assessment as a holistic process, issues in cross-cultural assessment, and the importance of embracing the testing and assessment process.

Section Two of the text addresses test worthiness and test statistics. The three chapters that make up this section examine how tests are created, scored, and interpreted. These chapters all use test statistics in some manner to explain the concepts being presented. In this section we demonstrate how collecting and interpreting test data is a deliberate and planned process that involves a scientific approach to the understanding of differences among people.

Chapter 3, on test worthiness, looks at four critical areas in test development and test usage: (1) validity: whether a test measures what it is supposed to measure; (2) reliability: whether the score an individual received on a test is an accurate measure of his or her true score; (3) cross-cultural fairness: whether the score the individual has obtained is a true reflection of the individual, and not a function of cultural bias inherent in the test, and (4) practicality: whether it makes sense to use a test in a particular situation. After examining these four factors, we conclude with a discussion of five steps to use in order to assure test worthiness when selecting a test to administer. The chapter also provides an explanation of two statistics: correlation coefficient and coefficient of determination. We present these statistics in this chapter as they are foundational to understanding much of what is presented in this and future chapters.

Chapter 4 starts with the basics: an examination of raw scores. In this chapter we note that raw scores generally provide little meaningful information about a set of scores, and we provide ways that we can manipulate those scores to make sense out of a set of data. Thus, in this chapter we examine how the following concepts are used to help us understand raw scores: frequency distributions; histograms and frequency polygons; cumulative distributions; the normal curve; skewed curves; measures of central tendency such as the mean, median and mode; and measures of variability, such as the range, interquartile range, and standard deviation.

Chapter 5, on creating new scores to interpret test data, examines how raw scores are converted to what are called "derived" scores so that individuals can more easily understand what their raw scores mean. We first distinguish between norm-referenced and criterion-referenced testing and then go on to discuss derived scores, such as (1) percentiles; (2) standard scores, including: z-scores, T-scores, Deviation IQs, stanines, sten scores, NCE scores, college entrance exam scores (e.g., SATs and ACTs) and publisher-type scores; and (3) developmental norms, such as age comparisons and grade equivalents. The chapter then examines standard error of measurement and standard error of estimate, both of which offer ways of understanding the range in which one's "true score" actually falls. The chapter concludes with a discussion of nominal, ordinal, interval, and ratio scales in which we explore each scale's unique attributes and note that different kinds of assessment instruments use different kinds of scales.

Section Three examines some of the commonly used tests and procedures used in a number of discrete realms of assessment as delineated by the chapters: Chapter 6: Assessment of Educational Ability, Chapter 7: Assessment of Intellectual and Cognitive Functioning, Chapter 8: Career and Occupational Assessment, Chapter 9: Clinical Assessment, and Chapter 10: Informal Assessment.

Chapter 6 examines tests typically given in schools to measure what students have learned and what they are capable of learning. First we define the purposes of tests of educational ability and then identify the various categories of educational ability tests, including survey battery achievement tests, diagnostic tests, readiness tests, and cognitive ability tests. Next, we examine some of the more popular tests in each category. Throughout the chapter we offer some insight into the world of high stakes testing and some of the important issues raised as the result of such laws as No Child Left Behind.

Chapter 7 explores intellectual and cognitive functioning and the tests associated with it. Thus, in this chapter we offer a brief history of both intelligence testing and neuropsychological assessment. In addition, we define intelligence testing and neuropsychological assessment and describe some of the differences between these kinds of assessment. The chapter also offers an overview of some of the more popular models of intelligences and we present some of the more common tests of intelligence and neuropsychological assessment.

Chapter 8 examines the kinds of tests that can help individuals make decisions about their occupational or career path. We begin with an examination of interest inventories, which are a type of personality assessment that generally look at individuals' likes and dislikes as well their personality orientation toward the world of work. We next explore multiple aptitude testing which can help individuals identify their range of skills and abilities that may be important in choosing an occupation. We conclude with a look at some of the more popular special aptitude tests which look at focused areas of ability, such as clerical skills, mechanical skills, artistic skills, and musical ability.

Chapter 9 examines the process of using tests for clinical assessment. We start by underscoring the fact that such assessment has a wide variety of applications and can be an important tool for the clinician or researcher. The chapter then defines clinical assessment and speaks to some of the critical issues that such assessment can address. The meat of the chapter is a review of a number of the more well known and used objective and projective clinical assessment procedures.

Chapter 10 covers informal assessment procedures. We start by defining informal assessment and then identify a number of different kinds of informal assessment techniques, including observation, rating scales, classification methods, environmental assessments, records and personal documents, and performance-based assessment. The second part of the chapter offers a discussion concerning test worthiness of informal assessment.

The last section of the text, Section Four examines how to make a diagnosis (Chapter 11), which is a type of an assessment of an individual, and then looks at the process of writing a comprehensive test report, which partly involves the use of diagnosis (Chapter 12).

Chapter 11 starts by discussing the importance of making a diagnosis and then describes the Diagnostic and Statistical Manual, Fourth Edition—Text Revision (DSM-IV-TR). We offer a brief history of the DSM-IV-TR and discuss its five axes that are used in making a diagnosis. We also show how a five axes diagnosis is made and present some case studies for additional practice. We conclude the chapter with a discussion of the importance of diagnosis in the total assessment process.

Chapter 12 takes a look at the process of interviewing a client and writing a test report. We begin by defining the purpose of the assessment report, and note that when you put "garbage in" to a report, you get a flawed report. We talk about the importance of accurately identifying the breadth and depth of the client's issues so that one can choose the appropriate assessment procedures to use in gathering information for the report. We also distinguish between three kinds of interviews: structured, unstructured, and semi-structured. We note that computers have become increasingly important in the writing of test reports in recent years. Finally, we give a detailed description of the categories of a test report and using a fictitious client, we offer an example of how to write one. The resulting five-page assessment report can be found in its entirety in Appendix F of the text. We think you will find this example helpful in writing your own assessment reports.

As noted earlier, at the end of the book we offer a glossary of all of the major words and terms used in the text. This should be helpful in remembering some of the basic concepts you read about. Also, as noted earlier, within each chapter you will find important concepts highlighted in the margins. At the end of the book you will find six appendices to enhance some of the issues identified in the text. Appendix A offers the websites of major professional associations and their accompanying ethical codes, Appendix B presents the assessment sections of ACA's and APA's ethical codes, Appendix C provides the Code of Fair Testing Practices in Education, Appendix D offers supplemental statistical equations to help guide you in some of aspects of tests statistics, Appendix E provides a conversion table of percentiles from z-scores, and Appendix F offers an example of a test report that should be helpful as a guide when you write your own report.

We believe this book is comprehensive without being overbearing. The text provides an overview of testing and assessment in a readable and we think, sometimes even enjoyable fashion. We hope that after reading it, you come away with a new appreciation of testing and assessment.

ACKNOWLEDGMENTS

We would like to give a special thanks to the assistance given from Brooks/Cole publishing, especially from: Seth Dobrin, Acquisition Editor, for his attention in getting this book revised; Rachel McDonald, Editorial Assistant, for her help with minutiae and her quick turn around time in responding to questions; Laurie Anderson who designed the beautiful cover; and Roberta Broyer for her help with obtaining the many permissions needed for a book of this kind. Our thanks also to Jared Sterzer, Senior Project Manager at Pre-Press PMG for his ongoing attention to the many changes in the text and to our Copy Editor, Kelly Birch. Finally, a special thanks to the many reviewers of the 1st edition who made a number of sound suggestions for changes to this edition, including: Jim Austin, University of Akron; Andy Beigel, Keuka College; Collen Biri, Lindenwood University; Richard Conti and David N. Perkins, College of Saint Elizabeth; Maria Galace, West Hills College; Robert B. Hensley, Mansfield University; Michael Johnson, University of Texas-Pan American; Karl Kelley, North Central College; Brenda M. Kilpatrick, Sue Norton, and William E. Roberts, Edinboro University of Pennsylvania; Gregory A. Lobb, Carlow University; Salvadore P. Massa, Marist College; Yvonne C. May, Bethune-Cookman University; Brad Mossbarger, Austin Peay State University; Deborah Partington, Ottawa University; John D. Sanders, Friends University; Joseph Spriner, Georgian Court University; Irene Staik, University of Montevallo; Franklin V. Thompson, University of Maine Presque Isle; Fredric J. Weiner, Holy Family University; and Robert J. Wright, Widener University.

HISTORY AND CURRENT PROFESSIONAL ISSUES

Section One of *Essentials of Testing and Assessment* includes two chapters: Chapter 1: History of Testing and Assessment, and Chapter 2: Ethical, Legal, and Professional Issues in Assessment. These chapters offer an overview of the field of testing and assessment and provide a link between the history of assessment and issues that continue to affect us today.

In the first chapter we examine the history of testing and assessment and see how the past has shaped current methods of assessment. We begin this chapter by discussing the differences between testing and assessment and pointing out how their current definitions are directly related to their history. Then we trace the history of assessment, starting with ancient history and working our way to the development of modern-day assessment instruments. Along the way, we highlight some of the people whose contributions were critical to the development of assessment measures, and we discuss some of the many controversial issues that arose.

Near the end of the chapter we examine current categories of assessment instruments, including ability testing (testing in the cognitive realm); personality assessment (testing in the affective realm); and informal assessment techniques. We also describe how the book is configured around the various kinds of assessment categories we just noted. The chapter concludes by raising a number of concerns that continue to face us today as we administer assessment instruments.

Chapter 2 examines the many complex ethical, legal, and professional issues that confront individuals who are assessing others. We start by identifying ethical codes that help guide the practice of mental health professionals, paying special attention to the codes of the American Counseling Association and the American Psychological Association. Both of these codes have a particularly strong emphasis on assessment, and this part of the chapter offers a brief overview of the assessment aspects of these important guidelines. Next, we summarize a number of standards that have been developed to help guide the practitioner when administering, scoring, and interpreting assessment procedures. This part of the chapter concludes with a discussion of ethical decision-making.

As Chapter 2 continues, we examine a number of laws that have been passed and lawsuits resolved that impinge on the use of tests. Most of these legal constraints involve issues of confidentiality, fairness, and test worthiness (reliability, validity, practicality, and cross-cultural fairness). The last section of the chapter begins by highlighting two professional associations in the field of assessment: The Association for Assessment in Counseling and Education (AACE) and Division 5 of the American Psychological Association: Evaluation, Measurement, and Statistics. Then we identify three organizations that address curriculum standards in the area of assessment, including the American Psychological Association (APA), the National Association of School Psychologists (NASP), and the Council for the Accreditation of Counseling and Related Educational Programs (CACREP). We then discuss an increasingly popular sub-specialty in assessment: forensic evaluation. As the chapter continues, we emphasize the importance of recognizing that assessment works best when it is a holistic process. Next, we explore ways in which assessment techniques can enhance the counseling process. The chapter concludes with a discussion of cross-cultural issues related to bias in testing.

HISTORY OF TESTING AND ASSESSMENT

"Pens and pencils down!" Those words still send chills down my spine. With millions of children and adults frightened by the thought of taking a test, this is not a pretty picture. But is there value in this sometimes-terrifying experience? We'll let you answer that question after you have finished reading this book. But how did test-taking start? That question will be answered in this chapter.

(Ed Neukrug)

In this chapter we will examine the history of testing and assessment. First, we will explore the differences between testing and assessment and point out how their current definitions are directly related to their history. We will then take a ride through the history of assessment, starting with ancient history and working our way to the development of modern-day assessment instruments. Along the way, we will highlight some of the people who were pioneers in the development of assessment measures and discuss some of the controversial issues that arose. As the chapter nears its conclusion, we will examine the current categories of assessment instruments, and we will finish by raising a number of ongoing concerns surrounding the use of assessment instruments.

DISTINGUISHING BETWEEN TESTING AND ASSESSMENT

Assessment
A broad array of evaluative procedures

Tests
Instruments that yield scores based on collected data—a subset of assessment

Today, the term assessment includes a broad array of evaluative procedures that yield information about a person (Hunsley, 2002). Assessment procedures include the clinical interview; informal assessment techniques such as observation, rating scales, classification methods, environmental assessment, records and personal documents, and performance-based assessment; personality tests such as objective tests, projective tests, and interest inventories; and ability tests, such as achievement tests and aptitude tests (see Figure 1.1).

Tests are a subset of assessment techniques that yield scores based on the gathering of collective data (e.g., finding the sum of correct items on a multiple-choice

3

FIGURE 1.1 | ASSESSMENT PROCEDURES

exam). Assessment procedures can be formal, which means they have been well-researched and shown to be scientifically sound, valid, and reliable; or informal, which implies that such rigor has not been demonstrated, although the procedure might still yield some valuable information.

Generally, the greater the number of procedures used in assessing an individual, the greater the likelihood that they will yield a clearer snapshot of the client. Thus, using multiple assessment procedures should always be considered when making important decisions about a client's life (Halperin & McKay, 1998; Joint Committee on Testing Practices, 2004; Meyer et al., 2001). In this text we will examine a broad array of formal and informal assessment procedures, all of which can be used in the decision-making process. But let's start at the beginning and see how events of the past have moved us toward our current use of assessment instruments.

Multiple assessment procedures should always be considered

THE HISTORY OF ASSESSMENT

The history of assessment goes back to ancient times, but it was not until the early part of the twentieth century that the modern era of assessment began. Let's examine some of the changes in assessment that have taken place over the centuries.

ANCIENT HISTORY

How long has assessment been around? We might say that Abraham's loyalty was assessed when God asked him to kill his son Isaac, and no doubt informal assessment procedures were around long before Abraham. The Chinese government is often given credit for developing one of the first widely used tests when it began to assess individuals for fitness to work in government positions in approximately 2200 B.C.E. (DuBois, 1970; Higgins & Sun, 2002). The selection process was grueling, with testing done in hundreds of small cubicles or huts. It was so bad that under the intense strain of the examinations, some examinees would die from exhaustion (Cohen & Swerdlik, 1999). The testing was finally abolished in 1905. Another ancient example of assessment is found in passages from Plato's (428–327 B.C.E.) writing that indicate the Greeks assessed both the intellectual and physical ability of men when screening for state service (Doyle, 1974).

PRECURSORS TO MODERN-DAY TEST DEVELOPMENT

Jean Esquirol
Used language to identify intelligence—forerunner of "verbal IQ"

Edouard Sequin
Developed the form board to increase motor control—forerunner of "performance IQ"

Sir Francis Galton
Examined relationship of sensory motor responses to intelligence

As experimental and controlled research spread throughout the scientific community during the 1800s, physicians and philosophers began to apply these research principles to the understanding of people, particularly in the area of cognitive functioning. For instance, the French physician Jean Esquirol (1772–1840) worked with individuals with mental retardation in the French mental asylums and began to use language to identify varying levels of intelligence of his patients (Zusne, 1984; Drummond, 2006). Then called "idiocy" (Esquirol, 1838, p. 76), until Esquirol came about mental retardation was viewed as an illness, and his efforts are often seen as the beginning of what later became known as the assessment of "verbal IQ." At around the same time, Edouard Sequin (1812–1880), another Frenchman who worked with individuals with mental retardation, suggest that the prognosis regarding intellectual deficits in children was worse if such deficits were associated with physiological problems. He suggested that physicians should "watch for a swinging walk, 'automatically busy' hands, saliva dripping from a 'meaningless mouth,' a 'lustrous and empty' look, and 'limited' or 'repetitive' speech" (Zenderland, 1987, p. 54). Eventually, Sequin developed the form board to increase his patients' motor control and sensory discrimination. Considered by some to be the forerunner of "performance IQ" measures (DuBois, 1970), versions of the form board, which is similar to the toy in which children place shapes in their respective grooves, are still used today in some performance-oriented IQ tests.

Meanwhile, intrigued by Charles Darwin's (1809–1882) theory of evolution, scientists during the mid-1800s became engrossed in trying to understand the development of the human species (Juve, 2008; Kerr, 2008). For instance, Sir Francis Galton (1822–1911), Darwin's cousin, became fascinated by differences among people (Gillham, 2001). Galton hypothesized that individuals who had a quicker reaction time and stronger grip strength might be superior intellectually. His curiosity led him to examine the relationship among such characteristics, and his research spurred others to develop the statistical concept of the correlation coefficient, which describes the strength of the relationship among variables (Dubois, 1970; Kerr). Calculating the correlation coefficient has become an important tool in the development and refinement of tests.

Wilhelm Wundt
Developed one of the first psychological laboratories

Wilhelm Wundt (1832–1920), another scientist intrigued with human nature, set out to create "a new domain of science" that he called physiological psychology. Around 1875, at the University of Leipzig, Wundt developed one of the first psychological laboratories that used experimental research (Nicolas, Gyselinck, Murray, & Bandomir, 2002). Many of the experiments in Wundt's laboratory studied reaction time of hearing, sight, and other senses in response to stimuli (Watson, 1968). A number of students who worked with Wundt helped to foster in the new age of psychological science. For instance, James McKeen Cattell (1860–1944), a doctoral student under Wundt who was later greatly inspired by Galton, became one of the earliest psychologists to use statistical concepts in understanding the person (Goodwin, 2008; Roback, 1961). Cattell's main emphasis became testing mental functions, and he is known for coining the term *mental test*. Another important figure, G. S. Hall (1844-1924), also worked with Wundt and eventually set up his own experimental lab at Johns Hopkins University. Hall became a mentor to other great American psychologists and was the founder and first president of the American Psychological Association in 1892 (Benjamin, 2008).

factor analysis

James Cattell
Brought statistics to mental testing —coined term mental test

G. S. Hall
Early experimental psychologist. First president of APA

THE EMERGENCE OF ABILITY TESTS (TESTING IN THE COGNITIVE DOMAIN)

Influenced by the new scientific approach to understanding human nature, researchers at the beginning of the twentieth century began to develop instruments that could scientifically measure an individual's abilities. This era saw the emergence of ability tests, including individual intelligence tests, neuropsychological assessments, and group tests of ability.

Alfred Binet
Created first modern intelligence test

INTELLECTUAL AND COGNITIVE FUNCTIONING: INTELLIGENCE TESTING AND NEUROPSYCHOLOGICAL ASSESSMENT Commissioned in 1904 by the Ministry of Public Education in Paris, Alfred Binet (1857–1911) was eager to develop an intelligence test that could be of assistance in integrating "sub-normal" children into the schools. Highly critical of the manner in which "mental deficiency" was diagnosed in children, Binet and his colleague Theophile Simon developed a scale that could be administered one-on-one, which would measure higher mental processes by assessing responses to a variety of different kinds of tasks (e.g., tracking a light, asking the individual to distinguish between different types of words) (Ryan, 2008). The information gained from their observations was then used to develop the first modern-day intelligence test (Watson, 1968). A relatively short time later, Lewis Terman (1877–1956), from Stanford University, began analyzing and methodically gathering extensive normative data on Binet and Simon's scale from hundreds of children in the Stanford, CA area (Jolly, 2008; Kerr, 2008). Based on the data, Terman made a number of revisions to the Binet and Simon scale. Originally called

Lewis Terman
Enhanced Binet's work to create Stanford-Binet intelligence test

BOX 1.1	DEVELOPING THE NOTION OF "IQ"

Lewis Terman wanted to develop a logical and relatively easy way of expressing an individual's intelligence. Using the data from his research, he quickly realized that he could compute a ratio score for each child by dividing a child's mental score (the age score at which the child performed) by the child's actual age. Thus, if a child was performing at the level of the average 12-year-old but was actually 9 years old, the ratio would be 12/9 or 1.33. Multiplying this number by 100 to eliminate the decimal point would yield an intelligence quotient ("IQ") of 133*. Use this method to determine the IQs of the children below, based on their mental age scores and their actual ages.

Child 1: mental age of 6 and chronological age of 8

Child 2: mental age of 16 and chronological age of 16.

Child 3: mental age of 10 and chronological age of 9.

Answers: Child 1: 75 (6/8 × 100), Child 2: 100 (16/16 × 100), Child 3: 111 (10/9 × 100).

*Note: IQ is no longer determined in this manner, and the current method of calculation will be discussed later in the text.

Intelligence quotient

Mental age divided by chronological age

the Stanford Revision of the Binet and Simon scale, the test later took on the name Stanford-Binet, which is the name the revised version continues to be known as today. Terman was the first to incorporate in his test the ratio of chronological age to mental age, calling it the "intelligence quotient" or "IQ" (see Box 1.1).

In addition to being interested in a person's intelligence, people have always been intrigued by the relationship between brain function and behavior. In fact, observations of behavioral changes following head injuries are found in 5,000-year-old Egyptian medical documents (Hebben-Milberg, 2002). More recently, research conducted during World War I examined behaviors of soldiers who suffered from brain injuries. Not surprisingly, with the testing movement in full swing, it was at this time that new screening and diagnostic measures to assess behavioral changes due to brain trauma were created (Lezak, Howieson, & Loring, 2004). During the twentieth century, as individuals became more interested in the nature of the brain and spurred on by the use of X-rays and other forms of brain imaging, the field of neuropsychology, or the study of brain function as it relates to behavior, was established. Today, when suspected changes occur in brain function due to disease or accidents, a neuropsychological assessment, which sometimes includes an intelligence test, is often used.

Robert Yerkes

Chairman of the committee that developed the Army Alpha

GROUP TESTS OF ABILITY (GROUP TESTING IN THE COGNITIVE DOMAIN)   Realizing the importance of obtaining accurate information from examinees, Terman and others developed standardized directions to use in testing and stressed the importance of having trained examiners administer tests individually (Geisinger, 1994; Jolly, 2008). However, it was soon evident that individual testing often took a particularly long time and was costly. During World War I, these practical concerns became paramount, because quickly administering tests of cognitive ability to large groups of recruits in order to place them in the military was of critical importance. Robert Yerkes, the president of the American Psychological Association, chaired a special committee appointed to create a screening test for these new recruits. The committee, composed of many well-known psychologists, including Terman,

BOX 1.2 | THE ARMY ALPHA TEST

The Army Alpha test was created to place recruits in the military (Jones, 2007; Mckean, 1985). Based on this test, it was found that the average mental age of the recruit was 13. Take the test below in the 3-minute time allotment given, then consider potential issues of bias and cultural fairness of the questions on the test.

The Army Alpha was used to determine placement in the armed forces during WWI. Below is an adaptation of the test, as printed in *Discover* magazine. Take the test and discuss your thoughts about it.

> *The average mental age of the recruits who took the Army Alpha test during WWI was approximately 13. Could you do better? You have three minutes to complete these sample questions, drawn verbatim from the original exam.* (McKean, 1985)

The following sentences have been disarranged but can be unscrambled to make sense. Rearrange them and then answer whether each is true or false.

1. Bible earth the says inherit the the shall meek.   true   false
2. a battle in racket very tennis useful is   true   false

Answer the following questions:

3. If a train goes 200 yards in a sixth of a minute, how many feet does it go in a fifth of a second?
4. A U-boat makes 8 miles an hour under water and 15 miles on the surface. How long will it take to cross a 100-mile channel if it has to go two-fifths of the way under water?
5. The spark plug in a gas engine is found in the: crank case   manifold   cylinder   carburetor
6. The Brooklyn Nationals are called the: Giants   Orioles   Superbas   Indians
7. The product advertised as 99.44 per cent pure is:
        Arm & Hammer Baking Soda   Crisco   Ivory Soap   Toledo
8. The Pierce-Arrow is made in: Flint   Buffalo   Detroit   Toledo
9. The number of Zulu legs is: two   four   six   eight

Are the following words the same or opposite in meaning?

10.   vesper–matin   same   opposite
11.   aphorism–maxim   same   opposite

Find the next number in the series:

12.   74,   71,   65,   56,   44,   Answer:
13.   3,   6,   8,   16,   18,   Answer:

14. Select the image that belongs in the mirror: 15. & 16. What's missing in these pictures?

      15.   16.

Answers: 1. true, 2, false, 3. twelve feet, 4, nine hours, 5. cylinder, 6. superbas, 7. Ivory Soap, 8. Buffalo, 9. two, 10. opposite, 11. same, 12. 29, 13. 36, 14. A, 15, spoon, 16. gramophone horn
Scoring: All items except 3, 4, 10, and 11 = 1.25 points. Items 3 and 4 = 1.875 points, Items 10 & 11 = .625 points. Add them all up, they equal your mental age. What is wrong with this test? Examine it for problems with content, history, cross-cultural contamination, and so forth.

Source: McKean, K. (1985). Intelligence: New ways to measure the wisdom of man. *Discover Magazine* 6(10), 28. Reprinted by permission of Disney Publications.

ILLUSTRATION 1.1 | RECRUITS TAKING AN EXAMINATION AT CAMP LEE, 1917

Source: U.S. Signal Corps photo number 11-SC-386 in the National Archives.

Army Alpha
First modern group test—used during WWI

prepared a draft of the test in just four months (Geisinger, 2000; Jones, 2007). The original test the committee developed was known as the Army Alpha (see Box 1.2 and Illustration 1.1).

Although the Army Alpha clearly had its problems, it was a large step toward the mass use of tests in decision-making and was administered to more than 1.7 million recruits in less than 2 years (Haney, 1981). Since there were many foreign-born recruits and large numbers of people who could not read, a second language-free version of the test, known as the Army Beta, was created. The Army Beta applied the use of form boards and mazes, and directions were given by pantomime so recruits could take the entire test without reading (Goodwin, 2008). Although crude by today's standards, the Army Alpha and Army Beta ushered in the era of group tests of ability.

In contrast with individual intelligence tests and neuropsychological assessments, which are given one-to-one, group tests of cognitive ability tend to be paper-and-pencil measures given to groups of individuals simultaneously in an effort to assess the academic promise of each individual in the group. Probably the most well known of these has been the Scholastic Aptitude Test (now the SAT Reasoning Test, or SAT). Developed by the Educational Testing Service after World War II, the test in many ways was the brain child of James Bryant Conant,

| **BOX 1.3** | Eugenics and the Testing Movement |

As the new scientific approach to knowledge increasingly began to examine differences among people, a number of scientists began attributing these differences to genetics. This information was used to bolster support for the emerging Eugenics Movement, whose members espoused a belief in selective breeding in order to improve the human race.

Individuals such as Galton, Terman, and Yerkes believed that the data retrieved from tests could help distinguish those who were naturally bright from those who, they argued, were less fortunate. The information derived from tests was used to advocate for providing incentives for the upper class to procreate and in finding methods to prevent the lower classes from having children (Gillham, 2001). Based on flimsy evidence and misguided thinking, this movement is also seen today as having racist undertones.

Believing that the Army Alpha and Army Beta measured innate ability, Terman, Yerkes, and others used the results of these tests to support the Eugenics Movement. However, the tests were a far cry from being a measurement of intelligence, as they were saturated with cultural bias and were largely based on measuring achievement, or what had been learned, as opposed to some kind of raw, inherent intelligence. Unfortunately, their beliefs about the test and what should be done as a result of the test data may have been one of many influences that led the U.S. government to manipulate whom it would allow to immigrate to the United States (Sokal, 1987). As a result, thousands—perhaps millions—of individuals were unable to emigrate from tyrannical governments in Europe and other parts of the world (Gould, 1996).

Question to Ponder: If a test could definitively identify those who were brighter than the rest of the population, would you support some kind of modified Eugenics Movement, such as encouraging individuals to mate only with individuals from a brighter gene pool?

James Bryant Conant

Developed SAT to equalize educational opportunities

president of Harvard. Believing in a democratic, classless society, Conant thought that such tests could identify the ability of individuals and ultimately help to equalize educational opportunities (Frontline, 1999). Unfortunately, many have argued that instead of fostering equality, the SATs have been used to separate the social classes, and many in the testing movement were not as magnanimous as James Bryant Conant (see Box 1.3)

Paralleling the rise of group tests of cognitive ability was the administration of group tests of achievement in the schools. Traditionally, such tests had been given orally, and later in essay fashion, but the practicality of administering objective tests of academic performance to large groups of students was obvious. With the new scientific approach to testing on the rise, Edward Thorndike (1874-1949), one of the pioneers of modern-day educational and psychological assessment, and others, thought that such tests could be given in a format that was more reliable than previous tests. This move toward group testing culminated with the development of the Stanford Achievement Test in 1923 (Armstrong, 2006). Today, these tests are commonplace and are given to students en masse in school systems throughout America.

Edward Thorndike

Developer of the Stanford Achievement Test

One last area where group testing became popular was in vocational counseling. With Frank Parsons (1909/1989) at its helm, vocational counseling became increasingly important at the turn of the twentieth century as large numbers of people moved to the bigger cities in search of employment. With vocational counseling seen as a process of (1) acquiring self knowledge, (2) acquiring knowledge of the

Frank Parsons

Leader in vocational counseling

world of work, and (3) finding a suitable match through a process called "true reasoning," thousands of individuals were anxious to discover what jobs might be a suitable match for them. And tests that could quickly measure large groups of peoples' likes and dislikes, as well as their abilities, could help do that. Thus, we began to see the rise of "multiple aptitude" tests. For example, the General Aptitude Test Battery (GATB) was developed by the United States Employment Service to measure abilities in a number of specific areas. These areas of ability could be directly matched with job characteristics to identify appropriate occupational choices.

GATB

Developed by U.S. Employment Service to measure multiple aptitudes

The Emergence of Personality Tests (Testing in the Affective Realm)

Paralleling the rise of tests in the cognitive domain, personality tests (or tests in the affective realm) began to be devised. Thus, around the turn of the twentieth century three types of personality assessment instruments were developed: interest inventories, objective personality tests, and projective personality tests. Let's take a brief look at each of these areas.

Interest Inventories and Vocational Assessment   In 1912, Edward Thorndike, one of the first to conduct research in the field of vocational assessment, published the results of a study that examined the interests of 100 students as they progressed from elementary school through college (DuBois, 1970). As the relationship of interests to vocational choice became more obvious, in 1922, J. B. Miner developed one of the first formal interest blanks (inventories) that was used to assist large groups of high school students in selecting occupations. Miner (1922) understood that his test was only part of the total assessment process, and he explained that his inventory was "the basis for individual interviews with vocational counselors" (p. 312).

J. B. Miner

Developed one of the first group interest inventories

On the heels of Miner's interest blank, in the mid-1920s Edward Strong (1884–1963) teamed up with a number of other researchers to develop what was to become the most well-known interest inventory (Cowdery, 1926; DuBois, 1970; Strong, 1926). Known as the Strong Vocational Interest Blank, the original inventory consisted of 420 items. Strong spent the rest of his life perfecting his vocational interest inventory. Having undergone numerous revisions over the years, this inventory continues to be one of the most widely used instruments in career counseling. Today, interest inventories like the Strong are often used in conjunction with multiple aptitude tests as part of the career counseling process.

Edward Strong

Founder of the Strong Vocational Interest Blank— derivative still used today

Objective Personality Assessment   Although Emil Kraeplin developed a crude word association test to study schizophrenia in the 1880s, Woodworth's Personal Data Sheet is considered to be the ancestor of most modern-day personality inventories. Woodworth's instrument, which was developed to screen WWI recruits for their susceptibility to mental health problems (DuBois, 1970), had 116 items to which individuals were asked to respond by underlining "yes" or "no" to indicate whether or not the statement represented them (see Box 1.4). These rather obvious questions were then related to certain types of neuroses and pathologies. Although the test had questionable validity compared to today's instruments, it became an

Emil Kraeplin

Developed early word association test

Woodworth's Personal Data Sheet

First modern personality inventory —used during WWI

BOX 1.4 | ITEMS FROM WOODWORTH'S PERSONAL DATA SHEET

Although crude by today's standards, Woodworth's Personal Data Sheet was one of the first instruments that attempted to assess one's personality. Below are some of original 116 items.

Answer the questions by underlining "Yes" when you mean yes, and by underlining "No" when you mean no. Try to answer every question.

1. Do you usually feel well and strong?   YES NO

3. Are you often frightened in the middle of the night?   YES NO

27. Have you ever been blind, half-blind, deaf or dumb for a time?   YES NO

51. Have you hurt yourself by masturbation (self abuse)?   YES NO

80. At night are you troubled by the idea that somebody is following you?   YES NO

112. Has any of your family been a drunkard?   YES NO

Source: Adapted from *A History of Psychological Testing* (pp. 160–163), by P. DuBois, 1970, Boston: Allyn and Bacon.

---

early model for a number of other, better refined instruments including the Minnesota Multiphasic Personality Inventory (MMPI).

PROJECTIVE TESTING   Clearing his mind and recording his associations to a number of stimulus words, Galton wrote:

> Experiments such as these allow an unexpected amount of illumination to enter into the deepest recess of the character, which are opened and bared by them like the anatomy of an animal under the scalpel of a dissector in broad daylight (Galton, 1879, p. 431).

These words of Galton speak to the premise of projective testing: present a stimulus to an individual in an attempt to tap into the unconscious mind and discover the inner world of that person. Recognizing the importance of Galton's work, Cattell examined the kinds of associations that mentally healthy individuals made to a standard list of words (DuBois, 1970).

Carl Jung
Used word associations to identify mental illness

By 1904, Carl Jung (1875–1961) had come up with 156 stimulus words that he used in one of the earliest word association tests. Examining the responses of his clients to his list of words, Jung came up with the word "complex" to describe sets of unusual and delayed responses that individuals had to groups of words that seemed to point to a problematic or neurotic area in their lives (Jung, 1918/1969; Jung & Riklin, 1904; Storr, 1973). However, it was Herman Rorschach (1884–1922), a student of Jung, who developed the most well-known projective test—the Rorschach Inkblot test. Rorschach created this test by selecting ten ink blots "thrown on a piece of paper, the paper folded, and the ink spread between the two halves of the sheet" (Rorschach, 1942, p. 1). Rorschach believed the interpretation of an individual's reactions to these forms could tell volumes about the individual's unconscious life. This test was the precursor to many other kinds of projective tests, such as Henry

Herman Rorschach
Developed famous Rorschach Inkblot test

Henry Murray
Developed Thematic Apperception Test (TAT)

Murray's Thematic Apperception Test, or TAT, which asks a subject to view a number of standard pictures and create a story that explains the situation.

THE EMERGENCE OF INFORMAL ASSESSMENT PROCEDURES

Informal assessment procedures
User-created and situational

The twentieth century saw the increased use of informal assessment procedures, which are assessment instruments that are often developed by the user and designed to meet a particular testing situation. For instance, as business and industry expanded during the 1930s, the situational test became more prevalent. In these tests, businesses took individuals who were potential hires or candidates for promotion and placed them into "contrived naturalistic situations" to assess their ability to respond to real-life situations. Meanwhile, as treatment of mental health clients improved, another informal procedure, the clinical interview, became prominent. The clinical interview became especially important as clients were increasingly being assessed for a diagnosis through the use of the *Diagnostic and Statistical Manual*, first developed by the American Psychiatric Association in 1952 (Neukrug & Schwitzer, 2006).

During the 1960s and 1970s the use of tests in the schools greatly increased and laws were passed that called for the assessment of students with disabilities. It was then that a number of informal techniques became popular, including observation, rating scales, classification techniques, and the review of records and personal documents to assess learning problems of children. Conducting an environmental assessment where many of these informal tools are used also become popular in recent years. For instance, knowing whether a particular home is a healthy place to raise a child has become an important aspect of the Child Protective Service worker's role. Finally, in recent years, performance-based assessment as an alternative way to measure ability has become increasingly popular. Today, informal assessment techniques, such as those mentioned above, are used in a variety of settings in a number of ways.

MODERN-DAY USE OF ASSESSMENT PROCEDURES

As complex statistical analyses became possible through the use of computers, the quality of assessment instruments advanced rapidly. Today, assessment instruments can be found in every aspect of society and their uses have been vastly expanded. Although one can categorize such instruments in many ways, we have found it helpful to classify them into the following groups: (1) testing in the cognitive domain, often called "ability testing," (2) testing in the affective domain, usually called "personality assessment," and (3) informal assessment procedures. Figures 1.2–1.4 are graphic displays of these domains and are followed in Box 1.5 by short definitions of the various categories.

In Section Two of the text, we will demonstrate how all of the assessment categories noted in Figures 1.2–1.4 and Box 1.5 are used today in a variety of ways. Below, you can see how the chapters in Section Three of the text correspond to the categories:

Chapter 6: Assessment of Educational Ability: Survey Battery, Diagnostic, Readiness, and Cognitive Ability Tests

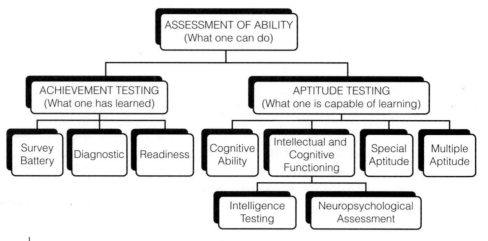

FIGURE 1.2 | TESTS IN THE COGNITIVE DOMAIN

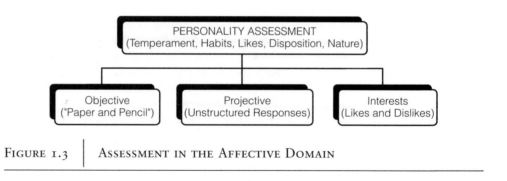

FIGURE 1.3 | ASSESSMENT IN THE AFFECTIVE DOMAIN

FIGURE 1.4 | INFORMAL ASSESSMENT PROCEDURES

BOX 1.5	BRIEF DEFINITIONS OF ASSESSMENT CATEGORIES

Assessment of Ability

Tests that measure what a person can do in the cognitive realm.

Achievement Testing

Tests that measure what one has learned.

Survey Battery Tests: Tests, usually given in school settings, which measure broad content areas. Often used to assess progress in school.

Diagnostic Tests: Tests that assess problem areas of learning. Often used to assess learning disabilities.

Readiness Tests: Tests that measure one's readiness for moving ahead in school. Often used to assess readiness to enter first grade.

Aptitude Testing

Tests that measure what one is capable of learning.

Intellectual and Cognitive Functioning: Tests that measure a broad range of cognitive functioning in the following domains: general intelligence, mental retardation, giftedness, and changes in overall cognitive functioning. Includes intelligence testing that leads to an "IQ" score and neuropsychological assessment that assesses changes in cognitive functioning over time.

Cognitive Ability Tests: Tests that measure a broad range of cognitive ability, these tests are usually based on what a student has learned in school and are useful in making predictions about the future (e.g., whether an individual might succeed in college).

Special Aptitude Tests: Tests that measure one aspect of ability. Often useful in determining the likelihood of success in a vocation (e.g., a mechanical aptitude test to determine potential success as a mechanic).

Multiple Aptitude Tests: Tests that measure many aspects of ability. Often useful in determining the likelihood of success in a number of vocations.

Personality Assessment

Tests in the affective realm used to assess habits, temperament, likes and dislikes, character, and similar behaviors.

Objective Personality Testing: Paper-and-pencil tests, often in multiple-choice or true/false formats, that assess various aspects of personality. Often used to increase client insight, to identify psychopathology, and to assist in treatment planning.

Projective Personality Tests: Tests that present a stimulus to which individuals can respond. Personality factors are interpreted based on the individual's response. Often used to identify psychopathology and to assist in treatment planning.

Interest Inventories: Tests that measure likes and dislikes as well as one's personality orientation toward the world of work. Generally used in career counseling.

Informal Assessment Instruments

Often developed by the user, they tend to be specific to the testing situation. Can assess broad areas of ability and personality attributes in a variety of settings.

Observation: Observing an individual in order to develop a deeper understanding of one or more specific behaviors (e.g., observing a student's acting-out behavior in class or assessing a client's ability to perform eye-hand coordination tasks as a means of determining potential vocational placement).

Rating Scales: Scales developed to assess any of a number of attributes of the examinee. Can be rated by the examinee or someone who knows the examinee well (rating a faculty member's teaching ability or a student's ability to make empathic responses).

Classification Methods: A mechanism whereby information is provided about whether or not an individual has, or does not have, certain attributes or characteristics (asking a person to check off those adjectives that seem to be most like him or her).

continued

BOX 1.5	BRIEF DEFINITIONS OF ASSESSMENT CATEGORIES *continued*

Environmental Assessment: A naturalistic and systemic approach to assessment in which information about clients is collected from their home, work, or school through observation or self-reports.

Records and Personal Documents: Items such as diaries, personal journals, genograms, school records, and so forth, that are examined to gain a broader understanding of an individual.

Performance-Based Assessment: The evaluation of an individual using a variety of informal assessment procedures that are often based on real-world responsibilities. Not highly loaded for cognitive skills, these procedures are seen as an alternative to standardized testing (e.g., a portfolio).

Chapter 7: Intellectual and Cognitive Functioning: Intelligence Testing and Neuropsychological Assessment

Chapter 8: Career and Occupational Assessment: Interest Inventories, Multiple Aptitude, and Special Aptitude Tests

Chapter 9: Clinical Assessment: Objective and Projective Personality Tests

Chapter 10: Informal Assessment: Observation, Rating Scales, Classification Methods, Environmental Assessment, Records and Personal Documents, and Performance-Based Assessment

QUESTIONS TO CONSIDER WHEN ASSESSING INDIVIDUALS

It is clear that today's assessment instruments have widespread applications. With the knowledge that many individuals have used assessment instruments for less than honorable reasons (e.g., the Eugenics Movement), it is critical that we remain vigilant about the use of such instruments. Keeping this in mind, we should continually be asking ourselves some important questions regarding the use of assessment instruments, including the following:

1. How valid is the information gained from assessment instruments, and how should that information be applied?
2. How do assessment instruments invade an individual's privacy, and does the government have, at times, the right to insist that an individual be assessed?
3. Can the use of some assessment instruments lead to labeling, and what are the implications for individuals who are "labeled"?
4. Are assessment procedures used to foster equality for all people, or do they tend to reinforce existing societal divisions based on class?

SUMMARY

We began this chapter by defining assessment and pointing out that assessment encompasses a broad range of techniques, including testing. We noted that modern-day assessment has been greatly influenced by the long history of assessment. Going back to 2200 B.C.E., we pointed out that the Chinese developed one of the first widely used tests and that hundreds of years ago the Greeks assessed intellectual and physical ability of men for state service. As we neared the modern era of testing, we pointed out that individuals such as Esquirol examined the relationship between language ability and intelligence, while others, such as Sequin, looked at the relationship between motor control and intelligence. We noted that Darwin's theory of evolution spurred on others such as Galton, Wundt, Cattell, and Hall to examine individual differences, a focus that would be critical to the nature of assessment.

Moving forward in time, we noted that the late 1800s saw Alfred Binet develop the first intelligence test. Later revised by Terman, the Stanford-Binet compared an individual's chronological age to his or her mental age. We pointed out that intelligence testing was also sometimes used as one aspect of neuropsychological assessments, which became more important with the advent of brain-imaging techniques and the use of additional methods to assess the relationship of brain function to behavior.

As the chapter continued, we noted that the early 1900s saw the development of group tests of ability, including the Army Alpha and Army Beta, achievement tests in the schools, and multiple aptitude tests. We then noted that during the 1900s individuals such as Galton, Yerkes, and Terman were influential in the Eugenics Movement. This misguided venture attempted to use test data to show intellectual differences among cultural groups and ended up influencing government policy, including laws regarding who would be allowed to immigrate to this country.

We pointed out that many of the first personality tests paralleled the development of ability tests. For instance, the early 1900s saw Thorndike, Miner, and Strong research the area of vocational assessment and develop some of the first interest inventories. Kraeplin developed a crude word association test, and Woodworth developed his "personal data sheet," which many consider the precursor of modern-day personality inventories. These early experiments were soon followed by the development of a word association test by Carl Jung, who sought to uncover what kinds of reactions caused complexes. Other early projective tests included Rorschach's Inkblot Test and Murray's Thematic Apperception Test. As the twentieth century continued, a number of informal assessment instruments were developed, including observational techniques, rating scales, classification schemes, records and personal documents, environmental assessments, and performance-based assessments.

Near the end of the chapter, we reviewed the definitions of the various assessment categories, including those assessment techniques that are found in the following domains: ability testing (achievement and aptitude), personality testing, and informal assessment instruments. The chapter concluded by highlighting a number of important issues in assessment, including test validity, invasion of privacy, caution regarding labeling, and the importance of assuring that assessment procedures foster equality.

CHAPTER REVIEW

1. Identify some of the ancient precursors to assessment.
2. Identify some of the precursors to modern-day assessment during the 1800s.
3. Discuss how the work of Darwin, Galton, Wundt, and Cattell has influenced the development of modern-day testing.
4. Identify some of the individuals involved and describe the precursors to modern-day intelligence testing.
5. What was the Eugenics Movement, and how did it influence government policy in the United States?
6. Identify some of the early group tests of ability, the main players in their development, and their uses.
7. Identify some of the early personality tests and the main players involved in their development.

8. Describe the contributions of some of the early developers of projective testing.
9. Draw four diagrams (see Figures 1.2–1.4) that list the various kinds of achievement testing, aptitude testing, personality assessment, and informal assessment. Define each

type of assessment category on your diagrams.
10. Make a list of every historical figure discussed in this chapter, and define each person's contribution to testing and assessment.

REFERENCES

Armstrong, T. (2006). *The best schools: How human development research should inform educational practice.* Alexandria, VA: Association for Supervision and Curriculum Development.

Benjamin, L. T. (2008). Psychology before 1900. In S. F. Davis, & W. Buskit (Eds.), *21st century psychology: A reference handbook* (vol. 1, pp. 2–11). Thousand Oaks, CA: Sage Publications.

Cohen, J., & Swerdlik, M. (1999). *Psychological testing and assessment: An introduction to tests and measurement* (4th ed.). Mountain View, CA: Mayfield.

Cowdery, K. (1926). Measurement of professional attitudes: Differences between lawyers, physicians and engineers. *Journal of Personnel Research, 5,* 131–141.

Doyle, K. (1974). Theory and practice of ability testing in ancient Greece. *Journal of the History of Behavioral Sciences, 10,* 202–212.

Drummond, R. J. (2006). *Appraisal procedures for counselors and helping professionals* (6th ed.). Upper Saddle River, NJ: Pearson.

DuBois, P. (1970). *A history of psychological testing.* Boston: Allyn and Bacon.

Esquirol, J. (1838). *Des maladies mentales considerees sous les rapports medical, hygienique, et medico-legal.* Paris: Bailliere.

Frontline. (1999). *The secrets of the SATs.* Retrieved November 23, 2008, from http://www.pbs.org/wgbh/pages/frontline/shows/sats/etc/script.html

Galton, F. (1879). Psychometric facts. *Nineteenth Century, 5,* 425–433.

Geisinger, K. (1994). Psychometric issues in testing students with disabilities. *Applied Measurement in Education, 7,* 121–140.

Geisinger, K. (2000). Psychological testing at the end of the millennium: A brief historical review. *Professional Psychology, Research, and Practice, 31,* 117–119.

Gillham, N. (2001). *A life of Sir Francis Galton: From African exploration to the birth of eugenics.* New York: Oxford University Press.

Goodwin, C. J. (2008). Psychology in the 20th century. In S. F. Davis & W. Buskit (Eds.), *21st century psychology: A reference handbook* (vol. 1, pp. 12–20). Thousand Oaks, CA: Sage Publications.

Gould, S. J. (1996). *The mismeasure of man* (Rev. and expanded). New York: Norton.

Halperin, J., & McKay, K. (1998). Psychological testing for child and adolescent psychiatrists: A review of the past 10 years. *Journal of the American Academy of Child and Adolescent Psychiatry, 37,* 575–583.

Haney, W. (1981). Validity, vaudeville, and values: A short history of social concerns over standardized testing. *American Psychologist, 36,* 1021–1033.

Hebben, N. & Milberg, W. (2002). *Essentials of neuropsychological assessment.* John Wiley & Sons: New York.

Higgins, L. T., & Sun, C. H. (2002). The development of psychological testing in China. *International Journal of Psychology, 37*(4), 246–254.

Hunsley, J. (2002). Psychological testing and psychological assessment: A closer examination. *American Psychologist, 57*(2), 139–140.

Joint Committee on Testing Practices. (2004). *Code of fair testing practices in education.* Washington, DC: American Psychological Association.

Jolly, J. L. (2008). Lewis Terman: Genetic study of genius—elementary school students. *Gifted Child Today, 31*(1), 27–33.

Jones, L. V. (2007). Some lasting consequences of U.S. Psychology programs in World Wars I and II. *Multivariate Behavioral Research, 42*(3), 593–608.

Jung, C. G. (1969) *Studies in word-association: Experiments in the diagnosis of psychopathological conditions carried out at the psychiatric clinic of the University of Zurich under the direction of C. G. Jung.* New York: Russell & Russell. (Original work published in 1918).

Jung, C., & Riklin, F. (1904). Untersuchungen über assoziationen gesunder. *Journal für Psychologie uünd Neurologie, 3,* 55–83.

Juve, J. (2008). Testing and assessment. In S. F. Davis, & W. Buskit (Eds.), *21st century psychology: A reference handbook* (vol. 1, pp. 383–391). Thousand Oaks, CA: Sage Publications.

Kerr, M. S. (2008). Psychometrics. In S. F. Davis, & W. Buskit (Eds.), *21st century psychology: A reference handbook* (vol. 1, pp. 374–382). Thousand Oaks, CA: Sage Publications.

Lezak, M., Howieson, D., & Loring, D. (2004). *Neuropsychological assessment* (4th Ed.). Oxford University Press: New York.

McKean, K. (1985). Intelligence: New ways to measure the wisdom of man. *Discover Magazine, 6* (10), 28.

Meyer, G. J., Finn, S. E., Eyde, L. D., Kay, G. G., Moreland, K. L., Dies, R. R., et al. (2001). Psychological testing and psychological assessment: A review of evidence and issues. *American Psychologist, 56*, 128–165.

Miner, J. (1922). An aid to the analysis of vocational interest. *Journal of Educational Research, 5*, 311–323.

Neukrug, E., & Schwitzer, A. (2006). *Skills and tools for today's counselors and psychotherapists: From natural helping to professional counseling.* Pacific Grove, CA: Brooks/Cole.

Nicolas, S., Gyselinck, V., Murray, D., & Bandomir, C. A. (2002). French descriptions of Wundt's laboratory in Leipzig in 1886. *Psychological Research, 66*(3), 208–214.

Parsons, F. (1989). *Choosing a vocation.* Garrett Park, MD: Garrett Park. (Original work published in 1909)

Roback, A. (1961). *History of psychology and psychiatry.* New York: Philosophical Library.

Rorschach, H. (1942). *Psychodiagnostics.* (P. V. Lamkau, Trans.). Bern, Switzerland: Verlag Hans Huber.

Ryan, J. J. (2008). Intelligence. In S. F. Davis, & W. Buskit (Eds.), *21st century psychology: A reference handbook* (vol. 1, pp. 413–421). Thousand Oaks, CA: Sage Publications.

Sokal, M. M. (1987). Introduction: Psychological testing and historical scholarship--questions, contrasts, and context. In M. M. Sokal (Ed.), *Psychological testing and American society: 1890–1930* (pp. 1–20). New Brunswick, NJ: Rutgers University Press.

Storr, A. (1973). *C. G. Jung.* New York: The Viking Press.

Strong, E. (1926). An interest test for personnel managers. *Journal of Personnel Research, 5*, 194–203.

Watson, R. (1968). *The great psychologists from Aristotle to Freud.* Philadelphia: Lippincott.

Zenderland, L. (1987). The debate over diagnosis: Henry Herbert Goddard and the medical acceptance of intelligence testing. In M. M. Sokal (Ed.), *Psychological testing and American society: 1890–1930* (pp. 46–74). New Brunswick, NJ: Rutgers Univesity Press.

Zusne, L. (1984). *Biographical dictionary of psychology.* Westport, CT: Greenwood.

2 | Ethical, Legal, and Professional Issues in Assessment

A friend of mine, a psychologist, complained to the ethics committee of her state professional association that a colleague of hers was continually writing incompetent test reports. She reported her colleague under the area of "incompetence," which includes the following:

> Psychologists provide services, teach, and conduct research with populations and in areas only within the boundaries of their competence, based on their education, training, supervised experience, consultation, study, or professional experience. (American Psychological Association, 2003, Section 2.01a)

and

> Psychologists undertake ongoing efforts to develop and maintain their competence. (Section 2.03)

My friend felt a sense of self-righteousness for having reported this psychologist. Much to her surprise, the colleague decided to report my friend on the grounds that she had not first approached her and tried to work out the situation informally. The colleague of my friend was not sanctioned, but my friend was.

> When psychologists believe that there may have been an ethical violation by another psychologist, they attempt to resolve the issue by bringing it to the attention of that individual...(Section 1.04)

In this chapter we will look at the complex ethical, legal, and professional issues that confront individuals who are assessing others. We will start by examining some of the ethical codes and standards that drive ethical decision-making and then we will review the ethical decision-making process as it relates to assessment. We will next examine some of the many laws and legal issues that have affected testing and assessment over the years. The chapter will conclude with an overview of some professional issues, such as associations and accreditation bodies that focus on assessment, conducting forensic evaluations, viewing testing as a holistic process, cross-cultural issues related to assessment, and the fear that many clinicians have concerning their use of assessment techniques.

ETHICAL ISSUES IN ASSESSMENT

This section of the chapter will offer (1) a brief overview of some of the aspects of the American Counseling Association's (ACA) and American Psychological Association's (APA) ethical codes that highlight assessment, (2) a brief overview of the many standards that have been developed to help guide the practitioner in the ethical use of assessment procedures, and (3) a discussion on the process of making ethical decisions.

OVERVIEW OF THE ASSESSMENT SECTIONS OF THE ACA AND APA ETHICAL CODES

Ethical codes
Professional guidelines for appropriate behavior

The ethical codes of our professional associations provide us with guidelines about how to respond under certain situations. Some codes, like those of the American Counseling Association (2005) and American Psychological Association (2003), include guidelines that specifically address issues of testing and assessment. The following discussion summarizes some of the more salient aspects of the assessment portions of these codes, including: choosing appropriate assessment instruments, competence in the use of assessment instruments, confidentiality, cross-cultural sensitivity, informed consent, invasion of privacy, proper diagnosis, release of test data, test administration, test security, and test scoring and interpretation. Please review the ethical guidelines of the professional associations, the websites of which can be found in Appendix A, as well as the actual portions of the assessment guidelines of ACA and APA which can be found in Appendix B.

Attend to test worthiness in choosing assessment instruments

CHOOSING APPROPRIATE ASSESSMENT INSTRUMENTS   Ethical codes stress the importance of professionals choosing assessment instruments that show test worthiness, which has to do with the reliability (consistency), validity (the test measuring what it's supposed to measure), cross-cultural fairness, and practicality of a test. Professionals must take appropriate actions when issues of test worthiness arise during an assessment so that the results of the assessment are not misconstrued. Test worthiness and how to choose an appropriate assessment instrument will be examined in detail in Chapter 3.

Competence in using tests
Requires adequate knowledge and training in administering an instrument

COMPETENCE IN THE USE OF TESTS   Competence to use tests accurately is another aspect that is stressed in the codes. The codes declare that professionals should have adequate knowledge about testing and familiarity with any test they may use. To establish who is qualified to give specific tests, the American Psychological Association (APA), in 1954, adopted a three-tier system for establishing test user qualifications. Although APA reevaluated this system and currently provides rather extensive guidelines of test user qualifications (see Turner, Demers, Fox, & Reed, 2001), many test publishers continue to use the original three-tier system, although they take into account the more involved guidelines. The original system labeled some tests according to the following three levels:

- Level A tests are those that can be administered, scored, and interpreted by responsible nonpsychologists who have carefully read the test manual and are familiar with the overall purpose of testing. Educational achievement tests fall into this category.
- Level B tests require technical knowledge of test construction and use and appropriate advanced coursework in psychology and related courses (e.g., statistics, individual differences, and counseling).
- Level C tests require an advanced degree in psychology or licensure as a psychologist and advanced training/supervised experience in the particular test. (American Psychological Association, 1954, pp. 146–148)

More specifically, an individual with a bachelor's degree who has some knowledge of assessment and is thoroughly versed with the test manual can give a Level A test and, under some limited circumstances, a Level B test. For example, teachers can administer most survey battery achievement tests. The master's level helping professional who has taken a basic course in tests and measurement can administer Level B tests. For example, counselors can administer a wide range of personality tests, including most interest inventories and many objective personality tests. However, they cannot administer tests that require additional training, such as most individual tests of intelligence, most projective tests, and many diagnostic tests. These Level C tests are reserved for those who have a minimum of a master's degree, a basic testing course, and advanced training in the specialized test (e.g., school psychologists, learning disabilities specialists, clinical and counseling psychologists, and master's-level therapists who have gained additional training).

Confidentiality
Ethical guideline to protect client information

CONFIDENTIALITY   Whether conducting a broad assessment of a client or giving one test, keeping information confidential is a critical part of the assessment process and follows similar guidelines to how one would keep information confidential in a therapeutic relationship. The importance of keeping information confidential is a professional responsibility, but sometimes it is contradicted by the law. Thus, professionals must sometimes grapple with difficult dilemmas pitting professional responsibility against the law (Remley & Herlihy, 2007). When can one reveal confidential information? Although one should always check the laws of the state in which one practices, practitioners are generally on fairly solid professional and legal ground in revealing information under the following conditions (Neukrug, 2007):

1. If a client is in danger of harming himself or herself or someone else;
2. If a child is a minor and the law states that parents have a right to information about their child;
3. If a client asks you to break confidentiality (for example, your testimony is needed in court);
4. If you are bound by the law to break confidentiality (for example, you are hired by the courts to assess an individual's capacity to stand trial);

5. To reveal information about your client to your supervisor in order to benefit the client;
6. When you have a written agreement from your client to reveal information to specified sources (for example, the court has asked you to send a test report to them).

Cross-cultural sensitivity

Ethical guideline to protect clients from discrimination and bias in testing

CROSS-CULTURAL SENSITIVITY   In reference to cross-cultural sensitivity, the codes tend to focus on the potential biases of assessment procedures when selecting, administering, and interpreting such procedures. In addition, they stress the importance of professionals being aware of and attending to the effects of age, color, cultural identity, disability, ethnicity, gender, religion, sexual orientation, and socioeconomic status on test administration and test interpretation. Later in this chapter, and in Chapter 3, we will discuss this important topic in greater detail.

Informed consent

Permission given by client after assessment process is explained

INFORMED CONSENT   Informed consent involves the right of clients to obtain information about the nature and purpose of all aspects of the assessment process and for clients to give their permission to be assessed. Although there are times when informed consent does not need to be obtained, such as when it is implied (e.g., giving of achievement tests in schools), or when testing is mandated by the courts (e.g., custody battles), generally test administrators should give their clients basic information about the assessment process and have obtained their permission to be assessed.

Invasion of privacy

Testing is an invasion of a person's privacy

INVASION OF PRIVACY   The codes generally acknowledge that, to some degree, all tests invade one's privacy and highlight the importance of clients understanding how their privacy might be infringed upon. Concerns about invasion of privacy are lessened if clients give informed consent, have real choice in accepting or refusing testing, and know the limits of confidentiality, as noted earlier.

Proper diagnosis

Choose appropriate assessment techniques for accurate diagnosis

PROPER DIAGNOSIS   Due to the delicate nature of diagnoses, the codes emphasize the important role that professionals play when deciding which assessment techniques to use in forming a diagnosis for a mental disorder and the ramifications of making such a diagnosis.

Release of test data

Test data are protected—client release required

RELEASE OF TEST DATA   Test data can be, and have been, misused. Thus, the codes assert that data should only be released to others if clients have given their consent. The release of such data is generally only given to individuals who can adequately interpret the test data and to those who will not misuse the information.

Test administration

Use established and standardized methods

TEST ADMINISTRATION   As you might guess, the codes reinforce the notion that tests should be administered in a manner that is in accord with the way that they were established and standardized. Alterations to this process should be noted and interpretations of test data adjusted if testing conditions were not ideal.

Test security

Ensure integrity of test content and test itself

TEST SECURITY   The codes remind professionals that it is their responsibility to make reasonable efforts to ensure the integrity of test content and the security of the test itself. Professionals should not duplicate tests or change test material without the permission of the publisher.

Test scoring and interpretation

Take into consideration problems with tests

TEST SCORING AND INTERPRETATION   The codes highlight the fact that when scoring tests and interpreting their results, professionals should reflect on how test worthiness (reliability, validity, cross-cultural fairness, and practicality) might affect the results. Results should always be couched in terms that reflect any potential problems with test interpretation. (These issues will be discussed in detail in Chapter 3).

STANDARDS FOR RESPONSIBLE TESTING PRACTICES

Standards in Assessment

Used to further ethical application of assessment techniques

A number of standards to help guide assessment practices have been developed in recent years. Partly a response to criticism of the manner in which tests have been used and abused over the years, these standards delineate the proper use of assessment techniques in educational, agency, and private practice settings. As an example of one standard, we have included the Code of Fair Testing Practices (2004) in Appendix C. Table 2.1 defines the purpose of the following seven well-known standards and offers references along with web addresses should you want to examine them in more detail:

- Standards for Qualifications of Test Users
- Responsibilities of Users of Standardized Tests
- Standards for Multicultural Assessment
- Code of Fair Testing Practices
- Rights and Responsibilities of Test Takers
- Competencies in Assessment and Evaluation for School Counselors
- Standards for Educational and Psychological Testing

TABLE 2.1 | STANDARDS OF RESPONSIBLE TEST USAGE

Name of Standard	Purpose	Developed/ Endorsed By*	Reference/ Web Address
Standards for Qualifications of Test Users (5 pages)	Addresses qualifications of counselors to use assessment instruments in following areas: test theory, test construction, test worthiness, test statistics, administration and interpretation of tests, cross-cultural issues, knowledge of standards and ethical codes.	ACA	ACA (2003). Standards for qualifications of test users. Alexandria, VA: Author. (www.theaaceonline.com/standards.pdf)
Responsibilities of Users of Standardized Tests (RUST) (5 pages)	"The intent of 'RUST' is to help counselors and other educators implement responsible testing practices"…in the following areas: qualifications of test users, technical knowledge, test selection, test administration, test scoring, interpreting test results, communicating test results." (p. 1)	AACE	AACE (2003). Responsibilities of users of standardized tests (RUST). Alexandria, VA: Author. (www.theaaceonline.com/resources.htm)
Standards for Multicultural Assessment (14 pages)	Addresses challenges in the assessment of diverse populations. Provides 68 standards across four areas, including; content and purpose in test selection; norming, reliability, and validity; administration and scoring; and interpretation and application.	AACE	AACE (2003), Standards for multicultural assessment. Alexandria, VA: Author. (www.theaaceonline.com/resources.htm)
Code of Fair Testing Practices (6 pages)	Intended to ensure that professionals "provide and use tests that are fair to all test takers regardless of age, gender, disability, race, ethnicity, national origin, religion, sexual orientation, linguistic background, or other personal characteristics" (¶ 1). Provides guidance for test developers and test users in four areas: developing and selecting appropriate tests, administering and scoring tests, reporting and interpreting test results, and informing test takers.	JCTP	(JCTP). (2004). Code of fair testing practices in education. Washington, DC: APA. (See Appendix C) (www.theaaceonline.com/codefair.pdf)

continued

25

TABLE 2.1 | CONTINUED

Name of Standard	Purpose	Developed/ Endorsed By*	Reference/ Web Address
Rights and Responsibilities of Test Takers (10 pages)	Delineates and clarifies "the expectations that test takers may reasonably have about the testing process, and the expectations that those who develop, administer, and use tests may have of test takers." (p. 1)	JCTP	JCTP (2000). Rights and responsibilities of test takers: Guidelines and expectations. Washington, DC: APA (http://aac.ncat.edu/resources.html)
Competencies in Assessment and Evaluation for School Counselors (4 pages)	Describes knowledge and skills needed by school counselors in assessment and evaluation in nine areas: selection, evaluation of tests, administration and scoring, interpreting, using results, interpreting and presenting data, evaluation of programs, use of surveys, familiarity with codes and standards.	ASCA/AACE	ASCA, AACE (1998). Competencies in assessment and evaluation for school counselors. Alexandria, VA: Author. (http://aac.ncat.edu/resources.html)
Standards for Educational and Psychological Testing (194 pages)	"...to provide criteria for the evaluation of tests, testing practices, and the effects of test use" (p. 2). Extensive explanation of testing practices in three broad areas: test construction, evaluation, and documentation; fairness in testing; testing applications.	AERA/APA/ NCME	AERA, APA, NCME (1999). *Standards for educational and psychological testing.* Washington, DC: AERA.

*ACA = American Counseling Association, AACE = Association of Assessment in Counseling and Education, JCTP = Joint Commission on Testing Practices, ASCA = American School Counseling Association, AERA = American Educational Research Association, APA = American Psychological Association, NCME = National Council on Measurement in Education

MAKING ETHICAL DECISIONS

Moral model
Consider moral principles involved in ethical decision-making

Because ethical codes are guidelines, it is important that practitioners rely on more than the codes when making ethical decisions. For instance, Remley and Herlihy (2007) have suggested a moral model of decision-making and have identified six moral principles often identified as important when making thorny ethical decisions. They include *autonomy*, which has to do with respecting the client's right of self-determination and freedom of choice; *nonmaleficence*, or ensuring that you "do no harm;" *beneficence*, which is promoting the well-being of others and of society; *justice*, such as providing equal and fair treatment to all people and being nondiscriminatory; *fidelity*, which has to do with being loyal and faithful to your commitments in the helping relationship; and *veracity*, which means that you will deal honestly with the client. The clinician who employs this model will not reject the use of codes but will refer to the codes while using these moral principles in his or her decision-making process.

Corey, Corey, and Callanan
Recommend an eight-step decision-making model

A hands-on, practical, problem-solving model espoused by Corey, Corey, and Callanan (2007) suggests that the practitioner go through eight steps when making complex ethical decisions:

1. identify the problem or dilemma,
2. identify the potential issues involved,
3. review the relevant ethical guidelines,
4. know the applicable laws and regulations,
5. obtain consultation,
6. consider possible and probable courses of action,
7. enumerate the consequences of various decisions, and
8. decide on what appears to be the best course of action.

Wise ethical decisions reflect higher cognitive development

Certainly, one can employ moral principles while using a model such as that suggested by Corey et al., (2007). In addition to the above principles and model, some suggest that regardless of the approach one takes in ethical decision-making, the ability to make wise ethical decisions may well be influenced by the clinician's level of ethical, moral, and cognitive development (Neukrug, Lovell, & Parker, 1996) (see Box 2.1). Those who are at higher levels of cognitive development, they state, view ethical decision-making in more complex ways than others (McAuliffe, Eriksen, & Associates, 2000). Certainly, this has broad implications for the training that takes place in clinical programs, as it would be hoped that students are challenged to make decisions that are comprehensive and thoughtful.

LEGAL ISSUES IN ASSESSMENT

Laws about testing
Created to protect the client or examinee

A number of laws have been passed and lawsuits resolved that impinge on the use of tests. Most of these legal decisions speak to issues of confidentiality, fairness, and test worthiness (reliability, validity, practicality, and cross-cultural fairness) (Swenson, 1997). In this section of the chapter we will summarize some of the more important laws that have been passed and legal cases resolved over the years, including the Family Education Rights and Privacy Act (FERPA); the Health Insurance Portability and Accountability Act (HIPAA); privileged communication laws; the Freedom of Information Act; various Civil Rights Acts (1964 and

BOX 2.1	MAKING ETHICAL DECISIONS

After reading this section, in small groups in class or as a homework assignment, use the moral principles identified and Corey's model of ethical decision-making to decide on your course of action in the following situation. Share your answers in class. You will have the opportunity to respond to additional vignettes in Box 2.5.

Situation: You have been asked to provide a broad personality assessment of a 17-year-old high school student who has been truant from school and has a history of acting-out behaviors. After meeting with her, conducting a clinical interview, and administering a number of projective tests and an MMPI-2 (an objective personality test), you find evidence that an uncle who is five years older than the client had sexually molested her when she was 12 years old. In addition, you believe that the young woman has been involved in some petty crimes, such as shoplifting and stealing audio equipment from the school. In writing your report, what should you include regarding her being molested and the crimes she has allegedly committed? Are you obligated to report this case to Child Protective Services? Do you have any obligation to contact the police? What are your obligations to this young person's parents, to the school, and to society?

---

amendments); the Americans with Disabilities Act (PL 101-336); the Individuals with Disabilities Education Improvement Act, which was an expansion of PL 94-142; Section 504 of the Rehabilitation Act; and the Carl Perkins Act (PL 98-24).

THE FAMILY EDUCATION RIGHTS AND PRIVACY ACT (FERPA) OF 1974

FERPA

Affirms right to access test records in the school

Sometimes called the Buckley Amendment, this law assures the right of privacy of student records, including test records, and applies to almost all schools that receive federal funds (K-12 and institutions of higher education) (U.S. Department of Education, 2007a). The law also gives the right to parents of students, or to the students themselves once they reach the age of 18 and are beyond high school, to review student records. If parents or the eligible student believe that school records are incorrect or misleading, they have the right to challenge them. If the school decides not to change the records, the parent or eligible student can ask for a formal hearing.

The law also states that if records are to be released, schools must receive written permission from parents or the eligible student, except in some specific circumstances (e.g., school officials acting in the educational interest of the student, accrediting organizations, to comply with a subpoena, for purposes of school evaluation, and other reasons).

THE HEALTH INSURANCE PORTABILITY AND ACCOUNTABILITY ACT (HIPAA)

HIPAA

Ensures privacy of medical and counseling records

In 1996 Congress passed the Health Insurance Portability and Accountability Act (HIPAA), and three main rules that underscore HIPAA's purpose subsequently went into effect (privacy, transaction rule, and security rules) (U.S. Department of Health and Human Services, 2007; Zuckerman, 2003). In general, HIPAA restricts the amount of information that can be shared without clients' consent and allows clients to have access to their records, except for process notes used in counseling. In fact, HIPAA requires agencies to show how they have complied with this act. Although HIPAA has far-reaching implications for the privacy and security of records and how confidential transactions are made, relative to testing, some of the more salient features of the law suggest that professionals must:

- Provide information to patients about their privacy rights and how that information can be used.
- Adopt clear privacy procedures for their practices.
- Train employees so that they understand the privacy procedures.
- Designate an individual to be responsible for seeing that privacy procedures are adopted and followed.
- Secure patient records. (APA Practice Organization, 2002, p. 2)

PRIVILEGED COMMUNICATION

Privileged communication
Legal right to maintain privacy of conversation

Privileged communication is a conversation conducted with someone that state or federal law identifies as a person with whom conversations may legally be kept confidential (i.e., therapist-patient, attorney-client, doctor-patient, clergy-penitent, husband-wife, etc.). In the case of clinicians, the goal of the law is to encourage the client to engage in conversations without fear that the clinician will reveal the contents of the conversation (e.g., in a court of law), thus ensuring the privacy and efficacy of the counseling relationship. The privilege belongs to the client, and only the client can waive that privilege (Attorney C. Borstein, personal communication, August 29, 2008; Swenson, 1997). Privileged communication should not be confused with confidentiality, which is the ethical, not legal, obligation of the counselor to keep conversations confidential (Glosoff, Herlihy, & Spence, 2000).

Jaffee v. Redmond
Affirms privileged communication laws

A 1996 ruling upheld the right to privileged communication (Jaffee v. Redmond, 1996). In this case, the Supreme Court upheld the right of a licensed social worker to keep her case records confidential. Describing the social worker as a "therapist" and "psychotherapist," the ruling has bolstered the right of all licensed therapists to have privileged communication (Remley, Herlihy, & Herlihy, 1997; Remley & Herlihy, 2007). (see Box 2.2)

THE FREEDOM OF INFORMATION ACT

Freedom of Information Act
Affirms right to access federal and state records

Originally passed in 1967 and amended in 2002, this law assures the right of individuals to access their federal records, including test records, if an individual makes a request in writing (The National Security Archive, 1995–2008). All states have enacted similar laws that assure the right to access state records.

CIVIL RIGHTS ACTS (1964 AND AMENDMENTS)

Civil Rights Act
Test must be valid for job in question

High Stakes Testing
The use of cut-off scores in important client decisions

In 1964 the Federal government passed the first of a number of laws to ban a broad spectrum of discrimination in the United States. This first act was focused on banning racial segregation in schools, public places, and employment. Since that time, a number of far-reaching amendments of the original law have been passed. Relative to testing, the laws assert that any test used for employment or promotion must be shown to be suitable and valid for the job in question. If not, alternative means of assessment must be provided. Differential test cutoffs are not allowed unless such scores can be shown to be based on valid educational principles (see Box 2.3).

BOX 2.2 | JAFFEE V. REDMOND

Mary Lu Redmond, a police officer in a village near Chicago, responded to a 'fight in progress' call at an apartment complex on June 27, 1991. At the scene, she shot and killed a man she believed was about to stab another man he was chasing. The family of the man she had killed sued Redmond, the police department, and the village, alleging that Officer Redmond had used excessive force in violation of the deceased's civil rights.

When the plaintiff's lawyers learned that Redmond had sought and received counseling from a licensed social worker employed by the village, they sought to compel the social worker to turn over her case notes and records and testify at the trial. Redmond and the social worker claimed that their communications were privileged under an Illinois statute.

They both refused to reveal the substance of their counseling sessions even though the trial judge rejected their argument that the communications were privileged. The judge then instructed jurors that they could assume that the information withheld would have been unfavorable to the policewoman, and the jury awarded the plaintiffs $545,000. (Remley et al., 1997, p. 214)

After a series of appeals, the Supreme Court heard the case on February 26, 1996. The Court decided that the licensed therapist did indeed hold privilege and that the judge's instruction to the jury was therefore unwarranted.

BOX 2.3 | THE CIVIL RIGHTS OF HIGH STAKES TESTING

Out of concern that college athletes were being recruited to play sports without regard for how they might do academically, in 1986, the National Collegiate Athletic Association (NCAA) implemented a rule that stated that high school student athletes would have to exceed specific scores on SAT or ACT college entrance exams to be eligible for athletic based scholarships and interscholastic competition (Waller, 2003). Schools that voluntarily chose to belong to the NCAA had to follow the rule. Many schools were and continue to be members of the NCAA, with non-membership potentially affecting the ability of a school to participate in competitive sports.

The results of this ruling was to disproportionately affect African-American high school students as a significantly higher percentage of them, as compared to White students, were found to not be eligible to play sports due to their scores. This also affected the ability of many high school athletes, particularly African-American athletes, to obtain sports scholarships and be accepted into college. On the other hand, a higher percentage of African American athletes were found to graduate college after this rule went into affect.

With federal civil rights law asserting that the use of tests could not disproportionately affect one group unless such use could be shown to be educationally sound, the NCAA was sued by African-American students for discrimination. Although the court has never definitively settled the cases, the uproar over the cut-off scores seems to have affected how the NCAA applied the rule. Now the NCAA uses a floating score: the higher your high school GPA, the lower the SAT or ACT score that the athlete is allowed.

With continuing concerns about the use of cut-off scores for such things as athletic scholarships, advancing in public school, and admission to college, the battle in the courts will probably continue. What do you think about the use of such high-stakes testing?

1. Should SAT and ACT scores be used to prevent student athletes from playing sports so that they can spend more time on their studies?

2. Should standardized test scores (e.g., SATs, ACTs, GREs, state achievement tests) be used to make educational decisions about placement into grade level, college, or graduate schools? Why or why not?

3. As the result of laws like No Child Left Behind which mandates that school systems must assure that all students achieve, there has been an increase in the average scores of minorities on some tests. What are the drawbacks and benefits of the continued use of such high stakes testing?

4. How might the use of high stakes testing affect those who are involved in the test-preparing process, such as teachers and administrators?

AMERICANS WITH DISABILITIES ACT (ADA) (PL 101-336)

ADA
Accommodations for testing must be made

In the United States today, close to 20% of Americans age 5 or older have a disability (U.S. Census Bureau, 2003). This includes 9.3 million (3.4%) with a sight or hearing disability, 21.2 million (8.2%) with a disability that limits physical activities, 12.4 million (4.8%) with a disability affecting learning, remembering, or concentration, and 6.8 million (2.6%) with a disability that affects their ability to dress, bathe, or get around their home. Despite such huge numbers, prejudice and discrimination has been commonplace for individuals with disabilities.As a result, in 1990, Congress passed the Americans with Disabilities Act (ADA).

Implemented in 1992, the ADA is a civil rights law that focuses on ensuring that individuals with disabilities are not discriminated against. The law banned discrimination in employment, public services and public transportation, public accommodations, and telecommunications. It mandated that in all these areas access to services had to be available, fair, and reasonable. One of its biggest impacts was in the area of employment, where the law prohibits "private employers, state and local governments, employment agencies and labor unions from discriminating against qualified individuals with disabilities in job application procedures, hiring, firing, advancement, compensation, job training, and other terms, conditions and privileges of employment" (U.S. Equal Employment Opportunity Commission, 1997, ¶ 1). Because testing is often used in the hiring and promotion of individuals in jobs, relative to testing, the law states that to ensure proper test administration, accommodations must be made for individuals with disabilities who are taking tests for employment and that testing must be shown to be relevant to the job in question.

INDIVIDUALS WITH DISABILITIES EDUCATION IMPROVEMENT ACT (IDEIA)

IDEIA
Assures right to be tested for learning disabilities in schools

In 1974 Public Law 94-142 was passed and guaranteed the right to a free and public education with appropriate accommodations for children with disabilities (Havey, 2003; Supporting Students with LD, 2008). Over the years, this law was expanded and in 2004 the most recent changes were made with the passing of IDEIA. Although IDEIA is far reaching, we will focus on the assessment aspect of the law, which assures the right of students to be tested, at the school system's expense, if they are suspected of having a disability that interferes with learning. The law, which applies to those from age 3 through age 21, asserts that if a student is assessed and found to have a disability, schools must ensure that the student is given accommodations for his or her disability and taught within the "least restrictive environment," which is often a regular classroom.

Students who are suspected of having a disability are generally referred for medical, psychological, communication, and/or vision and hearing evaluations. Any assessment that is conducted should be cross-culturally appropriate, and parents should be informed of the kinds of tests being used and give permission for the child to be tested. If the assessment indicates that a student is eligible for services, an IEP team must develop an Individualized Education Plan (IEP) within 120 days of the evaluation. The plan should address what services are needed and how they can be provided within the least restrictive environment. The IEP team often includes the parent(s), the child's teacher(s), a district representative who is able to provide or oversee the delivery of special education services, the child (when appropriate), representatives from the evaluation team, possible service providers, and other relevant people chosen by the parent or school.

SECTION 504 OF THE REHABILITATION ACT

Section 504
Assessment for programs must measure ability— not disability

This act applies to all federally funded programs receiving financial assistance and was established to create a "level playing field" and prevent discrimination based on disability. Based on this law, employers and organizations cannot:

- Deny qualified individuals the opportunity to participate in or benefit from federally funded programs, services, or other benefits.
- Deny access to programs, services, benefits or opportunities to participate as a result of physical barriers.
- Deny employment opportunities, including hiring, promotion, training, and fringe benefits, for which they are otherwise entitled or qualified (U.S. Department of Health and Human Services, n.d., ¶ 7).

Relative to assessment, any instrument used to measure appropriateness for a program or service must measure the individual's ability, not be a reflection of his or her disability.

CARL PERKINS CAREER AND TECHNICAL EDUCATION IMPROVEMENT ACT OF 2006

Carl Perkins Act
Ensures access to vocational assessment, counseling, and placement

This federally funded program, which gives financial grants to the states, assures that individuals in six identified "special populations" can have access to vocational assessment, counseling, and placement so that these individuals will be more likely to succeed in technical education programs and in their careers (U.S. Department of Education, 2007b). Originally passed in 1984, this fourth reiteration of the Carl Perkins Act applies to the following populations: (a) individuals with disabilities; (b) individuals from economically disadvantaged families, including foster children; (c) individuals preparing for non-traditional fields; (d) single parents, including single pregnant women; (e) displaced homemakers; and (f) individuals with limited English proficiency.

PROFESSIONAL ISSUES

Major professional associations
AACE of ACA and Division 5 of APA

This section of the chapter will begin by highlighting two professional associations in the field of assessment: The Association for Assessment in Counseling and Education (AACE) and Division 5 of the American Psychological Association: Evaluation, Measurement, and Statistics. We will then briefly mention two accrediting bodies that focus on assessment. This will be followed by a discussion about the growing professional field of forensic evaluation. Next, we will underscore the importance of recognizing that assessment works best when it is a holistic process; that is, when consideration is given for the use of multiple procedures when assessing an individual. The use of assessment techniques with minorities and women will then be highlighted, and the chapter will conclude with a discussion about importance of embracing the use of testing and assessment.

PROFESSIONAL ASSOCIATIONS

Although there are literally dozens of professional associations in the field that might pique your interest (see Appendix A), few specifically focus on assessment. Although we encourage you to join the professional association with which you feel the closest affinity, if you have a strong interest in assessment you might want to consider joining the following two associations.

The Association for Assessment in Counseling and Education (AACE), a division of ACA, "is an organization of counselors, educators, and other professionals that advances the counseling profession by providing leadership, training, and research in the creation, development, production, and use of assessment and diagnostic techniques" (AACE, 2008, ¶ 1). Consider joining AACE if you are interested in testing, diagnosis, the training and supervision of those who do assessment, and if you are fascinated by the process of developing and validating assessment products and procedures. AACE publishes a journal entitled *Measurement and Evaluation in Counseling and Development*.

Division 5 of the American Psychological Association: Evaluation, Measurement, and Statistics, is devoted to "promoting high standards in both research and practical application of psychological assessment, evaluation, measurement, and statistics" (Division 5, 2008, ¶ 1). Division 5 publishes two journals, *Psychological Assessment*, which is geared toward assessment, and *Psychological Methods*, which is research-oriented. Division 5 also publishes a quarterly newsletter, *The Score*, which focuses on business issues of the association as well as new issues in the field.

ACCREDITATION STANDARDS OF PROFESSIONAL ASSOCIATIONS

Accreditation bodies

Assist in setting curriculum standards (APA, NASP, and CACREP)

A number of the professional associations have accreditation standards that specifically speak to curriculum issues in the area of assessment. Such standards help to establish a common core of experience for students who enter their programs, regardless of the institution in which the program is housed. Thus, we find organizations such as the American Psychological Association (2000), the National Association of School Psychologists (2000), and the Council for the Accreditation of Counseling and Related Educational Programs (CACREP, 2008), setting standards that drive the curriculum for their graduate programs. In fact, much of what is covered in this text is a result of the authors examining these curriculum standards and trying to ensure that we cover them as fully as possible. If you get a chance, you may want to visit the websites listed in the references and examine the standards for each of these organizations.

FORENSIC EVALUATIONS

Forensic evaluations

Completed by forensic health evaluators and forensic psychologists

Increasingly, counselors, psychologists, and other mental health professionals are being called to testify in court and to offer expert witness about individuals they have worked with and have evaluated. Knowledge of assessment and legal and ethical issues clearly becomes paramount when dealing with such cases (Pennuto & Archer, 2008). To address the need of having accuracy in court, the specialized

| COMMON AREAS FOR FORENSIC HEALTH EVALUATORS AND FORENSIC PSYCHOLOGISTS

BOX 2.4

Civil	Criminal
• Child custody	• Juvenile waiver (from juvenile to adult court)
• Civil commitment	• Juvenile sentencing
• Deprivation of parental rights	• Competence to stand trial
• Divorce mediation	• Competence to be sentenced
• Employment litigation	• Competence to waive Miranda rights
• Guardianship	• Insanity defense
• Personal injury	• Diminished capacity
• Testamentary capacity	• Sentencing (including special issues related to capital sentencing)
• Workers' compensation	• Commitment of sex offenders ("sexually violent predators")

practices of forensic health evaluator and forensic psychology have become increasingly important and popular (Packer, 2008; Patterson, 2006). What areas do such specialists deal with? Packer identifies a wide range of common areas that such experts will often testify about (see Box 2.4)

Forensic evaluators and forensic psychologists need to know how to conduct forensic evaluations, which include the use of specific tests for the situation at hand, interviewing techniques that are focused on the goals of the court case, knowledge of ethical and legal issues relevant to expert testimony and the specific case, and how to write forensic reports that will be used in court. Although many of the tests and interviewing techniques used in this text can be applied to such evaluations, knowing how and when to use them is crucial. In addition, other assessment procedures are often involved in forensic evaluations. Thus, in order to assure the accuracy of such evaluations, the National Board of Forensic Evaluators (NBFE) certifies counselors and social workers as forensic health evaluators. In addition, psychologists interested in this area can now do residencies in forensic psychology or four years of postdoctoral forensic experience to become a diplomate in the American Board of Forensic Psychology (ABFP) (Packer, 2008). Finally, in 1991, Specialty Guidelines for Forensic Psychologists were published. Developed to provide a guide for best practices in forensic psychology, they are now in the process of being revised.

ASSESSMENT AS A HOLISTIC PROCESS

Holistic process
The importance of using multiple measures

As we will stress throughout this text, assessment of clients is much broader than simply giving an individual a test. In fact, one should generally "avoid using a single test score as the sole determinant of decisions..." and one should "Interpret test scores in conjunction with other information about individuals" (Joint Committee on Testing Practices, 2004, Section C-5). A good assessment will often involve a number of different kinds of instruments, including formal tests, informal assessment instruments, and a clinical interview. And, it is important to remember that tests tend not to measure certain aspects of a person, such as an individual's motivation, intention, and focus of attention (Preston, 2005). Ultimately, the examiner has to take into account test scores, assessment procedures, and these other aspects of the person if he or she is to make wise suggestions and decisions about the client. This holistic process can help us obtain a broader and more accurate view of the client than if we were to rely on just one test (Mislevy, 2004; Moss, 2004).

Assessment is a snapshot; clients continually change

In addition, assessment is not a static process; instead, it should be seen as continuous and ongoing. The assessment of a client occurs at a specific point in time; however, if we believe that a person can change, that point represents only a small sample of an individual's total functioning. Viewing assessment in this way allows us to understand that an individual's cognitive functioning and personality may, and probably will, change significantly throughout the lifespan. Seeing a client in this manner helps us develop treatment plans for the client in the here and now, while reminding us not to be held hostage to labels and diagnoses—for the individual may, and probably will, change.

CROSS-CULTURAL ISSUES IN ASSESSMENT

> [Mental health professionals] need to examine the quality and usefulness of available assessment activities relative to how such assessments may negatively affect clients, no matter the population group to which they may belong. Needed is a reorientation of assessment practices to promote the development of human talent and resources for all who are assessed. (Loesch, 2007, p. 204)

Cross-cultural issues

Bias in tests, bias in examiner, understanding affects on client

A review of contemporary articles on testing and assessment will quickly reveal that in recent years there has been increased attention to bias in testing and how it disproportionately affects minorities and women. Lawsuits have questioned the accuracy of some tests (see Box 2.3), laws have been passed preventing the use of other tests, and research has been conducted that demonstrates the negative impact of tests on minorities and women. In response to these problems, as you saw earlier in this chapter, ethical codes and standards that address assessment always include statements concerning how to choose, administer, and interpret tests and assessment instruments for minorities and women. In recent years, such codes and standards have stressed that individuals who give tests and use assessment procedures should, at the minimum, keep the following in mind (International Test Commission, 2008; Loesch, 2007):

1. Assume that all tests hold some bias.
2. Be in touch with your own biases and prejudices.
3. Only use tests that have been shown to be constructed using sound research procedures.
4. Only use tests that have good validity and reliability.
5. Know there are times when it is appropriate to test and times when it is not.
6. Know how to choose good tests that are relevant to the situation at hand.
7. Know how to administer, score, and interpret tests within the cultural context of the client.
8. Know and consider the implications that testing may have for the client.
9. Advocate for clients when tests are shown to be biased.
10. Treat people humanely during the assessment process.

In Chapter 3 we will discuss a number of matters related to cross-cultural issues and test worthiness. We will highlight the fact that a test should accurately measure a construct regardless of one's membership in a class, race, religion, or gender. We will discuss how the U.S. court system, public law, federal acts, and constitutional amendments have all supported the notion that testing must be fair for all groups of people and free from bias. We will note how tests cannot be used to track students and that as a result of the Supreme Court case of *Griggs v. Duke Power Company*, tests used for hiring and advancement at work must show that they can predict job performance for all groups. Also, as we highlighted in this chapter and will discuss in Chapter 3, a number of laws have been passed that impinge on the use of tests and assert the rights of all individuals to be tested fairly. In the future, we are likely to see an increased emphasis on understanding the inherent bias in tests, the creation of new tests that are less biased, and new efforts to properly administer, score, and interpret tests with the understanding that they will, to some degree, have bias.

BOX 2.5 | MAKING ETHICAL DECISIONS

Review the situations below, and then using the moral principles identified in the chapter, Corey's models of ethical decision-making, and your knowledge of legal and professional issues, decide on your probable course of action. Share your answers with the rest of the class.

Situation 1: A graduate-level mental health professional with no training in career development is giving interest inventories as she counsels individuals for career issues. Can she do this? Is this ethical? Professional? Legal? If this professional happened to be a colleague of yours, what, if anything, would you do?

Situation 2: During the taking of some routine tests for promotion, a company learns that there is a high probability that one of the employees is abusing drugs and is a pathological liar. The firm decides not to promote him and instead fires him. He comes to see you for counseling because he is depressed. Has the company acted ethically? Legally? What responsibility do you have toward this client?

Situation 3: An African-American mother is concerned that her child may have an attention deficit problem. She goes to the teacher, who supports her concerns, and they go to the assistant principal requesting testing for a possible learning disorder. The mother asks if the child could be given an individual intelligence test that can screen for such problems, and the assistant principal states, "Those tests have

been banned for minority students because of concerns about cross-cultural bias." The mother states that she will give her permission for such testing, but the assistant principal says, "I'm sorry, we'll have to make do with some other tests and with observation." Is this ethical? Professional? Legal? If you were a school counselor or school psychologist and this mother came to see you, what would you tell her?

Situation 4: A test that has not been researched to show that it is predictive of success for all potential graduate students in social work is used as part of the program's admission process. When challenged on this by a potential student, the head of the program states that the test has not been shown to be biased and the program uses other, additional criteria for admission. You are a member of the faculty at this program. Is this ethical? Professional? Legal? What is your responsibility in this situation?

Situation 5: An individual who is physically challenged and wheelchair bound applies for a job at a national fast food chain. When he goes in to take the test for a mid-level job at this company, he is told that he cannot be given this test because it has not been assessed for its predictive ability for individuals with his disability. You are hired by the company to do the testing. What is your responsibility, if any, to this individual and to the company?

EMBRACING TESTING AND ASSESSMENT PROCEDURES

Use assessment instruments! They allow clients better understanding of self

It's not a secret that many students are fearful of, and maybe even dreading, a course in assessment. And, if many students have this fear, one has to wonder if many students also leave a training program with an aversion to using tests and assessment procedures in their professional practice. We hope this is not the case. If you are one of those students, then this speaks directly to you. If you're not, our hats go off to you!

The bottom line: If you have an aversion to using assessment procedures, and you act on it, then you are not being fair to your clients. If clients are to get the most out of counseling, all avenues to increased self-knowledge should be made available to them, including the use of any assessment procedure that can help them gain such knowledge. In fact, one could argue that the proper use of assessment procedures should always be considered for all clients if we are to afford them the best services possible. Clinicians should embrace the appropriate use of assessment procedures as a possible enhancement to the counseling process. To not do so is bringing your fears and biases into the helping relationship.

SUMMARY

This chapter examined ethical, legal, and professional issues involved in assessment. We began be exploring ethical concerns, and first summarized ACA's and APA's assessment sections of their ethical codes, including (1) choosing assessment instruments, (2) competence in the use of tests, (3) confidentiality, (4) cross-cultural sensitivity, (5) informed consent, (6) invasion of privacy, (7) proper diagnosis, (8) release of test data, (9) test administration, (10) test security, and (11) test scoring and interpretation. We next briefly highlighted the purposes of seven important standards in assessment, including: Standards for Qualifications of Test Users, Responsibilities of Users of Standardized Test, Standards for Multicultural Assessment, Code of Fair Testing Practices, Rights and Responsibilities of Test Takers, Competencies in Assessment and Evaluation for School Counselors, and Standards for Educational and Psychological Testing.

As the section on ethical issues continued, we discussed the fact that good ethical decision-making is more than just relying on a code of ethics. We presented a moral model of ethical decision-making, which has to do with the importance of focusing on the *autonomy*, or self-determination, of the client; *nonmaleficence*, or

ensuring that you "do no harm"; *beneficence*, or promoting the well-being of society; *justice*, or providing equal and fair treatment; *fidelity*, or being loyal and faithful to your clients; and *veracity*, which means dealing honestly with your clients. We then presented Corey's eight-step model, which includes identifying the problem or dilemma, identifying the potential issues involved, reviewing the relevant ethical guidelines, knowing the applicable laws and regulations, obtaining consultation, considering possible and probable courses of action, enumerating the consequences of various decisions, and deciding on what appears to be the best course of action. We suggested that the ability to make wise ethical decisions might well be influenced by the counselor's level of ethical, moral, and cognitive development.

The next part of the chapter examined important legal issues involving the use of tests, including the Family Education Rights and Privacy Act (FERPA); the Health Insurance Portability and Accountability Act (HIPAA); privileged communication laws; the Freedom of Information Act; various Civil Rights Acts (1964 and amendments); the Americans with Disabilities Act (PL 101-336); the Individuals with Disabilities Education Improvement Act, which was an expansion of

PL94-142; Section 504 of the Rehabilitation Act; and the Carl Perkins Act (PL 98-24). Most of these laws have to do with issues of confidentiality, fairness, and test worthiness. This section of the chapter also offered a discussion of some of the implications of high-stakes testing.

In this chapter we examined a number of professional issues. First, we highlighted two professional associations in the field of assessment: the Association for Assessment in Counseling and Education (AACE), which is a division of ACA; and Division 5 of the American Psychological Association. We next highlighted three accrediting bodies in the helping professionals that address curriculum standards in assessment: APA, NASP, and CACREP. We then talked about the increasingly important field of forensics and the significance of becoming properly trained as a forensic evaluator or psychologist if one is to conduct such evaluations accurately. We next spoke of the importance of viewing assessment as a holistic process that should often involve assessing the client in multiple ways, including the use of formal tests, informal assessment instru-

ments, and the clinical interview. We pointed out that assessment should be viewed as an ongoing process because people change as they live and learn.

Relative to cross-cultural issues, we stressed that individuals who give tests and use assessment procedures should, at the minimum: only use tests that have been shown to be constructed using sound research procedures; only use tests that have good validity and reliability; know there are times when it is appropriate to test and times it is not; know how to choose good tests that are relevant to the situation at hand; know how to administer, score, and interpret tests within the cultural context of the client; know and consider the implications that testing may have for the client; advocate for clients when tests are shown to be biased; and treat people humanely during the assessment process. We noted that Chapter 3 would expand on the discussion of cross-cultural issues in assessment. Finally, we suggested that clinicians should remain open to using assessment instruments as part of their counseling process.

CHAPTER REVIEW

1. Relative to testing and assessment, identify and discuss some of the major themes addressed in ethical codes.
2. In addition to the ethical codes, other standards have been developed to guide individuals in test selection, administration, and interpretation. Describe some of these standards.
3. Describe APA's levels of test user competence.
4. Describe the moral model and Corey's problem-solving model of ethical decision-making.
5. Compare and contrast how individuals at different cognitive developmental levels would go about making ethical decisions.
6. Identify some of the major legal issues that have affected the selection, administration,

and interpretation of assessment instruments.
7. List two professional associations that specifically address assessment issues.
8. What is the role of accreditation in the delivery of curriculum content in the area of assessment?
9. What are some of the unique issues involved in forensic evaluation?
10. What is needed for a good assessment of an individual?
11. Why should assessment procedures often be considered when working with clients?
12. Describe the importance of having an understanding of cross-cultural issues when using assessment procedures.

REFERENCES

American Counseling Association. (2005). *Code of ethics* (Rev. ed.). Alexandria, VA: Author.

American Psychological Association. (1954). *Technical recommendations for psychological tests and diagnostic techniques.* Washington, DC: Author.

American Psychological Association. (2000). *Guidelines for principles and accreditation of programs in professional psychology.* Retrieved on January 22, 2009, from http://www.apa.org/ed/gp2000.html

American Psychological Association. (2003). *Ethical principles of psychologists and code of conduct.* Retrieved January 22, 2009, from http://www.apa.org/ethics

APA Practice Organization. (2002). Getting ready for HIPAA: What you need to know now: A primer for psychologists. Washington, DC: Author.

Association for Assessment in Counseling and Education. (2008). *AACE statements of purpose.* Retrieved August 29, 2008, from http://www.theaaceonline.com/about.htm

Corey, G., Corey, M., & Callanan, P. (2007). *Issues and ethics in the helping professions* (7th ed.). Pacific Grove, CA: Brooks/Cole.

Council for Accreditation of Counseling and Related Education Programs (CACRE). (2008). *2009 Standards.* Retrieved on August, 29, 2008, from http://www.cacrep.org/index.html

Division 5 (2008). *Division 5: APA Evaluation, measurement, and statistics.* Retrieved August 29, 2008, from http://www.apa.org/about/division/div5.html

Glosoff, H. L., Herlihy, B., & Spense, B. E. (2000). Privileged communication in the counselor-client relationship. *Journal of Counseling and Development,* 78(4), 454–462.

Havey, J. M. (2003). Inclusion, the law and placement decisions: Implications for school psychologists. In T. P. Remley, M. A. Hermann, & W. C. Huey (Eds.), *Ethical and legal issues in school counseling* (2nd ed., pp. 412–423). Alexandria, VA: American School Counselor Association.

International Test Commission. (2008). *Guidelines.* Retrieved September 1, 2008, from http://www.intestcom.org/guidelines/index.php

Jaffee v. Redmond, 518 U.S. 1 (U.S. Supreme Ct., 1996).

Joint Committee on Testing Practices (JCTP). (2004). Code of fair testing practices in education. Washington, DC: American Psychological Association.

Loesch, L. C. (2007). Fair access to and the use of assessment in counseling. In. C. C. Lee (Ed.), *Counseling for social justice* (2nd ed., pp. 201–222). Alexandria, VA: American Counseling Association.

McAuliffe, G., Eriksen, K., & Associates. (2000). *Preparing counselors and therapists: Creating constructivist and developmental programs.* Virginia Beach, VA: The Donning Company.

Mislevy, R. J. (2004). Can there be reliability without "reliability?" *Journal of Educational and Behavioral Statistics,* 29(2), 241–244.

Moss, P. (2004). The meaning and consequences of reliability. *Journal of Educational and Behavioral Statistics,* 29(2), 245–249.

National Association of School Psychologists (NASP). (2000). *Standards for training and field placement programs in school psychology.* Retrieved on August 29, 2008, from http://www.nasponline.org/standards/FinalStandards.pdf

Neukrug, E. (2007). *The world of the counselor.* Belmont, CA: Brooks/Cole.

Neukrug, E., Lovell, C., & Parker, R. (1996). Employing ethical codes and decision-making models: A developmental process. *Counseling and Values,* 40, 98–106.

Patterson, J. (2006, November). Attaining specialty credentials can enhance any counselor's career and knowledge base. *Counseling Today Online.* Retrieved, September 27, 2008, from http://www.counseling.org/Publications/CounselingTodayArticles.aspx?AGuid=20541921-5e69-4619-a587-79788a053249

Packer, I. K. (2008). Specialized practice in forensic psychology: Opportunities and obstacles. *Professional Psychology: Research and Practice,* 39(2), 245–249.

Pennuto, T. O., & Archer, R. P. (2008). MMPI-A forensic case studies: Uses in documented court decisions. *Journal of Personality Assessment,* 90(3), 215–226.

Preston, P. (2005). *Testing children: A practitioner's guide to the assessment of mental development in infants and young children.* Kirkland, WA: Hogrefe & Huber.

Remley, T. P., & Herlihy, B. (2007). *Ethical and professional issues in counseling.* Upper Saddle River, NJ: Merrill.

Remley, T. P., Herlihy, B., & Herlihy, S. B. (1997). The U.S. Supreme Court decision in *Jaffe v.*

Redmond: Implications for counselors. *Journal of Counseling and Development, 75,* 213–218.

Supporting Students with LD (2008). Supporting students with LD: Resources for Job Corps staff. Retrieved, August 29, 2008, from http://jccdrc.jobcorps.gov/ld/IDEA

Swenson, L. (1997). *Psychology and law for the helping professions* (2nd ed.). Pacific Grove, CA: Brooks/Cole.

The National Security Archive (1995–2008). *The Freedom of Information Act.* Retrieved, August 28, 2008, from http://www.gwu.edu/~nsarchiv/nsa/foia.html

Turner, S. M., DeMers, S. T., Fox, H. R., & Reed. G. M. (2001). APA's guidelines for test user qualifications: An executive summary. *American Psychologist, 56* (12), 1099–1113.

U.S. Census Bureau. (2003). *Disability status 2000: Census 2000 Brief.* Retrieved November 5, 2005, from http://www.census.gov/prod/2003pubs/c2kbr-17.pdf.

U.S. Department of Education. (2007a). *Family Educational Rights and Privacy Act (FERPA).* Retrieved, August 28, 2008, from http://www.ed.gov/policy/gen/guid/fpco/ferpa/index.html

U.S. Department of Education (2007b). *Carl D. Perkins Career and Technical Education Act of 2006.* Retrieved, September 1, 2008, from http://www.ed.gov/policy/sectech/leg/perkins/index.html#intro

U.S. Department of Health and Human Services. (n.d.). *Your rights under section 504 of the Rehabilitation Act.* Retrieved August 29, 2008 from http://www.hhs.gov/ocr/504.html

U.S. Department of Health and Human Services. (2007). *Protecting the privacy of patients' health information.* Retrieved August 28, 2008, from http://www.hhs.gov/news/facts/privacy2007.html

U.S. Equal Employment Opportunity Commission. (1997). *Facts about the Americans with Disabilities Act.* Retrieved August 28, 2008, from http://www.eeoc.gov/facts/fs-ada.html

Waller, J. M. (2003). A necessary evil: Proposition 16 and its impact on academics and athletics in the NCAA. *DePaul Journal of Sports Law and Contemporary Problems, 1*(2), p. 189–206.

Zuckerman, E. (2003). *The paper office: Forms, guidelines, and resources to make your practice work ethically, legally, and profitably* (3rd ed.). New York: Guilford Press.

TEST WORTHINESS AND TEST STATISTICS

SECTION | II

In Section Two we will examine how tests are created, scored, and interpreted. Chapters 3, 4, and 5 all explain a number of important concepts related to test statistics. Being able to understand these statistics and how they are applied to the assessment process is crucial if one is to interpret test data appropriately. As you read these chapters, we will show you that the development of tests and the interpretation of test data is a deliberate and planned process that involves a scientific approach to the understanding of differences among people. We try to present this information in a down-to-earth and comprehensible fashion.

Chapter 3 describes test worthiness and defines it as an involved, objective analysis of a test. To do this objective analysis, however, we must first understand a basic statistic called the correlation coefficient. Thus, the correlation coefficient is defined early in this chapter, and we subsequently show how this important statistic is used to conduct an analysis of many aspects of the four factors of test worthiness: (1) *validity*: whether the test measures what it's supposed to measure; (2) *reliability*: whether the score an individual has received on a test is an accurate measure of his or her true score; (3) *cross-cultural fairness*: whether the score the individual has obtained is a true reflection of the individual, and not a function of cultural bias inherent in the test or in the examiner, and (4) *practicality*: whether it makes sense to use a test in a particular situation. The chapter concludes with a list of five steps to use in test selection to assure test worthiness.

Chapter 4 starts with the basics: an examination of raw scores. We first show that raw scores generally provide little meaningful information about a set of scores, and then we look at various ways that we can manipulate raw scores to make sense out of a set of data. Thus, in this chapter we examine how a variety of basic statistics and graphs can help us understand raw scores. Some of these include frequency distributions; histograms and frequency polygons; cumulative distributions; the normal curve; skewed distributions; measures of central tendency such as the mean, median, and mode; and measures of variability such as the range, semi-interquartile range, and standard deviation.

Chapter 5 is a natural extension of Chapter 4, and in it we examine derived scores and explore how they are used to help us understand raw scores. We start by distinguishing norm-referenced testing and criterion-referenced testing because these two ways of understanding test scores are quite different, and derived scores are mostly associated with norm-referenced testing. Next, we discuss specific types of derived scores: percentiles; standard scores, including z scores, T scores, Deviation IQs, stanines, sten scores, college and graduate school entrance exam scores (e.g., SATs, GREs, and ACTs), NCE scores, and publisher-type scores; and developmental norms such as age comparisons and grade equivalents. The chapter nears its conclusion with a discussion of standard error of measurement and standard error of estimate. The chapter ends with a brief discussion of nominal, ordinal, interval, and ratio scales of measurement. We describe how each type of scale has unique attributes that may limit the statistical calculations we can perform, and we mention that different kinds of assessment instruments use different kinds of scales.

TEST WORTHINESS: VALIDITY, RELIABILITY, PRACTICALITY, AND CROSS-CULTURAL FAIRNESS

I'm walking down a Cincinnati street, and a man walks up to me and asks, "Want to take a test?" "Sure," I reply. He takes me to a storefront, gives me a test, and then goes to a back room to score it. A few minutes later he reappears and tells me, "Well, you're pretty bright and have a fairly good personality, but if you take Ron Hubbard's course in Scientology, you will be brighter and have a better personality." I tell him, "No thanks."
A few years later, I'm walking down a street in Minneapolis and a man comes up to me and inquires, "Want to take a test?" This time I say, "If you can show me that this test is a good test—that is, it has good reliability and validity—I'll take it." He says, "I'm sure it has good reliability and validity." I say, "Show me." He says, "Well, I know our New York office must have that information." I say, "Well, I tell you what, I'll buy Ron Hubbard's book, Dianetics, and if and when you can get me the information from the New York office, I'll read the book." I gave him my name and address. I never heard from him again.

(Ed Neukrug)

Test worthiness
Based on validity, reliability, cross-cultural fairness, and practicality

As you might expect from the above example, this chapter is about test worthiness, or how good a test actually is. Demonstrating test worthiness requires an involved, objective analysis of a test in four critical areas: (1) validity: whether it measures what it's supposed to measure; (2) reliability: whether the score an individual receives on a test is an accurate measure of his or her true score; (3) cross-cultural fairness: whether a person's score is a true reflection of the individual and not a function of cultural bias inherent in the test; and (4) practicality: whether it makes sense to use a test in a particular situation. After examining these four factors, we will conclude the chapter with a discussion of five steps to use in test selection to assure test worthiness. However, prior to examining the four critical factors of validity, reliability, cross-cultural fairness, and practicality, and before discussing test

43

selection, we will examine the concept of correlation coefficient because it is central to understanding much of what will be presented in this chapter.

CORRELATION COEFFICIENT

Correlation coefficient

Relationship between two sets of test scores

Correlation coefficient, which shows the relationship between two sets of scores, is a statistical concept frequently used in discussions of the critical factors listed above. Correlation coefficients range from −1.00 to +1.00 and generally are reported in decimals of one-hundredths (see Figure 3.1). A positive correlation shows a tendency for scores to be related in the same direction. For instance, if a group of individuals took two tests, a positive correlation would show a tendency for those who obtained high scores on the first test to obtain high scores on the second test, for those who obtained low scores on the first test to obtain low scores on the second test, and so forth. On the other hand, a negative correlation shows an inverse relationship between sets of scores; for instance, individuals who obtain high scores on the first test would be likely to obtain low scores on the second test.

A correlation that approaches −1 OR +1 demonstrates a strong relationship, while a correlation that approaches 0 shows little or no relationship between two measures or variables (see Figure 3.1). For instance, if I wanted to show that SAT scores predict college performance, I would have to show that the correlation coefficient does not approach zero and is significant enough to warrant its use (see Kobrin, Patterson, Shaw, Mattern, & Barbuti, 2008; Kuncel, & Hezlett, 2007). Similarly, if I wanted to show that my newly made test of depression was worthwhile, I could correlate scores on my new test with an established test of depression. In this case I would expect to find a relatively high correlation coefficient as evidenced by the fact that individuals who scored high on my test would have a tendency to score high on the established test, individuals who scored low on my test would have a tendency to score low on the established test, and so forth. As we discuss the four critical factors of validity, reliability, cross-cultural fairness, and practicality, you will see that correlation coefficient often plays an important role in many of them. If you would like to find out how to calculate a correlation coefficient, see Appendix D.

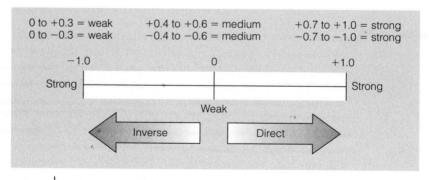

FIGURE 3.1 | CORRELATION COEFFICIENT

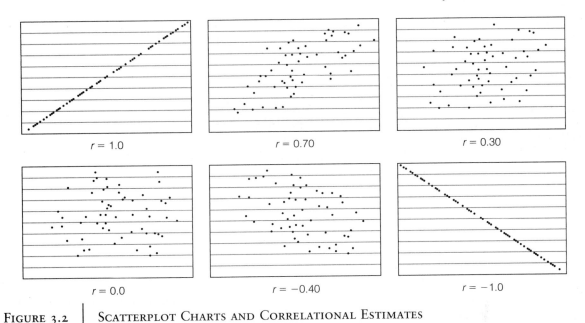

FIGURE 3.2 | SCATTERPLOT CHARTS AND CORRELATIONAL ESTIMATES

Scatterplot

Graph showing two or more sets of test scores

A correlation between two sets of variables, or test scores, can also be plotted on a graph. By placing an individual's first score on the horizontal (x) axis and second score on the vertical (y) axis, you can plot this person's scores on the graph. If you continue doing this for the remaining members of a group of people, each of whom has two sets of scores, you will end up with what's called a scatterplot (see Figure 3.2).

As illustrated in Figure 3.2, as the dots come close to forming a diagonal line, the scores on the x-axis are more closely related to scores on the y-axis, or the correlation becomes closer to plus or minus 1.0. As the dots become more random (little relationship between scores on the two tests), the correlation approaches zero. Additionally, it is called a positive correlation if the general slope of the dots rises from left to right and a negative correlation if it rises from the right to the left.

COEFFICIENT OF DETERMINATION (SHARED VARIANCE)

Coefficient of determination

Common factors that account for a relationship; square of the correlation coefficient

Squaring the correlation coefficient gives you the coefficient of determination, or shared variance between two variables. This variance is a statement about underlying factors that account for the relationship between two variables. Thus, if the correlation is .70, the square is .49, which represents a percentage of shared variance—in this case, 49 percent. For instance, in one study, a correlation of .85 was found between scores on a test of depression and scores on a test that measured anxiety (Cole, Truglio, & Peeke, 1997). Therefore, in this case it can be said that 72% of the variance is shared variance (.85 squared), or, in other words, a large percentage of similar factors underlie feelings of depression and anxiety as measured by these tests (see Figure 3.3). What might some of these factors be? An educated guess might lead us to think that they could be environmental stressors (e.g., job loss, relationship problems, etc.), cognitive schemata (ways of understanding the world), chemical imbalance, and so forth. All of these factors could trigger feelings of

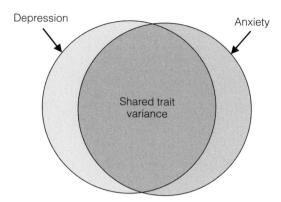

FIGURE 3.3 | SHARED VARIANCE BETWEEN DEPRESSION AND ANXIETY $(r = .85, r^2 = .72)$

depression and of anxiety. Of course, we need to keep in mind that 28% of the variance is not shared, which means that other factors differentially affect whether one feels depressed or anxious. Keep the concept of coefficient of determination in mind when you read the next section on validity.

VALIDITY

Validity
Evidence supporting the use of test scores

Validity is a unitary concept. It is the degree to which all of the accumulated evidence supports the intended interpretation of test scores for the intended purpose (American Educational Research Association, 1999, p. 11).

How well does a test measure what it's supposed to measure? That is the primary question that validity attempts to answer. Over the years a number of methods have been developed to determine the validity of a test. Logically, it makes sense that the more methods one can use to provide evidence that a test is valid, the stronger the case one can make that the interpretation of test scores is accurate for the manner in which the test is being used (American Educational Research Association, 1999). Various types of validity that help to provide the evidence needed to demonstrate the worthiness of a test include content validity; criterion-related validity, which includes concurrent validity and predictive validity; and construct validity, which includes methods of experimental design, factor analysis, discriminant validity, and convergent validity.

CONTENT VALIDITY

Content validity
Evidence that test items represent the proper domain

Probably the most basic form of validity is content validity. As with all types of validity, its name is reflective of what it attempts to show: Is the content of the test valid for the kind of test it is? In assuring content validity, a process is used to develop items for a test, such as examining established books in the field, gathering information from experts, and examining curriculum guides. In demonstrating content validity, test publishers need to do the following:

Step 1: Show that the test developer adequately surveyed the domain through the processes noted above.

Step 2: Show that the content of the test matches what was found in the survey of the domain.

Step 3: Show that test items accurately reflect the content.

Step 4: Show that the number of items for each content area matches the relative importance of these items as reflected in the survey of the domain (Wolfe & Smith, 2007).

To illustrate this process, let's look at the creation of a fourth-grade math achievement test to be used nationally. In demonstrating content validity, the test developer should do the following:

Step 1: Show that information for the test was gathered from places such as fourth-grade math books, teachers of fourth-grade math, curriculum specialists in the schools, professors at colleges who are training fourth-grade math teachers, and so forth.

Step 2: Show that the content was chosen based on the information that was gathered (e.g., addition, subtraction, multiplication, division, decimals, fractions).

Step 3: Show that the items reflect the content chosen.

Step 4: Show that the number of items for each content area reflects the relative importance of that area (e.g., multiplication and division might be emphasized more than the other items) (see Figure 3.4).

Despite one's painstaking attempts to assure content validity, not all fourth-grade teachers would be teaching the same math content, so the test might hold more validity for some fourth-grade classes than for others. Thus, content validity is somewhat contextual and depends on who is taking the test (Goodwin, 2002a, 2002b).

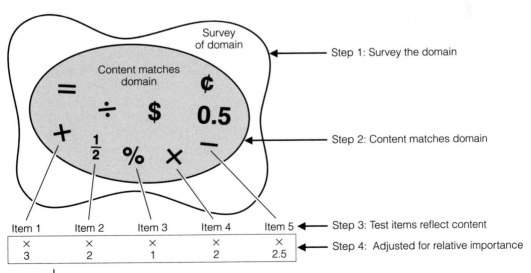

FIGURE 3.4 | ESTABLISHING CONTENT VALIDITY

Face validity
Superficial appearance of a test—not true validity

Face validity, which is not considered an actual type of validity, is sometimes confused with content validity. Face validity has to do with how the test superficially looks. If you were examining the test, would it appear to be measuring what it is supposed to measure? Although most tests should have face validity, some tests could be valid yet not have it. For instance, there might be some items on a personality test that, on the surface, do not seem to be measuring a quality that the test is attempting to assess. Look, for example, at the hypothetical item below that is assessing whether or not an individual may have a panic disorder:

In the past week, check the following symptoms that you have experienced:

_____ a. chills   _____ c. hot flashes   _____ e. depersonalization

_____ b. choking   _____ d. abdominal distress _____ f. unsteady feelings

Even though the symptoms listed above might not seem obvious to a person unfamiliar with panic disorder, they are often associated with the disorder, as noted in the *Diagnostic and Statistical Manual-IV-TR* (American Psychiatric Association, 2000). On the surface, this item might not seem to be measuring the construct, but individuals with panic disorder often have some or all of these symptoms, and thus such a question is conceivable and might be important to ask. Therefore, the item might be important to the content validity of the test.

EXERCISE 3.1 DEMONSTRATING CONTENT VALIDITY

In small groups, discuss how you might show content validity for a test that measures depression. Share your ideas in class.

CRITERION-RELATED VALIDITY

Criterion-related validity
Relationship between test scores and another standard

Concurrent validity
Relationship between test scores and another currently obtainable benchmark

Predictive validity
Relationship between test scores and a future standard

What is the relationship between a test and a criterion (external source) that the test should be related to? That is the essence of criterion-related validity. Two types of criterion-related validity generally described are *concurrent validity* and *predictive validity.*

Concurrent, or "here and now," validity occurs when a test is shown to be related to an external source that can be measured at around the same time the test is being given. For instance, suppose I develop a test to measure the tendency toward alcohol abuse. I might give this test to 500 individuals and then have significant people in each examinee's life rank order the examinee's use of alcohol to see if there is a correlation between alcohol abuse and use of alcohol (e.g., number of drinks per day). Clearly, I would suspect a high correlation (the higher the score, the more one drank), and if I did not find one, my test would be suspect.

Whereas concurrent validity relates a test to a "here and now" measure, predictive validity relates a test to a criterion in the future. This kind of validity is clearly important if a test should be predicting something about an individual. For instance, the GREs should have predictive validity for GPA in graduate school; otherwise they would not be valuable and should not be used. In actuality, the correlation

| TABLE 3.1 | AVERAGE ESTIMATED CORRELATIONS OF GRE GENERAL TEST (VERBAL, QUANTITATIVE, AND ANALYTICAL) SCORES AND UNDERGRADUATE GRADE POINT AVERAGE WITH GRADUATE FIRST-YEAR GRADE POINT AVERAGE BY DEPARTMENT TYPE |

Type of Department	Number of Departments	Number of Examinees	Predictors					
			V	Q	A	U	VQA*	VQAU*
All departments	1,038	12,013	.30	.29	.28	.37	.34	.46
Natural sciences	384	4,420	.28	.27	.26	.36	.31	.44
Engineering	87	1,066	.27	.22	.24	.38	.30	.44
Social sciences	352	4,211	.33	.32	.30	.38	.37	.48
Humanities & arts	115	1,219	.30	.33	.27	.37	.34	.46
Education	86	901	.31	.30	.29	.35	.36	.47
Business	14	196	.28	.28	.25	.39	.31	.47

V = GRE Verbal, Q = GRE Quantitative, A = GRE Analytical, U = Undergraduate grade point average
*Combination of individual predictors
Source: Graduate Record Examinations, 2004–2005. GRE materials selected from 2004–2005 Guide to the Use of Scores, p. 22. Reprinted by permission of Educational Testing Service, the copyright owner.

between the GREs and GPA in graduate school is about .34, which is not very high (see Table 3.1). However, when placed in the context of other possible predictors of college success (e.g., undergraduate GPA, extracurricular activities, and interviews), it's not so bad. And, if we combine the use of predictors of graduate school GPA, we increase our ability to make a prediction about students' success. For instance, the correlation between undergraduate GPA and grades in graduate school is .37, and when we combine the GRE scores and GPA in undergraduate school we find a correlation of .46 with grades in graduate school (see Table 3.1).

A practical application of predictive validity is the *standard error of the estimate* (SE*est*) which, based on one variable, allows us to predict a range of scores on a second variable. For example, if we know students' GRE scores and the correlation between GRE scores and first year grades in graduate school, we can predict the range of GPAs students are likely to obtain in graduate school. This range of scores is sometimes referred to as a confidence interval (e.g., where students GPAs will fall 68% of the time). Actually "seeing" how well one set of scores predicts a second set of scores can give us a more realistic sense of the whether or not such scores should be used in making important decisions about individuals' lives. In Chapter 5 we will show how a SE*est* is actually determined.

Another concept in the application of predictive validity is *false positives* and *false negatives*. A false positive is when an instrument incorrectly predicts a test taker will have an attribute or be successful when he or she will not. A false negative is when a test forecasts an individual will not have an attribute or will be unsuccessful when in fact he or she will. For example, let's say you are working in a high school and use the adolescent version of the Substance Abuse Subtle Screening Inventory (SASSI, 2008) to flag students who may have an addiction. After giving the instrument to 100 students, 10 are identified as having a high likelihood of having a substance dependency. If two of those students do not, in fact, have an addiction, that would be considered a false positive. If one of the 90 students whose scores indicated a low probability of a dependency, but in actuality had a diagnosable substance dependence, that would be considered a false negative. Although it would be better to have neither false positives or negatives, in the case of the SASSI, the designers chose to err toward having a greater chance of false positives than false negatives. Why do you think that is?

EXERCISE 3.2 DEMONSTRATING CRITERION-RELATED VALIDITY

In class, form small groups, some of which will examine concurrent validity while others will examine predictive validity. In your groups, choose a test from the list below or come up with another test. Next, discuss criteria with which you might compare your test.

Possible Tests:

High school achievement test	Depression test	Clerical aptitude test
SATs, GREs, MATs	Test of anxiety	First-grade reading test
Intelligence test	Test of hypochondriasis	

CONSTRUCT VALIDITY

Construct validity

Evidence that an idea or concept is being measured by a test

What is intelligence? When teaching an assessment class, we have found that this often becomes a "hot" topic for discussion, with students arguing over what they believe actually makes up this construct. Construct validity is the scientific basis for showing that a construct (idea, concept, or model) such as intelligence is being measured by a test. Showing evidence of construct validity is particularly important when developing tests that measure abstract domains, such as intelligence, self-concept, depression, anxiety, empathy, and many other personality characteristics. On the other hand, construct validity becomes much less of an issue when one is measuring well-defined areas, such as achievement in geometry.

To demonstrate construct validity it is often useful to provide multiple sources of evidence that the construct we are measuring is indeed being exposed. Although some have argued that almost any kind of validity is evidence that the construct being measured exists (Goodwin, 2002a), a more restrictive definition of construct validity includes an analysis of a test through one or more of the following methods: (1) experimental design, (2) factor analysis, (3) convergence with other instruments, and/or (4) discrimination with other measures.

Experimental design validity

Using experimentation to show that a test measures a concept

EXPERIMENTAL DESIGN VALIDITY   You've just developed your new test of depression, and you're very proud of it. Of course, you want to show that it is indeed valid. You already have shown that it has content validity by developing items through an examination of DSM-IV-TR, scholarly journal articles, and consultation with experts. However, now you want to show that the test indeed works— that it measures your construct. So you approach a number of expert clinicians who work with depressed clients and ask them to identify new clients on their caseloads who are depressed. You then request that they administer your depression test prior to and at the end of six months of treatment. What should you expect to find? Clearly, if the test is good and does measure the construct depression, it should be able to accurately reflect the change in these clients—in this case, a significant decrease in depression. If not, you need to go back to the drawing board. Experimentally based construct validity thus confirms the hypothesis you developed to scientifically show that your construct exists. Sometimes, when a number of studies are completed, you will find authors conducting a "meta-analysis," which statistically analyzes all of these studies in an effort to offer broader evidence of the existence of the construct being examined.

Factor analysis
Statistically examining the relationship between subscales and the larger construct

FACTOR ANALYSIS   Factor analysis, another method to show construct validity, demonstrates the statistical relationship among subscales or items of a test. Suppose, for instance, that your depression test has subscales that measure hopelessness, suicidal ideation, and self-esteem. Theoretically, you would expect them all to be related to your larger test score that measures depression. In addition, you would expect them to be somewhat related, but not largely related, to one another. After all, they are measuring something different from one another (although they all make up the larger test "depression"). If your factor analysis upholds these expectations, you have shown construct validity of your test.

Convergent validity
Relationship between a test and other similar tests

CONVERGENCE WITH OTHER INSTRUMENTS (CONVERGENT VALIDITY)   Believing strongly that your test does indeed measure depression, you would, of course, expect your test to be related to other existing well-known valid measures of depression (e.g., clinicians' ratings of clients or another test of depression). Thus, you decide to correlate your test with the Beck Depression Inventory II (BDI-II) (Beck, Steer, & Brown, 2004), a well-known test of depression. You give the BDI-II and your test to 500 subjects and you find a relatively high correlation between the two scores, perhaps .75. You're satisfied, perhaps even glad you didn't get a higher correlation. After all, isn't your test different (and a little better!) than the well-known existing test? Thus, you expect your correlation to be less than perfect. Thus, convergent validity occurs when you find a significant positive correlation between your test and other existing measures of a similar nature. Sometimes this relationship involves very similar kinds of instruments, but other times you would be looking for correlations between your test and variables that may seem only somewhat related. For instance, if you correlate your test with a test to measure despair, you would expect a positive correlation. However, because despair is theoretically different from depression, you would expect a lower correlation—maybe .4.

Discriminant validity
Showing a lack of relationship between a test and other dissimilar tests

DISCRIMINATION WITH OTHER MEASURES (DISCRIMINANT VALIDITY)   With convergent validity you're expecting to find a relationship between your test and other variables of a similar nature. Discriminant validity, in a sense, is the opposite in that you're looking to find little or no relationship between your test and measures of constructs that are not theoretically related to your test. For instance, with your test of depression, you might want to compare your test scores with an existing test that measures anxiety. In this case, you give 500 subjects your test of depression as well as a valid test to measure anxiety, looking to find little or no relationship. Consider how important discriminant validity might be in this case if you're working with clients. Clients who are dealing with high amounts of anxiety will often present with depressive features. If you were able to give your client a test that could discriminate depression from anxiety, you would get a better picture of your client. Making a more accurate diagnosis could dramatically affect your treatment plan, as approaches to working with depressed clients will vary from approaches to working with anxious clients.

EXERCISE 3.3   DEMONSTRATING CONSTRUCT VALIDITY

In small groups, show how you would develop the construct validity of a test that measures self-actualizing values (e.g., being in touch with feelings, being spontaneous, being accepting and nonjudgmental, showing empathy). Try to touch on many of the methods noted in this section of text, including experimental design, factor analysis, convergent validity, and discriminant validity. Present your group's proposal to the class.

RELIABILITY

Reliability

Degree of freedom from measurement error—consistency of test scores

Test reliability can be compared to eating at the same restaurant over and over again. If it's a highly reliable restaurant, the meals always taste great. On the other hand, a restaurant that has poor reliability can't be trusted. Too many bad ingredients are used and mistakes are made in putting the meals together. And, maybe the restaurant has an atmosphere that turns you off and makes you not enjoy your meal.

Similarly, a test with high reliability is put together well—it has the right ingredients. And when you take the test, it's in an environment that is conducive to you producing your best results. The test is made well and the environment is optimal for the test-taking situation. You can trust that if, hypothetically, you were the same person who had walked in the first time you took this test, and you were to take this test over and over again, you would score about the same each time (e.g., if it were an achievement test, you didn't look up the answers or study the content prior to taking the test again). On the other hand, if you were to take a test with poor reliability over and over again your scores would fluctuate—be higher or lower each time you took it. There are so many problems with the test and with the environment that you would answer items in a different manner every time you take it.

Reliability can be defined as "the degree to which test scores are free from errors of measurement" (American Educational Research Association, 1999, p. 180). Hypothetically, if we had a perfect test and the perfect environment, and a person who remained exactly the same each time he or she took the test, this individual would always score the same on the test, even if he or she took it one thousand times. As we all know, there are no perfect tests or environments, so we always end up with measurement error—or factors that affect one's score on a test. Clearly, the more we can reduce error on tests, the more accurate will be the examinee's score.

Have you ever taken a test and received a score that you felt didn't reflect how you actually performed on the test? Some of that difference may be attributed to measurement error. Many factors can cause such error, including poorly worded questions, poor test-taking instructions, test-taker anxiety or fatigue, and distractions in the testing room, to name just a few. On the other hand, part of the discrepancy may be due to lack of knowledge of the subject or lack of awareness of self, and sometimes it's easier to blame a test than ourselves for scores that we did not expect. If we know the amount of error on a test, as measured by reliability estimates, then we should be able to determine, to some degree, whether our unexpected score was due to error or to performance issues.

Test creators will evaluate their new instrument to determine if the scores it produces are reliable (consistent and dependable) and publish this information in the test manual, usually reported in the form of a reliability (correlation) coefficient. The closer the reliability estimate is to 1.0, the less error there is on the test. A good reliability estimate is sometimes a function of the kind of measurement being assessed, although there is no magic cut-off point for what makes a good reliability estimate (Heppner, Wampold, & Kivlighan, 2008). For instance, teacher-made tests generally will have lower reliability estimates, perhaps around .7, because they do not go through the same type of scrutiny as some other kinds of tests, such as national achievement tests that often have reliability estimates in the .90s. Also, personality tests generally have lower reliability estimates than ability tests because the construct being measured is more abstract and because personality tends to fluctuate and thus is more difficult to define and measure. Some ways of measuring reliability include test-retest, alternative forms, and internal consistency. After looking at these types of reliability, this section will conclude with a discussion about Item Response Theory, a more recent way of examining reliability.

TEST-RETEST RELIABILITY

Test-retest reliability

Relationship between scores from one test given at two different administrations

A relatively simple way to determine whether an instrument is reliable is to give the test twice to the same group of people. For example, imagine you have 500 people who come in to take a test. A day later they take the same test at the same place. You would then correlate the scores from the first test with those from the second test. The closer the two sets of scores, the more reliable the test. Although reliability coefficients provide individual test-takers with estimates about the stability of their individual scores, the actual process of gathering reliability information has to do with average fluctuation of many people's scores. Thus, although one person's score might fluctuate a lot, an instrument can still have high reliability if most scores have little fluctuation.

Accuracy of the test-retest method can be affected by several factors. For instance, depending on the time between test administrations, people may forget information. On the other hand, sometimes people might learn more about a specific subject by reading a book, listening to the radio, searching on the computer, and so on. Also, some people might score higher on a second test because they are more familiar with the test format. As you might expect, test-retest reliability tends to be more effective in areas that are less likely to change over time, such as intelligence.

ALTERNATE, PARALLEL, OR EQUIVALENT FORMS RELIABILITY

Alternate forms reliability

Relationship between scores from two similar versions of the same test

Another method for determining reliability is to make two or more *alternate, parallel,* or *equivalent* forms of the same test. These alternate forms are created to mimic one another, yet are different enough to eliminate some of the problems found in test-retest reliability (e.g., looking up an answer). In this case, rather than giving the same test twice, the examiner gives the alternate form the second time. Clearly, a challenge involved in this kind of reliability is to assure that both forms of the test use the same or very similar directions, format, and number of questions, and are equal in difficulty and content. Although creating alternate forms eliminates some of the problems found in test-retest reliability, difficulty can arise in ensuring that the two forms are truly parallel. Also, because creating a parallel form is labor intensive and costly, it is often not a practical kind of reliability to implement. If this kind of reliability is used, the burden is on the test creator to prove that both tests are truly equal.

INTERNAL CONSISTENCY

Internal consistency
Reliability measured statistically by going "within" the test

A third type of reliability is called internal consistency. In this case, a determination is made as to how scores on individual items relate to each other or to the test as a whole. For instance, it would make sense that individuals who score high on a test of depression should, on average, respond to all the items on the test in a manner that indicates depressive ideation. If not, one might wonder why a particular item is not assessing depression. This kind of reliability is called internal consistency because you are looking within the test itself, or not going "outside of the test" to determine reliability estimates as you would be with test-retest or parallel forms reliability. Some types of internal consistency reliability include split-half (or odd-even), Cronbach's Coefficient Alpha, and Kuder-Richardson, each of which will be discussed separately.

Split-half reliability
Correlating one half of a test against the other half

SPLIT-HALF OR ODD-EVEN RELIABILITY   The most basic form of internal consistency reliability is called split-half or odd-even reliability. This method, which requires only one form and one administration of the test, splits the test in half and correlates the scores of one half of the test with the other half. Again, imagine 500 individuals who come in to take a test. After they have finished, we gather their responses, split each of their tests in half, and score each half, almost as if each individual had taken two different tests. The scores on the two halves are then correlated with one another. Obviously, advantages of this kind of reliability include only having to give the test once and not having to create a separate alternate form. One potential pitfall of this form of reliability would arise if the two halves of the test were not parallel or equivalent, such as when a test gets progressively more difficult. In that case, you might end up correlating the first half of the test with the second nonequivalent half, which can give you an inaccurately low estimate of your reliability. One common method to alleviate this potential error is to split the test into odd-numbered items and even-numbered items, although even this method runs the risk of not producing parallel halves.

Another disadvantage of this kind of reliability is that by turning one test into two, you have made it half as long. Generally speaking, one obtains a more accurate reading of the reliability of a test the longer it is; consequently, shortening the test may decrease its reliability. One common method to mathematically compensate for shortening the number of correlations is to use the Spearman-Brown equation (Brown, 1910; Spearman, 1910). The generally used Spearman-Brown formula is:

$$\text{Spearman} = \text{Brown reliability} = \frac{2r_{hh}}{1 + r_{hh}}$$

where r_{hh} is the split-half or odd-even reliability estimate. For example, if the reliability is .70, you would multiply .70 by 2, and then divide by the sum of $1 + .70$. This would be 1.40 divided by 1.70, which gives you a reliability estimate of .82 for the whole test. So if a test manual states that split-half reliability was used, check to see if the Spearman-Brown formula was applied. If it was not, the test might be somewhat more reliable than actually noted.

Coefficient Alpha or Kuder-Richardson
Reliability based on a mathematical comparison of individual items with one another and total score

CRONBACH'S COEFFICIENT ALPHA AND KUDER-RICHARDSON   Although used for different kinds of tests, Coefficient Alpha and Kuder-Richardson forms of reliability are also considered internal consistency methods that attempt to estimate the reliability of all the possible split-half combinations (Cronbach, 1951). In brief, they do this by correlating the scores for each item on the test with the total score on the test and finding the average correlation for all of the items (Salkind, 2004). Clearly, individuals who are producing depressed scores should be responding to test items in a manner that indicates depression, and individuals who are producing scores that indicate they are not depressed should be responding to test items in a manner that do not indicate depression. If particular items are not able to discriminate between depressed and non-depressed individuals, there are likely some problems with those items and this will be reflected in an overall lower internal consistency estimate. Obtaining the correlation between each item and the whole test score for each person, and then finding the average of all those correlations, used to be a tedious process. However, with computers, such reliability estimates can now be configured in a millisecond and therefore have become very popular. The difference between these two formulas is that Kuder-Richardson can be used only with tests that have right and wrong answers, such as achievement tests, whereas Coefficient Alpha can be applied to assessment instruments that result in varied types of responses, such as rating scales. If you are interested in the actual formulas for Kuder-Richardson and Coefficient Alpha, you can find them in Appendix D.

VISUAL REPRESENTATION OF TYPES OF RELIABILITY

Figure 3.5 is a visual representation of the three types of reliability. Notice that test-retest is represented by the same test being given again with a time difference, alternative forms is represented by two similar forms that are not affected by time, and two types of internal consistency are shown: split-half, which is represented by a test being split, and Coefficient Alpha and Kuder-Richardson being shown as a grid which represents each item being related to the whole test. These visual representations can help you remember each form.

ITEM RESPONSE THEORY: ANOTHER WAY OF LOOKING AT RELIABILITY

IRT
Examining each item for its ability to discriminate as a function of the construct being measured

Most of the concepts in this book fall under the description of classical test theory. Item Response Theory (IRT) is an extension of this (Bechger, Maris, Verstralen, & Beguin, 2003; Brennan, 1998). Classical Test Theory, which originated with Spearman (1904), assumes that measurement error exists in every instrument. Hence, a respondent's true score is equal to his or her observed score plus or minus measurement error.

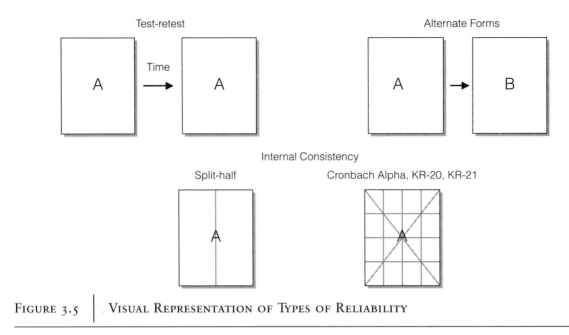

FIGURE 3.5 | VISUAL REPRESENTATION OF TYPES OF RELIABILITY

True score = observed score ± measurement error

Reliability is the opposite of measurement error, so we can see why it is important in classical test theory. As the reliability increases, the measurement error decreases. If we have a reliability alpha of .60, then we have a lot of measurement error, which makes it more difficult to estimate a true score. An instrument with .93 reliability has little error, allowing us feel more confident. In classical test theory, test items are viewed as a whole, with the desire to reduce overall measurement error (increase reliability) so that we can estimate the true score.

IRT, on the other hand, examines items individually for their ability to measure the trait being examined (Ostini & Nering, 2006). This provides IRT test developers with a slight advantage over classical test theorists for improving reliability, because IRT provides more sophisticated information regarding individual items (MacDonald & Paunonen, 2002). The item characteristic curve is a tool used in IRT that assumes that as people's abilities increase, their probability of answering an item correctly increases. We can plot examinees' ability along the x-axis and the probability of getting the item correct along the y-axis. If we were developing an IQ test using IRT, we could graph our sample data for each question using the item characteristic curve as seen in Figure 3.6. We can see that if someone has average ability (i.e., IQ of 100) along the bottom of the graph, he or she has a 50% chance of getting the item correct on the left side of the chart. If an individual has less ability, say an IQ of 85, his or her chance of getting the item correct has been reduced to 25%. Similarly, you can see as one's ability increases along the bottom toward the right, the chance of getting items correct begins to approach 100%.

FIGURE 3.6 | ITEM CHARACTERISTIC CURVE

The item characteristic curve provides a lot of information. We can see that if the shape of the "S" flattens out, the item has less ability to discriminate or provide a range of probabilities of getting a correct or incorrect response. If the S is tall, it means the item is creating strong differentiation across ability. IRT allows test developers to write items targeting specific ranges of ability. For example, we could write items that would have 50% probability of answering correctly at the 115 IQ level. If we were administering our test via computer, we could provide different questions for different abilities dependent on how the previous question was answered. If Jo Anne got our first question correct at the 100 IQ level, we could then give her a question at the 115 level. If she missed this item, we could give her one at the 107 level. We can continually fine-tune Jo Anne's score this way.

CROSS-CULTURAL FAIRNESS

Cross-cultural fairness

Degree to which cultural background, class, disability, and gender do not affect test results

Although inextricably related to the validity and reliability of a test, cross-cultural fairness deserves a separate section due to the importance we as a nation place on issues of fairness, especially with regard to diversity. Awareness of cross-cultural factors and how they impact the development, administration, scoring, and interpretation of assessment procedures are critically important and should always be considered when assessing an individual. When using tests, mental health professionals should take into account how such issues may impact a broad array of minorities and individuals with disabilities. For instance, the Standards for Qualifications of Test Users (American Counseling Association, 2003) states that those involved with testing should:

> …be committed to fairness in every aspect of testing. Information gained and decisions made about the client or student are valid only to the degree that the

test accurately and fairly assesses the client's or student's characteristics. Test selection and interpretation are done with an awareness of the degree to which items may be culturally biased or the norming sample not reflective or inclusive of the client's or student's diversity. Test users understand that age and physical disability differences may impact the client's ability to perceive and respond to test items. Test scores are interpreted in light of the cultural, ethnic, disability, or linguistic factors that may impact an individual's score. These include visual, auditory, and mobility disabilities that may require appropriate accommodation in test administration and scoring. Test users understand that certain types of norms and test score interpretation may be inappropriate, depending on the nature and purpose of the testing. (Standard 6)

Although much emphasis is placed on cross-cultural fairness today, this has not always been the case (recall the cultural bias of the Army Alpha described in Chapter 1). In fact, issues of bias in testing did not garner much attention until the civil rights movement of the 1960s when there was concern that African Americans and Hispanics were being compared unfairly against the White majority. In a series of court decisions, it was decided that some tests, such as IQ and achievement tests, could not be used to track students because minority students were being disproportionately placed in lower-achieving classrooms as the result of tests that may not have been accurately assessing their ability (see *Hobsen v. Hansen*, 1967; *Moses v. Washington Parish School Board*, 1969). And in 1971, the U.S. Supreme Court case of *Griggs v. Duke Power Company* asserted that tests used for hiring and advancement at work must show that they can predict job performance for all groups. Over the years, a number of laws have been passed that impinge on the use of tests and assert the rights of all individuals to be tested fairly (see Chapter 2 for expanded definitions of some of these laws). These laws, and their relationship to assessment, are briefly described below.

Many laws have affirmed the rights of minorities and others to fairness in testing

Americans with Disabilities Act. This law states that accommodations must be made for individuals who are taking tests for employment and that testing must be shown to be relevant to the job in question.

The Family Education Rights and Privacy Act (FERPA) of 1974. Also known as the Buckley Amendment, this law affirms the right of all individuals to review their school records, including test records.

Carl Perkins Act (PL 98-524). This law assures that individuals who have disabilities or who are disadvantaged have access to vocational assessment, counseling, and placement.

Civil Rights Acts (1964 and Amendments). This series of laws asserts that any test used for employment or promotion must be shown to be suitable and valid for the job in question. If not, alternative means of assessment must be provided. Differential test cutoffs are not allowed.

The Freedom of Information Act. This law assures the right of individuals to access their federal records, including test records. Most states have expanded this law so that it also applies to state records.

PL 94-142 and the Individuals with Disabilities Education Improvement Act (IDEIA). These legislative acts assure the right of students to be tested, at a

| **THE USE OF INTELLIGENCE TESTS WITH MINORITIES:** CONFUSION AND BEDLAM

The use of intelligence tests with culturally diverse populations has long been an area of controversy. Some states have found intelligence tests biased and have banned their use in certain circumstances with some groups (Gold, 1987; Swenson, 1997). Other states have not found widespread evidence of bias. If intelligence tests are used, the examiner needs to be alert to the proper way of administering and scoring the test with all clients.

The concern for bias in testing has gone so far in some circles that if the situation wasn't so serious, it would almost be comical. Take the case in California of Ms. Mary Amaya, who was concerned that her

son was being recommended for remedial courses he did not need. Having had an older son who was found to not need such assistance only after he was tested, Ms. Amaya requested testing with an intelligence test for her other son. However, since the incident with her first son, the state of California had decided that intelligence tests were culturally biased and thus banned their use for members of certain groups. Despite the fact that Ms. Amaya was requesting the use of an intelligence test, it was found that she had no legislative right to have the test given to her son.

school system's expense, if they are suspected of having a disability that interferes with learning. These laws assert that schools must make accommodations, within the least restrictive environment, for students with learning disabilities.

Section 504 of the Rehabilitation Act. Relative to assessment, any instrument used to measure appropriateness for a program or service must be measuring the individual's ability, not be a reflection of his or her disability.

Today, it is critical that cognitive differences among groups of individuals represent differences in ability, not differences that result from cultural identification, gender, age, or so forth, and that tests used for predictive purposes show that they predict accurately for all groups of people (e.g., the SATs, MATs, GREs) (Hartman, McDaniel, & Whetzel, 2004; Neisser et al., 1996; Roth, Bevier, Bobko, Switzer, & Tyler, 2001). However, it should also be stressed that such differences do exist, and one of the greatest challenges today is to understand why they exist in order to develop ways to eliminate such differences (Hartman et al.). These days, cognitive differences are generally traced to environmental factors, as is evidenced by the No Child Left Behind Act which assumes that all children can succeed in school and demands that school systems show that all children pass minimal competencies, regardless of their gender, culture, or disability (U.S. Department of Education, 2005, 2008a, 2008b).

EXERCISE 3.4   DIFFERENCES IN ABILITY SCORES AS A FUNCTION OF CULTURE

In small groups, discuss why there might be differences among cultural groups on their ability scores. Then discuss ways in which such differences could be ameliorated. Discuss your reasons and solutions in class.

PRACTICALITY

Practicality
Feasibility considerations in test selection and administration

Although tests should have good validity and reliability, as well as cross-cultural fairness, it is also important for the test to be practical. For instance, would it make sense to give a two-hour exam to first- or second-graders, or might a shorter test that may be somewhat less valid do nearly as well? Or, is it feasible to use a Wechsler Scale of Intelligence as pre-screening for learning disabilities to hundreds of possible learning disabled students in a school system? Such a test is given individually, takes 1 to 2 hours to administer, and requires another 1 to 2 hours to write up. Decisions about test selection should be made carefully because they have an impact on the person being tested, the examiner, and at times, the institutions that are requiring testing. Examples of a few of the major practical concerns examiners face include: time, cost, format, readability, and ease of administration, scoring, and interpretation.

TIME

As just noted, the amount of time it takes to administer a test can clearly affect whether or not it is used. Time factors tend to be related to the attention span of the client you are testing, to the amount of time allotted for testing in a particular setting, and to the final cost of testing (time is money!).

COST

With increasingly limited insurance reimbursements as well as funding cutbacks, counselors and therapists in private practice, public and private agencies, and school systems are forced to hold down expenses. Thus, the cost of testing is an important factor in making a decision about which test to use. For instance, it would be nice to have all high school seniors take an interest inventory to help them in their career decision-making process; however, given that this might cost about $10 per student, it may not be a wise economic decision for many school systems. And what decision would you make if you were working with a person who had just lost his or her job, was short on finances, and needed to take a battery of tests that might cost $500 when other tests, perhaps somewhat less valid and reliable, might cost $100?

FORMAT

The format of a test should also be considered when deciding which test to use. Some format issues include clarity of the print, print size, sequencing of questions, and the type of questions being used. Although there is a debate regarding the optimal number of distracters in multiple-choice questions, some have found that for many individuals, multiple-choice questions tend to lessen test anxiety while tests requiring constructive responses (i.e., open-ended, essay questions) generally increased test-taker anxiety, anxiety that could reduce cognitive clarity (Crocker & Schmitt 1987; Powers, 1988; Rodriguez, 2005). Also, the format of a test could affect scores differentially as a function of culture. In fact, one study across three different types of tests found that test-takers who are male or white tend to do better on multiple-choice tests than members of other groups (Bridgeman & Morgan, 1996). The format of a test should always be considered when choosing which test to use.

READABILITY

Readability, or the ability of the examinee to comprehend what he or she is reading, is of course critical for all tests other than vocabulary or reading level tests (Hewitt & Homan, 2004). No one should be surprised that the reliability of test scores are reduced when readability is not controlled for. Thus, it has been suggested that each item on a test be scrutinized for readability.

EASE OF ADMINISTRATION, SCORING, AND INTERPRETATION

In deciding how practical a test is to use, the ease of test administration, scoring, and interpretation should always be considered. This dimension involves a number of factors, including the following:

1. The ease of understanding and using test manuals and related information.
2. The number of individuals taking the test and whether or not their numbers affect the ease of administering the instrument.
3. The kind of training and education needed to administer the test, score the test, and interpret test results.
4. The "turnaround time" in scoring the test and obtaining the results.
5. The amount of time needed to explain test results to examinees.
6. Associated materials that may be helpful in explaining test scores to examinees (e.g., printed sheets generated by the publisher).

SELECTING AND ADMINISTERING A GOOD TEST

Now you know that a test should be valid, reliable, practical, and cross-culturally fair. But, with thousands of tests to choose from, how exactly does one find a test that meets the specific needs of the testing situation? A number of steps will assist you in the process, as described below.

STEP 1: DETERMINE THE GOALS OF YOUR CLIENT

The information-gathering process, which will be discussed in detail in Chapter 12, is critical to one's ability to determine what is happening with a client. As information is gathered from a client, client goals will become clearer and these goals will help you determine what assessment instruments might be valuable in helping to reach client goals.

STEP 2: CHOOSE INSTRUMENTS TO REACH CLIENT GOALS

Choosing the right instrument is not always an easy process. However, as soon as you have identified client goals, you have gained a sense of the kinds of instruments that may be helpful. For instance, if a client's goals include developing a career path and making a decision about a job, you might want to consider administering an interest inventory and a multiple aptitude test.

STEP 3: ACCESS INFORMATION ABOUT POSSIBLE INSTRUMENTS

A number of sources exist today to help you choose possible assessment instruments. Some of these are described below.

Source books on testing. Source books on testing provide important information about tests, such as the names of the author(s); the publication date; the purpose of the test; bibliographical information; information on test construction; the name and address of the publisher; the costs of the test; information on validity, reliability, cross-cultural issues, and practicality; reviews of the test (see Box 3.2); information on scoring; and other basic information about the test.

Mental Measurements Yearbook
A tremendous resource in finding and selecting tests

Two of the most important source books are the Buros Mental Measurements Yearbook (MMY) and its companion volume Tests in Print (Geisinger, Spies, Carlson, & Plake, 2007; Murphy, Spies, & Plake, 2006). The MMY, which is in its seventeenth edition, offers reviews of more than 2000 tests, instruments, and screening devices. Because there are thousands of possible tests, not all of them can be included in any one edition; consequently, it is often necessary to go back to previous editions to find a specific test that you might be looking for. Most large universities carry hardcover editions of these volumes, and the information is also available online. The MMY test reviews are classified into 18 major categories: achievement, behavior assessment, developmental, education, English and language, fine arts, foreign language, intelligence and general aptitude, mathematics, miscellaneous,

---

| BOX 3.2 | MENTAL MEASUREMENT REVIEW OF THE WAIS-III |

The following is part of the summary provided by the second reviewer of the Wechsler Adult Intelligence Scale-III (WAIS-III), as found in the Mental Measurement Yearbook. The actual two reviews run about 10 pages, single-spaced.

The WAIS-III is the oldest and most frequently used intelligence scale for individual administration to adults. It is composed of a set of 14 subtests that have been improved with extensive research while maintaining the historical continuity. Reviewers of the two previous editions have made criticisms and suggestions that have been addressed by the authors, and the changes appear to result in improvements for those practitioners and researchers who use the test. The scores from the test are reliable enough to be used in all of the designated age ranges and the validity evidence gives confidence that the test scores measure those intellectual constructs that it purports to measure. Psychologists in educational institutions will find it to be a useful tool for assessing those persons who are not adequately evaluated with group intelligence tests. Clinicians and clinical researchers will probably continue to employ the test as their primary instrument for assessing adult intelligence. The manuals are written in a clear, readable manner for those with proper training. Although there are areas in which the manuals can be improved, they provide more information than the manuals of most other tests. The WAIS-III gives promise of continuing the evolutionary trend toward improved measurement....(Rogers, 2001, p. 1340) neuropsychological, personality, reading, science, sensory-motor, social studies, speech and hearing, and vocations. Online searches of the MMY offer a quick mechanism for obtaining information about assessment instruments. For example, a quick search from the ninth to the seventeenth editions shows that the MMY holds 177 tests in the area of intelligence and general aptitude, 82 in the area of "personality," 54 in the area of neuropsychology, 43 in the area of "developmental," and 27 in the area of "miscellaneous." Plug in the word "love" and we find that 39 tests address this construct in some manner.

Publisher resource catalogs. Test publishing companies freely distribute catalogs that describe the tests they sell. Additional information about the tests usually can be purchased from the publisher (e.g., sample kits, technical manuals, and so on).

Journals in the field. Professional journals, especially those associated with measurement, will often describe tests used in research or give reviews of new tests in the field.

Books on testing. Textbooks that present an overview of testing are usually fairly good at highlighting a number of the better-known tests that are in use today.

Experts. School psychologists, learning disability specialists, experts at a school system's central testing office, psychologists at agencies, and professors are some of the many experts that can be called upon as providers of testing information.

The Internet. Today, publishing companies have home pages that offer information about tests they sell. In addition, the Internet has become an increasingly important place in which to search for information about testing. Of course, one needs to ensure that any information from the Internet is accurate.

STEP 4: EXAMINE VALIDITY, RELIABILITY, CROSS-CULTURAL FAIRNESS, AND PRACTICALITY OF THE POSSIBLE INSTRUMENTS

As you gather information about tests you might use, you may also have the opportunity to examine the validity, reliability, cross-cultural fairness, and practicality of possible instruments. However, if the sources do not offer this information, you can do a search of journal articles that may have examined these tests and you can contact the publisher to purchase a copy of the technical manual for the test. This manual should offer you all of the necessary information to make an informed judgment concerning whether or not to use the instrument in question.

STEP 5: CHOOSE AN INSTRUMENT WISELY

You've gone through your steps, and ideally you have some good options available to you. Most likely you narrowed your choices down to a few possible instruments. Now, it's time for you to be wise. Examine the technical information, consider the purpose of the testing, reflect on the ease and cost of the instrument, and make a wise choice—a choice that you will feel comfortable with and a choice that is right for your client.

SUMMARY

In this chapter we examined four components of test worthiness: validity, reliability, cross-cultural fairness, and practicality. We began by explaining the concept of correlation coefficient, and we noted that it ranges between −1.0 and +1.0 and describes the strength and direction of the relationship between two sets of variables such as test scores. We then noted that the coefficient of determination, or shared variance, is the square of the correlation (r^2), and is a statement about the commonality between variables.

We next examined validity, a broad evidence-based concept that attempts to verify that a test is measuring what it is supposed to measure. Content validity is based on evidence that test items accurately reflect the examinee's knowledge of the domain being measured. Criterion validity has two forms: concurrent, which demonstrates that the instrument is related to some criterion in the "now" (e.g., depression scores with clinical ratings of clients), or predictive, which examines how well the instrument forecasts some future event. We discussed how the standard error of the estimate, and false positives and false negatives are considerations in predictive validity. Construct validity shows whether the test is properly measuring the correct concept, model, or schematic idea. Evidence for construct validity is often available in the form of research studies, factorial analysis, and convergence and discrimination with other existing tests.

In the next part of the chapter we examined reliability, or the degree to which test scores are free from measurement error (i.e., consistent and dependable). We first examined three of the most common forms of reliability: test-retest; alternate, parallel, or equivalent forms; and internal consistency, which includes split-half or odd-even reliability, Cronbach's Coefficient Alpha, and Kuder-Richardson. Test-retest reliability is calculated by giving the same instrument twice to the same group of people and correlating the test scores. Alternate form reliability involves administering two equivalent forms of the test to the same group and correlating the scores. One type of internal consistency reliability, called split-half or odd-even reliability, is used when one-half of the test items are correlated with the other half. Other forms of internal consistency, such as Cronbach Alpha and Kuder-Richardson reliability, use more complex statistical calculations to find the average correlation of all test items. Finally, the section concluded with a brief look at Item Response Theory (IRT) which is a relatively new method of examining reliability. With IRT, each item is examined individually for its ability to discriminate from other items based on the construct being measured (e.g., intelligence).

The next area of test worthiness we discussed was cross-cultural fairness. We noted that a test should accurately measure a construct regardless of one's membership in a class, race, disability, religion, or gender. We saw how the legal system has supported the notion that testing must be fair for all groups of people and free from bias. We specifically highlighted the fact that tests that may be biased could not be used to track students and that as a result of the Supreme Court case of *Griggs v. Duke Power Company* (1971), tests used for hiring and advancement at work must be predictive of job performance for all groups. We also noted that a number of laws have been passed that assert the rights of all individuals to be tested fairly, including The Americans with Disabilities Act, The Family Education Rights and Privacy Act (FERPA), The Carl Perkins Act (PL 98-524), Civil Rights Acts (1964 and Amendments), The Freedom of Information Act, PL 94-142 and IDEIA, and Section 504 of the Rehabilitation Act.

Our last area of test worthiness was practicality, which includes the amount of time it takes to give the test, the cost of the test, the readability of the instrument, test format, and the ease of administration, scoring, and interpretation. We concluded the chapter by offering five steps for selecting a good test.

CHAPTER REVIEW

1. What are the four cornerstones of test worthiness? Briefly define each of the four types of test worthiness.
2. Explain what is meant by a correlation coefficient and describe how it is applied to the understanding of test validity and test reliability.
3. Describe the three main types and the various subtypes of validity.
4. Why is validity known as a "unitary concept"?
5. Why is "face validity" not considered a type of validity?
6. Describe the three main types and various subtypes of reliability.
7. Explain how Item Response Theory (IRT) is different from the more commonly used types of reliability.
8. Why have cross-cultural issues taken on such importance in the realm of tests and assessment?

9. Relative to cross-cultural issues and assessment, provide a brief explanation for each of the following:
   a. *Griggs v. Duke Power Company*
   b. Americans with Disabilities Act
   c. FERPA (The Buckley Amendment)
   d. Carl Perkins Act (PL 98-524)
   e. Civil Rights Acts (1964) and Amendments
   f. The Freedom of Information Act
   g. PL 94-142 and the IDEIA
   h. Section 504 of the Rehabilitation Act

10. Describe the main issues involved in assessing the practicality of an assessment instrument.
11. Describe the five steps critical to the selection of a good assessment instrument.

REFERENCES

American Counseling Association. (2003). *Standards for qualifications of test users*. Alexandria, VA: Author.

American Educational Research Association. (1999). *Standards for educational and psychological testing*. Washington, DC: AERA.

American Psychiatric Association. (2000). *Diagnostic and statistical manual of mental disorders* (4th ed., text revision). Washington, DC: Author.

Beck, A. T., Steer, R. A., Brown, G. K. (2004). *Beck depression inventory*, II. San Antonio, TX: Harcourt Assessment.

Bechger, T. M., Maris, G., Verstralen, H. H., & Beguin, A. A. (2003). Using classical test theory in combination with item response theory. *Applied Psychological Measurement, 27*, 319–334.

Brennan, R. L. (1998). Misconceptions at the intersection of measurement theory and practice. *Educational Measurement: Issues and Practice, 17*, 5–9, 30.

Bridgeman, B., & Morgan, R. (1996). Success in college for students with discrepancies between performance on multiple-choice and essay tests. *Journal of Educational Psychology, 88*, 333–340.

Brown, W. (1910). Some experimental results in the correlation of mental abilities. *British Journal of Psychology, 3*, 296–322.

Cole, D., Truglio, R., & Peeke, L. (1997). Relation between symptoms of anxiety and depression in children: A multitrait–multimethod–multigroup assessment. *Journal of Consulting and Clinical Psychology, 65*, 110–119

Crocker, L., & Schmitt, A. (1987). Improving multiple-choice test performance for examinees with different levels of test anxiety. *The Journal of Experimental Education, 55*, 201–205.

Cronbach, L. (1951). Coefficient alpha and the internal structure of tests. *Psychometrika, 16*, 297–334.

Geisinger, K. F., Spies, R. A., Carlson, J. F., & Plake, B. S. (2007). (Eds.). *The seventeenth mental measurements yearbook*. Lincoln, NE: Buros Institute of Mental Measurements.

Gold, D. L. (1987). *Civil-rights panel investigating I.Q. test ban in California*. Education Week. Retrieved on September 21, 2008, from http://www.edweek.org/ew/articles/1987/10/28/07330001.h07.html?print=1

Goodwin, L. (2002a). Changing conceptions of measurement validity: an update on the new standards. *Journal of Nursing Education, 41*, 100–106.

Goodwin, L. (2002b). The meaning of validity. *Journal of Pediatric and Gastroenterology and Nutrition, 35*, 6–7.

Griggs V. Duke Power Company, 401 U. S. 424 (1971).

Hartman, N., McDaniel, M., & Whetzel, D. (2004). Racial and ethnic difference in performance. In J. Wall & G. Watz (Eds.), *Measuring up: Assessment issues for teachers, counselors, and administrators* (pp. 99–115). Greensboro, NC: CAPS press.

Heppner, P. P., Wampold, B. E., & Kivlighan, D. M. (2008). *Research design in counseling* (3rd ed.). Belmont, CA: Thompson Brooks/Cole.

Hewitt, M. A., & Homan, S. P. (2004). Readability level of standardized test items and student performance: The forgotten validity variable. *Reading Research and Instruction, 43*, 1–16.

Kobrin, J. L., Patterson, B. F., Shaw, E. J., Mattern, K. D., & Barbuti, S. (2008). *Validity of the SAT for predicting first-year college grade point average*. Research Report No. 2008-5. Retrieved, September, 9, 2008 from http://professionals.college board.com/profdownload/Validity_of_the_SAT_ for_Predicting_First_Year_College_Grade_Point_ Average.pdf

Hobson v. Hansen, 269 F. Supp. 401 (D.D.C.,1967).

Kuncel, N. R., & Hezlett, S. A. (2007). Standardized tests predict graduate students' success. *Science. 315*(5815), 1080–1081.

MacDonald, P., & Paunonen, S. V. (2002). A Monte Carlo comparison of item and person statistics based on item response theory versus classical test theory. *Educational and Psychological Measurement, 62*, 921–943.

Moses v. Washington Parish School Board, 302 F.Supp. 362, 367 (ED La.1969).

Murphy, L. L., & Spies, R. A., Plake, B. S. (2006). *Tests in print VII: An index to tests, test reviews, and the literature on specific tests*. Lincoln, NB: Buros Institute of Mental Measurements.

Neisser, U., Boodoo G., Bouchard, T., Boykin, A., Brody, N., Ceci, S. et al. (1996). Intelligence: Knowns and unknowns. *American Psychologist, 51*(2), 77–101.

Ostini, R., & Nering, M. L. (2006). *Polytomous item response theory models*. Thousand Oaks, CA: Sage Publishing.

Powers, D. (1988). Incidence, correlates, and possible causes of test anxiety in graduate admission testing. *Advances in Personality Assessment, 7*, 49–75.

Rodriguez, M. C. (2005). Three options are optimal for multiple-choice items: A meta-analysis for 80 years of research. *Educational Measurement: Issues and Practice, 24*(2), 3–13.

Rogers, B. (2001). Review of the Wechsler Adult Intelligence Scale, Third Edition. In B. S. Plake and J. C. Impara (Eds.), *The Fourteenth Mental Measurement Yearbook* (pp. 1336–1340). Lincoln, NE: Buros Institute of Mental Measurements.

Roth, P., Bevier, C., Bobko, P., Switzer, F., & Tyler, P. (2001). Ethnic group differences in cognitive ability in employment and educational settings: A meta-analysis. *Personnel Psychology, 54*, 297–330.

Salkind, N. J. (2004). *Statistics for people who (think they) hate statistic*s (2nd ed.). Thousand Oaks, CA: Sage Publications.

SASSI [Substance Abuse Subtle Screening Inventory]. (2008). *SASSI Institute*. Retrieved on August 30, 2008, from http://www.sassi.com/sassi/index.shtml

Spearman, C. (1904). The proof and measurement of association between two things. *American Journal of Psychology, 15*, 72–101.

Spearman, C. (1910). Correlation calculated from faulty data. *British Journal of Psychology, 3*, 271–295.

Swenson, L. (1997). *Psychology and law for the helping professions* (2nd ed.). Pacific Grove, CA: Brooks/Cole.

U.S. Department of Education (2005). *Stronger accountability: The facts about making progress*. Retrieved November 23, 2008 from http://www. ed.gov/nclb/accountability/ayp/testing.html

U.S. Department of Education (2008a). *What is No Child Left Behind?* Retrieved, October 1, 2008, from http://answers.ed.gov/cgi-bin/education.cfg/ php/enduser/std_adp.php?p_faqid=4

U.S. Department of Education (2008b). *Fact sheets*. Retrieved, September 4, 2008, from http://www. ed.gov/news/opeds/factsheets/index.html?src=ln

Wolfe, E. W., & Smith, E. V., Jr. (2007). Instrument development tools and activities for measure validation using Rasch models: Part II – validation activities. *Journal of Applied Measurement, 8*, 204–234.

STATISTICAL CONCEPTS: MAKING MEANING OUT OF RAW SCORES

When my two daughters were nine and four, we had some pretty interesting conversations around the dinner table. One night we were talking about testing, and I was sharing the difficulty I sometimes have explaining the value of testing. Suddenly, my older daughter Hannah said, "Testing is good because teachers know what level you are at and then know what to teach you." I looked at her and said, "That's right." Then Emma chimed in, "[Test scores are important because] when somebody is sad, you should help them." They made it so simple!

(Ed Neukrug)

This chapter will help us understand how numbers are used to determine, as Hannah noted, what "level" individuals are at. Understanding this concept will enable us to do our job: help others. Whether it be an achievement test score that shows deficiencies in reading, or a personality test that indicates clinical depression (or as Emma noted, sadness), test scores can help us identify problem areas in a person's life.

To understand the importance of test scores, we will start with the basics: an examination of raw scores. After concluding that raw scores generally provide little meaningful information, we will look at various ways that we can manipulate those scores to make sense out of a set of data. Thus, in this chapter we will examine how the following are used to help us understand raw scores: frequency distributions; histograms and frequency polygons; cumulative distributions; the normal curve; skewed curves; measures of central tendency such as the mean, median and mode; and measures of variability, such as the range, interquartile range, and standard deviation. In Chapter 5, which is a natural extension of this chapter, we will examine derived scores and see how they too are used to help us understand raw scores. But let's start with the basics: raw scores.

RAW SCORES

Let's say Jeremiah receives a score of 47 on a test, and Elise receives a score of 95 on a different test. How have they done? If Jeremiah's score was 47 out of 52, one might assume he had done fairly well. But if 1000 people had taken this test and all others had received a higher score than Jeremiah, we might view his score somewhat differently. And to make things even more complicated, what if a high score represents an undesirable trait (e.g., cynicism, depression, schizophrenia)? Then clearly, the lower he scores compared to his norm (peer) group, the better he has done, and vice versa.

What about Elise's score? Is a score of 95 good? What if it is out of a possible score of 200, or 550, or 992? If 1000 people take the test and Elise's score is the highest and a higher score is desirable, we might say that she did well, at least compared with her norm group. But if her score is on the lower end of the group of scores, then comparatively she did not do well.

RULE NUMBER 1	RAW SCORES ARE MEANINGLESS

Raw scores alone tell us little, if anything, about how a person has done on a test. We must take an individual's raw score and do something to it to give it meaning.

Raw score
Untreated score before manipulation or processing

Because raw scores provide little information, we need to do something to make them meaningful. One simple procedure is to add up the various types of responses an individual makes (e.g., number of right or wrong items on an achievement test, number of different kinds of personality traits chosen). Although this can provide us with a general idea of the types of responses the person has made, comparing an individual's responses to those of his or her norm group can usually give us more in-depth information. Norm group comparisons are helpful for the following reasons:

- *They tell us the relative position, within the norm group, of a person's score.* For instance, Jeremiah and Elise, or others interested in Jeremiah's or Elise's scores (e.g., teachers, counselors), can compare their scores with those of people who took the same test and are like them in some important way (e.g., similar age, same grade in school).
- *They allow us to compare the results among test-takers who took the same test but are in different norm groups.* For instance, a parent who has two children, two grades apart, could determine which one is doing better in reading relative to his or her norm group (e.g., one child might score at the 50th percentile, the other at the 76th, relative to their respective norm groups). Or a school counselor might be interested in the self-esteem scores of all the fifth-graders as compared to all the third-graders.
- *They allow us to compare test results on two or more different tests taken by the same individual.* For instance, it is sometimes valuable for a teacher to know an individual's score on an achievement test and on an aptitude test because a discrepancy between the two tests might indicate the presence of a

learning disability. Or, when conducting a personality assessment, it is not unusual to give a number of different tests with an effort made to find similar themes running through the various tests (e.g., high indications of anxiety on a number of different tests).

To help us make some sense out of raw scores, a number of procedures have been developed to allow normative comparisons. In the rest of this chapter we will look at some of these procedures.

FREQUENCY DISTRIBUTIONS

Frequency distribution

List of scores and number of times a score occurred

One method of understanding test scores is to develop a frequency distribution. Such distributions order a set of scores from highest to lowest and list the corresponding frequency of each score (see Table 4.1). A frequency distribution allows one to easily identify the most frequent scores and is helpful in identifying where an individual's score falls relative to the rest of the group. For instance, by examining Table 4.1, we can easily see that most of the scores occurred around

TABLE 4.1 | A FREQUENCY DISTRIBUTION

Score	Frequency (f)
66	1
63	1
60	1
58	2
57	3
55	2
54	5
53	3
51	5
50	5
49	7
48	6
47	4
45	5
43	4
42	1
40	2
38	2
37	1
35	1
32	1

the 50 range, with fewer occurring as we move to the higher or lower ends. If an individual scored a 60, he or she can quickly see that such a score is higher than most.

HISTOGRAMS AND FREQUENCY POLYGONS

Histogram
Bar graph of class intervals and frequency of a set of scores

Class interval
Grouping scores by a predetermined range

Frequency polygon
Line graph of class intervals and frequency of a set of scores

Once a frequency distribution has been developed, it is relatively easy to convert it to either a histogram (similar to a bar graph) or to a frequency polygon. These visual representations of the frequency distribution are often easier for individuals to understand. In order to develop a histogram or frequency polygon, one has to first determine what class intervals are to be used.

Class intervals are derived from your frequency distribution and are groupings of scores that have a predetermined range. For example, we could take the frequency distribution from Table 4.1 and rearrange or group the scores by fives (the predetermined range), starting with the lowest score. The first class of scores would then be 32 to 36 (i.e., 32, 33, 34, 35, or 36). The next interval would be 37 to 41, and so forth. Table 4.2 illustrates the frequency distribution of the class intervals using a range of 5.

Of course, the class interval does not have to be 5. You could arrange the class interval to have any predetermined range, such as 3, 4, 6, 10, or whatever might be useful (see Box 4.1).

After you have constructed your class interval, the scores can be placed onto a graph in the form of a histogram or frequency polygon. To create a histogram, one places the class intervals along the x-axis and the frequency of scores along the y-axis (see Figure 4.1). In this case, a vertical line is placed at the beginning and end of each class interval and a horizontal line connects these two lines at the height (as measured along the vertical axis). The horizontal line represents the respective frequency of the specific interval being drawn.

To create a frequency polygon of the class interval of scores from Table 4.2, we would simply place a dot at the center of each class interval across from its respective frequency and then connect the dots (see Figure 4.2).

TABLE 4.2	SCORES ARRANGED WITH A CLASS INTERVAL OF 5
Class Interval	**Frequency (f)**
62–66	2
57–61	6
52–56	10
47–51	27
42–46	10
37–41	5
32–36	2

| BOX 4.1 | CONFIGURING THE NUMBER OF INTERVALS YOU WANT FOR YOUR GRAPH |

To determine how many numbers should be in your class interval, follow these instructions (Note: calculations are based on the data in Table 4.1)*:

1. Subtract the lowest number in the series of scores from the highest number: 66 − 32 = 34

2. Divide this number by the number of class intervals you want to end up with: 34/7 = 4.86

3. Round off the number you obtained in step 2: 4.86 is rounded off to 5

4. Starting with the lowest number in your series of scores, use the number obtained in step 3 (the number 5 in this case) as the number of scores you should place in each interval: 32–36, 37–41, 42–46, 47–51, 52–56, 57–61, 62–66

*Please note that this is a crude method of configuring the number of intervals you want and sometimes can be off by 1 interval.

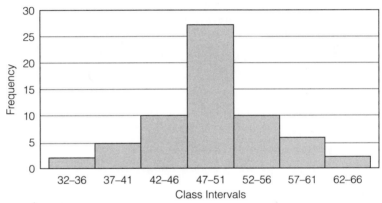

FIGURE 4.1 | HISTOGRAM WITH INTERVALS THAT HAVE A RANGE OF 5 (BASED ON TABLE 4.2)

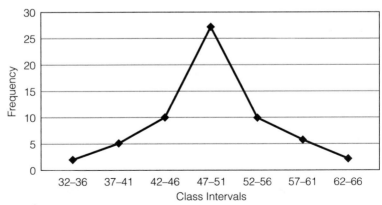

FIGURE 4.2 | FREQUENCY POLYGON WITH INTERVALS THAT HAVE A RANGE OF 5 (BASED ON TABLE 4.2)

CUMULATIVE DISTRIBUTIONS

Cumulative distribution

Line graph to examine percentile rank of a set of scores

Another method of visually displaying data from a frequency distribution is the cumulative distribution, sometimes called an *ogive curve*. Although the histogram and frequency polygon are the preferred methods for observing the shape of a distribution, the cumulative distribution is better for conveying information about the percentile rank. To create a cumulative distribution, you convert the frequency within each class interval to a percentage and then add it to the previous cumulative percentage of the distribution. In Table 4.3, we expand the scores and class intervals from Table 4.2 to include a column for the percentage and cumulative percentage.

We can now graph the cumulative percentage along the *y*-axis and our class intervals along the *x*-axis. As can be seen in Figure 4.3, we can quickly approximate the

TABLE 4.3 | PERCENTAGES CALCULATED FOR A CUMULATIVE DISTRIBUTION

Class Interval	*f*	%	Cumulative Percentage (%)
62–66	2	3	100
57–61	6	10	97
52–56	10	16	87
47–51	27	44	71
42–46	10	16	27
37–41	5	8	11
32–36	2	3	3
Total	62		

FIGURE 4.3 | CUMULATIVE DISTRIBUTION

percentage of any point of the distribution. If these were classroom test scores for a statewide proficiency achievement exam and the cutoff score for passing was 42, we could see from this distribution that about 19% of our students did not pass.

NORMAL CURVES AND SKEWED CURVES

As we collect data from test scores and create histograms or frequency polygons using class intervals, we will see that our distributions are sometimes skewed (asymmetrical) and other times represent what is called a normal or bell-shaped curve. Each of these types of curves has different implications for how we compare scores. Let's take a look at each of these types of curves and then see how measures of central tendency and measures of variability, two important measurement concepts, are applied to them.

THE NORMAL CURVE

Quincunx
Board developed by Sir Francis Galton to demonstrate bell-shaped curve

A number of years ago while I was visiting the Boston Museum of Science, I (Ed Neukrug) saw a device called a "quincunx" (also known as Galton's Board) through which hundreds of balls would be dropped onto a series of protruding points (see Figure 4.4). Each ball had a 50/50 chance of falling left or right every time it would hit one of the protruding objects. After all the balls were dropped, they would be collected and automatically dropped again. All day long this machine would drop the balls over and over again. Now, this process in and of itself was not so amazing. However, what did seem extraordinary was the fact that each time those balls were dropped, they would distribute themselves in the shape of a

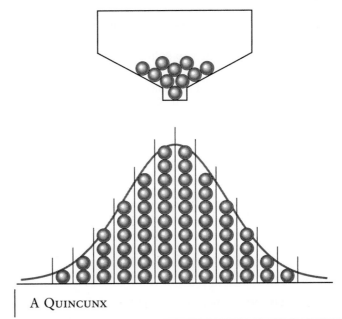

FIGURE 4.4 | A QUINCUNX

Normal curve

Bell-shaped distribution that human traits tend to fall along

normal curve (also called the bell-shaped curve). Now, mind you, they were not distributing themselves in that manner because they were being sent in that direction (see http://www.stattucino.com/berrie/dsl/Galton.html).

In point of fact, the resulting bell-shaped curve is a product of the natural laws of the universe and is explained through the laws of probability. So perfect are these natural laws that some people have given religious connotations to them. However, no matter how you explain these results, it is amazing that such a predictable pattern occurs over and over again. What does this have to do with testing? Like the balls dropping in this device, when we measure most traits and abilities of people, the scores tend to approximate a bell-shaped distribution. This is very convenient, for the symmetry of this curve allows us to understand measures of variability, particularly standard deviation, an important concept we will examine later in this chapter.

| RULE NUMBER 2 | "GOD DOES NOT PLAY DICE WITH THE UNIVERSE." (EINSTEIN PARAPHRASED*) |

So perfect are the laws of nature that some see this as the creation of a perfect God who has set in motion the wheels of the universe. Whether or not you believe this is a God-inspired phenomenon, it has great implications for testing. Concepts such as the bell-shaped curve are crucial to our understanding of norm-referenced testing and allow us to compare individuals

*As reported by Bryson (2003).

SKEWED CURVES

Skewed curve

Test scores not falling along a normal curve

Negatively skewed curve

Majority of scores at upper end

Positively skewed curve

Majority of scores at lower end

Sometimes a distribution of scores does not fall in a symmetrical shape or a normal curve. When this happens, the curve is called skewed or asymmetrical. If the majority of the scores fall toward the upper end, the curve is called negatively skewed. A positively skewed curve occurs when the majority of scores fall near the lower end (see Figure 4.5). If you split a normal curve in half, you will find the same number of scores in the first half of the curve as in the second half. This is not true of skewed curves. For instance, in a negatively skewed curve, there are more scores toward the high end of the curve as compared to the low end, and in a positively skewed curve, there are more scores at the lower end.

Negatively skewed

Normal curve

Positively skewed

FIGURE 4.5 | SKEWED AND NORMAL CURVES

MEASURES OF CENTRAL TENDENCY

Measures of central tendency tell us what is occurring in the midrange or "center" of a group of scores. Thus, if you know a person's score, you can compare that score to one of three scores that represent the middle of the group. Three measures of central tendency are the mean, median, and mode. Although measures of central tendency tell you little about the range of scores or how much scores vary, they do give you a sense of how close a score is to the middle of the distribution.

MEAN

Mean
Arithmetic average of a set of scores

The most commonly used measure of central tendency is the mean, which is the arithmetic average of a set of scores. The mean is calculated by adding together all of the scores and dividing by the number of scores. (See the formula below, where M is the mean, ΣX is the sum of all the scores, and N is the number of scores.)

$$M = \frac{\Sigma X}{N}$$

The first column of Table 4.4 shows how one determines the mean. By summing all of the scores and dividing by 11, we find the mean to be 85.55 (941/11).

MEDIAN

Median
Score where 50% fall above and 50% below

The median is the middle score, or the score at which 50% of scores fall above and 50% fall below. In Table 4.4 we can see that there are 11 total scores, and the middle score is the one that has 5 scores above it and 5 scores below it; hence, we

TABLE 4.4 | DETERMINING MEASURES OF CENTRAL TENDENCY

Mean	Median		Mode
97	97		97
94	94		94
92	92		92
89	89		89
89	89	5 ↑	89
87	87	Middle #	87
84	84	5 ↓	84
82	82		82
79	79		79
75	75		75
73	73		73
Sum = *941* N = 11 M = 85.55 (Mean)	Median = 87		Mode = 89

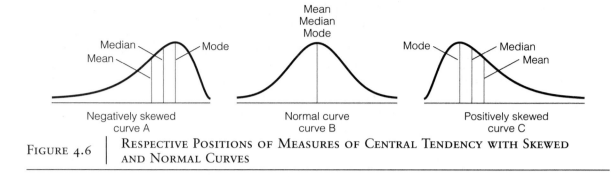

FIGURE 4.6 | RESPECTIVE POSITIONS OF MEASURES OF CENTRAL TENDENCY WITH SKEWED AND NORMAL CURVES

In a skewed distribution, the median is a better measure of central tendency

can see that in this case the middle score, or median, is 87. If there were an even number of scores, we would find not one middle score but two, and in this case we would simply take the average of the two middle scores. In situations involving a skewed set of scores, the median is generally considered a more accurate measure of central tendency because any unusually low or high scores do not distort the median as it would with the mean (because all scores are averaged to get the mean). For example, one can use the mean or median when trying to understand "average" salaries. If our community happens to have a relatively small number of individuals who make extremely large incomes, these incomes will be included when computing the mean. On the other hand, extremely large incomes would not affect the resulting median. Which measure of central tendency do you think would be more important if you were considering moving to a community that resembled this example?

MODE

Mode
Most frequently occurring score

The mode, the final measure of central tendency we will examine, is the score that occurs most often. In Table 4.4 you can quickly see that the mode is 89 because it is the only score that occurs twice. In smaller groups of scores, the mode may be erratic and not very accurate. However, with larger sets of numbers, the mode captures the peak or top of the curve. In addition, sometimes you can have multiple modes, such as when two numbers occur most often and the same number of times.

In examining the mode, consider our earlier example of incomes in a community. One could conceivably have a mean that is higher than the median (due to a few extremely high incomes), and a mode that is lower than the median (because the most commonly found incomes could fall below the median) (see Figure 4.6, curve C). As you review the skewed and normal curves in Figure 4.6, consider the reason why the mean, median, and mode are placed where they are, and then read Box 4.2.

BOX 4.2 | WHICH TO USE: MEAN OR MEDIAN?

A school system has asked you to determine the average reading score for its 50,000 fifth-grade students. The assistant superintendent wants to make sure the school system looks "as good as possible" because the press will get hold of the results. On the other hand, you realize that a sizable population of students read poorly and you want to make sure that their scores are included in your data so that their learning needs are focused upon. Which measure of central tendency do you use? What concerns do you have?

MEASURES OF VARIABILITY

Measures of variability tell us how much scores vary in a distribution. Three measures of variability are the *range*, or the number of scores between the highest and lowest scores on a distribution; the *interquartile range*, which measures the range of the middle 50% of a group of scores around the median; and the *standard deviation*, or the manner in which scores deviate around the mean in a standard fashion.

RANGE

Range
Difference between highest and lowest score plus 1

The simplest measure of variability, called the range, is calculated by subtracting the lowest score from the highest score and adding 1. Although the range tells you the distance from the highest to lowest score, it does little to identify where most of the scores fall. For example, if the highest score on an exam is 98 and the lowest score is 62, the range is 37 ($98 - 62 + 1 = 37$). However, this range gives no indication where the majority of scores may fall. Thus, the range is limited in function. A more complex and informative measure of variability is the interquartile range.

INTERQUARTILE RANGE

Interquartile range
Middle 50% of scores around the median

The interquartile range provides the range of the middle 50% of scores around the median. Because it eliminates the top and bottom quartiles, the interquartile range is most useful with skewed curves because it offers a more representative picture of where a large percentage of the scores fall (see Figure 4.7).

To calculate the interquartile range, first we subtract the score that is 1/4 of the way from the bottom from the score that is 3/4 of the way from the bottom and divide by 2. Next, we add and subtract this number to the median. For example, Table 4.5 has a set of 12 test scores. Let's find the interquartile range.

Since we have 12 scores, we first find the score that is 1/4 from the bottom (or 1/4 of 12). Since 1/4 of 12 = 3, we find the third score, or 81 (see Table 4.5) (round off if 1/4 of the N is not a whole number). Next, we find the score that is 3/4 from the bottom (or 3/4 of 12). Since 3/4 of 12 = 9, we find the ninth score,

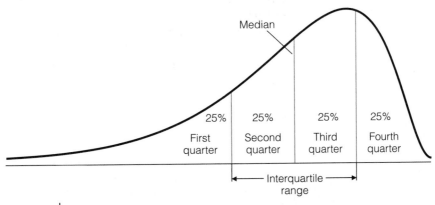

FIGURE 4.7 | INTERQUARTILE RANGE WITH SKEWED CURVE

TABLE 4.5 | EXAMPLE OF CALCULATING AN INTERQUARTILE RANGE

	Test Scores
	98
	97
	95
$\frac{3}{4}(N) = \frac{3}{4}(12) = $ 9th *score* ⟶	**92**
	90
	88
	87
	85
	83
$\frac{1}{4}(N) = \frac{1}{4}(12) = $ 3rd *score* ⟶	**81**
	80
	79

or 92 (see Table 4.5) (round off if 3/4 of the N is not a whole number). Next, we subtract our 1/4 score form our 3/4 score, or $92 - 81 = 11$. Finally, we divide 11 by 2 and add and subtract this number to the median (87.5 ± 5.5). So, our interquartile range is 82.0 through 93. A formula to find the interquartile range is:

$$Median \pm \frac{\frac{3}{4}N(find\ that\ score - \frac{1}{4}N(find\ that\ score)}{2}$$

Using the above example with the formula we find:

$$87.5 \pm \frac{\frac{3}{4}(12\ scores) - \frac{1}{4}(12\ scores)}{2}$$

or

$$87.5 \pm \frac{92 - 81}{2}$$

(Where "92" is the 9th score and "81" is the 3rd score)

or 87.5 ± 5.5 (82 through 93)

STANDARD DEVIATION

Standard deviation

How scores vary from the mean

In contrast to the interquartile range, which examines the spread of scores around the median, the standard deviation is a measure of variability that describes how scores vary around the mean. With normally distributed curves, the standard deviation is a powerful tool in helping us understand test scores. The standard deviation is important because in *all normal curves* the percentage of scores between standard deviation units is the same. For instance, between the mean and +1 standard deviation we find approximately 34% of the scores (see Figure 4.8). Similarly, between the mean and −1 standard deviation we also find 34% of the scores, as each side of the curve is the mirror image of the opposite side. In addition, as you can see in Figure 4.8, approximately 13.5% of the group falls between +1 and +2 standard deviations and another 13.5% between −1 and −2 standard deviations. Most of the rest of the group is between +2 and +3 standard deviations (2.25%), or −2 and −3 standard deviations (another 2.25%). As you can also see, approximately 68% of the group is between −1 and +1 standard deviations, and about 95% of scores will fall between −2 SD and +2 SD (13.5% + 34% + 34% + 13.5% = 95%), and so forth. Although standard deviations continue (e.g., 4 SDs, 5 SDs, and so forth), since 99.5% of people will fall within the first three standard deviations, we tend to focus only on these.

To understand standard deviation, let's suppose for a moment that a test has a mean of 52 and a standard deviation of 20. For this test, most of the scores (about 68%) would range between 32 and 72 (plus and minus one standard deviation; see Figure 4.8). On the other hand, a second test that had a mean of 52 and a standard deviation of 5 would have 68% of its scores between 47 and 57 (again, plus and minus one standard deviation). Clearly, even though the two tests have the same mean, the range of scores around the mean varies considerably. An individual's score of 40 would be in the average range on the first test but well below average on the second test. This example shows why measures of central tendency and measures of variability are both so important in understanding test scores. To actually determine the standard deviation of a group of scores, one uses the following formula (an alternative formula can be found in Appendix D):

$$SD = \sqrt{\frac{\Sigma(X - M)^2}{N}}$$

In this formula, X is each individual test score, M is the mean, and N is the number of scores. For example, let's say we want to find how far one standard

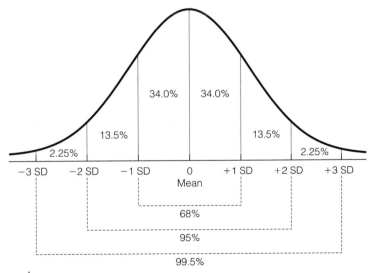

FIGURE 4.8 | STANDARD DEVIATION AND THE NORMAL CURVE

deviation is from the mean for a set of test scores in Table 4.6. First we generate a column for the $X - M$ for each score. Next we generate another column to calculate the $(X - M)^2$ for each score. Once this step is complete, we can sum all of the $(X - M)^2$, divide by the number of scores (N), and take the square root.

We calculate the mean (M) of the scores by summing them (42) and dividing by N, which is 6, so our $M = 7$. In the next column we subtract the mean from each score to get $X - M$. Now in the third column we square our results from column 2 to get $(X - M)^2$. Next, we sum our $(X - M)^2$ column and get 20. Now, we place the numbers in our equation as follows:

$$SD = \sqrt{\frac{\Sigma(X - M)^2}{N}} = \sqrt{\frac{20}{6}} = \sqrt{3.33} = 1.83$$

This result tells us that each standard deviation is 1.83 from the mean. Applying this to a normal curve would give us Figure 4.9.

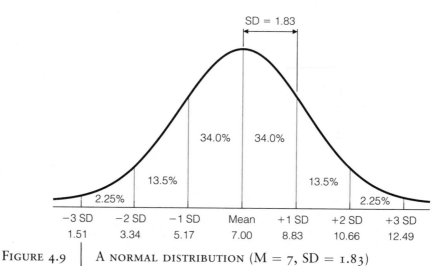

			SD = 1.83			
		34.0%	34.0%			
	13.5%			13.5%		
2.25%					2.25%	
−3 SD	−2 SD	−1 SD	Mean	+1 SD	+2 SD	+3 SD
1.51	3.34	5.17	7.00	8.83	10.66	12.49

FIGURE 4.9 | A NORMAL DISTRIBUTION (M = 7, SD = 1.83)

TABLE 4.6 | CALCULATING THE STANDARD DEVIATION

X	X − M	(X − M)²
10	$10 - 7 = 3$	$3^2 = 9$
8	$8 - 7 = 1$	$1^2 = 1$
7	$7 - 7 = 0$	$0^2 = 0$
7	$7 - 7 = 0$	$0^2 = 0$
6	$6 - 7 = -1$	$-1^2 = 1$
4	$4 - 7 = -3$	$-3^2 = 9$
$\Sigma = 42$		
$M = 42/6 = 7$		$\Sigma = 20$

Consequently, we can see that someone who scored a 5 falls slightly below -1 standard deviation (or at approximately the 15th percentile). Similarly, a person with a score of 11 is slightly above $+2$ standard deviations (or at approximately the 98th percentile). Standard deviation is a particularly important statistical concept when examining test scores relative to normal curves. In Chapter 5 we will examine how standard deviation is used to help us interpret a wide variety of test score data.

REMEMBERING THE PERSON

It is important to remember that individuals will have their own opinions about their performance. Thus, what is perceived as a high score by one person could be seen as a low score by another. The individual who consistently scores at the highest percentiles on a math test may feel upset about a score that is in the average range, while an individual who consistently scores low may feel good about that same score. Similarly, an individual who has struggled with lifelong depression may feel good about a moderate depression score on the Beck Depression Inventory, while another person might be concerned about such a score. As a helper, it is critical to always ask for feedback from the person who was assessed so that you can determine how he or she perceives the score that was received. Similarly, we should be careful to avoid letting our biases about what is a "good" or "bad" score interfere with hearing how an examinee feels about his or her score.

SUMMARY

We began this chapter by examining the usefulness of raw scores. First, we noted that raw scores are not particularly meaningful unless we manipulate them in some fashion, such as by comparing an individual's scores to his or her norm group. Such comparisons (1) tell the relative position, within the norm group, of a person's score, (2) allow for a comparison of the results among test-takers who took the same test but are in different norm groups, and (3) allow for a comparison of test results on two or more different tests taken by the same individual.

Next, we reviewed a series of mechanisms that one could use to make normative comparisons. We first looked at how to create a frequency distribution, because such a distribution can help us understand where most individuals fall. We then showed that data can be placed in class intervals and graphed as a frequency polygon or a histogram, which are visual representations of the norm group. We found that the cumulative distribution is helpful for gathering information about percentile rank.

We next examined the normal curve and distinguished it from skewed curves. We highlighted the amazing fact that due to the natural laws of the universe, many qualities, when measured, approximate the normal curve. We pointed out that the symmetry of the normal curve allows us to apply certain statistical concepts to it, such as measures of central tendency and measures of variability. We noted that in contrast, negatively and positively skewed curves are not symmetrical and have more scores at the higher (negatively skewed) or lower (positively skewed) ends of the distribution.

We went on to define three measures of central tendency: mean, or arithmetic average; median, or middle score; and mode, or most frequent score. We noted that in normal curves the mean, median, and mode are at the midpoint, cutting the curve into two halves. We contrasted this with a skewed curve where the mode is the highest point, the mean is drawn out toward the endpoint, and the median is between the mean and mode. Next we discussed three types of variability: the range, or the difference between the highest and lowest score +1; the interquartile range, or the middle 50% of scores around the median; and the standard deviation, or how scores deviate around the mean.

Relative to the normal curve, we explained how standard deviation can be used to understand where test scores fall. We noted that the percentage of scores between standard deviation units on a normally distributed curve is constant, with about 34% of scores falling between 0 and +1 standard deviation and another 34% between 0 and −1 standard deviation (68% total), that approximately 13.5% of the scores fall between +1 and +2 and another 13.5% between −1 and −2 standard deviations (27% total), and that approximately 2.5% of the scores fall between +2 and +3 and another 2.5% between −2 and −3 (5% total). Thus, if we know an individual's raw score as well as the mean and standard deviation of a test, we can approximate where on the curve the person's score falls.

As the chapter concluded, we highlighted the importance of always asking the individual who was assessed his or her perception of the score that was received. A high score for one person is a low score for someone else.

CHAPTER REVIEW*

1. Describe how norm group comparisons can make raw scores meaningful.
2. Using the scores below, create a frequency distribution.

1	2	4	6	12	16	14	17
7	21	4	3	11	4	10	
12	7	9	3	2	1	3	
6	1	3	6	5	10	3	

3. From the numbers in item 2, develop a histogram that uses class intervals of 3, a frequency polygon that uses class intervals of 4, and a cumulative distribution that uses class intervals of 4.
4. Describe the relationship between the mean, median, and mode on a negatively skewed curve, a positively skewed curve, and a normal curve.
5. Using the numbers in item 2, determine the mean, median, and mode of this group of scores (measures of central tendency).
6. Using the numbers in item 2, determine the range, interquartile range, and standard deviation of this group of scores (measures of variability).
7. If the scores in item 2 were the scores of a class of graduate students in counseling who took a national test of depression, and if the mean and standard deviation of the test nationally was 14 and 5 respectively for a group of moderately depressed clients, what statement might you be able to make about this group of students?
8. Using the national mean and standard deviation for moderately depressed clients (from item 7), at what approximate percentile has a person scored if he or she obtained a raw score of 9? What if he or she has a raw score of 19?
9. How might you feel if you scored a 19 on this test?
10. Describe the relationship between how a person does on a test, compared to a national mean and standard deviation, and how a person might feel about his or her score. For example, if I had a history of major depression and scored a 15 on the test just discussed, how might my interpretation of my score differ from an individual who has never dealt with depression and receives a score of 15?

REFERENCE

Bryson, B. (2003). *A short history of nearly everything*. New York: Broadway Books.

---

*Your instructor can find answers to the questions online a the "Companion Site" for this text.

STATISTICAL CONCEPTS: CREATING NEW SCORES TO INTERPRET TEST DATA

I remember taking an organic chemistry test in college and thinking afterwards that there was no doubt I had failed. This would have been the only test I had ever failed, and I was devastated. As I waited for my score, I pondered my future. Suddenly, a friend of mine burst into my dorm room and announced, "You passed. You got a D." I knew that even a score of D would have been impossible, so I asked, "What did I get on the test?" His response was, "You got a 17." By far, this was the lowest grade I had ever received. I responded, "Well, how could I have passed if I received a 17?" My friend explained, "He took the square root of each person's score and multiplied it by 10. Then he applied his usual 'curve,' and your score of 41 was a D." In essence, what had happened was that the professor had "converted" my score. I then understood that things are not always what they appear to be. As it was with my converted organic test score, many raw scores in the world of testing are converted so that they have new meaning. That is the topic of this chapter—varying ways that test publishers and others convert test scores for easier interpretation.

(Ed Neukrug)

In this chapter we will examine how raw scores are converted to what are called "derived" scores to make them easier to understand. We will start by distinguishing between norm-referenced testing and criterion-referenced testing, which are two different ways of understanding test scores. As we will see, derived scores are mostly associated with norm-referenced testing. Next, we will discuss specific types of derived scores, such as (1) percentiles; (2) standard scores, including z-scores, T-scores, Deviation IQs, stanines, sten scores, NCE scores, college and graduate school entrance exam scores (e.g., SATs, GREs, and ACTs), and publisher-type scores; and (3) developmental norms, such as age comparisons and grade equivalents. As we near the end of the chapter we will discuss standard error of measurement, which is a mechanism for estimating how close an individual's obtained score is to his or her true score. We will then discuss a related concept, standard error of estimate, which helps us predict a range of scores based on a criterion score. Finally, the chapter concludes with a short discussion of scales of measurement, which allow us to assign numerical values to non-numeric characteristics for purposes of testing.

NORM REFERENCING VERSUS CRITERION REFERENCING

Two testing experts pass each other in the hallway, and one turns to the other and says, "How are you doing?" The second expert replies, "Compared to whom?"

Norm referencing
Comparison of individual test scores to average score of a group

The terms *norm referencing* and *criterion referencing* are used to describe two different ways of understanding an individual's score. In norm referencing, each individual's test score is compared to the average score of a group of individuals, called the norm group or peer group. Thus, one could compare his or her score to the aggregate scores of students who took an organic chemistry test (as in the example at the beginning of the chapter), to the aggregate scores of thousands of individuals who took a national achievement test, or to a representative group of individuals who took a personality test. A large percentage of nationally made standardized tests are norm-referenced.

Criterion referencing
Comparison of test scores to a predetermined standard

Criterion referencing, on the other hand, compares test scores to a predetermined value or a set criterion. For example, an instructor may decide that a test score of 90 percent to 100 percent correct is an A, 80 percent correct to 89.9 percent correct is a B, 70 percent correct to 79.9 percent correct is a C, and so forth.

Criterion-referenced testing is generally used by state departments of motor vehicles (DMV), which often require a minimum score of 70 percent correct to pass their written exam. If the DMV used norm-referencing testing and decided that people would pass the test if they received a score above −1 standard deviation, approximately 16% of the individuals taking the test would consistently fail, even if they answered more than 70 percent of the questions correctly. In fact, if suddenly everyone who took this test was studying more diligently and the overall scores were higher, using norm-referenced testing would likely mean that 16% of the group would still fail. So those who fail might have higher scores than those who had previously passed. This could create an administrative mess for many DMVs and also result in a lot of angry people.

Many states have begun using criterion-referenced testing of students as a result of the No Child Left Behind legislation. In this case, the federal government mandated that all students must achieve minimum pre-set scores on statewide exams (e.g., 75 percent correct in reading) (see Box 5.1).

Table 5.1 shows some common tests that are norm-referenced or criterion-referenced. Obviously, the choice whether to use norm referencing or criterion referencing when considering test results is quite important.

BOX 5.1	HIGH STAKES TESTING: USING CRITERION-REFERENCED TES ASSURE THAT ALL STUDENTS WILL ACHIEVE

As you read the following paragraph, substitute the word "criterion" for the italicized word or phrase and you will see why NCLB is based on criterion-referenced testing.

As a result of the federal initiative called "No Child Left Behind" (NCLB), testing has become a critical method of assuring that all students will achieve in schools. In general, NCLB encourages each state to set a *passing score*, known as the "starting point," which is based on the performance of its lowest-achieving demographic group or of the lowest-achieving schools in the state, whichever is higher. The state then sets the level of *student achievement* that a school must attain after two years in order

to continue to show "adequate yearly progress." Subsequent thresholds must be raised at least once every three years until at the end of 12 years all students in the state are achieving at the proficiency level on state assessments in reading/language arts and math (U.S. Dept. of Education, 2005, 2008a, 2008b).

Although this is a noble effort, a major criticism of No Child Left Behind is the fact that the federal government has threatened to remove aid to schools if these thresholds are not met, even though little funding has been provided to assist school systems to meet higher standards of achievement (National Education Association, 2002–2008).

TABLE 5.1	EXAMPLES OF NORM-REFERENCED AND CRITERION-REFERENCED TESTS

Norm-Referenced	Criterion-Referenced
GREs, SATs, ACTs, MCATs, etc.	BDI-2 (Beck Depression Inventory)
IQ tests (Wechsler, Stanford-Binet, etc.)	College writing entrance or exit exam
Personality inventories (MBTI, CPI, MMPI-2, etc.)	Driver's licensing exam
Career inventories (Strong Interest Inventory, Self-Directed Search, etc.)	MAST (Michigan Alcohol Screening Test)
College exam scored on a "curve"	College exams scored against a standard (A = 90 percent right, B = 80 percent right, C = 70 percent right, etc.)

NORMATIVE COMPARISONS AND DERIVED SCORES

As discussed in Chapter 4, the relative position of an individual in his or her norm group is a reflection of how a person has performed. To review this point, consider the following question:

If John scores a 52 on a test and Marietta scores a 98, who has done better?

Reflecting back to Chapter 4, our answer as to who has done better must be based on a number of factors, including the following:

1. The number of items on the test and the highest possible score.
2. The relative positions of a score of 52 and a score of 98 compared with the rest of the group. If out of 1,000 examinees, the vast majority scored above 98, then the real difference between a 98 and 52 may be minimal.
3. Whether higher scores are better than lower scores. For instance, on a depression test, lower scores might be better.

4. How an individual feels about his or her score. A low score for some individuals may be a high score for others (e.g., some might be ecstatic with a score at the 80th percentile on a math test, while others might be disappointed).

As you can see from items 1 and 2 above, understanding an individual's relative position in a group is critical if we are to make judgments about that individual's score. Of course, relative position does not tell us whether a lower or higher score is better and does not indicate how a person feels about his or her score (items 3 and 4 above).

To determine an individual's relative position in his or her norm group, raw scores are often converted to frequency distributions, histograms, and polygons to provide a visual representation of what is happening with all the scores. We discussed this process in Chapter 4 and also introduced the concept of measures of central tendency and measures of variability in order to begin to examine how scores are related to the normal curve. In this chapter, we will introduce the concept of derived scores, which are conversions of raw scores that allow us to make further comparisons of an individual's score with those of his or her norm group. Derived scores include percentiles; standard scores such as z-scores, T-scores, Deviation IQs, stanines, sten scores, normal curve equivalents (NCEs), college and graduate school entrance exam scores (e.g., SATs, GREs, and ACTs), and publisher-type scores; and developmental norms, such as age comparisons and grade equivalents.

Derived score
Converted score based against a norm group

PERCENTILES

Percentile
Percentage of people falling at or below a score

Perhaps the simplest and most common method of comparing raw scores to a norm group is to use percentile rank, often just called percentile. A percentile represents the percentage of people falling below an obtained score and ranges from 1 to 99, with 50 being the mean. For example, if the median score on a sociology exam was a 45, and an individual scored a 45, his or her percentile score would be 50 (p = 50), meaning that 50 percent of the individuals who took the test scored below a 45. If the top score for that exam was 75, then that person would be at the 99th percentile. Be careful not to confuse percentile scores with the term "percentage correct," which refers to the number of correct items. In the example just given, the person with a percentile score of 99 could have answered 75 out of 125 questions correctly, which would have given that person a "percentage correct" score of 60 (75/125). Percentile ranking is considered norm referencing because it compares an individual's score with the scores of a larger group (the normative group).

By examining Figure 5.1, you can see that on the normal curve percentiles break down in the following approximate manner: −3 SD is a percentile that is less than 1, −2 SD is a percentile that is close to 2, −1SD is a percentile of about 16, 0 SD is a percentile of 50, +1 SD is a percentile of about 84, +2 SD is a percentile close to 98 and +3 SD is a percentile that is over 99.

STANDARD SCORES

Standard score
Derived score based on mean and standard deviation

Standard scores represent a number of different kinds of scores that are derived by converting an individual's raw score to a new score that has a new mean and new standard deviation. Standard scores are generally used to make interpretation of test material easier for the examinee. Some of the more common types of standard

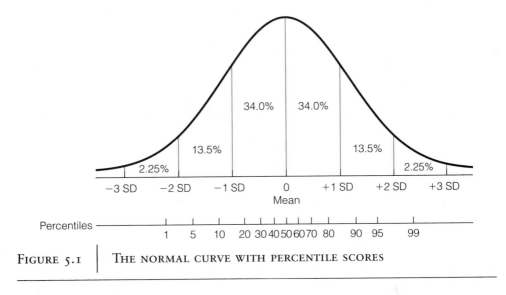

FIGURE 5.1 | THE NORMAL CURVE WITH PERCENTILE SCORES

scores include z-scores, T-scores, Deviation IQ (DIQ), stanines, sten scores, NCE scores, college and graduate school entrance exam scores (e.g., SATs, GREs, MATs, ACTs), and publisher-type scores.

z-score
Standard score with mean of 0 and SD of 1

z-SCORES   The most fundamental standard score is called a z-score, which is a simple conversion of an individual's raw score to a new score that has a mean of 0 and a standard deviation of 1. Thus, if an individual scored at the mean, the z-score would be 0; if an individual scored 1 standard deviation above the mean, the z-score would be 1; if an individual scored 1 standard deviation below the mean, the z-score would be -1; and so forth. Figure 5.2 demonstrates where z-scores lie on the normal curve.

Converting a raw score to a z-score is almost always the first step to take to understand the meaning of the raw score an individual obtained. Once the raw score has been converted to a z-score, almost any other type of derived score can be found, including percentiles, T-scores, Deviation IQs (DIQ), stanines, and so forth.

RULE NUMBER 3 | z-SCORES ARE GOLDEN*

z-scores are great for helping us see where an individual's raw score falls on a normal curve and are helpful for converting a raw score to other kinds of derived scores. That is why we like to keep in mind that z-scores are golden and can often be used to help us understand the meaning of scores.

---

*Rules 1 and 2 were introduced in Chapter 4:
Rule 1: Raw scores are meaningless.
Rule 2: God does not play dice with the universe.

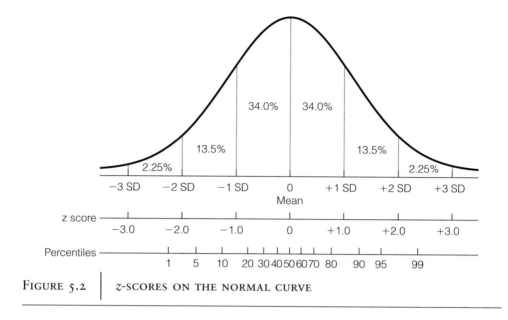

FIGURE 5.2 | z-SCORES ON THE NORMAL CURVE

That is why z-scores are so critical to our understanding of an individual's raw score (see Rule Number 3).

The formula for converting a raw score to a z-score is:

$$z = \frac{X - M}{SD}$$

where X is the raw score, M is the mean score, and SD is the standard deviation. For example, let's say an individual takes a psychology exam and the mean turns out to be 45 while the standard deviation is 10. To convert an individual's raw score of 65 on this test to a z-score, we would use the conversion formula in the following manner:

$$X = 65 \text{ (raw score)}$$
$$M = 45 \text{ (mean)}$$
$$S = 10 \text{ (standard deviation)}$$

We plug these values into our formula and get

$$z = \frac{X - M}{10} = \frac{65 - 45}{10} = \frac{20}{10} = 2.0$$

From this example we can see that the individual who scored a 65 on the exam has a z-score of +2.0. By examining Figure 5.2 you can see that this person has a percentile score of approximately 98.

Using the same formula, see if you can determine what the z-score would be for an individual who had a raw score of 30 on this same test. If you followed the formula correctly, you should have had a z-score of −1.5. Can you determine the approximate percentile that this person obtained? (All one need do is trace a line from the z-score to the percentile rank line on Figure 5.2.). In this case, you can see that the approximate percentile is a 7. If you would like an exact method for determining a percentile from a z-score, refer to Appendix E, which offers such a conversion formula. Additionally, Appendix E also includes a look-up table for quicker and easier conversions of z-scores to percentiles.

The main value of z-scores is to assist the test administrator in understanding where on the curve an individual falls compared with his or her peers, and as noted earlier, is the first step toward configuring other kinds of standard scores that are more readily understandable by clients. Explaining to a client that he or she had a z-score of −1.5 might be not only be useless but even counterproductive. However, we can convert the z-score to other kinds of derived scores (e.g., percentiles, stanines, DIQs, T-scores, and others) that are often more palatable for clients.

T-score
Standard score with mean of 50 and SD of 10

T-scores   One type of standard score that can be easily converted from a z-score is the T-score. T-scores have a mean of 50 and a standard deviation of 10 and are generally used with personality tests. Figure 5.3 shows T-scores on the normal curve.

To convert a z-score to a T-score, we use the following formula:

$$\text{Conversion score} = z(\text{SD}_{\text{of new desired score}}) + M_{\text{of new desired score}}$$

where the conversion score is the new standard score to which you are converting (e.g., T-score). In converting, one uses the standard deviation and mean of the score to which one is converting (in this case, T-scores; the SD = 10 and the M = 50). Continuing with our earlier example, the individual who has received a z-score of −1.5 has a T-score of 35 (−1.5 * 10 + 50 = 35). What about the person who had a raw score of 65 that converted to a z-score of 2.0? What would his or her T-score be? If you came up with a T-score of 70, you would be correct (2 * 10 + 50 = 70).

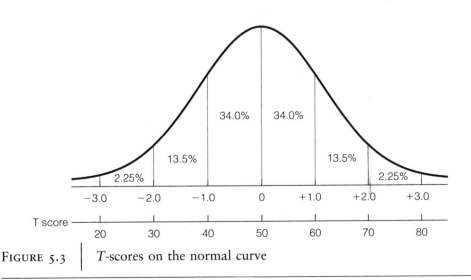

FIGURE 5.3 | *T-scores on the normal curve*

Deviation IQ
Standard score
with mean of 100
and SD of 15

DEVIATION IQ   Another commonly used standard score is Deviation IQ. The Deviation IQ has a mean of 100 and a standard deviation of 15. To apply this to the normal curve, see Figure 5.4.

Although most intelligence tests employ this standard of scoring, some caution should be exercised. For example, older versions of the Stanford-Binet Intelligence Test (Fourth Edition) used a mean of 100 and a standard deviation of 16; however, the most recent version (Fifth Edition; Riverside Publishing, 2004) uses a mean of 100 and a standard deviation of 15. To convert a z-score to a Deviation IQ (DIQ), we utilize the same conversion formula noted earlier [Conversion score = $z(SD_{of new desired score}) + M_{of new desired score}$]. However, in this case we use the standard deviation of 15 and the mean of 100. Using the example earlier in which an individual obtains a z-score of –1.5, we would find a DIQ of 77.5 (DIQ = –1.5 * 15 + 100). What is an individual's DIQ if his or her z-score is 2.0? If you came up with a DIQ of 130, you would be correct (2 * 15 + 100 = 130). And, finally what would a person's DIQ be if he or she had a z-score of 6 (see Box 5.2)?

Stanine
Standard score
with mean of 5
and SD of 2

STANINES   Another standard scoring system frequently used in the schools is stanines, which stands for "standard nines." Often used with achievement tests, stanines have a mean of 5 and a standard deviation of 2, and range from 1 to 9. For example, an individual who scores one standard deviation above the mean would have a stanine of 7 (mean = 5 + 1SD of 2). Similarly, if a student has a z-score of –1, his or her stanine would be 5 minus 2, which is 3. Figure 5.5 shows where stanines fall in comparison to z-scores and percentiles.

Unlike other forms of standard scoring we have examined thus far where a score could be identified with a specific z-score and percentile (e.g., T-score of 60 equals a z-score of 1 and percentile of 84), stanines represent a range of z-scores and percentiles. For instance, a stanine of 5 runs from a z-score of –.25 to a z-score of +.25 and from the 40th to 60th percentiles (see Figure 5.5). Similarly, a stanine of 6 runs from a z-score of +.25 to a z-score of +.75 and from the 60th

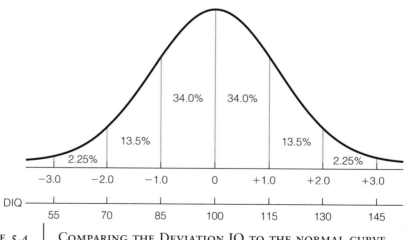

FIGURE 5.4 | COMPARING THE DEVIATION IQ TO THE NORMAL CURVE

| IQ, POPULATION, AND THE NORMAL CURVE

Have you ever heard anyone say he or she knows someone with an IQ of 200? I have. My grandmother told me that my cousin, Michael, had been tested and found to be brilliant, with an IQ over 200. Using the look-up table for percentiles (see Appendix E), you can see how rare people are at the outer edges of the normal or bell-shaped curve. Looking at the table, you will note that the fourth standard deviation ($z = 4.0$), which corresponds to an IQ of about 160, is extremely rare; only 3 out of 100,000 people are at this level. An IQ of 175 is found in only 3 out of 10 million people. That would mean there are only 88 people living in the United States with this IQ, assuming a U.S. population of 292 million (U.S. Census Bureau, n.d.). An IQ of 190 ($z = 6.0$) is found in only one out of a billion people, which means there are approximately six or seven people in the world with this IQ. As a matter of fact, I was speaking with Senior Project Director of the Stanford-Binet Intelligence Test (personal communication, Dr. Andrew Carson, October 7, 2004), and he said they have failed to ever find a person with an IQ above 160 because it is so rare. So the next time you hear of someone with a 200 IQ, you might want to question them further ... apparently they don't know a lot about the normal curve! –Charlie Fawcett

FIGURE 5.5 | STANINES COMPARED TO z-scores and percentiles

to 77th percentiles, and a stanine of 7 runs from a z-score of $+.75$ to z-score of $+1.25$ and from the 77th to 89th percentiles, and so forth. As you can see from Figure 5.5, any z-score that is below -1.75 or above $+1.75$ is a stanine of 1 or 9, respectively.

Changing z-scores to stanines is still done with our conversion formula $z(SD) + M$. Applying the formula for a z-score of -1.5, we would get

$$z = -1.5 \text{(given)}$$
$$SD = 2$$
$$M = 5, \text{so}$$
$$\text{Stanine} = z(SD) + M = -1.5(2) + 5 = -3 + 5 = 2$$

Consequently, a z-score of -1.5 converts to a stanine of 2. Similarly, a z-score of 2 converts to a stanine of 9 (stanine = $2 * 2 + 5$). Because stanines are reported only as whole numbers, in those cases where the use of the z-score in the conversion formula results in a fraction, the fraction should be rounded off to the nearest whole number. For example, a z-score of .87 converts to a stanine of 6.74 which is rounded off to 7 ($.87 * 2 + 5 = 6.74$, or in this case, 7).

As with most forms of standard scoring, stanines are an attempt to explain scoring so that the test-taker, or his or her parents, can easily understand test results. Unless you have happened to take a course like this one, it is usually easier

FIGURE 5.6 | STEN SCORES COMPARED TO z-scores and percentiles

to tell a parent that his or her daughter scored a 7 out of a range from 1 to 9 than to explain that the daughter has a z-score of .87.

Sten score

Standard score with mean of 5.5 and SD of 2

STEN SCORES   Sten scores are derived from the name "standard ten" and are commonly used on personality inventories and questionnaires. Stens have a mean of 5.5 and a standard deviation of 2. Stens divide the scale into ten units, each of which is one-half of a z-score, except for the first sten, which represents all scores below -2 z-scores, and the tenth sten, which represents all scores above $+2$ z-scores. Stens are similar to stanines in that they represent a range of scores rather than an absolute point. Figure 5.6 shows the relationship between stens, z-scores, and percentiles.

As you might expect, the conversion formula of $z(\text{SD}) + M$ also applies to sten scores. To use our example of a z-score of -1.5, we would determine our sten score to be 2.5:

$$z = -1.5(\text{given})$$
$$\text{SD} = 2$$
$$M = 5.5, \text{so}$$
$$\text{Sten} = z(\text{SD}) + M = -1.5(2) + 5.5 = -3 + 5.5 = 2.5$$

However, because stens, like stanines, are reported in whole numbers, we would round up a score of 2.5 to a sten of 3. What would be the sten score of an individual who obtained a z-score of 2? If you got 10, you would be correct ($2 * 2 + 5.5 = 9.5$, rounded off to 10).

Normal curve equivalent

Standard score with mean of 50 and SD of 21.06

NORMAL CURVE EQUIVALENTS (NCE) SCORES   A form of standard scoring frequently used in the educational community is Normal Curve Equivalents or NCE. The NCE has a mean of 50 and a standard deviation of 21.06. These units range from 1 to 99 in equal units along the bell-shaped curve. As can be seen in Figure 5.2, percentile ranks range from 1 to 99 but are not arranged in equal units along the curve. Consequently, the NCE and percentile ranks are the same at 1, 50, and 99 (see Figure 5.7 to compare NCEs with the normal curve). The standard formula for converting scores still applies to NCEs except that the limits are 1 and 99. The formula is NCE = $z(21.06) + 50$.

SAT/GRE type score

Standard score with mean around 500 and SD of 100

COLLEGE ENTRANCE EXAM SCORES   Probably, almost all of you have taken the SATs or ACT prior to entering college, and maybe you wondered how the score was derived. In this case, the SAT has three sections (critical reading, mathematics,

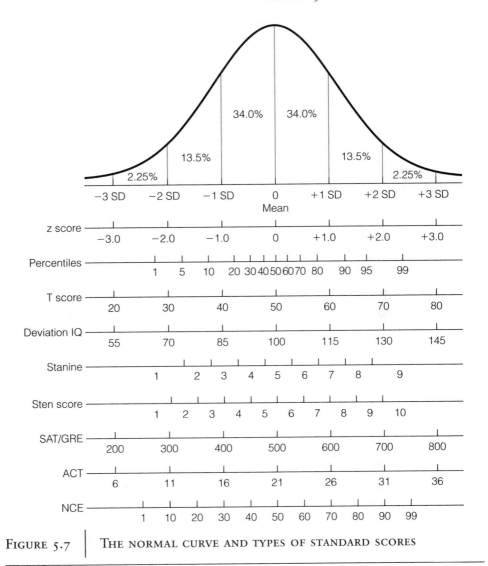

34.0% 34.0%

13.5% 13.5%

2.25% 2.25%

−3 SD   −2 SD   −1 SD   0   +1 SD   +2 SD   +3 SD
Mean

z score   −3.0   −2.0   −1.0   0   +1.0   +2.0   +3.0

Percentiles   1   5   10   20 30 40 50 60 70 80   90   95   99

T score   20   30   40   50   60   70   80

Deviation IQ   55   70   85   100   115   130   145

Stanine   1   2   3   4   5   6   7   8   9

Sten score   1   2   3   4   5   6   7   8   9   10

SAT/GRE   200   300   400   500   600   700   800

ACT   6   11   16   21   26   31   36

NCE   1   10   20   30   40   50   60   70   80   90   99

FIGURE 5.7 | THE NORMAL CURVE AND TYPES OF STANDARD SCORES

and writing), which use a standard score that has a standard deviation of 100 and a mean of 500. The norm group used in reporting the standard score consists of test results from 1990. However, rather than giving you a percentile as compared with that norm group, they determine an individual's percentile based on students who have taken the test over the past three years. Thus, an individual's standard score is compared to the 1990 norm group, but an individual's percentile is based on a more current norm group. Using the more current norm group·for an individual's percentile allows colleges and universities to see where an individual falls compared to other current students who are applying to college. Using our conversion formula, see if you can convert z-scores of −1.5 and 2 to an SAT-type score. If you got 350 and 700, you would be correct [SAT = −1.5 ∗ 100 + 500 = 350, and 2 ∗ 100 + 500 = 700].

The ACT, the ●ost widely used college entrance exam in the United States (ACT Inc., 2004a, 2004b), offers scores in four main subcategories, including English, mathematics, reading, and science as well as a combined composite average score. Like the SATs, the ACTs convert an individual's raw score to a standard score, which in this case uses a mean of 21 and a standard deviation of 5 for college-bound students. Like the SATs, an individual's raw score is compared to an earlier norm group, in this case 1994, and the percentile is determined from students who have taken the test over the past three years. Using the conversion formula, see if you can convert z-scores of -1.5 and 2 to an ACT type score. If you got 14 and 31, you would be correct [ACT $= -1.5 * 5 + 21 = 13.5$ or 14 rounded off, and $2 * 5 + 21 = 31$].

ACT score

Standard score with mean around 21 and SD of 5

Publisher-type scores

Test developer creates own standard score

PUBLISHER-TYPE SCORES   As you probably have come to realize, the conversion formula can be used to create a standard score with any pre-chosen mean and standard deviation. Consequently, sometimes test developers generate their own standard score. That is why it is common to see standardized achievement tests using unique test publisher scores that employ means and standard deviations of the publisher's choice. For instance, if Marietta took a standardized reading achievement test and received a raw score of 48, the scores on her actual profile sheet might look something like what you see in Box 5.3.

In the example in Box 5.3, Marietta's raw score is equivalent to a percentile score of 77, which is equivalent to a standard score of 588, which is equivalent to a stanine of 7. How did the publisher get these scores? First, they took her raw score and compared it to her norm group's mean and standard deviation to obtain a z-score (remember, z-scores are golden!). So, hypothetically, we may have seen something like the following: $z = (48 - 45)/4$, which equals a z-score of $+.75$. By looking at our graph (see Figure 5.2) we can see that a z-score of .75 is approximately a percentile of 77. Also, using our conversion formula, we can determine that a z-score of .75 is equal to a stanine of 7 ($.75 * 2 + 5 = 6.5$; rounded to 7). Finally, we can use our conversion formula to determine the publisher's standard score if we know the mean and standard deviation of the publisher's standard score (generally found in the publisher's manual and in this case given in Box 5.3). For instance, with a z-score of .75 we could determine that the publisher simply plugged the mean and standard deviation into the conversion formula: $.75 * 50 + 550 = 587.5$ (rounded to 588).

Unfortunately, test printouts usually only list the publisher's standard score without telling you the mean and standard deviation. This makes it quite difficult

BOX 5.3	MARIETTA'S READING SCORE

Raw Score*	Marietta Smartgirl Percentile	Grade 5.2 Stanine	Age: 10.5 Standard Score**
48	77	7	588

*Mean of raw score = 45; Standard deviation of raw score = 4
**Mean of publisher's standard score = 550; Standard deviation = 50

to determine what the score actually is based on. We sometimes call these publisher standard scores "magical scores," because they seem to magically appear with little explanation on the part of the publishing company. Thus, we usually suggest using other derived scores, such as percentiles or stanines, when interpreting test data for clients.

DEVELOPMENTAL NORMS

As opposed to standard scores, which in some manner convert an individual's raw score to a score that has a new mean and standard deviation, developmental norms, such as age comparisons and grade equivalents, directly compare an individual's score to the average scores of others at the same age or grade level.

Age comparison score

Comparison of individual score to average score of others at the same age

AGE COMPARISONS   Remember when you were a kid and you were always being compared to others of your age on those weight and height charts? The doctor was looking at where your height and weight fell compared to your norm group. Basically, the doctor would compare your height and weight to a bunch of kids who were the same age as you. So, if you were a 9-year, 4-month-old girl, and you were 55 inches tall, and the mean height for girls of your age was 52.5 inches with a standard deviation of 2.4 inches, your z-score would be $+1.04$ [$(55 - 52.5)/2.4)$]. This z-score converts to a percentile of approximately 85. One other way of using age norms is to see how your performance compares to the average performance of individuals at other age levels. Thus, for the 9-year, 4-month-old girl, we could say that she is at the average height for a 10-year, 11-month-old girl. If we were looking at an intelligence test, we might find that a 12-year, 5-month old has the mental age of the average 15-year, 4-month old (see Box 5.4).

Grade equivalent

Comparison of individual score to average score of others at the same grade level

GRADE EQUIVALENTS   Similar to age norms, grade equivalents compare an individual's score to the average score of children at the same grade level. Thus, if a student who was in the second month of the third grade (grade 3.2) took a reading test and scored at the mean, that student's grade equivalent would be 3.2. Unfortunately, this is where the comparison to age norms stops. Rather than actually comparing the raw score of a student to the raw scores of students at differing grade levels (e.g., comparing the raw score of the 3.2 grade student to the raw scores of students in the second grade, fourth grade, fifth grade, and so on),

---

| BOX 5.4 | IS YOUR HEAD TOO BIG? |

When my older daughter, Hannah, was two months old, the pediatrician measured her head size. He immediately said, "It's at the 98th percentile. Let's measure it again in a month." I asked him if he was concerned, knowing full well that her head size was "outside the norm" or not within the average range for her age group, which could suggest a number of medical problems. Thankfully there were no problems, and it turned out that some members of the family just have "big heads." However, such age norm comparisons can be critical to the identification of possible early developmental problems.

—*Ed Neukrug*

publishing companies usually extrapolate an individual's score. Thus, the student in the 3.2 grade who obtained a score at the 75th percentile when compared to her grade might end up with a grade equivalent of 4.5 despite the fact that she was never actually compared to students in the fourth grade, fifth month.

So, what can be said about a student's grade equivalent when it is either higher or lower than the mean score of students at his or her grade level? The best interpretation would be to state that a student has scored either lower or higher than students in his or her grade. For instance, a student in the 3.2 grade who obtains a grade equivalent of 5.4 has not mastered many of the concepts of the average student in grade 5.4; however, such a student is clearly doing much better than a large percentage of students in the third grade. Thus, it would make sense to say that this student is performing above the average for students at the 3.2 grade, but it may not be accurate to state that this student is performing at the 5.4 grade level. Similarly, another student in the 3.2 grade who obtains a grade equivalent of 2.2 has mastered many concepts that the average student at the 2.2 grade level has not even examined. Thus, it would make sense to say that this student is performing below the average for students at the 3.2 grade level, but probably not accurate to state that this student is performing at the 2.2 grade level.

You can see why it is important for test interpreters to read and understand how the test developer normed and calculated the grade equivalent score. It should be easy to see why having a strong background in testing and assessment is important in communicating test results.

PUTTING IT ALL TOGETHER

Now that we have learned that norm-referenced scores are based on the normal curve, we can use Figure 5.7 to examine the relationships between most of the various norm-referenced scores that we introduced in the chapter. You are encouraged to become familiar with these scores, as you will come across them often throughout your professional life.

STANDARD ERROR OF MEASUREMENT

Standard error of measurement

Range where a "true" score might lie

As we saw in Chapter 3, all tests have a certain amount of measurement error, which results in an individual's score being an approximation of his or her true score. By using some simple statistics, we can calculate the range or band in which a person's true score might actually lie. Known as the standard error of measurement, this range of scores is where we would expect a person's score to fall if he or she took the instrument over and over again (and was the same person each time he or she took it—e.g., no learning had taken place). As you will recall from Chapter 3, reliability is the degree to which a test is free of measurement error. Consequently, we can use the reliability to determine the standard error of measurement if we know the standard deviation of the raw score or of the standard score. The formula for calculating standard error of measurement (SEM) is:

$$\text{SEM} = SD\sqrt{1 - r}$$

where SD is the standard deviation of the raw score or of the standard score and *r* is the reliability coefficient of the test. As an example, let's say Latisha's "true" DIQ score is 120 (that is, if she were to take this test over and over again, the mean of all her scores would be 120). From reading the published data about the instrument, we know that it has a reliability coefficient of .95; we also know that DIQs have a standard deviation of 15. Applying this information to our formula, we get the following result:

$$SEM = SD\sqrt{1-r}$$
$$= 15\sqrt{1-.95}$$
$$= 15\sqrt{.05}$$
$$= 15 \times .22$$
$$= 3.35(\text{plus \& minus})$$

Now we know that if Latisha were to take the intelligence test over and over again, her score would fall plus or minus 3.35 of her score of 120, or between 116.65 to 123.35. As you may recall, the area under the normal curve of plus and minus one standard deviation equals 68 percent of the scores. Hypothetically, then, if Latisha were to take the test 1000 times, 68 percent of the time she would score between 116.65 and 123.35 (see Figure 5.8).

If we wanted greater accuracy, we could use plus or minus two 2 SEMs (two standard deviations around the mean), and that would tell us where her score would fall approximately 95 percent of the time. If we went out to 3 SEMs, we would know where her score would fall 99.5 percent of the time:

$$SEM = 2(SD)\sqrt{1-r}$$
$$SEM = 3(SD)\sqrt{1-r}$$

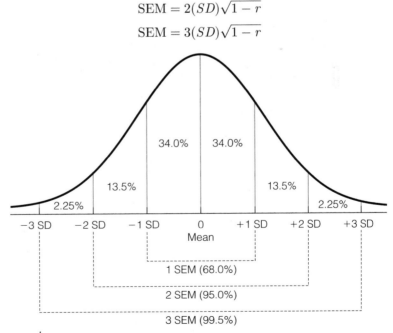

FIGURE 5.8 | STANDARD ERROR OF MEASUREMENT AND THE NORMAL CURVE

FIGURE 5.9 | EXAMPLE OF SEM ON TWO TEST REPORTS WITH DIFFERENT RELIABILITIES

So Latisha's 2 SEM score would be 3.35 times 2, or ±6.7; that is, 95 percent of the time her score would fall between 113.30 and 126.70, and 99.5 percent of the time her score would fall in the range of 109.95 to 130.05 (3 * 3.35 = ±10.05).

Reliability coefficient and SEM have an inverse relationship

At this point, you are probably beginning to see that there is an inverse relationship between the reliability coefficient and SEM; that is, as the reliability decreases, the SEM (the range of true scores) increases. Following the example of Latisha, let's say the intelligence test was not very reliable, with $r = .70$. How would this affect the SEM? Her SEM would increase. Calculating the SEM for the new reliability coefficient of .70, we would find:

$$SEM = SD\sqrt{1 - r}$$
$$= 15\sqrt{1 - .70}$$
$$= 15\sqrt{.30}$$
$$= 15 * .55$$
$$= ±8.22$$

So, if Latisha were to take this new intelligence test with a reliability coefficient of .70, 68 percent of the time her true score would fall in the range of 111.78 to 128.22. That range is quite a bit larger than the previous example when we used $r = .95$ and her SEM was determined to be between 116.35 and 123.35.

If you have observed test reports from the larger test publishers, you may have seen individual test scores with an "X" and with a line on either side of the "X" (see Figure 5.9). This line represents the SEM, or the range in which the true score might fall. Figure 5.9 shows how these bands may look on test reports showing Latisha's score on tests with reliability coefficients of .95 versus .70.

You can see that SEM is particularly important for the interpretation of test scores, because the larger the SEM, the more error and the larger the range where an individual's true score might fall (see Box 5.5)

STANDARD ERROR OF ESTIMATE

Standard error of estimate

Range where a predicted score might lie

A similar concept to standard error of measurement (SEM) is the standard error of estimate (SE$_{est}$), which was discussed briefly in Chapter 3. However, rather than giving a confidence interval around an obtained score as is done with SEM, SE$_{est}$ gives us a confidence interval around a predicted score. Based on the scores received on one variable (e.g., GREs), SE$_{est}$ allows us to predict a range of scores an individual might obtain on a second variable (e.g., first-year graduate school GPA).

BOX 5.5	DETERMINING STANDARD ERROR OF MEASUREMENT

Let's say Ed obtained a score on a test of depression that was a *T*-score of 60, and the test-retest reliability of the instrument was .75. Assuming that the higher the score, the more depressed a person is, answer the following questions:

1. What is Ed's percentile score on this test?
2. Determine what the SEM is 68 percent and 95 percent of the time.
3. What would be the range of Ed's *T*-score and percentile scores 68 percent of the time?
4. What would be the range of Ed's *T*-score and percentile scores 95 percent of the time?
5. What implications does the standard error of measurement have for interpreting Ed's score?

Answer:

1. About a percentile of 84.
2. SEM 68 percent of the time is $\pm 5 : (10\sqrt{1 - .75})$; SEM 95 percent of the time it is $\pm 10 : (10\sqrt{1 - .75}) * 2$.
3. 68 percent of the time Ed's score would fall between *T*-scores of 55 and 65 (percentiles of 70 to 93) (60 ± 5).
4. 95 percent of the time he would fall between *T*-scores of 50 to 70 (percentiles of 50 to 95) (60 ± 10).
5. Error has great implications for the interpretation of Ed's scores. The greater the error, the less we can rely on his score to be an indication of high levels of depression. At first it might seem that he has a fairly high level of depression (*T*-score of 60, percentile of 84), but as we consider the error and the range of his "true score," we lower our confidence that the score truly indicates somewhat high levels of depression.

The formula for calculating the standard error of estimate (SE$_{est}$) for two variables in which there is a correlation is:

$$SE_{est} = SD_Y \sqrt{1 - r^2}$$

where SD$_Y$ is the standard deviation of the variable to which you are predicting, (in this case, GPA) and *r* is the correlation between the two variables.

In continuing with our example from chapter 3, we know the correlation *(r)* between GRE scores and GPA is .34 (given in Chapter 3). If we know the mean and standard deviation of a fictional university department, we can determine the SE$_{est}$. For instance, if our mean GPA was 3.5 and the SD was .2 for our fictional department, using this SD of the GPA, we noted in Chapter 3, our mean GPA was 3.5 and the SD was .2 for the fictional department. So, using the SD of the GPA, we find the SE$_{est}$:

$$SE_{est} = SD_Y \sqrt{1 - r^2}$$
$$= .2\sqrt{1 - .34^2}$$
$$= .2\sqrt{1 - .12}$$
$$= .2\sqrt{.88}$$
$$= .2 \times .94$$
$$= .19$$

Next, if we know the *z*-score of a student's GREs, we can convert our GRE score to a GPA score using our conversion formula [*z*(SD$_{of\ new\ desired\ score}$) + *M* $_{of\ new\ desired\ score}$]. For instance, if the mean and standard deviation of the GREs is 500 and 100, and if an individual has obtained a 500, his or her *z*-score is 0 [$z = (X - M)/SD = (500 - 500)/100 = 0$). And, if we know the mean and standard deviation of the GPA, we can use our conversion formula to convert the GRE score to a GPA:

$$GPA_{conversion} = z(SD) + M$$

$$GPA = 0(.2) + 3.5 = 3.5$$

Now, if we add and subtract the obtained SE$_{est}$ (.19), we can see where this person's GPA is likely to fall 68% of the time: $3.5 \pm .19 = 3.31 - 3.69$. And, similar to the standard error of measurement, if we add and subtract it one more time, we can determine where this individual's GPA is likely to fall 95% of the time $(3.5 \pm .19(2) = 3.12 - 3.88)$.

Now, let's do the same thing with a person who scored a 300 on the GREs. His or her z-score is $-2 (z = \frac{X-M}{SD_x} = \frac{300-500}{100} = \frac{-200}{100} = -2)$.

Now, converting this z-score to a GPA score we get 3.1 $(z(SD) + M = -2 * .2 + 3.5 = 3.1)$. Now, if we add and subtract .19 to this score, we can see that 68% of the time this individual is likely to have a GPA between 2.91 and 3.29 and 95% of the time a GPA between 2.72 and 3.48. You can see why a program is more likely to take a risk with the students with the higher GRE when you look at the differences in ranges of likely GPA (Box 5.6 breaks this down into simple steps for you. (Read Rule Number 4).

SCALES OF MEASUREMENT

Now that we are finished discussing statistical concepts related to interpreting test scores and we are about to discuss commonly used assessment techniques (Section Three), it is important to consider that not all scores are the same. For instance, we can assign people to one of four categories of depression, such as none, low, medium, or high, and give each category a number, such as 0, 1, 2, or 3, respectively. Or we can take the same group of people and have them take a test for depression and examine the group scores, which would fall on a continuum from low to high, based on the number of items on the test. In the first example we can only

---

| BOX 5.6 | STEPS FOR CALCULATING STANDARD ERROR OF ESTIMATE |

Step 1: Obtain the correlation between your obtained scores and the scores you want to predict to (e.g., GRE and GPA).

Step 2: Obtain the standard deviation (SD) of the scores you want to predict to (e.g., GPA)

Step 3: Obtain your standard error of estimate by plugging the numbers you obtained in Steps 1 and 2 into the following formula:

$$SE_{est} = SD_Y \sqrt{1 - r^2}$$

Step 4: Calculate the z-score for you obtained score (e.g., GRE)

Step 5: Convert your obtained score to your predictor score (e.g., score on GPA) using your conversion formula: $[z (SD_{\text{of new desired score}}) + M_{\text{of new desired score}}]$

Step 6: Add and subtract your SE$_{est}$ in Step 3 to your obtained score in Step 5 to calculate your range of scores for 68% of the time. Add and subtract the SE$_{est}$ a second time to obtain your range of scores for 95% of the time.

RULE NUMBER 4	DON'T MIX APPLES AND ORANGES

As you practice various formulas in class, it is easy to use the wrong score, mean, or standard deviation. For instance, in determining the SE_{est} you can see how easy it would be to use the wrong standard deviation (GRE) instead of GPA—your predictor variable. This, obviously, would give you an erroneous answer. Thus, whenever you are asked to figure out a problem, remember to use the correct set of numbers (don't mix apples and oranges); otherwise your answer will be incorrect.

say that one group is higher or lower than another group. In the second example, however, we can make some judgment about the amount of depression an individual has, relative to another individual, and we can add and subtract the various scores.

To distinguish between different kinds of test scores and subsequently know what kinds of statistics can be applied to them, four kinds of scales of measurement have been identified: nominal scales, ordinal scales, interval scales, and ratio scales. Knowing which scale of measurement is being used for a specific instrument has profound implications for how the resulting scores can be manipulated statistically, and these implications are particularly important when conducting research. Although the kinds of tests we will examine in Section Three result in scores that are mostly of the interval type, some of the assessment procedures we will examine result in scores that fall into the nominal, ordinal, and ratio scales range. As you read through the text and review the various assessment instruments, you might want to consider which scale of measurement is being used for the instrument being discussed.

NOMINAL SCALE

Nominal scale
Numbers arbitrarily assigned to represent categories

The most basic or simple measurement scale is the nominal scale. In this scale numbers are arbitrarily assigned to represent different categories or variables. For example, race might be recorded as 1 = Asian, 2 = Latino, 3 = African American, 4 = Caucasian, etc. The assignment of numbers to these categories does not represent magnitude, so normal statistical calculations cannot be performed. All you can do is count the occurrences or calculate the mode.

ORDINAL SCALE

Ordinal scale
Numbers with rank order but unequal distances between

In the ordinal scale, magnitude or rank order is implied; however, the distance between measurements is unknown. An example of this would be asking someone how much they agree with the statement "The counseling I received was helpful in obtaining the goals I came in for" and then asking them to choose from: 1 = Strongly Disagree, 2 = Somewhat Disagree, 3 = Neutral, 4 = Somewhat Agree, 5 = Strongly Agree. These numbers represent rank or magnitude, but it is impossible to know the true distance between "somewhat agree" and "strongly agree."

INTERVAL SCALE

Interval scale
Numbers with equal distances between but no zero

The interval scale establishes equal distances between measurements but has no absolute zero reference point. The Graduate Record Exam (GRE) you may have taken for admission into school is an interval scale. A score of 530 is 20 equal units above a score of 510; however, there is no true zero point since the minimum possible score is 200. Some basic statistical analysis is appropriate, such as determining how many standard deviations an individual is from the mean, but one cannot say that a student who scores a 700 is twice as likely to succeed in graduate school as a student who scores a 350.

RATIO SCALE

Ratio scale
Numbers with equal intervals and meaningful zero

The ratio scale has a meaningful zero point and equal intervals; therefore, it can be manipulated by all mathematical principles. Very few behavioral measures fall into this category. Units such as height, weight, and temperature are all ratio scales since they have a true zero reference point. An example of a ratio scale would be the measurement of reaction times. If a researcher is attempting to measure brake response time by individuals with varying blood alcohol content (BAC) levels, both the BAC and the response time would be ratio scales. A BAC level of .00 (sober) might provide an average reaction time of .6 second, while a BAC level of .10 might correspond to an average reaction time of 1.2 seconds. Both the BAC and reaction time have true zero points, and therefore they are considered ratio scales. In other words, a reaction time of .6 second is twice as fast as 1.2 seconds.

SUMMARY

In this chapter we examined how raw scores are converted to what are called "derived" scores so that individuals can more easily understand the meaning of the raw scores. We started the chapter by pointing out that in norm-referenced testing, test scores are compared to a group of individuals called the norm group or peer group, but in criterion-referenced testing, test scores are compared to a predetermined value or a set criterion. We noted that although some tests are criterion-referenced, a large percentage are norm-referenced and employ a range of different kinds of derived scores in an attempt to make sense out of raw scores.

Relative to norm-referenced testing, we noted some factors that can affect our understanding of a raw score, including the number of items on a test and knowledge of what is the highest score possible, the relative position of an individual's score as compared to the scores of others who took the test, whether higher scores are better than lower scores, and how a person feels about his or her score on a test. We next identified a number of derived scores that are used to help us understand an individual's relative position in the norm group, such as (1) percentiles; (2) standard scores, including z-scores, T-scores, Deviation IQs, stanines, sten scores, NCE scores, college and graduate school entrance exam scores (e.g., SATs, GREs, MATs, and ACTs), and publisher-type scores; and (3) developmental norms, such as age comparisons and grade equivalents.

In examining derived scores, we first defined percentiles and distinguished percentiles from the concept of "percentage correct." We noted that percentiles represent the percentage of people falling below an individual's obtained score and range from 1 to 99.

Next, we examined standard scores, which are obtained by converting a raw score mean and standard deviation to a scale that has a new mean and standard deviation. First we highlighted the z-score, which is a standard score that has a mean of 0 and a standard deviation of 1, and offered a formula for obtaining it. We noted that an individual's z-score reflects where he or she falls on the normal curve. We pointed out that z-scores are so important to our understanding of derived scores that we might say "z-scores are golden," meaning that configuring a z-score is often the first critical step to finding all other derived scores.

We showed how to convert a z-score to a number of standard scores, including T-scores (SD = 10, M = 50), DIQs (SD = 15, M = 100), stanines (SD = 2, M = 5), sten scores (SD = 2, M = 5.5), SATs (SD = 100, M = 500), ACTs (SD = 5, M = 21), NCEs (SD = 21.06, M = 50), and publisher-type scores, where the standard deviation and mean vary depending on the publisher and the test.

As the chapter continued, we noted that developmental norms are also used to help us understand the relative position of an individual's raw score as compared with his or her norm group. We noted that age norms compare an individual's performance to the average performance of others in his or her age group (e.g., height, weight, mental ability), or to the average performance of individuals in other age groups (e.g., a 12-year-old might have the mental ability of the average 15-year-old). Grade equivalents, we noted, compare an individual's performance to the average performance of other students in his or her grade. We also cautioned that sometimes grade equivalents are misinterpreted because it is falsely assumed that a higher grade equivalent means an individual can perform at that higher grade level or that a lower grade equivalent means that the individual has not learned concepts at his or her own grade level.

Near the end of the chapter, we discussed standard error of measurement, which is a mechanism for estimating how close an individual's obtained score is to his or her true score. We noted that by using the formula to find the standard error of measurement, we can determine the range of scores in which an individual's true score is likely to fall 68 percent of the time ($\pm$ 1 SEM), 95 percent of the time ($\pm$ 2 SEM), or 99.5 percent of the time ($\pm$ 3 SEM). We noted that SEM has great implications for the interpretation of test data, because the higher the error, the less confidence we have about where the individual's true score actually lies. We then went on to discuss the standard error of estimate, which like the standard error of measurement can give a range of scores within which an individual might fall. However, in this case, it looks at the range of predicted scores as opposed to actual obtained scores. In discussing SE_{est} we highlighted our fourth rule: "Don't Mix Apples and Oranges"; that is, when computing any problem, make sure that you are using the correct sets of scores (e.g., correct mean and standard deviation).

Finally, we had a brief discussion of the four scales of measurement: nominal, ordinal, interval, and ratio. We noted that each type of scale has unique attributes that may limit the statistical and/or mathematical calculations we can perform and that different kinds of assessment instruments use different kinds of scales.

CHAPTER REVIEW

1. When might a criterion-referenced test be more appropriate to use than a norm-referenced test?

2. Discuss the strengths and weaknesses of using a criterion-referenced test instead of a norm-referenced test to measure progress as defined by No Child Left Behind.

3. Distinguish between the following kinds of derived scores: percentiles, standard scores, and developmental norms.

4. An individual receives a raw score of 62 on a national standardized test. Given that the mean and standard deviation of the test were 58 and 8, respectively, find the individual's z-score.

5. Using the *z*-score found in Item 4, find the following derived scores:
   a. Percentile (approximate)
   b. *T*-score
   c. Deviation IQ
   d. Stanine
   e. Sten score
   f. Normal curve equivalent (NCE)
   g. SAT-type score
   h. ACT score
   i. A publisher-type score that has a mean of 75 and standard deviation of 15

6. Define the term "developmental norms."

7. Explain what a grade equivalent is. What is a potential major downfall of using a grade equivalent type of score?

8. Find the *z*-score and approximate percentile of a 5.5-year-old child who is 46 inches tall when the mean and standard deviation of height for a 5.5-year-old child are 44 inches and 3 inches, respectively.

9. Referring to Item 5, b through i, find what the standard error of measurement would be 68 percent of the time for each of the scores if the reliability of the test is .84. Also determine what the individual's score would be for each of the items (b through i) 95 percent of the time.

10. If a student received a score of 24 on the ACT, what is the range of his or her likely GPA at the end of the first year in college given the following: (GPA Mean = 3.1, SD = .3; correlation between ACT and GPA is .45)?

11. Identify the four different types of scales of measurement and give examples of situations when some might be more appropriate to use than others.

_____

*Your instructor can find answers to these questions in the instructor's manual

REFERENCES

ACT, Inc. (2004a). *ACT information for life transitions.* Retrieved on April 26, 2004, from http://www.act.org

ACT, Inc. (2004b). *National distributions of "percent at or below" for ACT test scores, ACT-tested high school graduates of 2001, 2002, and 2003.* Retrieved on April 26, 2004, from http://www.act.org/aap/pdf/norms.pdf

National Education Association (2002–2008). *Issues in education: NEA's principles for ESEA/NCLB reauthorization.* Retrieved September 30, 2008, from http://www.nea.org/esea/policy.html

Riverside Publishing. (2004a). *Stanford-Binet Intelligence Scales, Fifth Edition.* Retrieved on April 21, 2004, from http://www.riverpub.com/products/clinical/sbis5/features.html

U.S. Census Bureau. (n.d.). *U.S. and world population clocks.* Retrieved April 3, 2004, from www.census.gov/main/www/popclock.html

U.S. Department of Education (2005). *Stronger accountability: The facts about making progress.* Retrieved September 4, 2008, from http://www.ed.gov/nclb/accountability/ayp/testing.html

U.S. Department of Education (2008a). *What is No Child Left Behind?* Retrieved, October 1, 2008, from http://answers.ed.gov/cgi-bin/education.cfg/php/enduser/std_adp.php?p_faqid=4

U.S. Department of Education (2008b). *Fact sheets.* Retrieved, September 4, 2008, from http://www.ed.gov/news/opeds/factsheets/index.html?src=ln

Commonly Used
Assessment Techniques

Section Three of the text examines some commonly used techniques for assessing educational ability, intellectual and cognitive functioning, career and occupational interests and aptitudes, clinical issues, and when conducting informal assessment. Not wanting to overwhelm the reader with dozens of tests that could be described in the above categories, we decided to identify and describe some of the more popular ones. We were partly driven by an examination of a number of studies that looked at some of the most frequently used tests (Hogan, 2005) (see Table 1). Thus, many of the 28 tests listed in Table 1 will be discussed in the following chapters.

In Chapter 6 we examine those tests typically given to assess what we have learned in school and which are used to determine a variety of educational issues. First we identify the purpose of the assessment of educational ability. We then define the different kinds of achievement and aptitude tests generally given to assess our learning and to make decisions about our futures, including survey battery achievement tests, diagnostic tests, readiness tests, and cognitive ability tests. Next, we examine some of the more popular tests in these categories (see Table 2).

Chapter 7 explores intellectual and cognitive functioning and the tests associated with it. Thus, in Chapter 7 we offer a brief history of both intelligence testing and neuropsychological assessment. In addition, we define intelligence testing and neuropsychological assessment. The chapter also offers an overview of some of the more popular models of intelligences, and we present some of the more common tests of intelligence and neuropsychological assessment (see Table 2).

In Chapter 8 we look at career and occupational assessment. We first define career and occupational testing and discuss its importance. Next, we look at interest inventories, multiple aptitude tests, and special aptitude tests, all of which are important in career and occupational assessment (see Table 2).

Our focus in Chapter 9 is clinical assessment. We start by defining clinical assessment and identifying its uses. Then we present a number of objective and projective tests used in clinical assessment (see Table 2).

TABLE 1 | FREQUENCY OF TEST USE BY DIFFERENT TYPES OF PSYCHOLOGISTS**

Ranking	Clinical	Counseling	Neuro	School
1	WAIS	MMPI	MMPI	WISC
2	MMPI	Strong*	WAIS	Peabody Individual Achievement Test
3	WISC	WAIS	Wechsler Memory Scale	House-Tree-Person*
4	Rorschach	Sentence Completion	Trail-Making Test	WAIS
5	Bender Visual-Motor Gestalt	WISC*	FAS Word Fluency Test	Human Figure Drawings*
6	TAT	TAT	Finger Tapping Test	Developmental Test of Visual-Motor Integration
7	WRAT	Sixteen PF	Halstead-Reitan	WRAT*
8	House-Tree-Person	Bender Visual-Motor Gestalt	Boston Naming Test	Kinetic Family Drawing
9	Wechsler Memory Scale	WRAT*	Category Test	Woodcock Johnson
10	Millon (MCMI)	Millon (MCMI)	WRAT*	Vineland Adaptive Behavior Scales
11	Beck Depression Test*	House-Tree-Person*	Beck Depression Test	Bender Visual-Motor Gestalt*
12	Trail Making Test	Rorschach Inkblot Test	Rey Complex Figure and Wisconsin Card Sorting Test	Peabody Picture Vocabulary and Child Behavior Checklist

*Tied with previous test
**Acronyms are spelled out in Table 2

Source: Hogan, T. P. (2005). Widely used psychological tests. In G. P. Koocher, J. C. Norcross, & S. S. Hill (Eds.), *Psychologists' desk reference* (2nd ed.) (pp. 101–104). New York: Oxford University Press.

In Chapter 10 we introduce various techniques of informal assessment and identify some positive and negative aspects of their use. We then offer an overview of a number of such instruments, but we stress that the ones we demonstrate are by no means an exhaustive list (see Table 2). Near the end of the chapter we discuss how to assess reliability and validity of informal assessment procedures.

Near the end of Chapters 6 through 10 we discuss the role that helpers play in using the assessment procedures being discussed in the particular chapter. Also, each chapter in this section concludes with a segment that places the assessment procedures within the context of the whole person and generally stresses the importance of using wisdom and sensitivity when assessing any person.

TABLE 2 | KEY ASSESSMENT INSTRUMENTS BY CHAPTER AND CATEGORY

CHAPTER 6: Assessment of Educational Ability	CHAPTER 7: Intellectual and Cognitive Functioning: Intelligence and Neuropsychological Assessment	CHAPTER 8: Career and Occupational Assessment	CHAPTER 9: Clinical Assessment	CHAPTER 10: Informal Assessment
Survey Achievement Tests • National Assessment of Educational Progress • Stanford Achievement Test • Iowa Test of Basic Skills • Metropolitan Achievement Test **Diagnostic Tests** • Wide Range Achievement Test 4 (WRAT4) • KeyMath3 • Peabody Individual Achievement Test • Wechsler Individual Achievement Test • Woodcock-Johnson(r) III **Readiness Tests** • Kindergarten Readiness Test • The Metropolitan • The Gesell	**Individual Intelligence Tests** • Stanford-Binet • Wechsler Scales of Intelligence (WPPSI, WISC, WAIS) • Kaufman Assessment Battery for Children **Nonverbal Intelligence Tests** • Comprehensive Test of Nonverbal Intelligence (CTONI) • The Universal Intelligence Test (UNIT). **Neuropsychological Assessment** • Halsted-Reitan Battery • Luria-Nebraska Neuropsychological Battery • Boston Process Approach	**Interest Inventories** • Strong Vocational Interest Inventory • Self-Directed Search • Career Occupational Preference System **Special Aptitude Tests** • Clerical Test Battery • Minnesota Clerical Assessment Battery • U.S. Postal Service's 470Battery Exam • Federal Clerical Exam • Skills Profiler Series • Mechanical Aptitude Test • Technical Test Battery • Wiesen Test of Mechanical Aptitude • ARCO Mechanical Aptitude & Spatial Relations Tests • Bennett Test of Mechanical Comprehension	**Objective Personality Tests** • Minnesota Multiphasic Personality Inventory (MMPI-2) • Millon Clinical Multiaxial Inventory (MCMI-III) • Beck Depression Inventory (BDI-II) • Myers-Briggs Type Indicator (MBTI) • The 16 PF • NEO PI-R • NEO-FFI • The PAI • The SASSI **Projective Personality Tests** • Thematic Apperception Test (TAT) • Rorschach Inkblot Test • Bender Visual-Motor Gestalt Test	**Informal Assessment Instruments** • Observation • Rating Scales • Classification Methods • Environmental Assessment • Records and Personal Documents • Performance-Based Methods

(continued)

TABLE 2 | CONTINUED

CHAPTER 6: Assessment of Educational Ability	CHAPTER 7: Intellectual and Cognitive Functioning: Intelligence and Neuropsychological Assessment	CHAPTER 8: Career and Occupational Assessment	CHAPTER 9: Clinical Assessment	CHAPTER 10: Informal Assessment
Cognitive Ability Tests • The Cognitive Ability Test • The Otis Lennon School Ability Test-8 (OLSAT 8) • Higher Education Admissions Tests: ACTs, SATs, GREs, LSATs, MCATs, MATs		• Music Aptitude Profile • Iowa Test of Music Literacy • Group Test of Musical Ability • Advanced Measures of Music Audiation **Multiple Aptitude Tests** • Armed Services Vocational Aptitude Battery • Differential Aptitude Test	• House-Tree-Person (HTP) • Kinetic-House-Tree-Person Test • Sentence Completion Series • EPS Sentence Completion • Kinetic Family Drawn • Draw-A-Man/Draw-A-Woman	

Assessment of Educational Ability: Survey Battery, Diagnostic, Readiness, and Cognitive Ability Tests

I woke up early, ready to take my test. I had studied hard, very hard, as hard as I ever had. I had taken an intensive course—10 hours a day for six days to make sure I was covering what I was supposed to cover. And now it was time to take "the test." I was confident— well, not really. Let's say I was as ready as I thought I could be. The big day was finally here.

I walk slowly to the testing center in the heart of Boston. Having stayed at a friend's house the night before, I notice my hip hurting as I marched my way to the test center. I walk in; "ID please," says a burly-looking character in a rough voice. I reach for my ID, thinking she does not have to be mean. After all, I am "choosing" to take this test. It starts late, and we're all getting more anxious. Finally, it comes. I take the test, and a few hours later I'm done. I soon notice that my hip pain is gone—it had been caused by my stress.

It's a few weeks later when I get my results—above the mean—slightly. I'm in. I'm now a licensed psychologist. I'm excited, but was it worth it? Perhaps, but does it really prove that I'm "better" than the 50 percent of doctoral level examinees who did not pass?

(Ed Neukrug)

Mass-produced tests of educational ability—we have all taken them, we have all sweated them, and they have affected all of us in some way. That's what this chapter is about—the types of widely used test that are given to assess what we have learned and to make decisions about our future. First we will identify and define the different kinds of achievement and aptitude tests generally given, including survey battery achievement tests, diagnostic tests, readiness tests, and cognitive ability tests. Next, we will look at some of the more popular kinds of tests in these categories. We will then provide an overview of some of the roles played by helpers in the assessment of educational ability and conclude with some thoughts about assessment in this important domain.

DEFINING ASSESSMENT OF EDUCATIONAL ABILITY

Whether it is the "Iowa," the "Stanford," the SAT, the ACT, or some other widely used test of educational ability, most students have taken many kinds of these tests, which are used to determine how we have been doing in school and to make decisions about our future. Tests of educational ability have broad applications. For instance, it is not unusual to find these tests being used for the following purposes:

1. To determine how well a student is learning.
2. To assess how well a class, grade, school, school system, or state is learning content knowledge.
3. As a method of detecting learning problems.
4. As a method of identifying giftedness.
5. To help determine if a child is ready to move to the next grade level.
6. To assess teacher effectiveness.
7. To help determine readiness or placement in college, graduate school, or professional schools.
8. To determine if an individual has mastered content knowledge for professional advancement (e.g., credentialing exams).

This chapter provides an overview of three kinds of achievement tests (survey battery, diagnostic, and readiness tests) and one kind of aptitude test (cognitive ability test). Together, these make up the four domains of educational assessment (see those domains bolded in Figure 6.1). Individual intelligence tests, and special and multiple aptitude tests, which largely do not focus on educational ability, are also sometimes used in the schools and have other broad applications. These tests will be covered in Chapter 7 and Chapter 8, respectively.

As you might recall from Chapter 1, we defined survey battery, diagnostic, readiness, and cognitive ability tests in the following ways:

Survey Battery Tests: Tests, usually given in school settings, which measure broad content areas. Often used to assess progress in school.

Diagnostic Tests: Tests that assess problem areas of learning. Often used to assess learning disabilities.

Readiness Tests: Tests that measure one's readiness for moving ahead in school. Often used to assess readiness to enter first grade.

Cognitive Ability Tests: Tests that measure a broad range of cognitive ability, these tests are usually based on what one has learned in school and are useful in making predictions about the future (e.g., whether an individual might succeed in school or in college).

You might also remember from Chapter 1 that sometimes the difference between Achievement Testing and Aptitude Testing has more to do with how the test is being used than what the test is actually measuring. For instance, although the SAT seems to be measuring content knowledge, or what you have learned in school, it is used to predict success in college and is therefore often listed in the Aptitude Section of Ability Testing. That is why there is a double-headed arrow in Figure 6.1—to remind us that many of these tests share much in common with one another—at least in

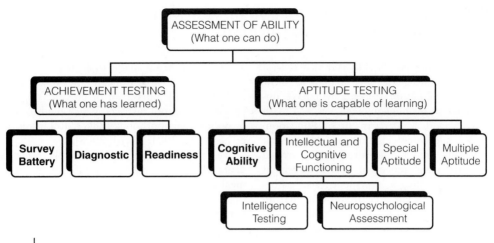

FIGURE 6.1 | Tests in the Cognitive Domain

terms of what they are measuring. In the rest of this chapter we will examine a number of survey battery, diagnostic, readiness, and cognitive ability tests and conclude with some final thoughts about the use and misuse of such tests.

SURVEY BATTERY ACHIEVEMENT TESTING

Survey battery tests

Paper-and-pencil tests measuring broad knowledge content

NCLB

Federal law ensuring all children succeed in school

With literally millions of children taking achievement tests every year, the achievement test industry is big business. It is therefore no surprise that a number of publishing companies spend a great deal of money on the development and refinement of survey battery achievement tests. Also, with "No Child Left Behind" (NCLB) mandating that states must show that "adequate yearly progress" is being made toward *all* students achieving at state-specified academic standards (U.S. Department of Education, 2005), survey battery achievement testing has taken on a bigger role, as these tests are used to document progress toward this goal (see Box 6.1).

Survey Battery Achievement Tests can be helpful on a number of levels. For instance, by providing individual profile reports, they can help a student, his or her parents, and his or her teachers identify strengths and weaknesses and develop strategies for working on weak academic areas. Similarly, profile reports at the classroom, school, or school system level can make it possible for teachers, principals, administrators, and the public to see how students are doing and when necessary, provide needed resources in areas where students seem to be struggling (see Figure 6.2). This section of the chapter will first review the testing process of the National Assessment of Educational Progress (NAEP), which uses achievement testing to assess how each state is doing compared to other states. Then, we will examine three of the most frequently used survey battery achievement tests given by various states, including the Stanford Achievement Test, the Iowa Test of Basic Skills (ITBS), and the Metropolitan Achievement Test.

BOX 6.1	HIGH STAKES TESTING: ACHIEVEMENT TESTING AND NO CHILD LEFT BEHIND

The No Child Left Behind (NCLB) Act is a federal law requiring that each state have a plan to show how, by the year 2014, *all* students will have obtained proficiency in reading/language arts and math (also see Box 5.1) (U.S. Department of Education, 2008a, b). Not surprisingly, scores on achievement tests are generally used to measure success toward NCLB. Thus, the development of new achievement tests, or the use of existing achievement tests, has become more important than ever in showing that all children are succeeding. For instance, Virginia has developed its own test, called the Standards of Learning (SOLs), which they use to show that progress has been made toward reaching proficiency as identified in NCLB.

The No Child Left Behind (NCLB) Act ties federal funding to the success of school districts and defines a number of actions that states must take to show that

attempts are being made to increase student scores (U.S. Department of Education, 2003). For good or bad, the NCLB puts a lot of pressure on the lower-performing school districts, which tend to be located in poorer neighborhoods (Baker, Robinson, Danner, & Neukrug, 2001; Lloyd, 2008).

Test scores not only allow schools to identify students who are not meeting specified levels of achievement but are also used to demonstrate how well each class, grade, school, district, or state is performing. As you might guess, there is a lot of pressure placed on teachers, principals, and superintendents, for if their class, school, or district does not show adequate progress, their jobs can be at stake. The upside: it is hoped that through NCLB, learning will improve, particularly among those who have traditionally been the most disenfranchised.

NATIONAL ASSESSMENT OF EDUCATIONAL PROGRESS (NAEP)

NAEP

The "Nation's Schools Report Card"

Partly because each state has a unique way of assessing its students, there was a push to develop one assessment procedure that would enable national comparisons to be made across all states. Sometimes called The National Report Card, the NAEP, which is sponsored by the U.S. Department of Education, samples students from all the states and compares them on a variety of subjects. Results are not provided for specific students, classes, or schools. In addition, it is important to emphasize that states cannot use the NAEP to show that adequate progress has been made toward No Child Left Behind.

All states are required to participate in the NAEP assessment in math and reading that occurs every two years, and most states also participate in periodic testing in writing and science. In addition, other subjects such as the arts, civics, economics, geography, and American history are sometimes assessed on a voluntary basis. Testing for the NAEP occurs at the fourth- and eighth-grade levels with each state carefully selecting a representative sample of 3000 students from 100 public schools (National Center for Education Statistics, 2008). For national data, a sample of between 10,000 and 20,000 public and nonpublic school students who are 9, 13, and 17 years old are assessed in mathematics and reading. Results are typically given as the percentage of students who scored above basic, proficient, or advanced achievement levels (See Table 6.1). In addition, scaled scores, which can be compared year to year within the state, to other states, and to a national sample, are provided. Scaled scores cannot be compared between subjects. Results can also be sorted by subject area, gender, ethnicity, and eligibility for national school lunch

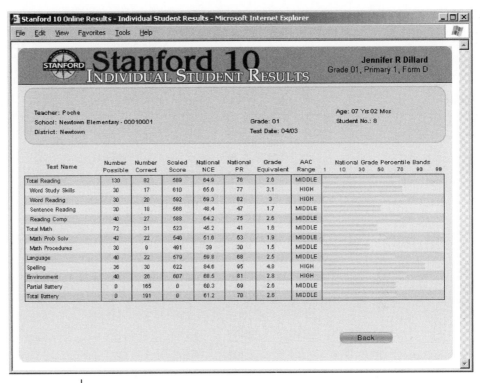

FIGURE 6.2 | **INDIVIDUAL STUDENT PROFILE ON THE STANFORD 10**

Source: Stanford 10 Results Online. Retrieved September 9, 2008, from http://pearsonassess.com/HAIWEB/Cultures/
en-us/Productdetail.htm?Pid=SAT10C&Mode=scoring&Leaf=SAT10C_4

programs. The tests appear to undergo a rigorous review process to ensure that
they are assessing national curricula and that they are reliable. The NAEP has become an important test that helps states examine whether or not they are achieving
at adequate levels. In Table 6.1, what trends do you see occurring in Florida on the
NAEP?

STANFORD ACHIEVEMENT TEST

SAT10

Assesses subject
areas in school

As mentioned in Chapter 1, the Stanford Achievement Test is one of the oldest survey battery achievement tests, having been introduced in 1923 (Carney, 2005;
Morse, 2005). Since that time it has gone through a number of revisions prior to
publication of its tenth edition in 2003. The Stanford Achievement Test (SAT10)
is given to students in grades K-12 and has been normed against hundreds of thousands of students (Harcourt Assessment, 2004).

This latest edition of the Stanford offers many options such as full-length or
abbreviated versions as well as content modules, which are tests for specific subjects such as reading, language, spelling, mathematics, science, social studies, and

TABLE 6.1 | HISTORY OF NAEP PARTICIPATION AND PERFORMANCE FOR FLORIDA

| Subject | Grade | Year | Scale Score | | Achievement Level | | |
| | | | State Avg. | [Nat. Avg.]* | Percent at or Above | | |
					Basic	Proficient	Advanced
Mathematics (scale: 0-500)	4	1992[n]	214	[219]	52	13	1
		1996[n]	216	[222]	55	15	1
		2003	234	[234]	76	31	4
		2005	239	[237]	82	37	5
		2007	242	[239]	86	40	6
	8	1990[n]	255	[262]	43	12	1
		1992[n]	260	[267]	49	15	1
		1996[n]	264	[271]	54	17	2
		2003	271	[276]	62	23	4
		2005	274	[278]	65	26	5
		2007	277	[280]	68	27	5
Reading (scale: 0-500)	4	1992[n]	208	[215]	53	21	3
		1994[n]	205	[212]	50	23	5
		1998	206	[213]	53	22	4
		2002	214	[217]	60	27	5
		2003	218	[216]	63	32	8
		2005	219	[217]	65	30	7
		2007	224	[220]	70	34	8
	8	1998	255	[261]	67	23	1
		2002	261	[263]	72	29	2
		2003	257	[261]	68	27	2
		2005	256	[260]	66	25	2
		2007	260	[261]	71	28	2
Science (scale: 0-300)	4	2005	150	[149]	68	26	2
	8	1996[n]	142	[148]	51	21	1
		2005	141	[147]	51	21	2
Writing (scale: 0-300)	4	2002	158	[153]	86	33	4
	8	1998	142	[148]	78	19	1
		2002	154	[152]	84	32	3
		2007	158	[154]	88	36	3

*Includes public schools only

[n]Accommodations were not permitted for this assessment

Source: National Center for Education Statistics (2006). *State profiles: Florida*. Retrieved September 4, 2008 from http://nces.ed.gov/nationsreportcard/states/profile.asp

writing (science and social science are merged into a heading called "environment" at the lower levels) (Carney, 2005). The Stanford Achievement Test also has sections that can be completed in open-ended format, requiring students to fill in the blank, respond with short answers, or write an essay that will be scored by the classroom teacher using criterion grading.

Reliability of the Stanford Achievement Test appears sound, with most subtests scoring in the mid .80s to low .90s using KR-20 internal consistency estimates. However, reliability estimates for the open-ended sections generally fell to the .60s to .80s and in some cases to the mid .50s (Harcourt Assessment, 2004). The Stanford Achievement Test appears to have sound validity, with content validity being established by working with content experts, teachers, editors, and measurement specialists. Evidence for construct validity was established by comparing scores on subtests with the Otis-Lennon School Ability Test, which produced a fairly high correlation. Criterion-related validity was addressed by numerous studies and is thorough and reasonable.

The Stanford Achievement Test, like other nationally made survey battery achievement tests, offers a number of interpretive reports, including Individual Profile Sheets, Class Grouping Sheets, Grade Grouping Sheets, and School System Grouping Sheets. Figure 6.2 shows an example of an Individual Student Profile, and Figure 6.3 shows data from 25 students in a fictitious third grade class disaggregated by ethnicity, socioeconomic status, limited English proficiency (LEP), and whether students have an Individualized Education Plan (IEP).

IEP:
Mandatory plan to accommodate students with special needs

Examine these profile sheets, and based on the information you learned in Chapter 5, see if you can make sense out of the data presented. Take particular note of how the data is disaggregated. This type of information is particularly useful for school systems because it allows them to target groups that are doing poorly.

Iowa Test of Basic Skills (ITBS)

ITBS
Measures skills to "satisfactorily" progress through school

One of the oldest and best known achievement tests is the Iowa Test of Basic Skills (ITBS). Initially developed in 1935, it has changed greatly from its early inception. Today, the test emphasizes the basic skills necessary to make satisfactory progress through school. The purposes of the instrument are "(a) to obtain information that can support instructional decisions made by teachers in the classroom, (b) to provide information to students and their parents for monitoring the student's growth from grade to grade, and (c) to examine yearly progress *of* grade groups as they pass through the school's curriculum" (Engelhard, 2007, ¶4).

The versions currently used are Form A (2001), Form B (2003), and Form C (2007). These versions of the test are geared for K through 8 and have numerous subtests, depending on the grade level, which may include language, reading comprehension, vocabulary, listening, word analysis, math, social studies, science, and sources of information (the ability of students to use maps, dictionaries, reference materials, charts, and so forth). Testing can run from 30 minutes for a single test to over six hours when a total battery is presented.

The authors of the test show strong evidence of content validity, which was guided by what is typically covered across the country, current teaching methods

		Total Reading									Total Math								
		Mean Raw Score	Mean Scale Score	Mean NCE	PR of Mean NCE	% in Quartile					Mean Raw Score	Mean Scale Score	Mean NCE	PR of Mean NCE	% in Quartile			
Group	N					1	2	3	4	N					1	2	3	4
Newtown	25	65.4	643.3	61.6	71	8	28	20	44	25	41.4	620.1	56.3	62	16	12	40	32
Male	9	67.6	628.7	54.0	57	22	22	33	22	9	43.3	614.9	53.7	57	22	0	56	22
Female	16	64.2	651.6	65.9	77	0	31	13	56	16	40.3	623.0	57.8	64	13	19	31	38
Asian	2	58.5	654.0	67.2	79	0	0	50	50	2	42.0	648.0	70.2	83	0	0	50	50
Black	1	44.0	605.0	41.3	34	0	100	0	0	1	37.0	620.0	57.0	63	0	0	100	0
Hispanic	2	56.5	657.5	68.7	81	0	50	0	50	2	37.5	635.5	62.4	72	0	50	0	50
White	17	73.1	651.5	66.0	78	6	18	24	53	17	43.4	616.9	54.8	59	24	6	35	35
Other	3	39.3	593.0	35.0	24	33	67	0	0	3	34.0	609.0	51.6	53	0	33	67	0
Low SES	3	70.3	603.3	43.4	38	33	33	33	0	3	36.7	577.7	34.4	23	67	0	33	0
Non Low SES	22	64.7	648.1	64.1	75	5	27	18	50	22	42.0	625.9	59.3	67	9	14	41	36
Non LEP	25	65.4	643.3	61.6	71	8	28	20	44	25	41.4	620.1	56.3	62	16	12	40	32
IEP	2	59.5	590.5	33.9	22	50	50	0	0	2	24.5	549.5	19.8	8	100	0	0	0
Non IEP	23	65.9	647.9	64.0	75	4	26	22	48	23	42.9	626.2	59.5	67	9	13	43	35

FIGURE 6.3 | CLASS/GRADE GROUPING SHEET

Source: Stanford 10 Results Online. Retrieved September 9, 2008, from http://pearsonassess.com/HAIWEB/Cultures/en-us/Productdetail.htm?Pid=SAT10C&Mode=scoring&Leaf=SAT10C_4

and textbooks used, and a review of national curricula (Engelhard, 2007; Lane, 2007). Reliability of most subtests are in the middle .80s to .low 90s, and the authors offer a *Guide to Research and Development Manual* (GRD) that stresses the strengths and weaknesses of the instrument. Finally, the publisher offers correlations in the low .70s to the low .80s, with the Cognitive Abilities Test (CogAT) offering additional validity evidence for the instrument and providing a mechanism to possibly identify learning problems if scores on the ITBS are considerably lower than those on the CogAT (See The Cognitive Ability Test later in the chapter).

METROPOLITAN ACHIEVEMENT TEST

Metropolitan Achievement Test

Assesses subject areas in school—has option for open-ended questions

First published during the 1930s, The Metropolitan Achievement Test is a popular paper-and-pencil test, the newest version of which is the eighth edition (Harwell, 2005; Lukin, 2005). It is designed to test students in grades K—12 for knowledge in a broad range of subjects such as reading, language arts, mathematics, science, and social studies. It has 13 test levels (K—12) and can be given in a short form that takes 90 minutes or the complete form that can take up to five hours. Test items consist of multiple-choice questions, which are graded correct or incorrect, and open-ended items, which are scored as 0 to 3. Although research based on extensive sampling data has been fairly exhaustive, some have suggested these samples might be too heavily weighted for rural class-rooms and underrepresent urban classrooms. As with the Stanford and ITBS, reliability estimates are quite high, usually between .8 and .9 or higher for most subtests, and content, criterion, and construct validity are sound.

DIAGNOSTIC TESTING

PL 94-142
Asserts right to be tested for learning disabilities

IDEIA
Extension of PL94-142

Diagnostic tests
Used to assess learning disabilities or difficulties

With the passage of Public Law 94-142 (PL94-142) in 1975 (Federal Register, 1977) as well as the more recent Individuals with Disabilities Education Improvement Act (IDEIA), millions of children and young adults between the ages of 3 and 21 who were found to have a learning disability were assured the right to an education within the least restrictive environment. These laws also assert that any individual who is suspected of having one of many disabilities that interfere with learning has the right to be tested, at the school system's expense, for the disability. Thus, diagnostic testing, usually administered by the school psychologist or learning disability specialist, has become one of the main ways to determine who might be learning disabled. These laws also state that a school team should review the test results and other assessment information obtained, and that any student identified as learning-disabled would be given an Individualized Education Plan (IEP) describing services that should be offered to assist the student with his or her learning problem.

Although diagnostic testing was certainly in existence prior to PL94-142 and IDEIA, its use, as well as the development of new diagnostic tests, greatly expanded as the result of these laws. In this section we will review three of the more common diagnostic tests of achievement often used to assess learning problems: the WRAT4, the Key Math Diagnostic Arithmetic Test, and the Peabody Individual Achievement Test. Throughout our discussion, keep in mind that dozens of diagnostic tests are in use today.

The Wide Range Achievement Test 4

WRAT4
Assesses basic learning problems in reading, spelling, math, and sentence comprehension

Significant differences between WRAT4 and IQ may indicate learning disability

The Wide Range Achievement Test 4 (WRAT4) was developed to assess basic reading, spelling, math, and sentence comprehension skills. It is "intended for use by those professionals who need a quick, simple, psychometrically sound assessment of important fundamental academic skills" (Wilkinson & Roberston, 2006, p. 3). It is called "wide range" because it can be used for populations from ages 5 to 94. The test takes between 15 and 45 minutes, depending on the age of the individual, and is administered individually since some sections are read aloud by the examinee. There are two equivalent forms of the exam called "blue" and "green" (Psychological Assessment Resources, 2005).

The WRAT4 attempts to ensure that the test is assessing the fundamentals of reading, spelling, and arithmetic, as opposed to comprehension, which is often the case when examinees are asked to read multiple-choice questions or paragraphs. Thus, the test is fairly simple to administer, as the individual being tested is asked by the examiner to "read" (pronounce) words, to spell words, to figure out a number of math problems, and with its latest revision, to provide a missing word or words to simple sentences to show that he or she understands the meaning of the sentence. The test includes the original three subtests, Word Reading, Spelling, and Math Computation, as well as the new, fourth subset called Sentence Comprehension. Combining the Word Reading and Sentence Comprehension subtests provides a Reading Composite score. The Spelling Comprehension and Math Computation subtests can be given in group format but the Word Reading and Sentence Comprehension must be administered individually.

Scores are presented in a number of ways, including grade equivalents, percentiles, NCEs, stanines, and a standard score that compares the individual by grade level or by age and uses a DIQ (mean of 100 and standard deviation of 15) (see Table 6.2). Confidence intervals, which are based on the WRAT4's standard error of measurement, are also provided for the standard score and suggest where the individual's "true score" falls 95% of the time. The DIQ is used so that the WRAT4 can be compared to scores on an intelligence test, such as the Wechsler Intelligence Scale for Children—III (WISC—III). This is important, because a significantly lower score on any of the scales of the WRAT4, as compared to the overall DIQ, could indicate the presence of a learning disability. Generally, more intensive testing for a learning disability would follow such findings.

Internal consistency reliability estimates are impressive and generally run in the .90s, and alternate form reliability averages in the mid 80s (Wilkinson & Robertson, 2006). The authors provide a rationale for the content of the test and demonstrate evidence of construct and criterion validity, such as moderate correlations with the WISC-III, the Wechsler Adult Intelligence Test—Revised (WAIS-R), and the Stanford Achievement Test.

KEYMATH-3 DIAGNOSTIC ARITHMETIC TEST

KeyMath3
Comprehensive test to assess for learning disabilities in math

The KeyMath has been described as "one of the very best test batteries for assessing a student's knowledge and understanding of basic mathematics and providing useful diagnostic information to teachers" (Wollack, 2001, "Summary"). Often used as a follow-up when there is a suspected math learning disability, the test is

---

TABLE 6.2 | SCORE SUMMARY TABLE (GREEN TEST FORM)

Subtest/Composite	Raw Score	Standard Score Norms: Age Norms	Confidence Interval 95%	% ile Rank	Grade Equivalent	NCE	Stanine
Word Reading	34	84	76–93	14	3.5	28	3
Sentence Completion	7	68	61–77	2	2.3	5	1
Spelling	27	85	76–95	16	3.7	29	3
Math Computation	37	105	94–115	63	7.3	57	6
Reading Composite*	152	74	69—80	4	N/A	13	2

*Reading Composite Raw Score = Word Reading Standard Score + Sentence Completion Standard Score

Source: Reynolds, C. R., Kamphaus, R., & PAR Staff. (2007). *RIAS™/WRAT4 discrepancy report*. Retrieved September 5, 2008, from http://www3.parinc.com/uploads/samplerpts/RIASWRAT4_Discrepancy_Simple.pdf

generally administered and interpreted by a person who has been well versed in both the test and in learning disabilities.

The most recent version of the instrument is the KeyMath-3, which has 10 subtests grouped under three broad math content areas: Basic Concepts (conceptual knowledge), Operations (computational knowledge), and Applications (problem solving) (Assessment for..., 2006). The test is appropriate for children in kindergarten through ninth grade or for individuals between the ages of 4½ and 21 if they are believed to be functioning within the K—9 grade levels. The test is untimed, but generally takes between 30 and 90 minutes to finish. Standard scores, scaled scores, percentiles, and grade or age equivalents are reported. This newest version was updated to reflect current curriculum standards and normed with a sample of 4,000 individuals to reflect gender, ethnicity, socioeconomic status, region of the country, and learning disabilities such as specific learning disability, speech and language impairment, intellectual disability, emotional/behavioral disturbance, and "other" impairment.

Internal consistency and alternate form reliability estimates tend to be quite high, often in the mid-.90s. The test shows correlations from the mid-.70s to the mid-.90s with the previous version of the test. To develop content validity, the authors reviewed state math standards and publications from the National Council of Teachers of Mathematics. Concurrent validity with the Kaufman Test of Educational Achievement, the ITBS, and with other instruments is quite good. To address issues of cross-cultural bias, "a sensitivity review was conducted to evaluate each item for fairness and appropriateness with respect to sex, race/ethnicity, cultural background, and geographic region" (KeyMath-3 DA Publication Summary Form, 2006, p. 11). Reviewers of various cultural backgrounds and from different areas of the United States participated in the review and made recommendations.

PEABODY INDIVIDUAL ACHIEVEMENT TEST

PIAT
Six content areas for screening K—12 students

The 1998 edition of the Peabody Individual Achievement Test—Revised—Normative Update (PIAT-R/NU) provides academic screening for children in grades K—12 and covers six content areas: General Information, Reading Recognition, Reading Comprehension, Mathematics, Spelling, and Written Expression (Cross 2001; Fager, 2001). Although renormed, the test is the same as the 1989 version. Except for General Information and Written Expression, the test is multiple choice. Individually administered, the instrument takes about one hour to give. Multiple derived scores can be obtained, including a standard score using Deviation IQ means and standard deviations, age equivalents, grade equivalents, percentile ranks, and NCEs. A developmental scaled score is used for the Written Expression Subtest (mean of 8, standard deviation of about 3). In addition, a convenient confidence interval is shown that uses 1 standard error of measurement for reported scores (see Table 6.3).

A wide variety of reliability estimates for the revised version show a median of approximately .94, although the written portion subtest, which is hand graded, has significantly lower interrater reliability (Cross, 2001; Fager, 2001). Content validity was established by using a number of school curriculum guides, and the manual

TABLE 6.3 | PEABODY INDIVIDUAL ACHIEVEMENT TEST RESULTS FEMALE, GRADE 2, AGE 8-7

Score Summary

Standard Scores were Derived from Age Norm Tables

Subtest or Composite	68% Confidence Level	Raw Score	Grade Equivalent	Age Equivalent	Standard Score	%ile Rank	NCE
General Information Subtest	+1.00 SEM	33		7-9	90	25	36
	Obtained Score	30	2.0	7-5	86	18	30
	−1.00 SEM	27		7-1	82	12	25
Reading Recognition Subtest	+1.00 SEM	25		7-2	82	12	25
	Obtained Score	23	1.5	6-11	80	9	22
	−1.00 SEM	21		6-8	78	7	19
Reading Comprehensi-on Subtest	+1.00 SEM	23		6-10	81	10	23
	Obtained Score	20	1.2	6-7	77	6	18
	−1.00 SEM	17		6-4	73	4	12
TOTAL READING	+1.00 SEM	47		6-11	79	8	21
	Obtained Score	43	1.3	6-9	77	6	18
	−1.00 SEM	39		6-6	75	5	15
Mathematics Subtest	+1.00 SEM	31		8-5	99	47	49
	Obtained Score	29	2.6	8-1	95	37	43
	−1.00 SEM	27		7-10	91	27	37
Spelling Subtest	+1.00 SEM	24		6-7	80	9	22
	Obtained Score	22	1.0	6-5	77	6	18
	−1.00 SEM	20		6-2	74	4	13
TOTAL TEST	+1.00 SEM	130		7-1	79	8	21
	Obtained Score	124	1.5	7-0	77	6	18
	−1.00 SEM	118		6-11	75	5	15

Written Expression II (Prompt A)

Raw Score = 17	Developmental Scaled Score = 2	Grade–based Stanine = 2

Written Language

Scaled Score Sum = 2 + 2 = 4	Age Standard Score = 74 +/− 4 %	Rank = 4	%ile Range = 2 − 7

Source: Sample PIAT-R/NU (2001). Retrieved September 5, 2008, from http://ags.pearsonassessments.com/pdf/piat.pdf

shows evidence of criterion and construct validity. The new normative sample ranged from 2,809 students for the Mathematics to 1,285 students for the Written Expression subtest. The instrument sampled well for sex, ethnicity, parental educational level, special education, and gifted students, but the Northeast and West are somewhat underrepresented.

OTHER DIAGNOSTIC TESTS

WIAT-II
Diagnostic test

Reviewing the dozens of other diagnostic tests available would exceed the scope of this book. However, two additional diagnostic instruments must be mentioned because of their popularity. The Wechsler Individual Achievement Test – Second Edition (WIAT-II) is an individually administered achievement test for ages 4 to 85 years old (Doll, 2003). The instrument provides composite scores in four domains: reading, mathematics, written language, and oral language. It is designed to work well with the other Wechsler intelligence scales (see Chapter 7) to aid in identifying disparities between ability and achievement (Pearson, 2008). The tests takes between 45 minutes and 2 hours, depending on age level, but an abbreviated version can be given in 15 to 30 minutes.

Woodcock-Johnson(r) III
Diagnostic test

Another comprehensive, individually administered diagnostic test is the Woodcock-Johnson(r) III, which is designed to assess "cognitive abilities, skills, and academic knowledge most recognized as comprising human intelligence and routinely encountered in school and other settings" (Cizek & Sandoval, 2003, ¶1). Although normed and applicable to individuals between the ages of 2 and 90, the instrument is generally used for students around the age of 10. The instrument, which shows strong evidence of test worthiness, actually consists of two batteries: (1) the Woodcock-Johnson Tests of Achievement, which examines academic strengths, and (2) the Woodcock-Johnson Tests of Cognitive Abilities, which looks at specific and general cognitive abilities. These tests, which can be given in standard and extended versions, were recently renormed with a diverse 8,800-subject sample.

READINESS TESTING

"All children in America will start school ready to learn."

(Goals 2000, 1996, ¶1)

Readiness tests
Assesses readiness for kindergarten or first grade

The Educate America Act, which many see as the predecessor to No Child Left Behind, had the above quote as one of its goals to be achieved by the year 2000. Although this goal may have been lofty, its basic concept was and continues to be strong. Today, one of the ways that we can assess a student's readiness to learn as he or she enters kindergarten or first grade is through a readiness test. Over the years, such tests have tended to be classified as either measurements of ability, such as reading or math achievement, or those that assess developmental level, such as psychomotor ability, language ability, and social maturity.

Because children change so rapidly at these young ages, and because the predictive ability of these tests tends to be weak, readiness testing has always been a questionable practice (Kim & Suen, 2000; Pyle 2002). In addition, because these assessments often carry cultural and language biases, children from low-income families, minority groups, and homes where English is not the first language will often obtain scores lower than their true ability. Thus, these tests need to be administered with care, if given at all. Despite problems with these tests, when a child's readiness to enter kindergarten or first grade is unclear, these instruments can sometimes be helpful and are used in many preschools and elementary schools. Generally, there are two categories of readiness testing—those that measure ability and those that measure developmental level, with ability readiness tests making up the bulk of readiness tests. Two ability readiness tests we will examine are The Kindergarten Readiness Test and the Metropolitan Readiness Test. The last readiness test we will briefly look at is the Gesell School Readiness Test, which measures developmental level.

KINDERGARTEN READINESS TEST

Kindergarten Readiness Test

Assesses broad range of cognitive and sensory motor skills

The Kindergarten Readiness Test, whose purpose is to determine if a child is ready to begin kindergarten, is administered individually, takes about 15 to 20 minutes, and assesses "Reasoning, Language, Auditory and Visual Attention, Numbers, Fine Motor Skills, and several other cognitive and sensory-perception areas" for children aged 4 to 6 (Slosson Educational Publications, n.d., ¶2)

Although administrative procedures and item quality are acceptable, items sometimes seem out of sequence and reliability and validity information is minimal (Beck, 1995; Sutton & Knight, 1995). Also, the sample population is drawn entirely from a four-state region in the Midwestern United States, which is not representative of the nation (Sutton & Knight, 1995). Despite these drawbacks, this instrument may be useful in determining whether a student is ready to begin kindergarten if the user believes that the content of the test matches the curriculum of the school the child will be attending.

METROPOLITAN READINESS TEST

MRT6

Assesses literacy development, reading, and mathematics

The Metropolitan Readiness Test, Sixth Edition (MRT6), is designed to assess beginning educational skills in preschoolers, kindergarteners, and first graders. Level 1 of the test is administered individually and assesses literacy development for preschoolers and beginning kindergarteners, while Level 2 assesses reading and mathematics development of kindergarteners through beginning first graders and is usually given in a group setting. The test generally takes between 80 and 100 minutes to administer, and the results are often used as an aid in determining whether a student should be placed in first or second grade. Results of the Metropolitan Readiness Test are generally reported using raw scores, stanines, or percentiles (Novak, 2001).

Reliability estimates for the composite test are strong and mostly hover around the .90s. Individual subtest reliabilities tend to deteriorate, often ranging from .53 to .77. Some have questioned the validity evidence of the MRT6 and its earlier versions. In fact, Kamphaus (2001) states that the Level 1 test shows no evidence of validity and that Level 2 has "virtually none" and is "unacceptable." However, others are more forgiving and find the MRT6 "useful in determining early academic or 'readiness' skills in reading and math" (Novak, 2001, "Summary").

GESELL SCHOOL READINESS TEST

Gesell School Readiness Test

Assesses developmental readiness

The Gesell School Readiness Test, Fifth Edition, was published in 1980 and is designed to assess personal and social skills, neurological and motor growth, language development, and overall adaptive behavior, or the ability of the child to adapt to new situations. The test is based on the work of Arnold Gesell, who spent years examining the normal development of children (Gesell Institute of Human Development, n.d). The test is administered in a non-threatening and comfortable environment by a highly trained examiner who observes the child's developmental maturity to assess the child's readiness to excel in different settings. This contrasts greatly with most other tests of readiness which use chronological age or intelligence in making decisions on child readiness (Bradley, 1985). The humanistic approach that the examiner takes when administering the test is appealing to many; however, there is quite a bit of examiner discretion in how the test is scored and interpreted.

Although the test provides some useful descriptive information about how children might perform in certain types of situations, overall, the test is weak in providing adequate information about its validity and reliability (Bradley, 1985; Waters, 1985). The test has also been criticized for its outdated norms, which are limited relative to ethnicity, geography, and social class. Although the test manual describes age-appropriate responses, the manual does not clearly specify how placement recommendations are made once an assessment has been completed. Therefore, school systems are not likely to use the instrument. Despite these problems, the test is sometimes used because it offers a view of readiness different from those that are based strictly on achievement in a content area. As far as Gesell was concerned, "achievement" involved more than getting high scores on a reading or math test (see Box 6.2)

BOX 6.2 | MEASURING ASSESSMENT: ABILITY OR DEVELOPMENTAL MATURITY?

When my daughter, Hannah, entered kindergarten, we asked her principal if she could be assessed for readiness for first grade, since her birthday missed the school system's deadline to enter first grade by only two days. Our daughter had gone to a very humanistically-oriented preschool, where achievement was not stressed but optimizing developmental level was. Between the preschool and some pretty good parenting (well, I think we did a good job!), our daughter clearly was mature for her age, socially adept, and seemed to be above average for most developmental milestones such as language and motor development. However, was she "smart enough" to enter first grade?

Hannah's public school was happy to give her a reading readiness test to see if she would "fit" into first grade. After taking the test, which was given by a reading specialist, we were told she would be a star in kindergarten and have some "catching up" to do in first grade. We were also told that it was our decision whether or not to move her into first grade. So

what to do—go with our sense of her developmental level or go with the reading test?

First, we consulted with her preschool teachers and experts in child development (after all, I do work in a College of Education). Boy, did we get mixed opinions! Knowing that such a decision should be based on many factors, not just one test, we considered Hannah holistically and hesitatingly decided to place her in first grade. We moved her to first grade, and as the reading specialist predicted, she did have some catching up to do. However, our decision seems to have been a good one, since she has excelled both in school and socially since that time. Maybe we made the best decision based on all the evidence, and maybe we just lucked out (she is now in ninth grade). Hannah's example shows how making a decision about early readiness is complex and highlights the importance of considering a variety of factors when in the decision-making process.

—Ed Neukrug

COGNITIVE ABILITY TESTS

Cognitive ability tests

Measures what one is capable of doing

As noted earlier, cognitive ability tests are aptitude tests that measure what one is capable of doing and are often used to assess a student's potential to succeed in grades K—12, college, or graduate school. First we will look at two K—12 tests: the Otis-Lennon School Ability Test and the Cognitive Ability Test. Then we will look at tests used to assess potential ability in college and graduate school, including: the American College Testing Assessment (ACT), the SAT Reasoning Test (SAT), the Graduate Record Exam (GRE), the Law School Admission Test (LSAT), and the Medical College Admission Test (MCAT).

OTIS-LENNON SCHOOL ABILITY TEST

OLSAT 8

Assesses abstract thinking and reasoning skills via verbal and nonverbal sections

The Otis-Lennon School Ability Test, Eighth Edition (OLSAT 8), is one of the more common cognitive ability tests. By assessing students' abstract thinking and reasoning skills via verbal and nonverbal sections, it provides educators with information about what to expect of students and why they may have challenges in certain subject areas. (Harcourt Assessment, 2008). Usually given in large group format and for students in K—12, the test assesses different clusters in the verbal and non-verbal realms. For instance, the two clusters for verbal ability include verbal comprehension and verbal reasoning. The three clusters for nonverbal ability include pictorial reasoning, figural reasoning, and quantitative reasoning. As you might expect, different grade levels are given different clusters, and each cluster has different subtests. Testing time is between 60 and 75 minutes, depending on the age of the student.

A variety of scores can be used in describing OLSAT 8 results, including a School Ability Index (SAI), which uses a mean of 100 and standard deviation of 16; percentile ranks based on age and grade; stanines; scaled scores; and NCEs based on grade. In addition, when given along with the Stanford 10, an Achievement/Ability Comparison (AAC) score can be obtained to give teachers insights into how students are actually doing in school compared to their potential. Significantly higher scores on a cognitive ability test (e.g., the OLSAT 8) as compared to an achievement test (e.g., Stanford 10) could be an indication of a learning disability. Figure 6.4 shows an Individual Profile Sheet from the OLSAT 8, and Figure 6.5 shows 20 of 56 students from a Grade Profile Sheet of the OLSAT 8.

The norm groups of the OLSAT 8 consisted of 275,000 students in the spring of 2002 and an additional 135,000 in the fall of 2002. Internal consistency measures of reliability based on the KR-20 for the composite score ranged from .89 to .94. Reliabilities for individual subtests using the KR-21 ranged from .52 to .82, with most falling in the .60s and .70s (Harcourt Assessment, 2002). Evidence of test content validity is somewhat vague, as the publisher notes that each user must determine if the content fits the population they are testing. Correlation coefficients for the OLSAT 8 composite scores with OLSAT 7 scores demonstrated coefficients in the range of .74 to .85, depending on grade level. Similarly, correlations among different levels of the OLSAT 8 were adequate. The test also showed reasonable correlations with the SAT10 (Harcourt Assessment).

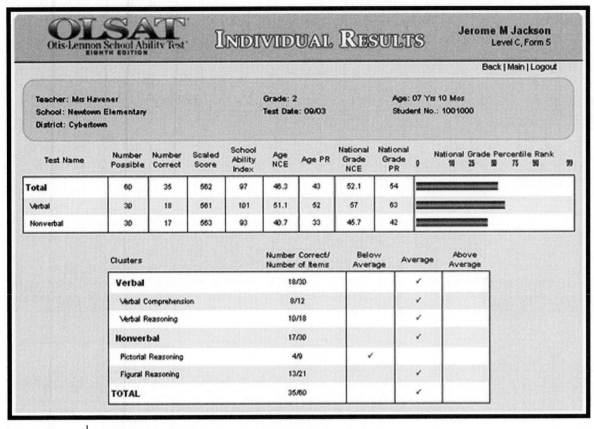

FIGURE 6.4 | OLSAT 8 INDIVIDUAL PROFILE SHEET

Source: OLSAT 8 Results Online. Retrieved September 9, 2008, from http://pearsonassess.com/haiweb/Cultures/en-US/Site/ProductsAndServices/Products/OLSAT8/OLSAT+8+Results+Online.htm

THE COGNITIVE ABILITY TEST

CogAT
Assesses verbal, quantitative, and nonverbal reasoning; uses Vernon's and Cattell's models of intelligence

Another common measure of cognitive ability, the Cognitive Ability Test (CogAT) has a name befitting of its test category. Form 6 of the CogAT is designed to assess cognitive skills of children from kindergarten through twelfth grade (Riverside Publishing, 2006). The purpose of this test is threefold, including: (1) to help a teacher understand the ability of each child in the classroom so that the teacher can optimize instruction for each child, (2) to provide a different means of measuring cognitive ability than traditional achievement tests, and (3) to identify students who might have large discrepancies between their cognitive ability testing and their achievement testing (DiPerna, 2005). Such discrepancies can be indicative of learning problems, lack of motivation, problems at home, problems at school, or self-esteem issues. Teachers and support staff should be cognizant of such discrepancies and make appropriate referrals as necessary (see Box 6.3).

Name	Student ID	Gender	Ethnicity	Verbal								Nonverbal							
				RS	SS	SAI	ANCE	APR	GNCE	NPR	PL	RS	SS	SAI	ANCE	APR	GNCE	NPR	PL
Wong, Jean	1000118	F	H	12	530	89	35.8	25	36.5	26	Average	19	575	101	51.1	52	53.2	56	Average
Wong, Connie	1000168	F	H	13	535	93	40.7	33	39.6	31	Average	20	580	106	58.1	65	55.9	61	Average
Wong, Christen	1000133	F	H	22	584	113	67	79	70.1	83	Above	25	617	118	73.7	87	73.7	87	Above
Sun, Vamsi	1000169	M	W	15	545	93	40.7	33	45.2	41	Average	18	569	96	44.7	40	48.9	48	Average
Sun, Johnny	1000128	M	W	18	561	101	51.1	52	57	63	Average	22	593	108	60.4	69	63.5	74	Average
Sun, James	1000157	M	W	20	572	110	62.9	73	63.5	74	Average	19	575	101	51.1	52	53.2	56	Average
Smith, Sharon D	1000143	F	H	22	584	113	67	79	70.1	83	Above	23	600	111	64.2	75	67	79	Above
Smith, Rebecca	1000165	F	H	17	556	97	46.3	43	54.3	58	Average	27	639	124	81.1	93	82.7	94	Above
Smith, Kathy	1000125	F	H	18	561	106	58.1	65	57	63	Average	26	627	123	79.6	92	78.2	91	Above
Smith, Kathleen M	1000137	F	B	23	591	116	70.9	84	73.7	87	Above	24	608	115	70.1	83	70.1	83	Above
Smith, Barbara	1000162	F	H	20	572	107	59.3	67	63.5	74	Average	27	639	126	84.6	95	82.7	94	Above
Mukkamala, Shari	1000136	F	B	13	535	92	39.6	31	39.6	31	Average	16	558	93	40.7	33	43	37	Average
Mukkamala, Connie	1000134	F	B	22	584	114	68.5	81	70.1	83	Above	21	587	107	59.3	67	59.8	68	Average
Malsbury, Jenny K	1000152	F	B	18	561	101	51.1	52	57	63	Average	23	600	111	64.2	75	67	79	Above
Malsbury, Jenny	1000126	F	B	12	530	89	35.8	25	36.5	26	Average	17	563	95	43.6	38	45.7	42	Average
Malsbury, Barbara	1000121	F	B	18	561	106	58.1	65	57	63	Average	20	580	106	58.1	65	55.9	61	Average
Hill, Tim	1000163	M	W	22	584	116	70.9	84	70.1	83	Above	19	575	104	55.3	60	53.2	56	Average
Hill, John E	1000138	M	W	27	628	128	86.9	96	89.6	97	Above	26	627	120	75.8	89	78.2	91	Above
Hill, Jerry C	1000144	M	W	21	578	110	62.9	73	67	79	Above	21	587	105	56.4	62	59.8	68	Average
Hill, Bryan M	1000140	M	W	18	561	101	51.1	52	57	63	Average	17	563	93	40.7	33	45.7	42	Average
Number Tested				56	56	56	56	56	56	56	56	56	56	56	56	56	56	56	56
Mean				19.2	569.2	106.9	59.0	64.3	60.9	67.3	NA	20.6	587.4	105.9	57.8	61.5	58.9	63.7	NA
Median				20.2	570.5	108.5	60.9	69.5	62.8	72.5	NA	20.4	579.9	105.5	56.9	62.5	58.1	60.9	NA

FIGURE 6.5 | OLSAT 8 GRADE PROFILE SHEET

Source: OLSAT 8 Results Online. Retrieved September 9, 2008, from http://pearsonassess.com/haiweb/Cultures/en-US/Site/ProductsAndServices/Products/OLSAT8/OLSAT+8+Results+Online.htm

The CogAT measures three broad areas of ability: verbal ability, quantitative ability, and nonverbal ability, and also offers a composite score. It is constructed with two models of intelligence in mind: Vernon's hierarchical model of abilities and Cattell's fluid and crystallized model of abilities (DiPerna, 2005; Rogers, 2005) (see Chapter 7). However, cognitive ability tests should never be viewed as substitutes for individual intelligence tests, because the manner in which they are created and administered is vastly different from that of intelligence tests, and they tend to focus primarily on traditional knowledge as obtained in school, particularly verbal and mathematical ability.

CogAT scores can be converted to standard scores that use a mean of 100 and standard deviation of 16, percentile ranks, and stanines. The entire test takes between two and three hours and is given in multiple administrations, depending on

BOX 6.3	IDENTIFYING NEEDED SERVICES

When I was in private practice, I worked with a third-grader who, a couple of years prior to my first meeting him, had been identified as having a math learning disability. This disability was first hypothesized after a large discrepancy was found between his cognitive ability score in math and his math achievement in school. Further testing verified the disability, and he was soon given an Individualized Education Plan that included three one-hour sessions of individualized assistance with math each week. After receiving this help, he soon began to do much better in math. However, after he had been getting higher math scores for about a year, the school discontinued tutoring services. I met him soon after this, following his parents' divorce, when his math scores had once again dropped. The scores had likely dropped due to the chaos at home as well as the removal of services. I immediately realized that this young man was not being given the extra help he was legally entitled to receive. I contacted the school, which agreed that he should be given assistance in math based on his Individualized Education Plan. Within a few weeks after obtaining this assistance, his math scores once again improved, and he was a noticeably happier child.

—*Ed Neukrug*

the age range of the student. In 2000, the authors of the CogAT normed its scores against a nationwide sample of more than 180,000 students. The sample was stratified to correctly weigh public, Catholic, and non-Catholic private schools, as well as socioeconomic status, geographic region, and racial/ethnic representation (Lohman & Hagen, 2002). Internal consistency reliability ranged from .86 to .96 for the verbal, quantitative, and nonverbal sections and from .94 to .98 from the composite score.

Because it is difficult to define any theoretical model that can clearly identify a knowledge base that predicts future ability, cognitive ability tests in general have a difficult time establishing content validity. However, the CogAT does offer a rationale by stating that the content domain was defined logically and through the sampling of student textbooks (Lohman & Hagen). Concurrent validity with the Iowa Test of Basic Skills (ITBS) was .83, and CogAT fourth grade scores correlated .79 with ninth-grade scores on the ITBS (Lohman & Hagen). Studies are in progress to correlate the CogAT Form 6 with the Woodcock-Johnson III and the Wechsler Intelligence Scale for Children III. Although some have questioned whether the instrument should be used to determine classroom learning, the test does show promise as a useful instrument in identifying student strengths and weaknesses and possible learning problems (DiPerna, 2005: Rogers, 2005).

COLLEGE AND GRADUATE SCHOOL ADMISSION EXAMS

A number of cognitive ability tests are used to predict achievement in college and graduate school. Some of the ones with which you might be familiar include the American College Testing Assessment (ACT), the SAT Reasoning Test (the SAT), the Graduate Record Exam (GRE) General Test and Subject Tests, the Miller Analogies Test (MAT), the Law School Admission Test (LSAT), and the Medical College Admission Test (MCAT). Despite much consternation over the use of these

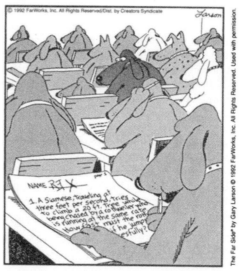

Before their admission to any canine university, dogs must first do well on the CATs.

Source: The "Far Side" by Gar Larson © 1992 FarWorks, Inc. All Rights Reserved. Used with permission

tests, research appears to support their use and indicates that such tests predict performance in undergraduate and graduate school about as well as or better than other indicators and are especially useful when combined with grade predictors (e.g., grades in high school or college grades) (Kobrin, Patterson, Shaw, Mattern, & Barbuti, 2008; Kuncel & Hezlett, 2007).

ACT

Assesses educational development and ability to complete college work

ACT The ACT, the most widely used admission exam at the undergraduate level, is designed to assess educational development and the ability to complete college-level work (ACT News, 2008). The test covers four skill areas, including English, Math, Reading, and Science. The ACT contains 215 multiple-choice questions and takes three and one-half hours to complete. Test scores range from 1 to 36 with a mean of 18 and a standard deviation of 5 for "average" high school students. However, the actual mean for the college-bound students taking the exam in 2008 was 21.2. The standard error of measurement (SEM) for the composite score is 1. The ACT publishers performed a major norm sampling in 1988 with more than 100,000 high school students and another re-sampling update in 1995 with 24,000 students stratified against the U.S. Department of Education figures for region, school size, affiliation, and ethnicity (ACT, Inc., 1997; ACT Technical Manual, 2007).

Reliability of the ACT has ranged between .85 and .91 for the four skill areas and is .96 for the composite score. Evidence of content validity is shown through the test development process by continually ensuring that test items show a

| BOX 6.4 | USE OF COLLEGE ADMISSION EXAMS |

Students in our testing and assessment classes frequently ask why universities continue to use college admission exams if the predictive validity correlation estimates are sometimes as low as the .30s or .40s (or about the same as correlation with high school GPA). This is a good question. There are many reasons to use these exams, but one important reason that is often overlooked is the fact that it levels the playing field. The range of academic difficulty in high schools varies considerably across the United States; that is, a 3.9 GPA performance in one high school may be equivalent to a 3.2 GPA in another. Perhaps the student with the 3.2 GPA went to an extraordinarily difficult and rigorous high school and took many advanced classes, whereas the student with the 3.9 GPA might have coasted in relatively easy classes at a school that graded liberally. The college admission exam gives both of these students a fair and equal chance to show what they know. One additional reason for using the ACT or SAT is that predictions of how a student will do in college are more accurate if scores on the tests are used in conjunction with high school GPA.

—Charlie Fawcett

relationship to how students have "developed the academic skills and knowledge that are important for success in college" (ACT Technical Manual, 2007, p. 62). The ACT publishers also performed studies that showed a sound correlation between students' ACT scores and their high school GPAs. Predictive validity studies correlating ACT scores and first-year college GPA had a median of .42. Combining ACT scores with high school GPA increased the predictive validity to .53. Numerous other studies of validity are available in the ACT technical manual.

SAT
Assesses reading, math, and writing— predicts mildly well for college grades

SAT   The other major undergraduate college exam is the SAT Reasoning Test. The SAT measures critical thinking and problem-solving skills in three areas: reading, mathematics, and a writing section that has multiple-choice questions as well as a writing sample. On each of the three sections students earn a score that ranges between 200 and 800 as well as a percentile score that compares the examinee's results to those of students who have taken the test recently. On the writing section, students also receive a writing score that is based on their essay and ranges between 1 and 6 (6 being a better score) and is evaluated by two or three readers.

On the mathematics and critical reading sections, longitudinal comparisons can be made as test scores are compared to a 1990 norm group that had its mean "set" at about 500 and its standard deviation "set" at about 100. Thus, if the mean mathematics score of students in a recent year is 580 and the standard deviation is 108, it can be said that this group is doing better than an earlier norm group with a lower mean and similar standard deviation. Such comparisons make it possible to determine whether today's students are doing better or worse in mathematics and reading than students in past years.

Internal consistency reliability estimates for a national sample of the SAT were .93 for critical reading, .92 for mathematics, and .83 for the multiple-choice section of the writing. On the essay portion of the writing exam, using a variety of types of reliability, estimates were quite a bit lower and hovered around .60

(Ewing, Huff, Andrews, & King, 2005; Breland, Kubota, Nickerson, Trapani, & Walker, 2004). A 2006 sample of over 150,000 students showed that correlations for SATs with first-year GPA in college were the following: .51 for the writing test, .48 for the critical reading test, and .47 with the math test (Kobrin, Patterson, Shaw, Mattern, & Barbuti, 2008). High school grades correlate .54 with first-year GPA in college, and when combining high school grades with the scores on all three tests of the SATs there is a correlation of .62. The test predicts a little better for White students than "underrepresented groups" for first year GPA in college, with correlations ranging from .46 to .51 for White students and from .40 to .46 for underrepresented groups (Mattern, Patterson, Shaw, Kobrin, & Barbuti, 2008). Correlations were slightly higher for females as compared to males.

GRE

Assesses verbal reasoning, quantitative reasoning, and analytical writing; predicts graduate school success

GRE GENERAL TEST   The GRE General Test is a cognitive ability test frequently required by U.S. graduate schools. The General Test contains three sections: verbal reasoning, quantitative reasoning, and analytical writing. The scoring for the verbal and quantitative reasoning sections is similar to the SAT and ranges from 200 to 800. However, the Educational Testing Service does not "set" the mean or standard deviation and instead uses a scaled score with a mean and standard deviation that floats over time. For instance, the mean on the verbal reasoning section for those who took the test between July 1, 2003 and June 30, 2005 was 465 and the standard deviation was 117, while the mean and standard deviation for quantitative reasoning were 584 and 149, respectively (Graduate Record Examinations, 2007). Thus, it is probably prudent to look at percentile ranks as opposed to scaled scores. Percentiles allow examinees to see how they are doing compared to those who are currently taking the exam. The analytical section is scored by two trained readers, and scores range from 0 to 6 (a third reader is brought in if the two scores are more than 1 point apart). The mean and standard deviation for this section of the test was 4.1 and 0.9, respectively, for those who took it between July 1, 2003 and June 30, 2005.

Reliability estimates for the GREs are in the low .90s for the verbal and quantitative reasoning sections and .72 for the analytical writing section. Correlations for the GRE General Test (Verbal and Quantitative) with a number of different predictors are as follows: first-year graduate GPA, .34 and .46; comprehensive exam scores, .44 and .51; and faculty ratings, .42 and .50 (Graduate Record Examinations, 2007). Correlations between combined scores on the verbal and quantitative sections with graduate school GPA for specific graduate school majors are often much higher (e.g., .51 for psychology; .66 for Education (Burton & Wang, 2005).

GRE SUBJECT TESTS   In addition to the GRE General Test, a number of subject tests are provided for those graduate programs that wish to assess more specific ability. The available subject tests include biochemistry, cell and molecular biology; biology; chemistry; computer science; literature in English; mathematics; physics; and psychology. Like the GRE General Test, the subject tests use a floating mean and standard deviation; however, the Subject Test's scaled score ranges between

200 and 990, as opposed to 200 and 800 on the General Test (Graduate Record Examinations, 2007). Means and standard deviations can vary dramatically among subject tests. For instance, the mean and standard deviation for those examinees who took the biochemistry, cell and molecular biology test between July 2003 and June 2006 were 519 and 99, respectively, while the mean and standard deviation for experimental psychology during that time were 598 and 101. Reliability of the subject tests tend to be in the low to mid-.90s. Correlations between subject scores and grades in graduate school tend to run between .33 and .47.

MAT

Uses analogies to assess analytical abilities; predicts graduate school success

MAT   Another test used for admission to graduate school is the Miller Analogies Test, which "measures your ability to recognize relationships between ideas, your fluency in the English language, and your general knowledge of the humanities, natural sciences, mathematics, and social sciences" (Miller Analogies Test, 2008—2009, p. 2). The test, which has 120 analogies, can be taken on a computer or by hand and takes one hour to complete. A scaled score based on all who took the test between January 2001 and December 2003 is given and ranges from 200 to 600 with a mean set at 400. Percentile scores are also compared to the examinee's intended major and to the total group who took the test. Internal reliability coefficients range from .91 to .94. Predictive validity studies for students entering graduate school in 2005 showed correlations with first-year GPA to be .27. Other correlations were .21 with the GRE Verbal Score, .27 with the GRE Quantitative Score, .11 with the GRE Writing Score, and .24 with undergraduate GPA. Although all but the Writing score were statistically significant, their correlations are in the weak to moderate level (Meagher, 2008).

LSAT

Assesses acquired reading and verbal reasoning skills; predicts grades in law school

LSAT   The Law School Admissions Test (LSAT) is a half-day test that consists of four sections used to determine admission to law school. The test includes three multiple-choice sections measuring reading comprehension, analytical reasoning, and logical reasoning and a fourth section that asks for a writing sample that is not scored but sent directly to Law Schools to which the applicant is applying. A fifth section is unscored and is used to pretest new questions. The LSAT has a unique scoring method that ranges from 120 to 180 based on item difficulty and how the examinee has scored compared to others. Percentiles are also given. The median correlation between LSAT scores and grades in the first year of law school is .33, and the correlation increases to .47 when the test is combined with undergraduate grade-point average (LSAT & LSDAS Information Book, 2008–2009). Reliability estimates are quite high, ranging from .90 to .95

MCAT

Assesses knowledge of physical biological sciences, verbal reasoning, and writing skills; predicts grades in medical school

MCAT   Most medical schools use the Medical College Admission Test (MCAT) as one factor in determining admissions. The test consists of four sections: physical sciences, biological sciences, verbal reasoning, and a writing sample. For all but the writing section, examinees receive a scaled score that ranges from 1–15 as well as a total score that is a simple adding together of the physical sciences, biological sciences, and verbal reasoning scores. For the writing sample, examinees receive a letter from J through T that is reflective of the average score of two readers (the closer to T, the better the score). The mean and standard deviation of the scaled scores can vary, but each examinee is given a separate sheet that states the mean and standard deviation for the test they took as well as their percentile ranking (Medical College Admission Test, 2005). Although some research appears to support the predictive validity of the MCAT (see Annotated Bibliography…, 1995–2008), additional research that examines both its validity and reliability would be helpful.

THE ROLE OF HELPERS IN THE ASSESSMENT OF EDUCATIONAL ABILITY

In addition to teachers, a variety of helping professionals can play critical roles in assessing educational ability. For instance, school counselors, school psychologists, learning disabilities specialists, and school social workers often work together as members of the school's special education team to assess eligibility for assessment of learning disabilities and to help determine a child's Individualized Education Plan (IEP). School psychologists and learning disability specialists are generally the testing experts who are called upon to do the testing to identify learning problems. Sometimes outside experts in assessment, such as clinical and counseling psychologists, are called upon to do additional assessments or to contribute a second opinion to the school's assessment.

Because school counselors are some of the few experts in assessment who are housed at the school (school psychologists generally float from school to school), they will sometimes assist teachers in understanding and interpreting educational ability tests. In addition, by disaggregating the data from achievement tests, school counselors can play an important role in helping to identify students and classrooms that might need additional assistance in learning specific subject areas. Finally, licensed professionals in private practice need to know about the assessment of educational ability when working with children who are having problems at school. In fact, it is often critical that these clinicians consult with professionals in the schools to ensure that the child is making adequate progress (see Box 6.5).

| BOX 6.5 | ASSISTING TEACHERS TO INTERPRET STANDARDIZED TESTING |

A school system once hired me to run a series of workshops for their teachers on how to interpret the results of national standardized testing, such as survey battery achievement test scores. I was quite surprised to learn that few of them had ever taken a course on how to interpret such data and thus had no idea of the important information that could be gained from analyzing the data. I was, however, impressed with the content knowledge that these teachers possessed. It was almost as though I was teaching them Greek (basic test statistics used in test interpretation) and they were teaching me Latin (the meaning of the content areas that were being reported on the test reports). It was certainly a learning experience for all of us!

—Ed Neukrug

FINAL THOUGHTS ABOUT THE ASSESSMENT OF EDUCATIONAL ABILITY

As you can see from this chapter, the assessment of educational ability has become an important aspect of testing in the United States. Despite the widespread use of these tests, many criticisms have arisen, including the following:

1. Teachers are increasingly being forced to teach to the test. This prevents them from being creative and limits the kind of learning that takes place in the schools.
2. Testing leads to labeling and this can cause peers, teachers, parents, and others to treat the child as the label. For the child, the label sometimes becomes a self-fulfilling prophecy that prevents him or her from being able to transcend the label.
3. Some tests, particularly readiness tests and cognitive ability tests, are just a mechanism to allow majority children to move ahead and to keep minority children behind.
4. Testing fosters competitiveness and peer pressure, creating a failure identity for a large percentage of students.

On the other hand, many have spoken positively about tests of educational ability and have made the following points:

1. Tests allow us to identify children, classrooms, schools, and school systems that are performing poorly. This, in turn, allows us to address weaknesses in learning. In fact, evidence already exists that as a result of state standards of learning and the achievement testing associated with them, poor children, minority children, and others who traditionally have not done as well in schools have been doing better academically (Achievement Tech., 2002).
2. Without diagnostic testing we could not identify those children who have a learning disability, and we would not be able to offer them services to help them learn.
3. Testing allows a child to be accurately placed in his or her grade level. This ultimately provides a better learning environment for all children.
4. Testing helps children identify what they are good at and pinpoint weak areas that require added attention.

Probably both the criticism and praises of educational ability testing hold some truth. Perhaps as we realize the positive aspects of such testing we should also pay attention to the criticisms and find ways to address them.

SUMMARY

In this chapter we examined the assessment of educational ability. We started by noting that such tests have a variety of purposes, including determining if students are learning; assessing content knowledge of classes, schools, and school systems; identifying learning problems; determining

giftedness; deciding whether a child is ready to move to the next grade level; as a measure to assess teacher effectiveness; and to help determine readiness and placement in college and graduate school.

We identified four kinds of educational ability testing, including three kinds of achievement tests (survey battery, diagnostic, and readiness) and one kind of aptitude test (cognitive ability testing). We defined each of these test categories and noted that often the difference between achievement testing and aptitude testing involves how the test is used as opposed to what it is measuring.

In this chapter we looked at four types of survey battery achievement tests: the National Assessment of Educational Progress, which is sponsored by the U.S. Department of Education and offers a "National Report Card" on how schools are doing in educating our students. We next looked at three achievement tests often used by states in assessing how their students are doing: the Stanford Achievement Test, Iowa Test of Basic Skills, and the Metropolitan Achievement Test. We noted that these tests tend to have very good validity and reliability and in recent years have become particularly important in measuring progress in meeting states' standards of learning and guidelines as set by No Child Left Behind. In the age of high stakes testing and No Child Left Behind, these tests have shown to be good at identifying the individual strengths and weaknesses of students and how well individual teachers, schools, and school systems are doing at teaching content areas.

Next, we noted that diagnostic testing has become increasingly important in the identification and diagnosis of learning disabilities. This is partly due to the passage of PL94-142 and the Individual with Disabilities Education Improvement Act (IDEIA), which state that all students with a learning disability must be given accommodations for their disability within the least restrictive environment. We noted that Individualized Education Plans address any accommodations that need to be made to help the student learn.

In discussing the measurement of disabilities, we highlighted three diagnostic achievement tests: the Wide Range Achievement Test 4, which looks at whether an individual has learned the basic codes for reading, spelling, and arithmetic; the Key-Math-3, which offers scrutiny of a child's math ability when he or she is suspected of having a math disability; and the Peabody Individual Achievement Test, which provides academic screening for K–12 students in a wide range of content areas. As with the survey battery tests, these tests tend to have good validity and reliability. Additionally, we briefly mentioned some other common diagnostic tests, including the Wechsler Individual Achievement Test—Second Edition and the Woodcock-Johnson(r) III.

The final area of achievement testing we looked at was readiness testing. Although the validity information on readiness testing is weak, these tests are sometimes helpful in determining whether a child is ready to begin kindergarten or first grade. Three readiness tests we examined included the Kindergarten Readiness Test, which assesses reasoning, language, auditory and visual attention, numbers, fine motor skills, and several other cognitive and sensory-perception areas; the Metropolitan Readiness Test, which measures literacy development for kindergarteners and reading and mathematics for first graders; and the Gesell, which assesses personal and social skills, neurological and motor growth, language development, and overall adaptive behavior, or the ability of the child to adapt to new situations.

As the chapter continued, we reviewed a number of cognitive ability tests, starting with the Otis-Lennon School Ability Test 8 (OLSAT 8). We noted that this was one of the more common cognitive ability tests and that it assesses students' abstract thinking and reasoning skills via verbal and nonverbal sections. We also highlighted the Cognitive Ability Test (CogAT), which measures cognitive skills for children from kindergarten to twelfth grade. Somewhat based on Vernon's and Cattell's theories of intelligence, this test provides scores in three areas: verbal, quantitative, and nonverbal reasoning abilities. We noted that cognitive ability tests such as these are particularly helpful in identifying students who have potential to do well in school but are not succeeding due to such things as learning disabilities, motivation, problems at home, problems at school, or self-esteem issues. We warned that tests such as these should not be confused with individualized intelligence tests.

Next, we went on to examine cognitive ability tests that are used to predict achievement in college and graduate school. For instance, we identified the American College Testing Assessment (ACT) and the SAT Reasoning Test as two tests that predict how well an individual will do in college with about the same level of predictive accuracy as high school GPA. On the graduate level, we identified the Graduate Record Exam (GRE) General Test and Subject Tests, which predict grades moderately well, and the Miller Analogies Test (MAT). We also noted that the Law School Admission Test (LSAT) and the Medical College Admission Test (MCAT) both are fairly good predictors of achievement in law school or medical school.

As the chapter neared its conclusion, we identified some of the important roles played by school counselors, school social workers, school psychologists, and learning disabilities specialists in the schools relative to the assessment of educational ability. We also highlighted the importance of private practice clinicians knowing about such types of assessment.

The chapter concluded with some final thoughts about the assessment of educational ability. We noted that such tests have been attacked for forcing teachers to teach to the test, labeling children, hindering progress of minority children, and fostering competitiveness and peer pressure. On the other hand, they have been praised because they can identify which children, classrooms, schools, and school systems are performing poorly; signal the presence of learning disabilities; allow children to be accurately placed in their grade levels; and help students identify what areas they need to focus upon. We stressed that probably both the criticism and praises of educational ability testing hold some truth.

CHAPTER REVIEW

1. Discuss applications of tests for assessing educational ability.
2. Define the following types of tests of educational ability: survey battery tests, readiness tests, diagnostic tests, and cognitive ability tests.
3. Discuss some of the benefits and drawbacks of No Child Left Behind in terms of the "high stakes testing" atmosphere it tends to promote.
4. From your reading in the chapter, identify two or three survey battery tests and discuss how they might be applied.
5. Relative to survey battery achievement tests, what are some of the uses of classroom, school, and school system profile reports?
6. Discuss the relevance of diagnostic testing to PL94-142 and to the IDEIA.

7. Identify and describe two or three diagnostic tests discussed in this chapter.
8. Compare and contrast a readiness test such as the Metropolitan with one like the Gesell.
9. Identify one or more cognitive ability tests that are typically used in the schools and discuss their applications. In particular, how are they important for the identification of learning problems?
10. Discuss two or more types of cognitive ability tests that are typically used for admission into college or graduate school.
11. Discuss the role of school counselors, school psychologists, learning disability specialists, school social workers, and private practice clinicians in the assessment of educational ability.

REFERENCES

Achievement Tech. (2002). *Effectiveness report: South Plainfield schools' quest to leave no child behind*. Retrieved on September 26, 2004, from http://www.achievementtech.com/pdf/SouthPlainField.pdf

ACT, Inc. (1997). *ACT Assessment technical manual.* Iowa City, IA: Author.

ACT News. (2008). *Facts about the ACT.* Retrieved September 9, 2008, from http://www.act.org/news/aapfacts.html

ACT Technical Manual. (2007). Iowa City, IA: Author.

Annotated Bibliography of... (1995–2008). *Annotated bibliography of MCAT research*. Retrieved September 9, 2008, from http://www.aamc.org/students/mcat/research/bibliography/start.htm

Assessment for... (2006). *Assessments for specialized education needs: KeyMath3*. Retrieved September 5, 2008, from http://ags.pearsonassessments.com/group.asp?nGroupInfoID=aKeymath3

Baker, S. R., Robinson, J. E., Danner, M. J. E., Neukrug, E. (2001). *Community social disorganization theory applied to adolescent academic achievement* (Report No. UD034167). (ERIC Document Reproduction Service No. ED453301).

Beck, M. (1995). Review of the Kindergarten Readiness Test. In J. C. Conoley and J. C. Impara, (Eds.), *The Twelfth Mental Measurements Yearbook*. Lincoln, NE: Buros Institute of Mental Measurements. Retrieved from Mental Measurements Yearbook database.

Bradley, R. (1985). Review of the Gesell Readiness Test. In J. V. Mitchell, Jr. (Ed.), The *Twelfth Mental Measurements Yearbook*. Lincoln, NE: Retrieved from Mental Measurements Yearbook database.

Breland, H., Kubota, M., Nickerson, K., Trapani, C., & Walker, W. (2004). *New SAT writing prompt study: Analyses of group impact and reliability*. Retrieved September 9, 2008, from http://professionals.collegeboard.com/research/pdf/04497newsatwritrr041_34556.PDF

Burton, N. W., & Wang, M. (2005). *Predicting long-term success in graduate school: A collaborative validity study*. Princeton, NJ: Educational Testing Service

Carney, R. N. (2005). Review of the Stanford Achievement Test, Tenth Edition. In R.A. Spies and B.S. Plake Eds.), *The Sixteenth Mental Measurements Yearbook*. Lincoln, NE: Buros Institute of Mental Measurements. Retrieved from Mental Measurements Yearbook database.

Cizek, G. J., & Sandoval, J. (2003). Review of the Woodcock-Johnson® III. In B.S. Plake, J.C. Impara, and R. A. Spies (Eds.), *The Fifteenth Mental Measurements Yearbook*. Lincoln, NE: Buros Institute of Mental Measurements. Retrieved from Mental Measurements Yearbook database.

Cross, L. (2001). Review of the Peabody Individual Achievement Test—Revised [1998 normative update]. In B.S. Plake and J.C. Impara (Eds.), *The Fourteenth Mental Measurements Yearbook*. Lincoln, NE: Buros Institute of Mental Measurements. Retrieved from Mental Measurements Yearbook database.

DiPerna, J. C. (2005). Review of the Cognitive Abilities Test, form 6. In R.A. Spies and B.S. Plake (Eds.), *The Sixteenth Mental Measurements Yearbook*. Lincoln, NE: Buros Institute of Mental Measurements. Retrieved from Mental Measurements Yearbook database.

Doll, B. J. (2003). Review of the Wechsler Individual Achievement Test—Second edition. In B.S. Plake, J.C. Impara, and R.A. Spies (Eds.), *The Fifteenth Mental Measurements Yearbook*. Lincoln, NE: Buros Institute of Mental Measurements. Retrieved from Mental Measurements Yearbook database.

Engelhard, G. (2007). Review of the Iowa Tests of Basic Skills: Forms A and B. In K.F. Geisinger, R.A. Spies, J.F. Carlson, and B. S. Plake (Eds.), *The Seventeenth Mental Measurements Yearbook*. Lincoln, NE: Buros Institute of Mental Measurements. Retrieved from Mental Measurements Yearbook database.

Ewing, M., Huff, K., Andrews, M., & King, K. (2005). *Assessing the reliability of skills measured by the SAT*. Retrieved September 9, 2008, from http://professionals.collegeboard.com/research/pdf/RN-24.pdf

Fager, J. J. (2001). Review of the Peabody Individual Achievement Test—Revised [1998 normative update]. In B.S. Plake and J.C. Impara (Eds.), *The Fourteenth Mental Measurements Yearbook*. Lincoln, NE: Buros Institute of Mental Measurements. Retrieved from Mental Measurements Yearbook database.

Federal Register, 42(163), 42474-42518. (1977). *Regulation implementing Education for All Handicapped Children Act of 1975* (PL94-142).

Gesell Institute of Human Development. (n.d.). *Developmental screening*. Retrieved September 5, 2008, from http://www.gesellinstitute.org/layout.aspx?pageid=0

Goals 2000 (1996). *The national education goals*. Retrieved September 8, 2008, from http://www.ed.gov/G2K/ProgRpt96/natgoals.html

Graduate Record Examinations. (2007). *Guide to the use of scores (2007–2008)*. Retrieved September 9, 2008, from http://www.ets.org/Media/Tests/GRE/pdf/994994.pdf

Harcourt Assessment. (2002). *OLSAT 8 technical manual.* San Antonio, TX: Author.

Harcourt Assessment. (2004). *Stanford Achievement Test Series, Tenth Edition: Technical data report.* San Antonio, TX: Author.

Harcourt Assessment. (2008). *OLSAT 8 Brochure.* Retrieved September 9, 2008, from http://pearson assess.com/hai/images/dotCom/olsat8/OLSAT_Brochure.pdf

Harwell, M. (2005). Review of the Metropolitan Achievement Tests, Eighth Edition. In R.A. Spies and B.S. Plake (Eds.), *The Sixteenth Mental Measurements Yearbook.* Lincoln, NE: Buros Institute of Mental Measurements. Retrieved from Mental Measurements Yearbook database.

KeyMath-3 DA Publication Summary Form. Retrieved September 5, 2008, from http://ags.pearsonassess ments.com/keymath/km3-da-pub-summary.pdf

Kim, J., & Suen, H.K. (2000). *The relationship between early assessment of children and later achievement: a validity generalization study.* Paper presented at the annual meeting of the American Educational Research Association, New Orleans, LA.

Kamphaus, (2001). Review of the Metropolitan Readiness Test, Sixth Edition. In B.S. Plake and J.C. Impara (Eds.), *The Fourteenth Mental Measurements Yearbook.* Lincoln, NE: Buros Institute of Mental Measurements. Retrieved from Mental Measurements Yearbook database.

Kobrin, J. L., Patterson, B. F., Shaw, E. J., Mattern, K. D., & Barbuti, S. (2008). *Validity of the SAT for predicting first-year college grade point average.* Research Report No. 2008-5. Retrieved September, 9, 2008 from http://professionals.collegeboard. com/profdownload/Validity_of_the_SAT_for_Predi cting_First_Year_College_Grade_Point_Average.pdf

Kuncel, N. R., & Hezlett, S. A. (2007). *Standardized tests predict graduate students' success. Science, 315*(5815), 1080–1081.

Lane, S. (2007). Review of the Iowa Tests of Basic Skills: Forms A and B. In K.F. Geisinger, R.A. Spies, J.F. Carlson, and B.S. Plake (Eds.), *The Sixteenth Mental Measurements Yearbook.* Lincoln, NE: Buros Institute of Mental Measurements. Retrieved from Mental Measurements Yearbook database.

Lloyd, S. C. (2008). *Stat of the week: Sanctions and low-performing schools.* Retrieved September 4, 2008, from http://www.edweek.org/rc/articles/2008/03/04/sow0304.h27.html

Lohman, D., & Hagen, E. (2002). *CogAT form 6 research handbook.* Itasca, IL: Riverside Publishing.

LSAT & LSDAS Information Book (2008–2009). Retrieved September 9, 2008, from http://www. lsac.org/pdfs/2008-2009/InformationBook08web. pdf

Lukin, L. (2005). Review of the Metropolitan Achievement Tests, Eighth Edition. In R.A. Spies and B.S. Plake (Eds.), *The Sixteenth Mental Measurements Yearbook.* Lincoln, NE: Buros Institute of Mental Measurements. Retrieved from Mental Measurements Yearbook database.

Mattern, K. D., Patterson, B. F., Shaw, E. J., Kobrin, J. L., & Barbuti, S. (2008). *Differential validity and prediction of the SAT. Research Report No. 2008-4.* Retrieved September, 9, 2008 from http://professio nals.collegeboard.com/profdownload/Differential_ Validity_and_Prediction_of_the_SAT.pdf

Meagher, D. (2008). *Miller Analogies Test: Predictive validity study.* Retrieved September 9, 2008, from http://pearsonassess.com/NR/rdonlyres/423607BB-F273-467C-8232-0E2613093D23/0/MAT_White paper.pdf

Medical College Admission Test (2005). *Explanation of scores.* Retrieved September 9, 2008, from http:// www.aamc.org/students/mcat/sendscores/exofscores. pdf

Miller Analogies Test (2008–2009). *Candidate information booklet.* Retrieved September 9, 2008, from http://pearsonassess.com/NR/rdonlyres/37A8 B113-C0F4-4830-B9BD-0CB9D0B8E277/0/MAT_ CIB_2007_Final.pdf#page=i

Morse, D. T. (2005). Review of the Stanford Achievement Test, Tenth Edition. In R.A. Spies and B.S. Plake (Eds.), *The Sixteenth Mental Measurements Yearbook.* Lincoln, NE: Buros Institute of Mental Measurements. Retrieved from Mental Measurements Yearbook database.

National Center for Education Statistics (2006). *State profiles: Florida.* Retrieved September 4, 2008 from http://nces.ed.gov/nationsreportcard/states/ profile.asp

National Center for Education Statistics. (2008). *The nation's report card: Frequently asked questions.* Retrieved September 4, 2008, from http://nces.ed. gov/nationsreportcard/faq.asp#ques26

Novak, C. (2001). Review of the Metropolitan Readiness Test, Sixth Edition. In B.S. Plake and J.C. Impara (Eds.), *The Fourteenth Mental Measurements Yearbook.* Lincoln, NE: Buros

Institute of Mental Measurements. Retrieved from Mental Measurements Yearbook database.

Pearson (2008). *Wechsler Individual Achievement Test–Second Edition* (WIAT-II). Retrieved September 9, 2008, from http://harcourtassessment. com/HAIWEB/Cultures/en-us/Productdetail.htm? Pid=015-8983-505&Mode=summary

Psychological Assessment Resources, Inc. (PAR). (2005). *Wide Range Achievement Test 4 (WRAT4).* Retrieved September 9, 2008, from http://www3.par inc.com/products/product.aspx?Prod uctid=WRAT4

Pyle, R.P. (2002). Best practices in assessing Kindergarten readiness. *The California School Psychologist, 7,* 63–73.

Reynolds, C. R., Kamphaus, R., & PAR Staff. (2007). *RIAS™/WRAT4 discrepancy report.* Retrieved September 5, 2008, from http://www3.parinc.com/ uploads/samplerpts/RIASWRAT4_Discrepancy_ Simple.pdf

Riverside Publishing. (2006). *Cognitive Abilities Test, Form 6.* Retrieved September 9, 2008, from http:// www.riverpub.com/products/cogAt/index.html

Rogers, B. G. (2005). Review of the Cognitive Abilities Test, form 6. In R.A. Spies and B.S. Plake (Eds.), *The Sixteenth Mental Measurements Yearbook.* Lincoln, NE: Buros Institute of Mental Measurements. Retrieved from Mental Measurements Yearbook database.

Sample PIAT-R/NU (2001). Retrieved September 5, 2008, from http://ags.pearsonassessments.com/pdf/ piat.pdf

Slosson Educational Publications (n.d.). *The Kindergarten Readiness Test.* Retrieved September 10, 2008, from http://www.slosson.com/onlineca-talogstore_i1003393.html?catId=51574

Sutton, R., & Knight, C. (1995). Review of the Kindergarten Readiness Test. In J.C. Conoley and J.C. Impara (Eds.), *The Twelfth Mental Measure-ments Yearbook.* Lincoln, NE: Buros Institute of Mental Measurements. Retrieved from Mental Measurements Yearbook database.

U.S. Department of Education (2003). *Elementary and secondary education: Accountability.* Retrieved September 4, 2008 from http://www.ed.gov/nclb/ accountability/index.html

U.S. Department of Education (2005). *Stronger ac-countability: The facts about making progress.* Retrieved September 4, 2008, from http://www.ed. gov/nclb/accountability/ayp/testing.html

U.S. Department of Education (2008a). *What is No Child Left Behind?* Retrieved October 1, 2008, from http://answers.ed.gov/cgi-bin/education.cfg/ php/enduser/std_adp.php?p_faqid=4

U.S. Department of Education (2008b). *Fact sheets.* Retrieved September 4, 2008, from http://www.ed. gov/news/opeds/factsheets/index.html?src=ln

Waters, E. (1985). Review of the Gesell Readiness Test. In. J.V. Mitchell, Jr. (Ed.), *The Twelfth Mental Measurements Yearbook.* Lincoln, NE: Buros Institute of Mental Measurements. Retrieved from Mental Measurements Yearbook database.

Wilkinson, G. S., & Robertson, G. J. (2006). *Wide Range Achievement Test professional manual.* Lutz, Fl: Psychological Assessment Resources.

Wollack, J. (2001). Review of the KeyMath Revised: A diagnostic inventory of essential mathematics [1998 normative update]. In B. S. Plake and J. C. Impara, (Eds.), *The Fourteenth Mental Measurements Yearbook* (pp. 640–641). Lincoln, NE: Buros Institute of Mental Measurements.

Intellectual and Cognitive Functioning: Intelligence Testing and Neuropsychological Assessment*

John is a 9-year-old, fifth-grade student. His teachers reported that he was "a wiz at math and was the first student in the class to memorize all the state capitols." On his fourth-grade report card, John received all A's. This past year, John was riding his bike after school to a friend's house. He was not wearing his helmet and was struck by an oncoming vehicle. John was rushed to the emergency room and sustained what was then considered to be a "minor head injury." He was released a few days later from the hospital. When John returned to school, his teachers began noticing that John took longer to complete tasks, had difficulty staying on task, and had problems with his short-term memory. His grades dropped from A's to mostly B's and C's. John's parents were concerned about these changes and scheduled an appointment for John to be tested by a local clinical neuropsychologist.

This chapter is going to examine one of the most interesting and perplexing aspects of what it's like to be human—how we think and how our cognitive processes function—in other words, how our brains work! Within the chapter we will look at models of intelligence and how intelligence is measured, and then we will examine the interesting world of neuropsychology, which looks at changes in brain functioning over time. For example, with John above, we might want to administer an intelligence test and a neuropsychological battery. The intelligence test, which is sometimes included as part of a complete neuropsychological workup, will help us see how John is doing compared to his peers and might also pick up on some cognitive impairments. A neuropsychological battery will look at a broad range of

---

*Written by: Craigen, L, Neurkrug, E., & Fawcett, R. C.

cognitive functioning *and* will help us make a determination about possible changes in John's brain functioning over time. If we did test John in this manner, we might find that the intelligence scores reflect average intellectual ability while the neuro-psychological battery shows a number of cognitive impairments that are reflective of changes since the bicycle accident. This case exemplifies how the neuropsychological battery is more concerned with comparing one's premorbid levels (prior to the accident) to one's post-morbid levels (after the accident) rather than comparing one's level of functioning to a normative group, as is done in intelligence testing.

The chapter will begin with a brief history and definition of intelligence testing and then provide an overview of some models of intelligence. Next, we will examine some of the better-known individual intelligence tests, including measures of nonverbal intelligence. We will then examine the field of neuropsychology and explain neuropsychological assessment. In this section we will provide a brief history and definition of neuropsychology, discuss the domains assessed in neuropsychological assessment, and introduce two common methods used in neuropsychological assessment: a fixed battery and a flexible battery approach. As the chapter nears its conclusion, we will look at some of the roles helpers have in the assessment of intellectual and cognitive functioning and include some final thoughts about the assessment of these important domains.

A BRIEF HISTORY OF INTELLIGENCE TESTING

As noted in Chapter 1, the emergence of ability testing can be traced back thousands of years and can be found in Biblical passages, Chinese history, and ancient Greek writings. Centuries later, the first individual intelligence test was pioneered in France by Alfred Binet (1857–1911) and his colleague, Theophile Simon. Shortly thereafter, at Stanford University, Lewis Terman (1877–1956) gathered and analyzed normative data and made revisions to Binet's measure. Terman's alterations were extensive, and the test was later renamed the Stanford-Binet. This revised version (and many subsequent revisions since then) has stood the test of time and continues to be used today in clinical and educational settings.

Over the years, new models of intelligence have emerged, and concurrently, new intelligence tests have been developed. The following sections will explore current definitions of intelligence testing, introduce a variety of models that attempt to explain intelligence, and describe some of the more commonly used intelligence tests.

DEFINING INTELLIGENCE TESTING

As mentioned in Chapter 1, intelligence testing is a subset of intellectual and cognitive functioning and assesses a broad range of cognitive capabilities that generally results in an "IQ" score (see Figure 1.2 and Box 1.5). Like special aptitude testing, multiple aptitude testing, and cognitive ability testing, intelligence testing measures aptitude, or what one is capable of doing. Special and multiple aptitude testing will be examined in Chapter 8 as types of testing for occupational and career counseling. Cognitive ability tests were examined in Chapter 6 as a type of educational ability testing, and although intelligence tests are often used to measure educational ability, they tend to have much broader applications. Intelligence tests are used for a variety of purposes, including the following:

1. To assist in determining giftedness.
2. To assess for mental retardation.
3. To identify certain types of learning disabilities.
4. To assess intellectual ability following an accident, the onset of dementia, substance abuse, disease processes, and trauma to the brain.
5. As part of the admissions process to certain private schools.
6. As part of a personality assessment battery to aid in understanding the whole person.

We will begin this chapter by presenting a number of models of intelligence, and this will lead into a discussion of some of the more frequently used types of intelligence tests. As you read the chapter, reflect on how these intelligence tests reflect the models we are about to discuss.

MODELS OF INTELLIGENCE

In an attempt to define intelligence, a number of theoretical models have been proposed. These models are sometimes quite involved, and in this text we offer a brief overview of a few of the more prevalent ones, including Spearman's Two-Factor Approach, Thurstone's Multifactor Approach, Vernon's Hierarchical Model of Intelligence, Guilford's Multifactor/Multi-Dimensional Model, Cattell's Fluid and Crystal Intelligence, Piaget's Cognitive Development Theory, and Gardner's Theory of Multiple Intelligences.

SPEARMAN'S TWO-FACTOR APPROACH

Spearman
Known for his *g* and *s* factors of intelligence

When Alfred Binet created the first widely used intelligence test, he developed a number of subtests that assessed a range of what he considered to be intellectual tasks, and then he determined the average scores on the test of individuals belonging to different age groups. Consequently, when one took the Binet scale, one could compare his or her score to the average score of groups of individuals at different ages. Asserting that such a test was a hodgepodge or "promiscuous pooling" of factors, Charles Edward Spearman (1863–1945) was critical of Binet and others (Spearman, 1970, p. 71). Spearman, in other words, felt that Binet had lumped a number of different factors together in a spurious fashion.

Spearman (1970) believed in a two-factor approach to intelligence that included a general factor (*g*) and a specific factor (*s*), both of which he considered important in understanding intelligence. He contended that the importance or "weight" of *g* varied as a function of what was being measured. For example, he stated that the "talent for classics" (e.g., understanding the ancient worlds of Rome and Greece) had a ratio of *g* to *s* of 15 to 1; that is, general intelligence is much more significant than any specific ability in understanding the ancient worlds. Conversely, he purported that the ratio of general intelligence (*g*) to specific talent for music (*s*) was a ratio of 1 to 4, meaning that having music ability was much more significant in having talent for music than was general intelligence

(Spearman). Although Spearman's theory was one of the earlier models of intelligence, many still adhere to the concept that there is a *g* factor that mediates general intelligence and *s* factors that speak to a variety of specific talents.

THURSTONE'S MULTIFACTOR APPROACH

Thurstone
Believed in seven different mental abilities

Using multiple-factor analysis, Thurstone developed a model that included seven primary factors or mental abilities. Although Thurstone's research did not substantiate Spearman's general factor (*g*), he did not rule out the possibility that it existed since there appeared to be some amount of commonality among the seven factors (Thurstone, 1938). The seven primary mental abilities he recognized were verbal meaning, number ability, word fluency, perception speed, spatial ability, reasoning, and memory.

VERNON'S HIERARCHICAL MODEL OF INTELLIGENCE

Vernon
Developed hierarchy of intelligence approach that is still used by most tests today

Perhaps one of the greatest and most widely adopted models of intelligence has been Vernon's hierarchical model. Philip Vernon believed that subcomponents of intelligence could be added in a hierarchical manner to obtain a cumulative (*g*) factor score. His hierarchical model comprised four levels, with factors from each lower level contributing to the next level on the hierarchy. Vernon's top level was similar to Spearman's general factor (*g*) and was considered to have the most variance of any of the factors, while the second level had two major factors: *v:ed*, which stands for verbal and educational abilities, and *k:m*, which represents mechanical-spatial-practical abilities. The third level is composed of what was called minor group factors, while the fourth level is made of what was identified as specific factors (Vernon, 1961), as illustrated in Figure 7.1.

GUILFORD'S MULTIFACTOR/MULTI-DIMENSIONAL MODEL

Guilford
Developed 180 factors in his model, shaped as a cube

Guilford (1967) originally developed a model of intelligence with 120 factors. As if that were not enough, he later expanded it to 180 factors (Guilford, 1988). His three-dimensional model can be represented as a cube and involves three kinds of cognitive ability: *operations*, or the general intellectual processes we use in understanding; *content*, or what we use to perform our thinking process; and the *products*, or how we apply our operations to our content (see Figure 7.2). Different mental abilities will require different combinations of processes, contents, and products. All of the possible combinations are combined to create the $(6 * 6 * 5) = 180$ factors. Guilford's multifactor model provides a broad view of intelligence (Guilford, 1967); however, his model is sometimes considered too unwieldy to implement and has not significantly influenced the testing community.

CATTELL'S FLUID AND CRYSTAL INTELLIGENCE

During the 1940s, after attempting to remove cultural bias from intelligence tests, Cattell observed marked changes from the original test scores of individuals and subsequently suggested there were two types of intelligence (Cattell, 1971).

FIGURE 7.1 | DIAGRAM ILLUSTRATING VERNON'S HIERARCHICAL STRUCTURE OF ABILITIES

FIGURE 7.2 | GUILFORD'S MULTIFACTOR MODEL OF INTELLIGENCE

Source: Guilford, J. (1988). Some changes in the structure of the intellect model. *Educational and Psychological Measurement, 48,* 1-4, p. 3.

Piaget
Cognitive developmental model highlights assimilation and accommodation in learning

Cattell
Differentiated fluid (innate) from crystallized (learned) intelligence

He realized that as information based on learning was removed from the intelligence test (the portion most affected by cultural influences), the raw or unlearned abilities provided a different score. He then considered the possibility that two "general factors" made up intelligence: "fluid" (g_f) intelligence, or that culture-free portion of intelligence that is inborn and unaffected by new learning; and "crystallized" intelligence (g_c), which is acquired as we learn and is affected by our experiences, schooling, culture, and motivation (Cattell, 1979). He eventually estimated that heritability variance within families for fluid intelligence was about .92, which basically means if your parents have it, you are likely to have it (Cattell, 1980). Abilities such as memory and spatial capability are aspects of fluid intelligence.

As one might expect, crystallized intelligence will generally increase with age, while many research studies have found that fluid intelligence tends to decline slightly as we get older (See Box 7.1). Therefore, many theorists believe that overall intelligence (g) is maintained evenly across the lifespan (see Figure 7.3). As we look at specific intelligence tests later in the chapter, see if you can identify how Cattell's ideas have influenced their development.

BOX 7.1 | EXAMPLE OF FLUID AND CRYSTALLIZED INTELLIGENCE

At our university, we have a good mix of traditional-aged as well as older adult (35-year-old+) students. It is interesting to observe students when we give exams. The last five or six students left taking an exam will invariably be almost all of the older adult students. Sure, some of the reason is that they may be more careful, but the decrease in fluid intelligence could also be a major factor. Are the older students' scores lower? Absolutely not. As a matter fact, they are at least equal to the younger students, if not higher. Why is this? It might be due to the fact that older students may be experiencing a decrease in fluid intelligence, but their crystallized intelligence is making up for the difference!

—*Charlie Fawcett*

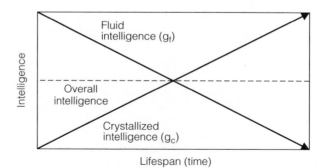

FIGURE 7.3 | FLUID AND CRYSTALLIZED INTELLIGENCE ACROSS THE LIFESPAN

PIAGET'S COGNITIVE DEVELOPMENT THEORY

Piaget
Cognitive developmental model highlights assimilation and accommodation in learning

Piaget (1950) approached intelligence from a developmental perspective rather than a factors approach. Spending years observing how children's cognitions were shaped as they grew, he developed the now familiar four stages of cognitive development: sensorimotor, preoperational, concrete operational, and formal operational. Piaget believed that cognitive development is adaptive; that is, as new information from our environment is presented, we are innately programmed to take it in and make sense of it in some manner in order to maintain a sense of order and equilibrium in our lives.

Piaget believed that we adapt our mental structures to maintain equilibrium through two methods: assimilation and accommodation. *Assimilation* is incorporating new stimuli or information into existing cognitive structures. On the other hand, *accommodation* is creating new cognitive structures and/or behaviors based on new stimuli. For example, a parent might teach a young child that the word "hot" means that one should stay away from certain items (e.g., a stove, iron, etc.) because touching those items can result in something bad happening. The child then learns that stoves are "hot" and should be avoided. In addition, every time the child is near a hot object, he or she knows to avoid it (e.g., match, coal, frying pan, etc.). The new object has been assimilated as something to be avoided.

As the child grows older, he or she comes to realize that not all hot items are hot all the time, and the child accommodates to this new information. For instance, as the child comes to understand the stove is not "hot" all the time, he or she creates a new meaning for the concept "stove," which now is seen as an object that can be hot or cold. Consequently, the child's behavior around a stove will change as he or she has accommodated this new meaning into his or her mental framework.

Consider how assimilation and accommodation are also important in the learning of important concepts in school, such as the shift between addition and multiplication (multiplication being a type of advanced addition). Also, consider how you have assimilated or accommodated information from this text into your existing structures of understanding! Although Piaget's understanding of cognitive development does not speak directly to the amount of learning taking place, it does highlight the process of learning—a critical concept for teachers and helpers to understand.

GARDNER'S THEORY OF MULTIPLE INTELLIGENCES

Gardner
Theory of multiple intelligences is novel but difficult to apply

Gardner (1983, 1999), who is vehemently opposed to the current construct of intelligence measurement, refers to the predominant notion of intelligence as the "dipstick theory" of the mind; that is, it holds that there is a specific amount or level of intelligence in the brain, and if you could place a dipstick in the brain and pull it out, you should be able to accurately read how smart a person is (Gardner, 1996). In contrast to this approach, he believes that intelligence is too vast and complex to be measured accurately by our current methods.

Based on his research of brain-damaged individuals, as well as literature in the areas of the brain, evolution, genetics, psychology, and anthropology, Gardner developed his Theory of Multiple Intelligences which asserts there are eight or nine intelligences, and with more research, others might even be found. Below are the nine identified intelligences, although research on the ninth type of intelligence, existential intelligence, has not clearly established its validity at this point (see below) (Gardner, 2003).

1. *Verbal-Linguistic Intelligence*: well-developed verbal skills and sensitivity to the sounds, meanings, and rhythms of words
2. *Mathematical-Logical Intelligence*: ability to think conceptually and abstractly, and capacity to discern logical or numerical patterns
3. *Musical Intelligence*: ability to produce and appreciate rhythm, pitch and timbre
4. *Visual-Spatial Intelligence*: capacity to think in images and pictures, to visualize accurately and abstractly
5. *Bodily-Kinesthetic Intelligence*: ability to control one's body movements and to handle objects skillfully
6. *Interpersonal Intelligence*: capacity to detect and respond appropriately to the moods, motivations, and desires of others
7. *Intrapersonal Intelligence*: capacity to be self-aware and in tune with inner feelings, values, beliefs, and thinking processes
8. *Naturalist Intelligence*: ability to recognize and categorize plants, animals, and other objects in nature
9. *Existential Intelligence*: sensitivity and capacity to tackle deep questions about human existence, such as the meaning of life, why do we die, and how did we get here (Educational Broadcasting Corporation, 2004, section: "What is...")

Gardner's understanding of intelligence is revolutionary and not yet mainstream. However, agreement with this theory appears to be growing in academic and non-academic settings. Not only are his identified categories novel, but his understanding of how intelligence manifests itself is different, as noted below:

1. All human beings possess a certain amount of all of the intelligences.
2. All humans have different profiles or amounts of the multiple intelligences (even identical twins!).
3. Intelligences are manifested by the way a person carries out a task in relationship to his or her goals.
4. Intelligences can work independently or together, and each is located in a distinct part of the brain (Gardner, 1983, 2003).

THEORIES OF INTELLIGENCE SUMMARIZED

As you can see, the manner in which intelligence is conceptualized varies depending on the theory. Thus, how an intelligence test is constructed will reflect the model one believes is most true to the nature of this construct. Table 7.1 summarizes some of the major points of each theory discussed in this chapter. Consider what you might measure if you were developing an intelligence test based on one or more of these theories.

TABLE 7.1 | SUMMARY OF MODELS OF INTELLIGENCE

Theoretical Model	Number of Factors or Attributes	Nature of Factors or Attributes
Spearman's Two Factor Approach	Two: g and s	The g factor mediates general intelligence and s factor mediates specific abilities. Ratio of g to s varies depending on ability.
Thurstone's Multifactor Approach	Seven	Research on multiple factor analysis led to the belief that there are seven primary factors which may be related to g. They include: verbal meaning, number ability, word fluency, perception speed, spatial ability, reasoning, and memory
Vernon's Hierarchal Model of Intelligence	Four hierarchical levels	The four levels included: (1) g, the highest level, with the largest source of variance between individuals; (2) major group factors, including verbal-numerical-educational (*v:ed*) and practical-mechanical-spatial-physical (*k:m*) ability, (3) minor group factors, and (4) specific factors.
Guilford's Multifactor/ Multi-dimensional Model	Three dimensional model with 180 factors	Three kinds of cognitive ability: *operations*, or the 6 processes we use in understanding; *contents*, or the 6 ways we perform our thinking process; and the *product*, or the 5 possible ways we apply our operations to our content ($6 * 6 * 5 = 180$ possible paths)
Cattell's Fluid and Crystal Intelligence	Two: fluid g_{f}, and crystallized intelligence g_c	Two g factors: fluid intelligence (g_f): culture-free intelligence with which we are born; and crystallized intelligence (g_c): acquired as we learn, and affected by experiences, schooling, culture, and motivation
Piaget's Cognitive Development Theory	Two: assimilation and accommodation	Process model, not a cognitive gain model. Assimilation is adapting new stimuli or information into existing cognitive structures, and accommodation is creating new cognitive structures and/or behaviors from new stimuli. We learn through these processes.
Gardner's Theory of Multiple Intelligences	Eight, maybe nine	Non-traditional model of eight or nine intelligences which all people have at different levels: Verbal-Linguistic, Mathematical-Logical, Musical, Visual-Spatial, Bodily-Kinesthetic, Interpersonal, Intrapersonal, Naturalist, and maybe Existential

INTELLIGENCE TESTING

It would make sense that to some degree, theories of intelligence are the basis for intelligence tests. So, it is not surprising that over the years a number of intelligence tests have been devised to measure such factors as general intelligence (g), specific intelligence (s), fluid and crystal intelligence, and other factors traditionally seen to be related to intellectual ability. Intelligence tests do not tend to measure mental ability as defined by Gardner, whose nontraditional notion of intelligence highlights concepts not usually seen as being related to intelligence. Instead, traditional intelligence tests measure intelligence based on traditional constructs. Today, these tests are standardized and administered individually by a highly trained examiner. Although a number of intelligence tests are available today, the Stanford-Binet and the three Wechsler Scales of Intelligence are the most widely used. Thus, we will examine these tests as well as another popular intelligence test known as the Kaufman Assessment Battery for Children. We will also briefly introduce the concept of nonverbal intelligence tests and introduce the CTONI and the UNIT, two tests that assess intelligence in this manner.

STANFORD-BINET

SB5
Uses routing test, basal and ceiling levels to determine start and stop points; measures verbal and non-verbal intelligence across five factors

Probably the most well known intelligence test is the Stanford-Binet, which, as noted earlier, dates back to the original work of Alfred Binet in 1904. Published in 2003, the Stanford-Binet Fifth Edition (SB5) is its most recent revision. This version of the test takes between 45 and 60 minutes to administer individually and can be given to individuals from 2 to 90 years of age (Riverside Publishing, 2006). In order to administer the test in a reasonable amount of time to individuals of all ages, the Stanford-Binet uses a vocabulary routing test, almost a pretest, to determine where an individual should begin. For example, a 35-year-old engineer does not need to answer all the questions in the mathematics section that would normally apply to an elementary school student. Instead, using the routing test, the examiner determines the age level at which to begin testing. Next, a basal level is determined, which is the highest point where the examinee is able to get all the questions right on two consecutive age levels. Testing continues until the ceiling level is reached, which is the point where the individual misses 75% of the questions on two consecutive age levels. Basal and ceiling levels are important because they help the examinee avoid feeling bored and they lessen the likelihood that the examinee will experience a sense of failure, which could happen if the examinee was asked to respond to all questions on the test. Basal and ceiling levels are also found in other kinds of assessment procedures and are an important concept to understand.

The SB5 measures verbal and nonverbal intelligence across five factors: fluid reasoning, knowledge, quantitative reasoning, visual-spatial processing, and working memory. These divisions create ten subtests (2 domains × 5 factors) (see Table 7.2). Discrepancies among scores on the subtests as well as between scores on the verbal and nonverbal factors can be an indication of a learning disability.

Although previous versions of the Stanford-Binet used a mean of 100 and a standard deviation of 16, the SB5 has now joined most other intelligence tests by using a mean of 100 and a standard deviation of 15. Subtests use a mean of 10 and a SD of 3, and other standardized scoring methods are available, such as percentile ranks, grade equivalents, and a descriptive classification (average, low average, etc.). A nice feature of this latest edition is that the publishers also offer a compatible program called the SB5 Scoring Pro™. This Windows-based software program allows the examiner to enter raw scores which are converted to standard scores, and it provides various profiles related to areas that are assessed. Figure 7.4 provides example of the Interpretive Worksheet of the Stanford-Binet.

TABLE 7.2 | ORGANIZATION OF THE STANFORD-BINET, FIFTH EDITION

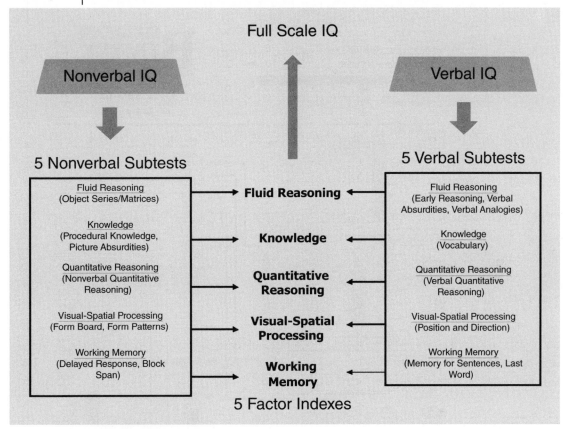

The SB5 norm group was based on a stratified random sample of 4,800 people gathered from the 2000 U.S. Census. Each item was examined for bias in gender, ethnicity, regional, and socioeconomic status. Split-half and test-retest reliabilities for individual subtests by age averaged between .66 and .93, while full-scale IQ reliability was very high and ranged between .97 and .98 for all age groups (Roid, 2003). Content validity included professional judgment of items over a seven-year development process and item analysis using advanced statistical methods. Criterion-related validity showed a "substantial" correlation of .90 with the previous version of the Stanford-Binet (SB IV). Sound predictive validity was also shown with a variety of special groups such as individuals who are gifted, mentally retarded, and learning disabled. Correlations with other instruments ranged from .53 to .84 for the SB5 with the Wechsler Scales, Woodcock-Johnson III Tests of Cognitive Abilities, Woodcock-Johnson III Tests of Achievement, and Wechsler Individual Achievement Test (WAIT) (Roid). Finally, the 217-page technical manual is filled with other advanced statistical analyses that show evidence of reliability and validity.

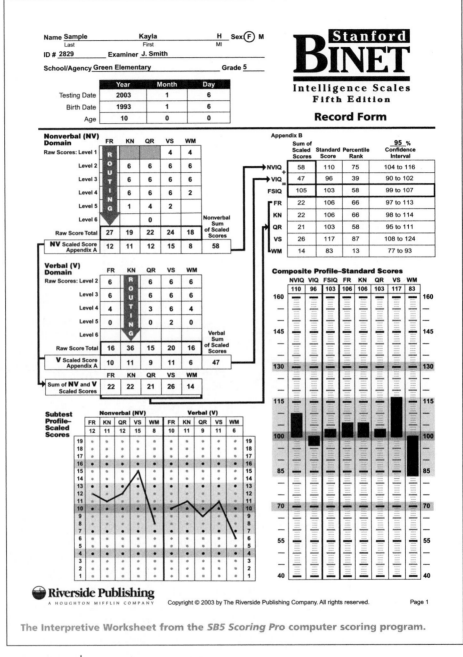

FIGURE 7.4 | THE SB5 INTERPRETIVE REPORT

On the above interpretive report you can see the following (going counter-clockwise): 1) basic demographic information, 2) the routing score to help determine the basal age, 3) verbal and non-verbal subtest raw and scaled scores (M = 10, SD = 3), 4) comparison of non-verbal IQ, verbal IQ, Full Scale IQ using DIQ, percentile rank, and confidence intervals (range of true scores), 5) comparison of non-verbal IQ, verbal IQ, Full Scale IQ, and subtest scores using DIQ.

Source: Wechsler Intelligence Scale for Children—Fourth Edition (WISC-IV). Copyright © 2003 by NCS Pearson, Inc. Reproduced with permission. All rights reserved. "Weschler Intelligence Scale for Children" and "WISC" are trademarks, in the US and/or other countries, of Pearson Education, Inc. or its affiliates.

Wechsler Scales

Wechsler scales
Three different
tests for three dif-
ferent age groups

Although the Stanford-Binet may be the best-known intelligence test, the three Wechsler scales of intelligence are the most widely used intelligence tests today. In contrast to the Stanford-Binet, which assesses intelligence of individuals from a broad spectrum of ages, each Wechsler test measures a select age group. For instance, the WPPSI-III (Wechsler Preschool and Primary Scale of Intelligence—Third Edition) assesses children between the ages of 2 years, 6 months and 7 years, 3 months; the WISC-IV (Wechsler Intelligence Scale for Children—Fourth Edition) is geared for children between the ages of 6 and 16; and the WAIS-IV (Wechsler Adult Intelligence Scale—Fourth Edition) was developed to assess adults aged 16 through 90.

All three versions of the Wechsler tests are useful in assessing general cognitive functioning, in helping to determine mental retardation and giftedness, and in assessing probable learning problems. All three tests share many similar features, such as similar subtests, except that they are geared for their unique age groups. In the development of each of the tests, the publishers used a random sample of approximately 2,000 children or adults that were stratified for age, sex, race, parent education level, and geographic region. In addition, they worked hard to ensure content validity, based on their ongoing view of intellectual functioning, and showed a variety of different kinds of criterion-related and construct validity. Overall reliability estimates for each of the tests tend to be high, in the mid-.90s, although some of the subtests will dip down into the .70s (Hess, 2001; Maddle, 2005; Pearson, 2008).

WISC-IV
Subtests measure
broad range of
cognitive ability;
ten subtests com-
bine for a compo-
site score (*g*)

*Composite scores
are useful in
identifying learn-
ing disabilities*

Because the tests are similar in nature, to give you a sense of what these tests are like, the following is an overview of the WISC-IV, the most widely used of the three Wechsler Intelligence Scales. In Table 7.3 you can see a short description of the 15 subtests of the WISC-IV (Wecshler, 2003), many of which are similar to those in the WPPSI-III and WAIS-IV. Each subtest measures a different aspect of cognitive functioning, although there is some overlap among certain subtests (see Table 7.3).

The WISC-IV provides a Full-Scale IQ as well as four additional composite score indexes in areas called Verbal Comprehension Index (VCI), Perceptual Reasoning Index (PRI), Working Memory Index (WMI), and Processing Speed Index (PSI). The subtests that are associated with each of their respective composite score indexes are listed in Table 7.4. The ten subtests not italicized in Table 7.4 are used to find the Full-Scale IQ, while each of the five italicized subtests can be used if a subtest is invalidated for some reason (e.g., given incorrectly, not appropriate for a child due to his or her specific disability) or if additional information is warranted.

The four composite score indexes provide important information concerning the child being tested, including identifying strengths and weaknesses of a child as well as helping to identify a possible learning disability. Subtest scores use scaled scores (standard scores) that have a mean of 10 and a standard deviation of 3, while the Full-Scale IQ is reported with a mean of 100 and standard deviation of 15. The front page of the WISC-IV Record Form offers a summary of the child's test scores. Figure 7.5 shows the form, which offers six parts, A–F.

TABLE 7.3 | ABBREVIATIONS AND DESCRIPTIONS OF SUBTESTS

Subtest	Abbreviation	Description
Block Design	BD	While viewing a constructed model or a picture in a Stimulus Book, the child uses red-and-white blocks to re-create the design within a specified time limit.
Similarities	SI	The child is presented two words that represent common objects or concepts and describes how they are similar.
Digit Span	DS	For Digit Span Forward, the child repeats numbers in the same order as presented aloud by the examiner. For Digit Span Backward, the child repeats numbers in the reverse order of that presented aloud by the examiner.
Picture Concepts	PCn	The child is presented with two or three rows of pictures and chooses one picture from each row to form a group with a common characteristic.
Coding	CD	The child copies symbols that are paired with simple geometric shapes or numbers. Using a key, the child draws each symbol in its corresponding shape or box within a specified amount of time.
Vocabulary	VC	For Picture Items, the child names pictures that are displayed in the Stimulus Book. For Verbal Items, the child gives definitions for words that the examiner reads aloud.
Letter-Number	LN	The child is read a sequence of numbers and letters and recalls the numbers in ascending order and the letters in alphabetical order.
Matrix Reasoning	MR	The child looks at an incomplete matrix and selects the missing portion from five response options.
Comprehension	CO	The child answers questions based on his or her understanding of general principles of social situations.
Symbol Search	SS	The child scans a search group and indicates whether the target symbol(s) matches any of the symbols in the search group within a specified time limit.
Picture Completion	PCm	The child views a picture and then points to or names the important part missing within a specified time limit.
Cancellation	CA	The child scans both a random and a structured arrangement of pictures and marks target pictures within a specified time limit.
Information	IN	The child answers questions that address a broad range of general knowledge topics.
Arithmetic	AR	The child mentally solves a series of orally presented arithmetic problems within a specified time limit.
Word Reasoning	WR	The child identifies the common concept being described in a series of clues.

Source: Wechsler, D. (2003). *WISC-IV Administration and scoring manual. San Antonio*, TX: Harcourt Assessment, Inc. pp. 2–3.

Part A presents the child's age at testing and the date of testing. Part B presents the raw score of each of the subtests given as well as the scaled (standard) scores. In this case, you can see that although two additional subtests were used to gather more information (cancellation and arithmetic), they are not included when

TABLE 7.4	SUBTESTS AND COMPOSITE INDEXES*

VCI	PRI	PSI	VMI
Similarities	Block Design	Coding	Digit Span
Vocabulary	Picture Concepts	Symbol Search	Letter-Number Sequencing
Comprehension	Matrix Reasoning	*Cancellation*	*Arithmetic*
Information	*Picture Completion*		
Word Reasoning			

*Subsets not italicized are used to determine Full-Scale IQ.

FIGURE 7.5	WISC-IV RECORD FORM

Source: Wechsler Intelligence Scale for Children—Fourth Edition (WISC-IV). Copyright © 2003 by NCS Pearson, Inc. Reproduced with permission. All rights reserved. "Weschler Intelligence Scale for Children" and "WISC" are trademarks, in the US and/or other countries, of Pearson Education, Inc. or its affiliates.

deriving the Full-Scale IQ. Part C offers the sum of the scaled scores. Part D offers a summary of the four composite indexes as well as the Full-Scale IQ. Here, the sums of all of the scaled scores are offered as well as converted scores using a mean of 100 and standard deviation of 15. Corresponding percentiles are also presented, and confidence intervals (standard error of measurement) show the probability that 95 percent of the time the score is likely to fall within the range given.

Part E shows the breakdown of the specific subtests grouped by composite index. This visual representation allows one to readily see an individual's strengths and weaknesses as based on the composite indexes. Part F shows a visual representation of the composite indexes and the Full-Scale IQ using a mean of 100 and standard deviation of 15. Thus, comparisons can be made to each of the composite indexes with the Full-Scale IQ.

The Wechsler tests in general have good validity and excellent reliability. For example, the WISC-IV internal consistency for the full scale is .97. Individual subtest reliabilities tend to average in the .80s (Wechsler, 2003). The WISC-IV technical manual has 51 pages dedicated to providing evidence of validity, including evidence based on test content, internal structure, factor analysis, and relationships with numerous other variables (Wechsler, 2003). As you can see, the WISC-IV, as well as its first cousins the WPPSI-III and WAIS-IV, offers a comprehensive picture of the cognitive functioning of the individual. These instruments are all useful in determining such things as mental retardation, giftedness, learning problems, and other suspected cognitive problems.

Kaufman Assessment Battery for Children

KABC-II
Measures cognitive ability for ages 3 to 18; provides choice of theoretical model of intelligence

The Kaufman Assessment Battery for Children, Second Edition (KABC-II) is an individually administered test of cognitive ability for children between the ages of 3 and 18. Depending on the age range, test times can vary from 25 to 70 minutes. Subtests and scoring allow for a choice between two theoretical models, one of which is Cattell's model of fluid and crystallized intelligence. However, both methods examine visual processing, fluid reasoning, and short-term and long-term memory. Scores are age-based and have a mean of 100 and a SD of 15, but also can be reported as a percentile rank or age equivalent (Pearson, 2006).

The norm group for the KABC-II was based on a sample of 3,025 that was stratified against the U.S. population for gender, race, SES, religion, and special education status. Reliability estimates are quite sound, ranging from .87 to .95 for composite score means. Subtest reliabilities are generally strong, falling within the .80s range. Additional psychometric data such as validity is available in the manual.

Nonverbal Intelligence Tests

Nonverbal intelligence tests are different from traditional measures of intelligence in that they rely on little or no verbal expression. Nonverbal scales are appropriate

Nonverbal intelligence tests
Intelligence tests that rely on little or no verbal expression

for children who may be disadvantaged by traditional verbal and language-based measures. For example, nonverbal measures assess intelligence for children with autism, specific language-based learning disabilities, poor expressive abilities, hearing impairments, differences in cultural background, and certain psychiatric disorders (Aylward, 1996). Two commonly used nonverbal intelligence tests are the Comprehensive Test of Nonverbal Intelligence (CTONI) and the Universal Intelligence Test (UNIT).

CTONI and UNIT
Two nonverbal tests of intelligence

COMPREHENSIVE TEST OF NONVERBAL INTELLIGENCE (CTONI) The CTONI is a nonverbal instrument designed to measure intellectual functioning from ages 6 years, 0 months to 18 years, 11 months. The test is composed of six subtests that measure different nonverbal intellectual abilities (pictorial analogies, geometric analogies, pictorial categories, geometric categories, pictorial sequences, geometric sequences). The CTONI was normed on a stratified sample of 2,129 children and adolescents from 23 states with careful attention paid toward gender, ethnicity, and geographic area (Aylward, 1996; van Lingen, 1996). Reliability estimates for the subtests are strong, ranging from .86 to .92, and for composite scores, from .93 to .97. Criterion validity was not particularly impressive, showing significant correlations with only two subtest of the WISC-III (Similarities and Object Assembly). However, one small study of 32 deaf students between the ages of 8 and 18 showed correlations from .85 to .90 between the CTONI and the performance IQ section of the WISC (Aylward, van Lingen).

THE UNIVERSAL INTELLIGENCE TEST (UNIT) The UNIT is a nonverbal instrument designed to measure intelligence of children ages 5 to 17 years. Composed of six subtests (symbolic memory, cube design, spatial memory, analogic reasoning, object memory, and reasoning), the UNIT includes an abbreviated, standard, and extended battery and is unique because it relies entirely on nonverbal test administration and response style (Bandalos, 2001).

The UNIT was standardized on a national sample of 2,100 children stratified against gender, race, Hispanic origin, region, parental educational attainment, community setting, and classroom placement (regular or special education). All versions of the UNIT show reliability estimates that range from the mid-.80s to mid-.90s, and the test showed a correlation of .80 with the WISC-III. Predictive validity coefficients were weaker, with correlations between the UNIT standard battery full scale scores and the Woodcock Johnson-Revised broad knowledge scale at .51, .56, and .66 for samples of learning disabled, mentally retarded, and intellectually gifted students, respectively (Bandalos, 2001).

NEUROPSYCHOLOGICAL ASSESSMENT

Neuropsychological assessment is a new field compared to intelligence testing and offers a broad array of ways to examine the cognitive functioning of individuals. The following offers a brief history of neuropsychological assessment, defines the purposes and uses of this kind of assessment, and provides a quick look at a couple of the more common tests used when conducting a neuropsychological assessment.

A Brief History of Neuropsychological Assessment

Neuropsychology
A domain of psychology that examines brain-behavior

Although the professional identity of neuropsychology emerged in the early 1970s, interest in how the brain functions has been around for centuries. For instance, observations of behavioral changes following head injuries are found in 5,000-year-old Egyptian medical documents (Hebben-Milberg, 2002). In modern days, interest in brain injury was piqued during World War I because significant numbers of soldiers suffered brain trauma, and it was at this point that screening and diagnostic measures were created (Lezak, Howieson, & Loring, 2004). This early research on war-damaged veterans is said to be the catalyst for the birth of clinical neuropsychology.

During the 1950s it was realized that what might be considered the same kind of brain damage in different individuals could in fact affect people differently. In other words, brain injury was found to be unique among people with traumatic injuries in the sense that it could lead to a wide variety of behavioral patterns (McGee, 2004). More recently, the advent of modern-day technology has significantly contributed to changes to the relatively new field of neuropsychology. For instance, the invention of diagnostic scanning techniques such as magnetic resonance imaging (MRI) and positron emission tomography (PET) makes many of the former neuropsychological assessments unnecessary (Kolb & Whishaw, 2008). However, the most sensitive measure of brain capacity is behavior, which is not measured by these scanning devices. Thus, neuropsychological assessment continues to play a significant role in explaining brain-behavior relationships. The following section defines the complex field of neuropsychology and neuropsychological assessment.

Defining Neuropsychological Assessment

Clinical Neuropsychology
The assessment and intervention principles related to the central nervous system

Neuropsychology is a domain of psychology that examines brain-behavior relationships. A subdiscipline of neuropsychology is clinical neuropsychology, which includes both the assessment of the central nervous system and interventions that may result from an assessment (Hebben & Milberg, 2002). Neurological assessments are generally employed following a traumatic brain injury, an illness that affects brain function, or because of suspected changes in brain function from the aging process.

In the assessment process, neuropsychological assessment can measure a number of domains related to brain-behavior, including memory, intelligence, language, visuo-perception, visual-spatial thinking, psychosensory and motor abilities, academic achievement, personality, and psychological functioning (Lezak et al., 2004). Uses of such an assessment can vary dramatically. For example, results can be used in the following ways:

- As a diagnostic tool used to identify the root of a condition and the extent of the brain damage
- To measure change in an individual's functioning (e.g., cognitive ability, movement, reaction time)

- To compare changes in cognitive or functional status to others within the normative sample
- To provide specific rehabilitation treatment and planning guidelines for individuals and families
- To provide specific guidelines for educational planning in the schools (Kolb & Whishaw, 2008)

Neurospsychological assessment shares both similarities and differences with intelligence testing. In fact, many neuropsychological assessments begin with a measure of general intelligence (Kolb & Whishaw, 2008). Further, some intelligence scales have been adapted for neuropsycholological purposes; most notably the Weschler Intelligence Scale (WAIS-R-NI). Despite these parallels, there are notable differences between an intellectual assessment and a neuropsychological evaluation. You may remember these differences from the opening case study of this chapter. Intelligence testing compares the individual's response to normative data based on a sample of normal individuals. In contrast, neuropsychological assessment compares an individual's current levels of functioning to his or her estimated premorbid level of functioning (Lezak et al., 2004). In the following section we will take a closer examination of what a neuropsychological assessment looks like.

METHODS OF NEUROPSYCHOLOGICAL ASSESSMENT

Early assessment procedures relied on single, independent instruments to assess brain damage. However, most modern approaches to neuropsychology have moved away from the idea that there is one single test for brain damage and rely on "battery approaches" to assessment (Kolb & Whishaw, 2008). With this being said, there is still no universal approach to neuropsychological assessment. That is, current assessment practices utilize a continuum of approaches, from a fixed battery approach to a flexible battery approach. This section will introduce each approach and will also include their respective strengths and weakness.

Fixed Battery
The rigid and standardized administration of a uniform group of instruments

FIXED BATTERY APPROACH AND THE HALSTED-REITAN   A fixed battery approach to neuropsychological assessment involves the rigid and standardized administration of a uniform group of instruments. That is, with fixed battery approaches all individuals requiring assessment receive the same set of tests. The majority of fixed batteries have cutoff scores that reflect the degree of severity of the impairment and also differentiate between impaired and unimpaired individuals. Two common fixed neuropsychological batteries are the Halsted-Reitan Battery and the Luria-Nebraska Neuropsychological Battery. This section will provide a description of the Halsted-Reitan Battery.

The Halsted-Reitan was developed by Ward Halstead in the 1950s and modified by Halstead's graduate student Ralph Reitan (Hebben & Millberg, 2002). Two children's versions also exist: the Reitan Indiana Neuropsychological Test Battery (ages 5 to 8) and the Halstead Neuropsychological Test Battery for Older Children (ages 9 to 14). The Halsted-Reitan provides individuals with a cutoff score, or index of impairment, which discriminates brain-damaged from normal

Halstead-Reitan
A widely utilized fixed battery neuropsychological assessment consisting of eight core tests

functioning individuals. Information about specific areas of the brain that are damaged and information about the severity of the damage can also be garnered from this battery. The Halstead-Reitan battery takes approximately five to six hours to complete and consists of eight core tests as follows (Dean, 1985; Encyclopedia of Mental Disorders, n.d.; Hebben & Milberg):

1. *Category Test*: 208 pictures consisting of geometric figures are presented to the examinee. With each picture, individuals are asked whether the figure reminds them of the number 1, 2, 3, or 4. Test-takers then press a key corresponding to their response. This core test evaluates abstraction ability and the ability to draw specific conclusions from general information.

2. *Tactual Performance Test*: A form board consisting of ten cut-out shapes and ten wooden blocks matching those shapes are presented in front of the blindfolded test-taker. Individuals are instructed to place the blocks in their appropriate square on the board, first with their dominant hand, then with their nondominant hand, and then with both hands. Then, the form board and blocks are removed. Still blindfolded, participants are then instructed to draw the form board and shapes in their proper locations. This core test evaluates sensory ability, memory for shapes and the special location of shapes, motor functions, and transferability between both hemispheres of the brain.

3. *Trail Making Test*: This is a two-part core test. Part A consists of a page with 25 circles numbered and randomly arranged. Individuals are instructed to draw lines, circle to circle, in numerical order, until they reach the circle labeled "End." Part B consists of a page with circles containing the letters A through L as well as 13 numbered circles intermixed and randomly arranged. Individuals are instructed to connect the circles by drawing lines alternating between numbers and letters in sequential order, until they reach the circle labeled "End." This core test evaluates information-processing speed, visual scanning ability, the integration of visual and motor functions, letter and number recognition and sequencing, and the ability to maintain two different trains of thought.

4. *Finger Tapping Test*: Test-takers place their index finger on a lever that is attached to a counting device. Then, they are instructed to tap their fingers as quickly as possible for ten seconds. The trial is repeated five to ten times for each hand to measure motor speed, manual dexterity, and hand dominance. This test is helpful in determining the particular area(s) of the brain that may be damaged.

5. *Rhythm Test*: A total of 30 pairs of rhythmic beats are presented to the test-taker. With each pair, he or she decides if the two sounds are the same or different. This core test evaluates auditory attention and concentration and the ability to discriminate between nonverbal sounds.

6. *Speech Sounds Perception Test*: A total of 60 nonsense syllables containing the vowel sound "ee" are presented. After each syllable, the test-takers underline, from a set of four written alternatives, the spelling that represents the sound they just heard. This core test examines auditory attention and concentration and the ability to discriminate between verbal sounds.

7. *Reitan-Indiana Aphasia Screening Test*: Here, test-takers are presented with a variety of questions and tasks, including naming pictures aloud, writing the name of the picture without saying the name aloud, reading material aloud, repeating words, drawing shapes without lifting the pencil, and more. This core test detects possible signs of aphasia, which is the loss of ability to understand or use written or spoken language, usually as a result of brain damage, illness, or deterioration.

8. *Reitan-Klove Sensory-Perceptual Examination*: Test-takers are asked to participate in different test procedures, including: (a) specifying whether touch, sound, or visible movement is occurring on the right, left, or both sides of the body; (b) identifying numbers "written" on their fingertips while eyes are closed; (c) recalling numbers assigned to particular fingers (the examiner assigns numbers by touching each finger and stating the number with the individual's eyes closed); and (d) identifying the shape of a wooden block placed in one hand by pointing to its shape on a form board with the opposite hand. This core test detects whether individuals are unable to perceive stimulation on one side of the body when both sides are stimulated at the same time.

The Halstead-Reitan is perhaps the most widely used, most rigorous, and best researched of all fixed neuropsychological batteries. However, this and other fixed battery approaches have notable weaknesses. For example, the length of time required to complete the battery requires a great deal of patience and financial cost to the individual. Further, since fixed batteries give the same test to all individuals, some information may be missed or some unnecessary information may be gathered. In addition, the 102-page testing manual fails to provide psychometric data concerning the validity, reliability, and norming procedures of the Halstead-Reitan. Failure to include this information makes the interpretation of the instrument somewhat problematic and should be a "red flag" indicating that test administrators should utilize this battery with some amount of caution.

Flexible Battery
Combination of tests dictated by the referral questions and unique needs of the client

Boston Process Approach
A well-known flexible battery method of assessment

FLEXIBLE BATTERY APPROACH AND THE BOSTON PROCESS APPROACH (BPA)   In the flexible battery approach to neuropsychological assessment, the use of a combination of tests is dictated by the referral questions and the unique needs and behaviors of the client. In this case, a series of tests is chosen that may evaluate different areas of neuropsychological functioning. Generally speaking, clinicians will utilize an exhaustive list of tests within a flexible battery. The Boston Process Approach (BPA) is one example of the flexible battery approach. This approach requires careful observation of the test-taker during test administration. With the Boston Process Approach and additional flexible battery approaches, there is a strong emphasis on garnering qualitative data. For example, the clinician may be more concerned with how the test-taker solves the problem, may give additional time to the test-taker for answering the problem, and may adapt the exercise to the individual's specific needs (Milberg, Hebben & Kaplan, 1996).

There are clear strengths and weaknesses of using the flexible battery approach in neuropsychological assessment. For instance, whereas this approach allows the test administrator to give a wide variety of tests that are tailored to the presenting problem, as a consequence, some critical areas may be overlooked. Additionally, a flexible battery approach requires a great deal of training specific to neuropsychology (Vanderploeg, 2000). Flexible batteries have also been criticized because they gather limited psychometric data. Finally, the flexible battery approach has undergone a considerable amount of scrutiny from within the courts system. For example, certain neuropsychological evidence resulting from the flexible battery approach has been excluded from trials because it was deemed to not be as scientific as a fixed battery approach.

Both the fixed and flexible battery approaches to neuropsychological assessment require specific training to adequately and ethically administer the tests to others. As discussed earlier, this is also the case for intelligence tests. The following section will examine the specific role that helpers, or test administrators, play in the assessment of cognitive functioning.

THE ROLE OF HELPERS IN THE ASSESSMENT OF INTELLECTUAL AND COGNITIVE FUNCTIONING

The assessment of intelligence and neurological impairment takes advanced training, which is generally given in school psychology programs and many doctoral programs in counseling, clinical psychology, and clinical neuropsychology. Although other helpers, such as learning disabilities specialists, licensed clinical social workers, and licensed professional counselors can also obtain such training, many graduate programs in special education, counseling, and social work do not automatically offer these courses.

When a helper does have this training, he or she can provide a wide range of services to individuals, including the assessment of intelligence to help determine learning problems, mental retardation, giftedness, potential for learning, and possible neurological impairment. For those helpers who do not have the training to give an assessment in the intellectual and cognitive realms, it is still imperative that they have sufficient knowledge of these kinds of tests so that they will know when to refer clients who might need such an assessment and be able to participate in the development of treatment plans for their clients who have received an assessment in this area.

FINAL THOUGHTS ON THE ASSESSMENT OF INTELLECTUAL AND COGNITIVE FUNCTIONING

Intelligence testing and neuropsychological assessment can be used in a variety of ways, and if one is not careful, can be abused. Abuses over the years have been many, including the miscalculation of intelligence of minorities, over-classification of individuals who are learning disabled, "proof" of racial differences of ability, and a means of differentiating social classes. However, the astute examiner knows that the assessment of cognitive functioning is complex and a number of factors including the examinee's culture, the environment, genetics, and biology should be considered in assessments. Thus, any conclusions about an individual should be made within the context of knowing the whole person as well as the complex societal issues that are involved.

SUMMARY

We started this chapter by looking at a young man who had neurological impairment as result of a bicycle accident. We noted that the use of both an intelligence test and a neurological assessment would be critical to understanding his cognitive functioning after the accident.

The chapter then offered a brief review of the history of intelligence testing and presented a definition of intelligence testing. We noted that intelligence tests are types of aptitude tests that measure a range of intellectual ability and offer a broad assessment of one's cognitive capabilities. We pointed out that intelligence tests are used in a variety of ways, such as assisting in determining giftedness, mental retardation, and learning disabilities; helping to assess intellectual ability following an accident, the onset of dementia, substance abuse, disease processes, and trauma to the brain; as part of the admissions process for some private schools; and as part of a personality assessment to help understand the whole person.

We next offered a brief introduction of models of intelligence, including Spearman's Two-Factor Approach, Thurstone's Multifactor Approach, Vernon's Hierarchical Model of Intelligence, Guilford's Multifactor/Multi-Dimensional Model, Cattell's Fluid and Crystal Intelligence, Piaget's Cognitive Development Theory, and Gardner's Theory of Multiple Intelligences. A summary of these models was presented in Table 7.1.

Relative to intelligence testing, we discussed three commonly used intelligence tests: the Stanford-Binet, Fifth Edition, the Wechsler tests (focusing on the WISC-IV), and the Kaufman Assessment Battery for Children. We also introduced the concept of nonverbal intelligence tests.

With the Stanford-Binet, we noted that the test measures cognitive functioning of individuals from age 2 through 90. We also pointed out that it assesses verbal and nonverbal intelligence across five factors: fluid reasoning, knowledge, quantitative reasoning, visual-spatial processing, and working memory. We noted that it uses a vocabulary routing test to help determine the basal age of the examinee, or the point where testing is started, and that ceiling ages are used to determine when the testing should be completed. This test has been one of the most popular tests of cognitive functioning and continues to be widely used today.

Next, we discussed the Wechsler tests, particularly the WISC-IV. We identified 15 subtests that can be assessed when administering the WISC-IV, although only ten are used in determining the examinee's Full-Scale IQ. We noted that subtests are specific to four Composite Score Indexes which include Verbal Comprehension Index (VCI), Perceptual Reasoning Index (PRI), Working Memory Index (WMI), and Processing Speed Index (PSI). These indexes are important in determining possible learning problems. We pointed out that the Wechsler tests are probably the most widely used tests of mental ability and are used to assess mental retardation, giftedness, learning problems, and general cognitive functioning.

We next examined the Kaufman Assessment Battery for Children, Second Edition (KABC-II), which measures cognitive ability of children from ages 3 to 18 and specifically focuses on visual processing, fluid reasoning, and short-term and long-term memory. We pointed out that the test can be scored based on a couple of models of intelligences, one of which is Cattell's model of fluid and crystallized intelligence.

The last intelligence tests we examined were the CTONI and the UNIT, two commonly used nonverbal intelligence measures. The CTONI was designed to measure nonverbal intellect from ages 6 years, 0 months to 18 years, 11 months. The CTONI is composed of six subtests (pictorial analogies, geometric analogies, pictorial categories, geometric categories, pictorial sequences, and geometric sequences). The UNIT was designed to measure nonverbal intelligence of children from ages 5 to 17 years. The UNIT is composed of six subtests (symbolic memory, cube design, spatial memory, analogic reasoning, object memory, and reasoning).

As the chapter continued we introduced the concept of neuropsychology. More specifically, this section focused on how neuropsychological assessment assesses a wide variety of problems related to brain-behavior relationships. We noted that although the field of neuropsychology is relatively new, interest in brain functioning goes back thousands of years. We pointed out that neuropsychological assessments are generally called for following a traumatic brain injury, an illness that affects brain function, or because of suspected changes in brain function from the aging process. We highlighted the fact that the results of a neurological assessment can be used as a diagnostic tool in identifying root causes and the extent of brain damage, to measure changes in functioning, to compare cognitive functioning to a norm group, to help in treatment and planning for individuals and their families, and to offer guidelines for educational planning.

Relative to neurological assessment we highlighted two methods of assessment: a fixed and a flexible battery approach. In a fixed battery approach, all individuals requiring assessment receive the same set of standardized tests. Two well-known tests of this kind are the Halsted-Reitan Battery and the Luria-Nebraska Neuropsychological Battery. Some of the categories assessed in the Halsted-Reitan include: Category Test, Tactual Performance Test, Trail-Making Test, Finger Tapping Test, Rhythm Test, Speech Sounds Perception Test, Aphasia Screening Test, and the Sensory-Perceptual Examination. This section of the chapter concluded with a discussion of The Boston Process Approach (BPA), which is one example of a flexible battery approach. This approach requires careful observation of the test-taker during test administration and is much more qualitative in nature.

As the chapter neared its conclusion, we noted that only some helpers are given the advanced training needed for the assessment of cognitive ability. For those helpers who do not have such training, we pointed out the reasons it is still imperative that they have the basic knowledge of these kinds of tests.

Finally, we shared that over the years the examination of cognitive functioning has been abused by miscalculating the intelligence of minorities, over-classifying individuals with learning disabilities, "proving" racial differences of ability, and differentiating social classes. We suggested that the astute examiner know that the assessment of cognitive functioning is complex, is based on the environment, genetics, and biology, and that conclusions should be drawn tentatively and done within the context of knowing the whole person.

CHAPTER REVIEW

1. Discuss some of the many ways that intelligence tests are used.
2. Highlight the major points of the following theories of intelligence:
   a. Spearman's Two-Factor Approach
   b. Thurstone's Multifactor Approach
   c. Vernon's Hierarchical Model of Intelligence
   d. Guilford's Multifactor/Multi-Dimensional Model
   e. Cattell's Fluid and Crystal Intelligence
   f. Piaget's Cognitive Development Theory
   g. Gardner's Theory of Multiple Intelligences
3. Why is Gardner's Theory of Multiple Intelligences revolutionary as compared to the more traditional models of intelligence?
4. Describe the concepts of basal level and ceiling level. How are these levels used in the Stanford-Binet?
5. Explain the differences between the WAIS-IV, WISC-IV, and WPPSI-III.
6. Discuss the purposes of the Composite Indexes on the Wechsler tests of intelligence.
7. Although there are many similarities between the Stanford-Binet and the Wechsler tests of intelligence (e.g., both measure global intelligence, both compare nonverbal

and verbal intelligence), some major differences exist. Discuss these differences and the strengths and weaknesses of both tests.

8. Discuss the purpose of nonverbal intelligence tests. What population(s) are they suited for?
9. Define neuropsychological assessment.
10. What domains are measured in neuropsychological assessment?
11. What are the two major approaches to neuropsychological assessment. Give a description of each.
12. Discuss the role of helpers in the administration and interpretation of tests of intelligence and neuropsychological assessment.

References

Aylward, G.P. (1996). Review of the Comprehensive Test of Nonverbal Intelligence. In J.C. Impara and B.S. Plake (Eds.), *The Thirteenth Mental Measurements Yearbook*. Lincoln, NE: Buros Institute of Mental Measurements. Retrieved from Mental Measurements Yearbook database.

Bandalos, D.L. (2001). Review of the Universal Nonverbal Intelligence Test. In B.S. Plake and J.C. Impara (Eds.), *The Thirteenth Mental Measurements Yearbook*. Lincoln, NE: Buros Institute of Mental Measurements. Retrieved from Mental Measurements Yearbook database.

Cattell, R. (1971). *Abilities: Their structure, growth, and action*. Boston, MA: Houghton Mifflin.

Cattell, R. (1979). Are culture fair intelligence tests possible and necessary? *Journal of Research and Development in Education, 12*, 3–13.

Cattell, R. (1980). The heritability of fluid, g_f, and crystallized, g_c, intelligence, estimated by a least squares use of the MAVA method. *British Journal of Educational Psychology, 50*, 253–265.

Dean, R. (1985). Review of the Halstead–Reitan Neuropsychological Battery. In J.V. Mitchell (Ed.), *The Ninth Mental Measurements Yearbook*. Lincoln, NE: Buros Institute of Mental Measurements. Retrieved from Mental Measurements Yearbook database.

Educational Broadcasting Corporation (2004). Concept to classroom: What is the theory of multiple intelligences (M. I.)? Retrieved, September 26, 2008, from http://www.thirteen.org/edonline/concept2class/mi/index.html

Encyclopedia of Mental Disorders (n.d.). Halstead-Reitan battery. Retrieved on September 15, 2008, from http://www.minddisorders.com/Flu-Inv/Halstead-Reitan-Battery.html

Gardner, H. (1983). *Frames of mind*. New York: Basic Books Inc.

Gardner, H. (1996). *MI: intelligence, understanding and the mind* [motion picture]. (Available from Media into the classroom, 10573 W. Pico Blvd. #162, Los Angeles: CA 90064)

Gardner, H. (1999). *Intelligence reframed: Multiple intelligence for the 21st century*. New York, NY: Basic books.

Gardner, H. (2003). Multiple intelligences after twenty years. Paper presented at the American Educational Research Association. Chicago: April 21, 2003. Retrieved September 23, 2008, from: http://www.pz.harvard.edu/PIs/HG_MI_after_20_years.pdf

Gould, S. J. (1996). *The mismeasure of man* (Rev. and expanded). New York: Norton.

Guilford, J. (1967). *The nature of human intelligence*. New York, NY: McGraw-Hill.

Guilford, J. (1988). Some changes in the structure of the intellect model. *Educational and Psychological Measurement, 48*, 1–4.

Hebben, N. & Milberg, W. (2002). *Essentials of neuropsychological assessment*. John Wiley & Sons: New York.

Hess, A.K. (2001). Review of the Wechsler Adult Intelligence Scale-Third Edition. In B.S. Plake and J.C. Impara (Eds.), *The Thirteenth Mental Measurements Yearbook*. Lincoln, NE: Buros Institute of Mental Measurements. Retrieved from Mental Measurements Yearbook database.

Kolb, B. & Whishaw, I. (2008). *Fundamentals of human neuropsychology* (6th ed.). Palgrave Macmillan, United Kingdom.

Lee, G. (n.d.). Neuropsychological assessment. Retrieved September 25, 2008, from http://www.nldontheweb.org/neuropsych_assessment.htm

Lezak, M., Howieson, D., & Loring, D. (2004). *Neuropsychological Assessment* (4th ed.). Oxford University Press: New York.

Madle, R.A. (2005). Review of the Wechsler Preschool and Primary Scale of Intelligence. In R.A. Spies and B.S. Plake (Eds.), *The Sixteenth Mental Measurements Yearbook*. Lincoln, NE: Buros Institute of Mental Measurements. Retrieved from Mental Measurements Yearbook database.

McGee, J. (2004). Neuroanatomy of behavior after brain injury or You don't like my behavior? You'll have to discuss that with my brain directly. Retrieved September 22, 2008, from http://www.premier-out look.com/pdfs/article_archive/summer_2004/ INSIGHTSUMMER2004.pdf

Milberg, W.P., Hebben, N., & Kaplan, E. (1996). The Boston Process Approach to neuropsychological assessment. In I. Grant & K. Adams (Eds.), *Neuropsychological assessment of neuropsychiatric disorders* (pp. 58–80). United States: Oxford University Press).

Pearson. (2006). KABC-II: Kaufman Assessment Battery for Children, Second Edition. Retrieved September 22, 2008, from http://ags.pearsonassess-ments.com/group.asp?nGroupInfoID=a21000

Pearson (2008). Weschler Adult Intelligence Scale, Fourth Edition. Retrieved September 26, 2008, from http://pearsonassess.com/haiweb/Cultures/ en-US/Site/AboutUs/NewsReleases/NewsItem/ NewsRelease082808.htm

Piaget, J. (1950). *The psychology of intelligence* (M. Piercy & D. Berlyne, Trans.). London: Routledge & Kegan.

Riverside Publishing (2006). The Stanford-Binet Intelligence Scales, Fifth Edition. Retrieved September 21, 2008, from http://www.riverpub. com/products/sb5/index.html

Roid, G. (2003). *Stanford-Binet Intelligence Scales, Fifth Edition, technical manual*. Itasca, IL: Riverside Publishing.

Spearman, C. (1970). *The abilities of man*. New York, NY: AMS Press. (Original work published in 1932).

Thurstone, L. (1938). *Primary mental abilities*. Chicago, IL: University of Chicago Press.

Vanderploeg, R. (Ed.) (2000). *Clinician's guide to neuropsychological assessment*. Tampa, Fl: Lawrence Erlbaum Associates.

VanLingen, G. (1996). Review of the Comprehensive Test of Nonverbal Intelligence. In J.C. Impara and B.S. Plake (Eds.), *The Thirteenth Mental Measurements Yearbook*. Lincoln, NE: Buros Institute of Mental Measurements. Retrieved from Mental Measurements Yearbook database.

Vernon, P. (1961). *The structure of human abilities* (2nd ed.). London: Methuen & Co. Ltd.

Wechsler, D. (2003). *WISC-IV administration and scoring*. San Antonio, TX: Harcourt Assessment.

CAREER AND OCCUPATIONAL ASSESSMENT: INTEREST INVENTORIES, MULTIPLE APTITUDE, AND SPECIAL APTITUDE TESTS

A friend of mine was struggling with whether or not to continue working toward his doctoral degree in psychology. He already had a master's degree, had worked a while in the field of mental health, and had begun his first semester toward his Ph.D. Every day he would come home from school and have panic attacks. He simply was not sure that this was the career path he wanted to take. He decided to take a Strong Interest Inventory, and his concerns were reinforced when the test revealed that he viewed learning more as a means to an end than as something to embrace. His personality orientation toward the world of work also did not quite fit those of most psychologists. He decided to quit his Ph.D. program and become a ski instructor. Later, he went into investment banking, and today he's a very successful insurance broker —and much happier. What a switch!

When I was 35 and making a paltry salary as an assistant professor, I thought, "If I joined the Reserves, I could make some extra money pretty easily." So I went down to the local recruiting center, where they told me, "First, you need to take this test." It was the Armed Services Vocational Aptitude Test Battery (the ASVAB). I knew about it because I had taught a brief overview of it in my testing class. It measured general cognitive ability as well as specific vocational aptitudes. I said, "Sure." A couple of weeks later, a recruiter called and said, "We want you." I had scored high on all the scales and moderately high on mechanical aptitude. I pondered joining the Reserves but then called him back and said, "Thanks, but I think I'll pass." Despite my ability, I decided I didn't quite have the interest or inclination to be in the military.

(Ed Neukrug)

This chapter is about tests that can help an individual make a decision about his or her academic or vocational path. Whether it's an interest inventory such as the one my friend took, or a multiple aptitude test such as the one I took, these instruments can be critical in helping an individual choose an occupation or a career. Thus, in this chapter we will examine tests that are used in occupational and career counseling, including interest inventories, which are a type of personality assessment, and special aptitude and multiple aptitude tests, which help an individual determine what he or she is good at. We will also examine some of the various roles helpers play in career and occupational assessment and conclude with some final thoughts about this important domain.

DEFINING CAREER AND OCCUPATIONAL ASSESSMENT

Career and occupational assessment can take place at any point in an individual's life, but it is often most critical at transition points such as when an adolescent moves into high school and begins to ponder an occupation or a career, when a young adult finds a job or goes on to college, when an adult decides to crystallize his or her career choices, when a middle-aged adult makes a career shift, or when an older adult considers shifting out of his or her career. Although talking with a counselor can make these transitions smoother, tests provide a vital adjunct to this counseling process. Three kinds of tests are sometimes used in the vocational counseling process: interest inventories, multiple aptitude tests, and special aptitude tests.

In Chapter 1 interest inventories were defined as a type of personality assessment, similar to objective personality tests that are discussed in that chapter, but generally classified separately because of their popularity and very specific focus (see Figure 1.3). Our definition from Chapter 1 suggested that interest inventories are used to determine a person's likes and dislikes as well as an individual's personality orientation toward the world of work, and are almost exclusively used in the career counseling process. In contrast, we noted in Chapter 1 that multiple aptitude tests measure a number of homogeneous abilities and are used to predict the likelihood of success in any of a number of vocations, while special aptitude tests usually measure one homogenous area of ability and are used to predict success in a specific vocational area. Interest inventories, which focus on likes and dislikes, and special and multiple aptitude tests, which focus on ability, complement each other and are sometimes given together. In this chapter we will explore interest inventories, take a look at multiple aptitude tests, and conclude by discussing special aptitude tests.

INTEREST INVENTORIES

Interest inventories

Determine likes and dislikes from a career perspective; good at predicting job satisfaction

With an estimated 3,000,000 interest inventories administered each year, interest inventories have been particularly successful as an adjunct to the career counseling process and have become big business in the world of assessment (Hansen, 1995; Zytowski, 1994). This is probably partially due to the fact that interest inventories are fairly good at predicting job satisfaction based on occupational fit (Jagger, Neukrug, & McAuliffe, 1992; Ton & Hansen, 2001). For instance, if a person takes an interest inventory and chooses a job that seems to match his or her personality type, then that person is more likely to be satisfied in that occupation than a person whose personality type does not match his or her job. It should be noted, however, that interest in an area does not necessarily correlate with ability in that same area. For example, you might want to be a rock star, but if you lack certain musical abilities, your career may be short-lived.

Three of the most common interest inventories we will examine include the Strong Vocational Interest Inventory (Consulting Psychologists Press, 2004), the Self-Directed Search (SDS; PAR 2001), and the Career Occupational Preference System Interest Inventory (COPS) (EdITS, n.d.).

STRONG INTEREST INVENTORY®*

One of the most commonly used career inventories is the "Strong." First developed in 1927 and published as the Strong Vocational Interest Blank (Strong, 1926), its latest version is called the Strong Interest Inventory (SII). The 291-item SII, which was recently reduced from 317 items, is given to people aged 16 or older, takes 35 to 40 minutes to administer, and can be administered individually or in a group setting (Consulting Psychologists Press, 2004; Kelly, 2003). The latest version uses a 5-point Likert scale that asks people to rate themselves from strongly like to strongly dislike in six broad areas (occupations, subject areas, activities, leisure activities, people, and characteristics). The SII test report offers five different types of interpretive scales or indexes in the following areas:

- General Occupational Themes
- Basic Interest Scales
- Occupational Scales
- Personal Style Scales
- Response Summary

Strong—General Occupational Themes

Uses Holland's theory of personality type (RIASEC)

GENERAL OCCUPATIONAL THEMES   The most commonly used score on the Strong is the one found on the General Occupational Themes, which offers a three-letter code based on Holland's hexagon model (see Figure 8.1). Holland defines six personality types: Realistic, Investigative, Artistic, Social, Enterprising, and Conventional. These classifications are further explained in Box 8.1. The SII identifies the test-taker's top three Holland codes and places them in hierarchical order.

On the hexagon, codes adjacent to one another share more elements in common than nonadjacent ones. For example, a typical counselor or social worker will have a Holland code of SAE, codes that are on adjacent corners of the hexagon and share many common elements. In contrast, people in the Artistic realm tend to have little interest in jobs or tasks in the Conventional category (located on the opposite side of the hexagon), such as accounting or bookkeeping.

---

*Strong Interest Inventory is a registered trademark of CPP, Inc.

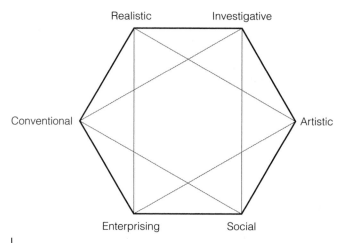

FIGURE 8.1 | HOLLAND'S HEXAGON MODEL OF PERSONALITY TYPES

BOX 8.1 | HOLLAND'S PERSONALITY AND WORK TYPE

Realistic: Realistic persons like to work with equipment, machines, computer hardware, or tools, often prefer to work outdoors, and are good at manipulating concrete physical objects. These individuals prefer to avoid social situations, artistic endeavors, or abstract tasks.

Occupational settings in which you might find realistic individuals include filling stations, farms, machine shops, construction sites, computer repair labs, and power plants.

Investigative: Investigative persons like to think abstractly, solve problems, and investigate. These individuals feel comfortable with the pursuit of knowledge and enjoy manipulating ideas and symbols. Investigative individuals prefer to avoid social situations and see themselves as introverted. Some settings in which you might find investigative individuals include research laboratories, hospitals, universities, and government-sponsored research agencies.

Artistic: Artistic individuals like to express themselves creatively, usually through artistic forms such as drama, art, music, and writing. They prefer unstructured activities in which they can use their imagination and express their creativity. Some settings in which you might find artistic individuals include the theater, concert halls, libraries, art or music studios, dance studios, orchestras, photography studios, newspapers, and restaurants.

Social: Social people are nurturers, helpers, and caregivers who have a high degree of concern for others. They are introspective and insightful and prefer work environments in which they can use their intuitive and caregiving skills. Some settings in which you might find social people include government social service agencies, counseling offices, churches, schools, mental hospitals, recreational centers, personnel offices, and hospitals.

Enterprising: Enterprising individuals are self-confident, adventurous, bold, and enjoy working with other people. They have good persuasive skills and prefer positions of leadership. They tend to dominate conversations and enjoy work environments in which they can satisfy their need for recognition, power, and expression. Some settings in which you might find enterprising individuals include life insurance agencies, advertising agencies, political offices, real estate offices, new and used car lots, sales offices, and management positions.

Conventional: Individuals of the Conventional orientation are stable, controlled, conservative, and cooperative. They prefer working on concrete tasks and like to follow instructions. They value the business world, clerical tasks, and tend to be good at computer programming or database operations. Some settings in which you might find conventional people include banks, business offices, accounting firms, computer software companies, and medical records departments.

Strong—Basic Interest Scales

Identify broad areas of interest

BASIC INTEREST SCALES   The Basic Interest Scales identify the respondent's interest in 30 broad areas, such as science, performing arts, marketing, teaching, law, and so on. The individual is shown his or her top five interest areas and can also view the 30 interest areas together with their corresponding Holland Codes (see Figure 8.2). Using T scores, individuals can compare themselves to the average scores of people of their own gender. The higher the T-score (remember that 50 is the mean and 10 is the standard deviation), the more interest a person will have in a particular area as compared with others. Interest areas greater than one standard deviation (i.e., 60 or above) are considered very high.

Strong—Occupational Scales

Compares interests to those of others with the same job

OCCUPATIONAL SCALES   These scales provided the original basis for the 1927 Strong and allow an individual to compare his or her interests to the interests of individuals of the same sex who are satisfied in their jobs. Thus, respondents can compare how they scored on the Strong to the scores of individuals in 244 commonly held jobs who also took the Strong. The Strong lists the 10 occupations to which the respondent is most similar (see Figure 8.3), and then separately lists the T-scores of the client as compared to all 244 occupations (not shown in the figure). The higher the T-score, the more similar are the respodent's interests to those of satisfied people in the stated job.

Strong—Personal Style Scales

Assesses work style, learning environment, leadership style, risk taking, and team orientation

PERSONAL STYLE SCALES   These scales gives an estimate as to how comfortable the test-taker is in certain activities, including work style (alone or with people), learning environment (practical vs. academic), leadership style (taking charge vs. letting others take charge), risk taking/adventure (risk taker vs. non risk taker), and team orientation (working on a team vs. independently). T-scores are used to compare individuals to men, women, or a combined group.

THE RESPONSE SUMMARY   Response Summary provides a percentage breakdown of the client's responses across all of the six interest areas measured by the Strong (e.g., occupations, subject areas, etc.). The summary offers the total percentages of each of the Likert response types, varying from "strongly like" to "strongly dislike." In addition, there is a new typicality index that assists in identifying or flagging examinees who may be making random responses, which has been found to be 95% accurate. A score of 16 or lower indicates an inconsistent pattern of item selection (Consulting Psychologists Press, 2004).

The Strong can be scored in a number of ways. The test booklet can be mailed to the testing center, on-site scoring software can be purchased and used, or the assessment can be administered over the Internet to produce immediate scoring reports. Norm data were updated for the latest version of the Strong and contained an equal number of men and woman (n = 2,250) and a similar distribution of racial and ethnic groups compared to U.S. Census data (Consulting Psychologists Press, 2004). The sample included people representing 370 different occupations. Reliability coefficient alphas for the General Occupational Themes (Holland codes) were between .91 and .95 with test-retest reliabilities ranging from .88 to .95. The Basic Interest Scales had a median alpha of .87. The Occupational Scales had test-retest reliability median average of .86 between tests taken two to seven months apart. The five Personal Style Scales had coefficient alphas that ranged from .82 to .87. Evidence of

Strong Interest Inventory® Profile   JANE SAMPLE | Page 3

BASIC INTEREST SCALES   **SECTION 2**

The Basic Interest Scales represent specific interest areas that often point to work activities, projects, course work, and leisure activities that are personally motivating and rewarding. As with the General Occupational Themes, your interest levels (Very Little, Little, Moderate, High, Very High) were determined by comparing your scores against the average scores for your gender.

As you review your results in the charts below, note your top interest areas and your areas of least interest, and think about how they relate to your work, educational, and leisure activities. Take time to consider any top interest areas that are not currently part of your work or lifestyle and think about how you might be able to incorporate them into your plans.

YOUR TOP FIVE INTEREST AREAS	Areas of Least Interest
1. Writing & Mass Communication (A)	Management (E)
2. Performing Arts (A)	Computer Hardware & Electronics (R)
3. Visual Arts & Design (A)	Military (R)
4. Culinary Arts (A)	
5. Law (E)	

ARTISTIC — Very High

BASIC INTEREST SCALE	STD SCORE & INTEREST LEVEL	STD SCORE
Writing & Mass Communication	VH	71
Performing Arts	VH	71
Visual Arts & Design	VH	70
Culinary Arts	VH	67

INVESTIGATIVE — Moderate

BASIC INTEREST SCALE	STD SCORE & INTEREST LEVEL	STD SCORE
Research	H	57
Science	M	56
Medical Science	M	52
Mathematics	L	40

SOCIAL — Moderate

BASIC INTEREST SCALE	STD SCORE & INTEREST LEVEL	STD SCORE
Social Sciences	H	59
Counseling & Helping	M	58
Religion & Spirituality	M	53
Human Resources & Training	M	48
Healthcare Services	M	46
Teaching & Education	M	45

ENTERPRISING — Moderate

BASIC INTEREST SCALE	STD SCORE & INTEREST LEVEL	STD SCORE
Law	VH	66
Marketing & Advertising	VH	65
Politics & Public Speaking	H	58
Entrepreneurship	M	46
Sales	L	41
Management	VL	33

CONVENTIONAL — Moderate

BASIC INTEREST SCALE	STD SCORE & INTEREST LEVEL	STD SCORE
Finance & Investing	M	55
Office Management	M	50
Taxes & Accounting	M	43
Programming & Information Systems	L	39

REALISTIC — Little

BASIC INTEREST SCALE	STD SCORE & INTEREST LEVEL	STD SCORE
Nature & Agriculture	M	50
Protective Services	M	47
Athletics	M	45
Mechanics & Construction	M	40
Military	L	36
Computer Hardware & Electronics	VL	33

FIGURE 8.2 | STRONG INTEREST INVENTORY® PROFILE SHEET FOR BASIC INTEREST SCALES

Source: Reproduced with permission of the Publisher, CPP, Inc., from the Strong Interest Inventory® Profile. Copyright 2004 by CPP, Inc. All rights reserved. Strong Interest Inventory is a registered trademark of CPP, Inc.

Strong Interest Inventory® Profile   JANE SAMPLE | Page 4

OCCUPATIONAL SCALES   **SECTION 3**

This section highlights your Profile results on the Occupational Scales of the *Strong*. On the next three pages you will find your scores for 122 occupations. The 10 occupations most closely aligned with your interests are listed in the summary chart below. Keep in mind that the occupations listed in your Profile results are just *some* of the many occupations linked to your interests that you might want to consider. They do not indicate those you "should" pursue. It is helpful to think of each occupation as a single example of a much larger group of occupational titles to consider.

Your score on an Occupational Scale shows how similar your interests are to those of people of your gender who have been working in, and are satisfied with, that occupation. The higher your score, the more likes and dislikes you share with those individuals. The Theme Codes associated with each occupation indicate the GOTs most commonly found among people employed in that occupation.

YOUR TOP TEN STRONG OCCUPATIONS	Occupations of Dissimilar Interest
1. Librarian (A)	Physical Education Teacher (SRC)
2. Technical Writer (AIR)	Physicist (IRA)
3. Broadcast Journalist (AE)	Athletic Trainer (RIS)
4. Graphic Designer (ARI)	Mathematician (IRC)
5. Photographer (ARE)	Mathematics Teacher (CIR)
6. Reporter (A)	
7. Chef (ERA)	
8. Attorney (A)	
9. Editor (AII)	
10. Translator (A)	

As you read through your Occupational Scales results on this and the following pages, note the names of those occupations for which you scored "Similar." Those are the occupations you might want to explore first. If you have no scores in this range, take a look at those in the midrange and begin there. You might also consider occupations of least interest or for which you scored "Dissimilar"; however, keep in mind that you are likely to have little in common with people in those types of work and probably would contribute to such occupations in a unique way. Your career professional can guide you further in this process.

You can learn about occupations from information found in a public library, in the career library of a college or university near you, in a professional career center, or on the Internet. A recommended online source for occupational information is the O*NET™ database at http://online.onetcenter.org. You can also learn a lot about an occupation by talking to people who are working in that particular occupation. These people can describe their day-to-day work and tell you what they like and dislike about it.

FIGURE 8.3 | STRONG INTEREST INVENTORY® PROFILE SHEET FOR OCCUPATIONAL SCALES

convergent validity was demonstrated when scores from the most recent version of the General Occupational Themes had a .95 correlation with the previous version. Regression analysis of the Basic Interest Scales revealed that they, as a group, explained 68 to 78 percent of the variance in the broader occupational groups. Evidence of discriminant validity is suggested within the five Personal Style Scales through comparing the divergence of correlations between scales. Results indicate correlations from .03 to .55, suggesting that each Personal Style Scale is analyzing a unique aspect of preferred work environment (Consulting Psychologists Press).

SELF-DIRECTED SEARCH

SDS

This is a self-administered, scored, and interpreted test that was created by Holland and uses his personality types

The Self-Directed Search (SDS; PAR, 2001) was created by John Holland and is based on the Holland hexagon shown in Figure 8.1. As the name of the instrument suggests, the SDS can be self-administered, self-scored, and self-interpreted, although it is suggested that a counselor guide a client in his or her exploration. Although the instrument is based primarily on interests, it also includes self-estimates of competencies and ability. Once the instrument is scored and the client obtains his or her 3-letter Holland code, he or she can cross-reference the code with the Occupations Finder, which classifies more than 1,300 occupations by Holland type, or with a book entitled the Dictionary of Holland Occupational Codes (Gottfredson & Holland, 1996), which lists more than 12,000 occupational codes.

The SDS is available in four forms. Form R (Regular), is designed for high school students, college students, and adults; Form E (Easy-to-Read) is written at the fourth-grade level and can be used with students or adults who have limited reading ability; Form CE (Career Explorer) is for middle school and junior high students; and Form CP (Career Planning) is designed for professional-level employees (Brown, 2001). The SDS can be administered by hard copy booklet, computer software, or on the World Wide Web at www.self-directed-search.com (PAR, 2001).

Scoring for the test is done by simply adding the raw scores of each of the six types of personality, with the three highest scores, from highest to lowest, providing the individual's "Holland Code." Norm data for form R were based on 2,602 people between the ages of 17 and 65 from 25 different states. Internal reliability coefficients ranged from .90 to .94 for the combined scales (Brown, 2001). Form E was normed against 719 people from ages 15 to 72 and has slightly higher reliability coefficients than Form R. Form CP was administered to only 101 working people aged 19 to 61, most of whom had been to college, and had slightly lower reliability estimates than the other forms (Brown). Validity of the SDS has been shown by correlating resulting codes of the most recent version of the Self-Directed Search with an earlier one and finding scales correlating greater than .94. In fact, half of individuals had the same 3-letter Holland code for both, and two-thirds had the same first two Holland codes (Brown). Research on the Holland codes has consistently shown moderate to high validity with job satisfaction (Jagger et al., 1992; Ton & Hansen, 2001).

COPSYSTEM

COPSystem

Three instruments that measure interests, abilities, and values

The COPSystem is a career measurement package that contains three instruments that can be used individually or together to aid in making career decisions. The three instruments measure interests, abilities, and values (see Table 8.1).

The tests can be hand scored, mailed to EdITS for machine scoring, or scored with on-site scoring software purchased from the publisher.

COPS

Assesses interests along career clusters

CAREER OCCUPATIONAL PREFERENCE SYSTEM INTEREST INVENTORY (COPS) The COPS is designed for individuals from seventh grade to adult and consists of 168 items that are based on high school and college curricula as well as sources

TABLE 8.1 | COPSystem Assessments and Administration Times

Measurement	Acronym	Full Name	Administration Time
Interests	COPS	Career Occupational Preference System Interest Inventory	20 to 30 minutes
Abilities	CAPS	Career Ability Placement Survey	50 minutes
Work Values	COPES	Career Orientation Placement and Evaluation Survey	30 to 40 minutes

of occupational information. Scores on the instrument are related to a unique career cluster model that is used to guide the individual to a number of career areas (see Figure 8.4). Although the publisher suggests the instrument can be used for a wide age group, norms are based on high school or college samples (EdITS, n.d.). The instrument takes 20 to 30 minutes to administer and about 15 minutes to hand score.

CAPS

Measures abilities in the work environment that relate to career clusters

CAREER ABILITY PLACEMENT SURVEY (CAPS)   The CAPS test measures abilities across eight different dimensions that relate to the COPS career clusters (outer circle of Figure 8.4). The test allows individuals to identify which career fields are best suited to their abilities or identify careers for which more training may be required. The instrument is designed for middle school students through adults. Norm

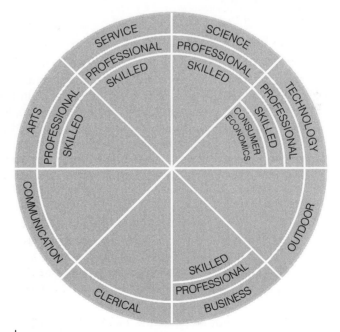

FIGURE 8.4 | COPS CAREER CLUSTERS

TABLE 8.2	THE COPES SCALES	
Investigative	vs.	Accepting
Practical	vs.	Carefree
Independence	vs.	Conformity
Leadership	vs.	Supportive
Orderliness	vs.	Flexibility
Recognition	vs.	Privacy
Aesthetic	vs.	Realistic
Social	vs.	Reserved

data are available for eighth- through twelfth-graders and for college students. Each of the eight subtests takes five minutes to administer, and the total test time is about 50 minutes. Hand scoring requires an additional 15 to 20 minutes.

COPES
Values in job selection related to career clusters

CAREER ORIENTATION PLACEMENT AND EVALUATION SURVEY (COPES)   COPES is an assessment of values that are important in occupational selection and job satisfaction. Scales are based on eight dichotomous poles (Table 8.2), which then are keyed to the career clusters in Figure 8.4 to assist in using values in choosing a career.

As with the CAPS and COPS, however this instrument is designed for middle school students through adults, norm data are available only from high school and college students.

OTHER COMMON INTEREST INVENTORIES

Today, dozens of interest inventories are available for client use. However, a few stand out as being especially popular. For instance, The Campbell Interest and Skill Survey (CISS) is a self-report instrument measuring both interests and skills for a variety of occupations. It is intended for people 15 years or older, and is primarily for college-bound students or college-educated adults (NCS Pearson, 2008a). SIGI 3 is a computer-based (stand-alone, networked, or online) career self-assessment program primarily for high school and college students. It also provides up-to-date career information such as educational requirements, income, job satisfaction, and so on (Valpar, 2008). The Career Assessment Inventory—Enhanced Version is another instrument for career development and guidance for individuals 15 years and older. It also uses the familiar Holland codes (RIASEC) (NCS Pearson, 2008b). Clearly, experts in career and occupational assessment have many good tests from which to choose.

MULTIPLE APTITUDE TESTING

Multiple aptitude tests

Measure abilities and predict success in several fields

Multiple aptitude tests, as the name implies, measure several abilities at one time and are used to predict how an individual might perform in many different types of jobs. For example, the Armed Services Vocational Aptitude Battery (ASVAB), which will be discussed in greater detail, measures auto and shop knowledge, mechanical comprehension, general science, electronics knowledge, and so on. This type of information helps military administrators with placement decisions and is useful for those who are considering entering the armed services or who want to get a better idea of the skills they possess. Obviously, someone who has high mechanical aptitude and enjoys that type of work might be better suited to repairing jet aircraft or tank engines than working as a desk clerk.

FACTOR ANALYSIS AND MULTIPLE APTITUDE TESTING

Factor analysis
Helps developers determine differences and similarities between subtests

As you may recall from Chapter 3, test developers use factor analysis in demonstrating evidence of construct validity for their tests. This common statistical technique allows researchers to analyze large data sets to determine patterns and calculate which variables have a high degree of commonality. Using this process allows multiple aptitude test developers to assess the differences and similarities in the many abilities they are attempting to measure. For example, if you wanted to create a multiple aptitude test that assessed a variety of sports abilities, you could develop a number of tests, such as a softball throw, a 100-meter dash, a long jump, a 5-km run, a baseball throwing accuracy test, and a 50-meter swim. After giving the tests to your norm group and applying factor analysis to your data, you may find that the softball throw and the baseball accuracy test have so much overlap that you decide to remove one of them from your instrument or combine the two subtests into one. Two commonly used multiple aptitude tests that use factor analysis to show the purity of their component parts include the Armed Services Vocational Aptitude Battery and the Differential Aptitude Test.

ARMED SERVICES VOCATIONAL APTITUDE BATTERY AND CAREER EXPLORATION PROGRAM

ASVAB
Measures many abilities required for military and civilian jobs

The Armed Services Vocational Aptitude Battery (ASVAB) is the most widely used multiple aptitude test in the world (ASVAB, 2008). Originally developed in 1968, it has gone through many improvements since that time. The latest revision is called the ASVAB Career Exploration Program (CEP) and consists of two instruments: the traditional ASVAB aptitude test and a new interest inventory called FYI (Find Your Interests). The ASVAP CEP also includes other components such as a career exploration guide, online resources, and a short video program.

The ASVAB (2008) battery consists of eight "power tests," a term used to describe a test that has generous time limits (in contrast to a "speed test" such as a one-minute typing test). The tests include General Science, Arithmetic Reasoning, Word Knowledge, Paragraph Comprehension, Mathematics Knowledge, Electronics Information, Auto and Shop Information, and Mechanical Comprehension. The test contains 200 items and takes 170 minutes to administer (see typical sample questions, Box 8.2). Scores for each of the eight tests, as well as three career exploration (composite) scores, are provided to the examinee. Combinations of the eight tests are used to form the three composite scores in the areas of verbal skills, math skills, and science and technical skills. These three areas tend to be important for success in a number of jobs and contrast with the one general score that is given in many individual intelligence tests. The composite scores can be associated with job classifications in the U.S. Department of Labor's Occupational Information Network

BOX 8.2 | SAMPLE ASVAB QUESTIONS

General Science
1. An eclipse of the sun throws the shadow of the
A. moon on the sun.
B. moon on the earth.
C. earth on the sun.
D. earth on the moon.

2. Substances that hasten chemical reaction time without themselves undergoing change are called
A. buffers.
B. colloids.
C. reducers.
D. catalysts.

Word Knowledge
3. The wind is variable today.
A. mild
B. steady
C. shifting
D. chilling

Math Knowledge
4. If 50 percent of X = 66, then X =
A. 33
B. 66
C. 99
D. 132

5. What is the area of this square?
A. 1 square foot
B. 5 square feet
C. 10 square feet
D. 25 square feet

Electronics Information
6. Which of the following has the least resistance?
A. wood
B. iron
C. rubber
D. silver

7. In this circuit diagram, the resistance is 100 ohms, and the current is 0.1 amperes. The voltage is
A. 5 volts.
B. 10 volts.
C. 100 volts.
D. 1,000 volts.

Automotive and Shop Information
8. A car uses too much oil when which of the following parts are worn?
A. pistons
B. piston rings
C. main bearings
D. connecting rods

9. A chisel is used for
A. prying.
B. cutting.
C. twisting.
D. grinding.

Mechanical Comprehension

10. In this arrangement of pulleys, which pulley turns fastest?
A. A
B. B
C. C
D. D

Solutions

1. B; 2. D; 3. C; 4. D; 5. D;
6. D; 7. B; 8. B; 9. B; 10. A

Source: Adapted from ASVAB (Armed Services Vocational Aptitude Battery). (2004). The ASVAB career exploration program counselor manual. Retrieved June 7, 2004, from http://www.asvabprogram.com/downloads/asvab_counselor_manual.pdf

(O*NET). Although the ASVAB began as a test strictly for the military, over the years it has been altered and is now useful for both civilian and military occupations.

ASVAB scores were normed against two large samples that in combination contained approximately 10,700 men and women ranging from tenth grade up to age 23 from the Profile of American Youth project in 1997. The 18 and older group was oversampled for Hispanic and African American youth (ASVAB, 2008). ASVAB developers employed Item Response Theory (IRT) techniques to estimate reliabilities, which ranged between .69 and .88 for the eight subscales for 10th, 11th, and 12th grades. The three composite scores (math, verbal, and science and technical skills) ranged between .88 and .91. Content validity and content construction focused on knowledge required to perform specific jobs rather than the entire content domain. For example, instead of testing the complete domain of math, the math domain is geared toward knowledge and skills needed in the typical work environment. Numerous validity studies show correlations that range from a moderate .36 to an impressive .77 for predicting success in military occupations. Regarding construct validity, one study found a .79 correlation between ASVAB and ACT scores (Nicewander as cited by ASVAB). Another study found correlations ranging from .70 to .86 with the California Achievement Test (Streicher & Friedman as cited by ASVAB).

In addition to the traditional ASVAB, the "ASVAB Career Exploration Program" now also offers the FYI (Find Your Interests), a newly developed interest inventory to assist high school students in determining what they would *like* to do rather than what they *can* do (ASVAB). It is based on Holland's RIASEC personality types and provides individuals their three highest codes. FYI contains 90-items and can be taken online at the ASVAB Web site or with paper-and-pencil. The paper-and-pencil version takes approximately 15 minutes to complete and score (ASVAB, 2008). It uses a 3-point Likert scale asking individuals if they would like, be indifferent to, or dislike certain activities.

In 2008, coefficient alpha reliabilities ranged from .92 to .94 while test-retest reliabilities ranged from .89 to .93 for each of the Holland Codes (ASVAB, 2008). Evidence of validity has been demonstrated for the FYI through several methods. Adherence to proper development processes suggest adequate content validity. Factorial analysis suggesting internal structure and correlation with the Strong Interest Inventory help demonstrate construct validity. The FYI correlated with the Strong General Occupation Themes ranging from .68 to .85, the Strong Basic Interest Scales from .44 to .59, and the Strong Occupation Scales from .54 to .61. Although useful for any student, the FYI can be particularly helpful for the approximately 70 percent of students who do not go on to college, because they can be hopeful about their futures when they see occupations that are in range of their interests and skills (J. Styers, personal communication, October 3, 2008).

DIFFERENTIAL APTITUDE TESTS

The Differential Aptitude Tests (DAT), Fifth Edition, is a long-standing series of tests for students in grades 7 through 12 that measures adolescents' abilities across

DAT

Measures abilities and interests to assist with career decision making

vocational skills (Hattrup & Schmitt, 1995; Pearson, 2008). Often administered and interpreted by school counselors, the DAT takes approximately 1½ to 2½ hours to complete, depending on whether the full or abbreviated version is used. The DAT has eight separate tests that measure verbal reasoning, numerical reasoning, abstract reasoning, perceptual speed and accuracy, mechanical reasoning, space relations, spelling, and language usage. The DAT also includes a Career Interest Inventory (CII) to determine what the student is good at as well as what careers might be of interest to him or her. It is easy to see how both sets of these scores can be useful to a school counselor when assisting a student in determining a possible occupation or college major. Raw scores are converted to percentiles and stanines.

Internal consistency reliability measures for the DAT are high, ranging between .80 and .95 for the different tests. Regarding construct validity, correlations with the DAT and several other major aptitude tests (ACT, ASVAB, SAT, and the California Achievement Test) range between .68 and .85 (Hattrup & Schmitt, 1995). Although correlations with DAT scores and high school grades were sound, no data have been provided regarding predictive validity in job performance. A healthy norm sample of approximately 170,000 students proportionately represented by geography, gender, socioeconomic status, ethnicities, and other factors was used for the Fifth Edition.

DAT PCA

Often used by employers to assess ability

An alternative version of the DAT for adults is called the Differential Aptitude Battery for Personnel and Career Assessment (DAT PCA). The DAT PCA measures ability and aptitude across eight different areas, similar to the DAT, and is often used for hiring purposes. It allows employers to determine one's current ability and aptitude for learning new skills during training. Like the DAT, the DAT PCA uses percentiles and stanines. Reliability estimates are sound, ranging between .88 and .94 (Wilson & Wing, 1995). The norm sample consisted of twelfth-grade students, which is a bit of a leap from the adult population for which the test is intended. However, predictive validity correlations comparing DAT PCA scores with grades, job supervisors' ratings, and job performance were low, ranging from .1 to .4 (Wilson & Wing).

SPECIAL APTITUDE TESTING

Special aptitude tests

Designed to predict success in a vocational area

As noted earlier, special aptitude tests measure a homogenous area of ability and are generally used to predict success in a specific vocational area of interest. Thus, they are frequently used as a screening process to assess one's ability to perform a certain job or to master a new skill at work. Hiring and training employees is an expensive operation for any size of company, so you can imagine how useful these tests might be. Similarly, specialized vocational training in areas such as art, music, plumbing, and mechanics all require aptitudes that not everyone possesses. Hence, educational institutions frequently rely on special aptitude testing during the admission process.

The tests we will briefly examine in this section include the Clerical Test Battery, the Minnesota Clerical Assessment Battery, the U.S. Postal Service's 473 Battery Examination, the Mechanical Aptitude Test, the Wiesen Test of Mechanical Aptitude, the Arco Mechanical Aptitude and Spatial Relations Tests, the Technical Test Battery, the Bennett Test of Mechanical Comprehension, the

Music Aptitude Profile, the Iowa Test of Music Literacy, the Keynotes Music Evaluation Software Kit, the Group Test of Musical Ability, and the Advanced Measures of Music Audiation.

CLERICAL APTITUDE TESTS

Clerical aptitude tests

Used for screening applicants for clerical jobs

Several tests are available to measure one's aptitude at performing clerical tasks. The Clerical Test Battery (CTB2), published by Psytech (2006), measures clerical skill across a range of abilities, including verbal reasoning, numerical ability, clerical checking, spelling, typing, and filing. The CTB2 takes only 27 minutes to administer, and it can be completed with paper and pencil or on a personal computer. Reliability estimates for the subtests are sound and fall between .81 and .90. Reasonable evidence of validity is provided in the test manual. A similar type of clerical test is the Minnesota Clerical Assessment Battery, which measures traits such as typing, proofreading, filing, business vocabulary, business math, and clerical knowledge. Reliability estimates for the subtests are acceptable; however, Fitzpatrick (2001) questioned whether the publisher had provided adequate evidence of validity.

More than 500,000 people each year take the U.S. Postal Service's entrance examination (Learning Express, 2001). The new Test 473 for Major Entry-Level Jobs (also known as 473 Battery Exam) recently replaced the 470 Battery (USPS, 2007). This test is required for most entry-level positions in the U.S. Postal Service such as clerk, mail handler, carrier, mark-up clerk, mail processor, flat sorter, and distribution clerk. The "473" measures aptitudes such as address checking, forms completion, coding, memory, and an inventory of personal experiences. The instrument has 398 items and examinees are given 129 minutes to complete it. A score of 70% is considered passing, but those hired generally have scores 90% or greater (USPS).

MECHANICAL APTITUDE TESTS

Mechanical aptitude tests

Measure ability to learn mechanical principles and manipulate mechanical objects

Have you ever known people who could look at almost any mechanical-related problem (stalled car, leak underneath the sink, malfunctioning household appliance) and fix it? Obviously there is some learned information (crystallized intelligence) involved, but some people just seem to have a knack for it (fluid intelligence). Mechanical aptitude is generally considered the ability to learn physical and mechanical principles and manipulate mechanical objects. Put another way, it is the ability to understand how mechanical things work. Some people seem to have it, and some don't. (The authors of this book are in the second category.)

Many mechanical aptitude tests are available today, and small manufacturing companies, governmental agencies, and technical institutes frequently use them when they want to measure this ability before hiring or training someone. The Mechanical Aptitude Test (MAT-3C; Raymond Corporation, 2008) was developed to reduce the impact of gender and race on the measurement of mechanical aptitudes. The 36 items were written to relate to everyday things and focus on household objects, work production, science and physics, and hand and power tools.

This paper-and-pencil instrument can be taken in 20 minutes and self-scored. Reliability alphas in one published sample were .72 (Raymond Corporation). The test has been shown to correlate with technical college GPAs, mechanical knowledge, manager ratings of employees (predictive validity), and other measures of mechanical aptitude (convergent validity).

The Wiesen Test of Mechanical Aptitude (WTMA; Criteriacorp, 2008) is a similar test with a focus on predicting job performance in the operation and maintenance of tools, machinery, and equipment. It has 60 items and takes 30 minutes to complete. It attempts to remove gender and race bias and has a Spanish version. The reliability with the norm sample was .97 and it had a high correlation with the Bennett Mechanical Comprehension Test. Other common mechanical ability tests include the Technical Test Battery (TTB2), the Arco Mechanical Aptitude and Spatial Relations Tests, Fifth Edition, and the Bennett Test of Mechanical Comprehension.

ARTISTIC APTITUDE TESTS

Artistic aptitude tests

Frequently used for art school admissions

Rating artistic ability is not an easy task, and although some tests have been developed (see Figure 8.5), they have not been widely used and have questionable reliability and validity (e.g., Meir Art Test, Graves Design Judgment Test). To demonstrate artistic ability, professional art schools require applicants to submit a portfolio. One of the drawbacks to this process is that usually, a faculty member must subjectively score each portfolio, which can cause problems with reliability. One way to improve reliability is to have two or more individuals (raters) practice rating items similar to the ones they will eventually rate. Generally, as the parameters of what they are rating become more clearly defined (e.g., form, appeal, use of color, and so on), their ratings should increasingly be similar. Once they reach a high degree of agreement in their ratings, they are ready to rate the students' pieces (called "interrater reliability," this concept will be discussed in more detail in Chapter 10).

MUSICAL APTITUDE TESTS

One of the challenges of measuring musical aptitude is to be able to distinguish between one's ability to learn a distinct knowledge base, such as musical theory, history, and rhythm and cadence, and one's ability to actually play an instrument. Although several tests attempt to distinguish the ability to learn information from the ability to perform, they do so with some difficulty.

Musical aptitude tests

Assess knowledge of music

The Music Aptitude Profile, which is designed for students in grades 4 through 12, involves having the student listen to two musical excerpts and then answer a series of questions pertaining to the music. Traits that are measured include the student's ability to assess harmony, tone, melody, tempo, balance, and style. Unfortunately, test administration is lengthy, running 2½ hours. Split-half reliability coefficients were .90 for composite scores. Although evidence of validity appears fair, when comparing this test with what is defined as musical intelligence by Gardner (see Chapter 7), there is some question as to whether it actually conforms to Gardner's understanding of this trait (Cohen, 1995).

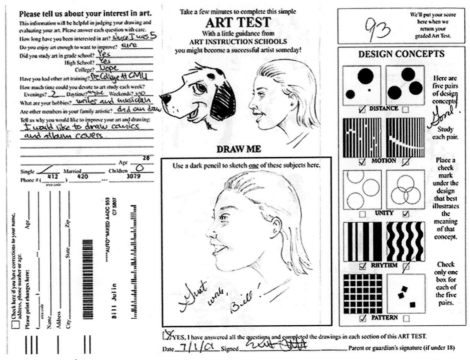

FIGURE 8.5 | COMMONLY SEEN ART TEST GRAPHICS FROM LOCAL ART SCHOOLS

Some art schools ask individuals to draw or copy pictures and are told professionals would judge them. Unfortunately, this judging is generally not valid or reliable and is often a mechanism to attract students. Professional art schools are more likely to ask individuals to provide complex portfolios that are judged by a number of individuals.

Source: TNY [*The New Yinzer*]. (2002, August). The results of my art test by Bill Julin. Retrieved on December 5, 2008, from http://www.newyinzer.com/version1/issue13/r-julin.html Reprinted by permission.

Another music test designed to measure students' "audiation," or the process of thinking about music in one's mind without it actually being there, is the Iowa Test of Music Literacy (Revised). Although it may be classified as an achievement test, it can also be used to determine a student's aptitude for music training. In this test the examinee not only listens to music, but is also required to read sheet music and compare what he or she is reading with what is being played (Radocy, 1998). Another music test, the Keynotes Music Evaluation Software Kit, is designed for classroom teachers to assess their students' musical aptitude (Brunsman & Johnson, 2000). For students aged 9 to 14, this 65-item instrument is taken on a computer with speakers or headphones and provides scores for pitch discrimination, pattern recognition, and the ability to read music. Unfortunately, no reliability or validity data is supplied in the manual (Brunsman & Johnson). Still other musical aptitude tests include the Group Test of Musical Ability and the Advanced Measures of Music Audiation.

THE ROLE OF HELPERS IN OCCUPATIONAL AND CAREER ASSESSMENT

A wide range of helpers provide occupational and career assessment. For instance, middle school counselors administer interest inventories to help students begin to examine their occupational likes and dislikes. High school counselors and college counselors provide such inventories to help students begin to think about occupational choices and to help them make tentative choices about their college major. High school counselors can also be found orchestrating the administration of multiple aptitude tests and helping students interpret those tests to identify possible vocational strengths. Similarly, private practice clinicians can be found giving interest inventories and aptitude tests to help their clients examine what they are good at and to identify which occupational areas might best fit their personalities. Today, the administration of career and occupational assessment has become big business, and we can even find businesses that specifically focus upon such assessments. Although many of these tests are used by a wide range of helpers and do not require advanced training to administer and interpret, any professional who administers such instruments should obtain the necessary basic training to be able to administer them accurately and interpret them wisely.

FINAL THOUGHTS CONCERNING OCCUPATIONAL AND CAREER ASSESSMENT

The tests discussed in this chapter can be fundamental in helping an individual make important decisions regarding occupational and career choices. However, as with all testing, occupational and career assessment should not be done in a vacuum. Understanding the complexities of why one has interests and even abilities and why one ultimately chooses a particular occupation or career can be related to a myriad of reasons including psychodynamic issues (e.g., parental influences), social pressures (e.g., racism, sexism, peer pressure), environmental concerns (e.g, the economy), and family issues (e.g., sibling order). As colleges and universities have increasingly moved toward "career management centers," as opposed to career counseling centers, these issues have become paramount. Choosing a career or occupation should never be based solely on taking a test.

SUMMARY

We began this chapter by highlighting the fact that career and occupational assessment can occur at any point in an individual's life but is often most critical at transitional points. We noted that interest inventories, multiple aptitude tests, and special aptitude tests are often used to assist an individual during these transitions, but that these tests are best used within a counseling context. We defined interest inventories as personality tests that measure likes and dislikes as well as one's personality orientation toward the world of work; multiple aptitude tests as tests that measure a number of homogeneous areas of ability and are used to predict likelihood of success in any of a number of vocational areas; and special aptitude tests as tests that usually measure one homogenous area of ability and are used to predict success in a specific vocational area. We first looked at interest inventories, then examined multiple aptitude tests and special aptitude tests.

The first interest inventory we examined was the Strong, one of the oldest career interest inventories. Its newest version focuses on five areas. The General Occupational Theme uses a Holland code to match personality type with occupations. The Basic Interest Scales also use the Holland code, this time to show how closely an individual's personality aligns with 30 broad interest areas. The Occupational Scales allow an individual to compare his or her interests to the interests of same-sex individuals from 244 occupations. The Personal Style Scales gives estimates as to the test-taker's work style (alone or with people), learning environment (practical vs. academic), leadership style (taking charge vs. letting others take charge), risk taking/adventure orientation (risk taker vs. non risk taker), and team orientation (working on a team vs. independently). Finally, the Response Summary allows the examiner to see how the client responded to the test overall and can be important in flagging individuals who are making random responses.

The Self-Directed Search (SDS), which was created by John Holland, also uses the Holland Codes and provides a personality orientation based on the client's self-estimates of interests, competencies, and ability. This easy-to-use instrument comes in a number of forms depending on the age and professional level of the client and can be cross-referenced with occupations having a Holland code similar to the client's code.

The next interest inventory we examined was the COPSystem, which is a career measurement package that contains three instruments. The Career Occupational Preference System Interest Inventory (COPS) measures interests, the Career Ability Placement Survey (CAPS) measures ability, and the Career Orientation Placement and Evaluation Survey (COPES) measures values. The scores on these tests can be cross-referenced with a number of career clusters that define occupations in key areas. We ended this section by discussing a few other common interest inventories such as CISS and SIGI 3.

In the next part of the chapter we took a look at two Multiple Aptitude Tests: the Armed Services Vocational Aptitude Battery (ASVAB) Career Exploration Program and the Differential Aptitude Test (DAT). We pointed out that these assessments often use factor analysis to assure that the various tests that collectively make up the whole instrument are unique and share little in common with one another.

The ASVAB, which is the most widely used multiple aptitude test, consists of eight power tests in the areas of General Science, Arithmetic Reasoning, Word Knowledge, Paragraph Comprehension, Mathematics Knowledge, Electronics Information, Auto and Shop Information, and Mechanical Comprehension. Scores for each of the eight tests, as well as three career exploration (composite) scores, are provided to the examinee. The composite scores can be associated with job occupations in the U.S. Department of Labor's Occupational Information Network (O*NET). The ASVAB Career Exploration Program has an interest inventory called FYI (Find Your Interests), which uses the Holland RIASEC (Realistic, Investigative, Artistic, Social, Enterprising, Conventional) types, to assist students in determining their interests as a supplement to the ASVAB data regarding their abilities.

The Differential Aptitude Test (DAT) is for students in grades 7 through 12 and consists of eight separate tests that measure verbal reasoning, numerical reasoning, abstract reasoning, perceptual speed and accuracy, mechanical reasoning, space relations, spelling, and language usage. An alternative version of the DAT for adults called the Differential Aptitude Battery for Personnel and Career Assessment (DAT PCA) is also available and allows employers to determine an individual's current ability and aptitude for learning new skills during training.

In the last part of the chapter we reviewed a number of different kinds of special aptitude tests that are frequently used as a screening process to assess one's ability to perform a certain job or to master a new skill at work. We briefly examined special aptitude tests in the areas of clerical ability, mechanical ability, music ability, and artistic ability.

As the chapter neared its conclusion, we noted that a wide variety of helpers offer career and occupational assessment. Although advanced training is not needed to administer and interpret such instruments, these helpers must obtain the skills needed to be able to administer these tests accurately and interpret the results wisely.

The chapter concluded with a discussion of how occupational and career assessment should not be done in a vacuum. We pointed out that there are frequently a myriad of reasons why a person chooses an occupation or a career, including psychodynamic issues, social pressures, environmental concerns, and family issues. We concluded that choosing an occupation or a career should never be the result of only taking a test and that counseling, in addition to assessment, should often be used.

CHAPTER REVIEW

1. Distinguish between interest inventories, multiple aptitude tests, and special aptitude tests.
2. On the Strong Interest Inventory, there are five different types of interpretive scales or indexes. Describe each of them:
   a. General Occupational Themes
   b. Basic Interest Scales
   c. Occupational Scales
   d. Personal Style Scales
   e. Response Summary
3. The Self-Directed Search uses the Holland code to assist in identifying possible personality fit with occupations. Describe how it does this.
4. Describe some possible advantages of the COPSystem over the Strong and the Self-Directed Search.
5. Discuss why factor analysis is important to the development of a good multiple aptitude test.

6. Compare and contrast the different subtests of the ASVAB and the DAT. Which test would you prefer to take?
7. Describe the advantage of a multiple aptitude test, like the DAT or ASVAB, having an interest inventory attached to it.
8. Identify three or four special aptitude tests and discuss why they might be used in lieu of a multiple aptitude test.
9. What might be some disadvantages of special aptitude tests that measure vague constructs like music and art?
10. Discuss the role of the helper in the selection, administration, and interpretation of career and occupational assessment instruments. What kind of training do you think is necessary for an examiner in this area of assessment?

REFERENCES

Armed Service Vocational Aptitude Battery (ASVAB). (2008). *The ASVAB career exploration program counselor manual*. Retrieved September 20, 2008, from http://www.asvabprogram.com/downloads/asvab_counselor_manual.pdf

Brown, M. (2001). Review of the Self-Directed Search, 4th edition [Forms R, E, and CP]. In B.S. Plake and J.C. Impara (Eds.), *The Fourteenth Mental Measurements Yearbook* (pp. 1105–1107). Lincoln, NE: Buros Institute of Mental Measurements.

Brunsman, B. A., & Johnson, C. (2000). Review of the Keynotes Music Evaluation Software Kit. In B. S. Plake, J. C. Imapara and R. A Spies (Eds.), The *Fifteenth Mental Measurements Yearbook*. Lincoln, NE: Buros Institute of Mental Measurements.

Cohen, A. (1995). Review of the Musical Aptitude Profile 1988 revision. In J. C. Conoley and J. C. Impara (Eds.), *The Tweflth Mental Measurements Yearbook* (pp. 663–666). Lincoln, NE: Buros Institute of Mental Measurements.

Consulting Psychologists Press. (2004). *Technical brief for the newly revised Strong Interest Inventory assessment:* Content, reliability, and validity. Retrieved on September 20, 2008, from http://

www.cpp.com/products/strong/StrongTechnical Brief.pdf

Criteriacorp. (2008). *Solutions: Wiesen Test of Mechanical Aptitude (WTMA)*. Retrieved on September 21, 2008, from http://www.criteriacorp.com/solution/wtma.php

EdITS. (n.d.). COPS: *Career Occupational Preference System Interest Inventory. Interest inventory assessment for career exploration and counseling.* Retrieved on September 20, 2008, from http://www.edits.net/cops.html

Fitzpatrick, R. (2001). Review of the Minnesota Clerical Assessment Battery. In B.S. Plake and J. C. Impara (Eds.), *The Fourteenth Mental Measurements Yearbook* (pp. 769–771). Lincoln, NE: Buros Institute of Mental Measurements.

Gottfredson, G. D. & Holland, J. (1996). *Dictionary of Holland occupational codes* (3rd ed.). Lutz, FL: Psychological Assessment Resources.

Hansen, J. C. (1995). *Interest assessment* (Report No. EDO-CG-95-13). Greensboro, NC: ERIC Clearinghouse on Counseling and Student Services. (ERIC Document Reproduction Service No. ED 389-961.)

Hattrup, K. & Schmitt, N. (1995). Review of the Differential Aptitude Test, Fifth Edition. In J. C. Conoley and J. C. Impara (Eds.), *The Twelfth Mental Measurements Yearbook* (pp. 301–305). Lincoln, NE: Buros Institute of Mental Measurements.

Jagger, L., Neukrug, E., & McAuliffe, G. (1992). Congruence between personality traits and chosen occupation as a predictor of job satisfaction for people with disabilities. *Rehabilitation Counseling Bulletin, 36,* 53–60.

Kelly, K. (2003). Review of the Strong Interest Inventory. In B.S. Plake, J. C. Imapara, and R. A Spies (Eds.), *The Fifteenth Mental Measurements Yearbook* (pp. 893–897). Lincoln, NE: Buros Institute of Mental Measurements.

Learning Express. (2001). *Postal worker exam* (2nd ed.). Retrieved June 12, 2004, from http://www.learnatest.com/shop/BookDetail.cfm?coreID=1576853314&type=B&seqNum=0&mbc=POST & sbc=POSTAL

NCS Pearson. (2008a). CISS: *Campbell Interest and Skill Survey.* Retrieved on September 20, 2008, from http://www.pearsonassessments.com/tests/ciss.htm

NCS Pearson. (2008b). *Career Assessment Inventory–The Enhanced Version.* Retrieved on September 20, 2008, from http://www.pearsonassessments.com/tests/cai_e.htm

Psychological Assessment Resources, Inc. (PAR). (2001). *Welcome to the Self-Directed Search by John L. Holland.* Retrieved on July 25, 2004, from http://www.self-directed-search.com/index.html

Pearson. (2008). *Differential Aptitude Tests, Fifth Edition (DAT®).* Retrieved on September 20, 2008, from http://pearsonassess.com/HAIWEB/Cultures/en-us/Productdetail.htm?Pid=015-4060-47X&Mode=summary

Psytech. (2006). *Clerical Test Battery 2 (CTB2).* Psyctech International. Retrieved on September 21, 2008, from http://www.psytech.co.uk/tests/ctb2.htm

Radocy, R. (1998). Review of the Iowa Test of Music Literacy Revised. In J.C. Impara and B.S. Plake (Eds.), *The Thirteenth Mental Measurements Yearbook* (pp. 552–555). Lincoln, NE: Buros Institute of Mental Measurements.

Raymond Corporation. (2008). *Mechanical Aptitude Test MAT-3C RR110-C.* Retrieved on September 21, 2008, from http://www.ramsaycorp.com/products/ mechanicalaptitude.asp

Strong, E. (1926). An interest test for personnel managers. *Journal of Personnel Research, 5,* 194–203.

Ton, M., & Hansen, J. (2001). Using a person-environment fit framework to predict satisfaction and motivation in work and marital roles. *Journal of Career Assessment, 9*(4), 315–331.

USPS. (2007). *Post office jobs. Federal Jobs Net.* Retrieved on September, 21, 2008, from http://federaljobs.net/usps.htm

Valpar. (2008). SIGI 3: *Educational and career planning software.* Retrieved on September 20, 2008, from http://www.valparint.com

Wilson, V. & Wing, H. (1995). Review of the Differential Aptitude Test for Personnel and Career Assessment. In J. C. Conoley and J. C. Impara (Eds.), *The Twelfth Mental Measurements Yearbook* (pp. 305–309). Lincoln, NE: Buros Institute of Mental Measurements.

Zytowski, D. G. (1994). Tests and counseling: We are still married and living in discriminant analysis. *Measurement and Evaluation in Guidance, 15,* 15–21.

CHAPTER 9

CLINICAL ASSESSMENT: OBJECTIVE AND PROJECTIVE PERSONALITY TESTS

Several years ago I was asked to assess a client who had been diagnosed with a dissociative identity disorder. At our first meeting, she told me that she had 254 personalities. I was fascinated. However, I was not testing her for the disorder, as she was in treatment, accepted her disorder, and was working hard on integrating her personalities. However, she had been denied Social Security disability compensation, and I had been asked to assess her ability to work. Thus, I needed to carefully choose the tests that I would use to assess her. When I had finished administering the tests, I concluded that she was not able to work at that time, but in a year she might be able to do so. She was not happy with my conclusion.

One of my former students was doing her dissertation on the relationship between self-actualizing values and the number of years one had meditated. She went to an Ashram and obtained permission from dozens of meditators to participate in her study. Using a test to measure self-actualizing values, she tested the meditators and correlated their test results with the number of years they had been meditating. She was quite surprised to find no relationship and subsequently came up to me and said, "There must be something wrong with this study, because I know there is a relationship!" I suggested that there was nothing wrong with her study and that not finding a relationship did not mean that meditation wasn't worthwhile, and indeed, it had already been found to be related to many attributes such as reduced stress levels. She ended up a bit dejected, but with a broader understanding of the limitations of objective tests.

I once was asked to do a broad personality assessment for a high school student some teachers were concerned about. I conducted a clinical interview and gave him some objective and projective tests and was somewhat surprised when a number of the projective tests clearly had a theme of destruction. I duly noted this in my report and warned the school about what I had found. Shortly afterward, he was arrested for property destruction!

(Ed Neukrug)

This chapter is about clinical assessment, which often includes a clinical interview, objective testing, and/or projective testing. As you can see from the examples above, such assessments have a wide variety of applications and can be an important tool for the clinician or researcher. In this chapter we will define clinical assessment and examine some of the major objective and projective tests used in the clinical assessment process.

DEFINING CLINICAL ASSESSMENT

Clinical assessment involves assessing clients through one or more of the following methods: the clinical interview (see Chapter 12), the administration of informal assessment techniques (Chapter 10), and the administration of objective and projective tests (this chapter). This process is used to gather information from clients for the following purposes:

1. To help clients gain greater insight,
2. To aid in case conceptualization and mental health diagnostic formulations,
3. To assist in making decisions concerning the use of psychotropic medications,
4. To assist in treatment planning,
5. To assist in court decisions (e.g., custody decisions; testing a defendant in a child molestation case),
6. To assist in job placement decisions (e.g., candidates for high-security jobs),
7. To aid in diagnostic decisions for health-related problems (e.g., Alzheimer's),
8. To identify individuals at risk (e.g., students at risk for suicide or students with low self-esteem).

In this chapter we will only look at a small number of objective and projective tests used in the clinical assessment process, but remember that clinical assessment can involve a broad range of assessment instruments. Let's start with a review of some of the more popular objective personality tests.

OBJECTIVE PERSONALITY TESTING

Objective personality tests

Paper-and-pencil tests to assess various aspects of personality

As discussed in Chapter 1, objective personality testing is a type of personality assessment that uses paper-and-pencil tests, often in multiple-choice or true/false formats, to assess various aspects of personality. Each objective personality test measures different aspects of an individual's personality based on the specific constructs defined by the test developer. For example, the Minnesota Multiphasic Personality Inventory (MMPI) measures psychopathology and is used to assist in the diagnosis of emotional disorders. The Myers-Briggs Type Indicator (MBTI)® measures personality based on a construct created by Carl Jung related to how people perceive and make judgments about the world, and Coopersmith's Self-Esteem Inventory (SEI) measures self-esteem based on one's perception of self. Although these three tests measure very different aspects of personality, they all can be useful in developing a picture of a client. Let's take a look at some of the more common objective personality tests and explore how they are used.

COMMON OBJECTIVE PERSONALITY TESTS

Objective personality tests assess various aspects of personality and may increase client insight, identify pathology, and assist in treatment planning; however, how they do this can vary dramatically. In this section we will highlight nine objective personality tests, each of which has a slightly different emphasis (see Table 9.1). In addition, some other popular objective tests will be briefly noted at the end of this section of the chapter.

MMPI-2

Assists in identifying psychopathology; takes skill to interpret

MINNESOTA MULTIPHASIC PERSONALITY INVENTORY—2 The most widely used diagnostic personality test is the Minnesota Multiphasic Personality Inventory (MMPI) which was originally developed by Hathaway and McKinley in 1942. Today, there are currently three versions available: the full version, called the MMPI-2, which was introduced in 1989 (Butcher, Dahlstrom, Graham, Tellegen, & Kaemmer, 1989); an adolescent version, MMPI-A, released in 1992; and a shorter version called the Restructured Form (MMPI-2-RF), which became available in 2008. Both the MMPI-2 and the MMPI-A can be administered individually or in groups and require approximately 90 minutes for test-takers to complete the 567 items by hand. A computerized version is somewhat faster (Groth-Marnat, 2003). The MMPI-2-RF has only 338 items so it can be taken by paper-and-pencil in about 45 minutes or completed on the computer in 30 minutes (Pearson, 2008a). Although administration and scoring of the MMPIs is relatively straightforward, interpretation of the test is not. The MMPI-2 manual states, "Interpreting it demands a high level of psychometric, clinical, personological, and professional sophistication as well as a strong commitment to the ethical principles of test usage" (Butcher et al., 1989, p. 11). To be qualified to administer the test, examiners must have taken a minimum of a graduate level course in psychological testing and a graduate level course in psychopathology.

TABLE 9.1 | OBJECTIVE PERSONALITY TESTS AND THEIR GENERAL USE

Test Name	General Use
Minnesota Multiphasic Personality (MMPI-2)	Psychopathology and Axis I disorders Inventory
Millon Clinical Multiaxial Inventory (MCM-III)	Personality disorders and Axis II symptomatology
Personality Assessment Inventory (PAI)®	Psychopathology (Axis I), some personality disorder features (axis II), and interpersonal traits
Beck Depression Inventory II (BDI-II)	Presence and severity of depression
Myers-Briggs Type Indicator (MBTI)®	Personality types based on Jung's theory of personality (non-clinical population)
16 Personality Factors (16PF)®	General personality characteristics (non-clinical) based on Cattell's work
NEO Personality Inventory-Revised (NEO PI-R)™	Assesses non-clinical personality dimensions using the Big Five personality traits
Coopersmith's Self-Esteem Inventory (SEI)	Level of self-esteem
Substance Abuse Subtle Screening Inventory (SASSI)	Detection of substance dependence

Three of six valid-ity scales are particularly important for interpretation, and ten basic (clinical) scales are helpful in diagnosis

The MMPI-2 provides six validity scales, ten basic (clinical) scales, and fifteen content scales. However, the most commonly used scales are three of the validity scales and the ten basic scales (see Figure 9.1 and Table 9.2).

In interpreting the MMPI, it is important to understand the meaning of each scale. For example, a high L (Lie) score does not necessarily indicate compulsive lying but does indicate that the client is having trouble acknowledging his or her faults and that the entire test results are suspect and may have been "spoiled" (Butcher et al., 1989, p. 23). The Basic or Clinical Scales are particularly useful in diagnosis and treatment planning, and patterns of responses by clients are often used in making decisions about clients as opposed to examining an individual score on any one scale. Since hundreds of patterns can arise from ten scales, computerized scoring is helpful in quickly finding a diagnosis, interpreting client issues, and treatment planning. The MMPI-2 defines "clinical significance" as a T-score of 65 or greater, whereas the older MMPI established clinical significance as a T-score of 70 or higher.

The Content Scales, which are not as frequently used, identify 15 specific traits such as anxiety, fears, anger, cynicism, and low self-esteem, and are useful in creating

FIGURE 9.1 | MMPI-2 PROFILE FORM FOR BASIC SCALES

Based on the clinical interview of Mr. A, above, and his MMPI-II profile, he has a diagnostic impression of dysthymia with hypochondriacal features.

Source: Butcher et. al., (1989). *Manual for administration and scoring: MMPI-2.* Minneapolis, MN: University of Minnesota Press.

TABLE 9.2 | MOST COMMONLY USED SCALES OF THE MMPI—2

Abbreviation and Scale Number	Name	Brief Description
Validity Scales		
L	Lie	Lacks ability to admit minor faults or character flaws; does not necessarily indicate "lying," but that test scores may have been "spoiled."
F	Infrequency	Reflects random scoring which may indicate unwillingness to cooperate, poor reading skills, or "faking bad" to gain special attention.
K	Correction	Tendency to "slant" or "spin" answers to minimize appearance of poor emotional control or personal ineffectiveness.
Basic (Clinical) Scales		
Hs – 1	Hypochondriasis	Excessive concern regarding health with little or no organic basis, and rejecting reassurance of no physical problem.
D – 2	Depression	Depression and/or a depressive episode with feelings of discouragement, pessimism, and hopelessness.
Hy – 3	Conversion Hysteria	Conversion disorders where a sensory or motor problem has no organic basis; denial and lack of social anxiety often accompany symptoms.
Pd – 4	Psychopathic deviant	Frequent hostility toward authority, law, or social convention, with no basis in cultural deprivation, subnormal intelligence, or other disorders.
Mf – 5	Masculinity-femininity	Gender-role confusion and attempting to control homoerotic feelings; also emotions, interests, hobbies differing from one's gender group.
Pa – 6	Paranoia	Paranoia marked by interpersonal sensitivities and tendency to misinterpret intentions and motives of others.
Pt – 7	Psychasthenia	Obsessive-compulsive concerns (excessive worries and compulsive rituals) as well as generalized anxiety and distress.
Sc – 8	Schizophrenia	Wide range of strange beliefs, unusual experiences, and special sensitivities; often accompanied by social or emotional alienation.
Ma – 9	Hypomania	Displaying symptoms found in a manic episode such as hyper-activity, flight of ideas, euphoria, or emotional excitability.
Si – 0	Social introversion	High scores indicate increasing levels of social shyness and desire for solitude; low scores indicate the opposite (social participation).

a more detailed perspective of the client as well as identifying other considerations for counseling.

As compared to the original MMPI, the MMPI-2 has 82 rewritten items. However, these items are so "psychometrically equivalent" to the original test that they have a .98 correlation; hence, the clinical scales are virtually unchanged (Graham, 2000, p. 189). To renorm the MMPI-2 against the non-clinical population, it was restandardized against a sample that included 2600 people living in seven states and was fairly representative of the 1980 U.S. Census; however, both Hispanic and Asian-Americans were slightly underrepresented in the sample (Butcher et al., 1989). Test-retest reliabilities for the basic scales range between .67 and .92 for normal males and .58 and .91 for a similar sample of women. Internal consistency estimates using the Cronbach alpha for the basic scales ranged between .34 and .87. The only evidence of validity provided in the MMPI-2 manual is discriminant validity. As you may recall, discriminant validity is the ability of the instrument to differentiate between different constructs. For example, MMPI-2 scores in depression should be minimally related to scores in hypochondriasis or conversion hysteria. However, the intercorrelations between scales were found to be quite high, primarily because many of the scales share test items (Groth-Marnat, 2003).

The 338 items in the MMPI-2-RF are a subset taken from the lengthier MMPI-2. Consequently, the developers were able to use the same normed data from the MMPI-2 for the newer Restructured Form. A major difference between the MMPI-2 and the MMPI-2-RF, besides the latter's shorter length, is that the MMPI-2-RF has new validity scales, additional High-Order scales, and restructured clinical scales, as well as somatic/cognitive and internalizing scales, externalizing, interpersonal and interest scales, and psychopathology scales (Pearson, 2008a). However, the test best known for measuring severe clinical syndromes including Axis-II personality disorders is the Millon.

MCMI

Used to assess personality disorders (Axis II) and clinical symptomatology

MILLON CLINICAL MULTIAXIAL INVENTORY, THIRD EDITION   The Millon Clinical Multiaxial Inventory (MCMI) has become the second most used objective personality test (Camara, Nathan, & Puente, 2000). The latest version of this test is designed to assess DSM-IV-TR personality disorders and clinical symptomatology (Pearson, 2008b). The MCMI-III, which is generally called the "Millon" (Mill-*on*), focuses on DSM-IV-TR Axis II disorders in contrast to the MMPI's focus on Axis I disorders (Groth-Marnat, 2003). The Millon has 175 true/false items, is written at an eighth-grade reading level, and is designed for individuals 18 years or older. Hence, there is also an adolescent version for ages 13 to 19 called the Millon Adolescent Clinical Inventory or MACI (Pearson, 2008c).

The MCMI-III is much quicker to administer than the MMPI, requiring only 25 minutes (Pearson, 2008b). It can be taken via paper-and-pencil or on a computer. Scoring the Millon can be accomplished by using computer software, hand scoring, optical scan scoring, or a mail-in scoring service. The Millon has six different major scales: Clinical Personality Pattern Scales, Severe Personality Pathology Scales, Clinical Syndrome Scales, Severe Clinical Syndrome Scales, Modifying Indices, and a Validity Index. The sub-scales to these major scales can be seen in Table 9.3.

The Millon uses a unique scoring method called the Base Rate (BR) that converts a raw score to a more meaningful standardized score based primarily on the psychiatric population. To do this, the publishers changed the actual median for a

TABLE 9.3 | THE MILLON CLINICAL MULTIAXIAL INVENTORY-III SCALES

Major Scales	Sub-Scale	Name
Clinical Personality Pattern Scales		
	Scale 1	Schizoid
	Scale 2A	Avoidant
	Scale 2B	Depressive
	Scale 3	Dependent
	Scale 4	Histrionic
	Scale 5	Narcissistic
	Scale 6A	Antisocial
	Scale 6B	Aggressive/Sadistic
	Scale 7	Compulsive
	Scale 8A	Passive-Aggressive
	Scale 8B	Self-Defeating
Severe Personality Pathology Scales		
	Scale S	Schizotypal
	Scale C	Borderline
	Scale P	Paranoid
Clinical Syndrome Scales		
	Scale A	Anxiety
	Scale H	Somatoform
	Scale N	Bipolar: Manic
	Scale D	Dysthymia
	Scale B	Alcohol Dependence
	Scale T	Drug Dependence
	Scale R	Post-Traumatic Stress Disorder
Severe Clinical Syndrome Scales		
	Scale SS	Thought Disorder
	Scale CC	Major Depression
	Scale PP	Delusional Disorder
Modifying Indices		
	Scale X	Disclosure
	Scale Y	Desirability
	Scale Z	Debasement
Validity Index		
	V	Validity

non-psychiatric, or normal person, by setting it at 35, while the actual median for the psychiatric population is also changed and set at 60. A BR of 75 indicates that some of the features of that characteristic are present, while a BR of 85 indicates that the trait is clearly present (Groth-Marnat, 2003).

The norms for the interpretive report came from a clinical sampling of 998 people with a wide variety of diagnoses (Pearson, 2008b). There is also an additional norm group that can be used for a special Corrections Report that is based on 1,676 incarcerated inmates. The Corrections Report provides information that may be of value when doing a forensic evaluation, such as whether there is a need for mental health or anger management services, if the individual has suicidal tendencies, whether the person may be an escape risk, and so on.

Reliability coefficient alphas ranged from .67 to .90 for the scales and were predominately in the .80s (Millon as cited in Groth-Marnat, 2003). With regard to evidence of validity based on other variables (convergent validity), the MCMI-2 scales have been correlated with several other scales and measures such as the MMPI and the BDI. In general, most of the correlations were healthy and expected. One surprise was a low correlation (.29) between the MCMI-III Paranoid scale and the MMPI-2 Paranoia scale. Other studies using the MCMI-2 have demonstrated moderate to high predictive validity for the instrument with DSM-IV-TR diagnoses.

PAI

Aid in making diagnosis, treatment planning, and screening for psychopathology

PERSONALITY ASSESSMENT INVENTORY® The Personality Assessment Inventory (PAI®) is designed to aid in making clinical diagnoses, screening for psychopathology, and assist in treatment planning (Boyle & Kavan, 1995; PAR, 2005a). This instrument was designed in 1991 by Leslie Morey and continues to gain popularity with both clinicians and researchers. Some have argued that the PAI may be more effective than the MMPI-2 (McDevitt-Murphy, Weathers, Flood, Eakin, & Benson, 2007; White, 1996).

The PAI is for use with adults 18 years and older, contains 344 items, which are written at a fourth-grade reading level, and takes 50 to 60 minutes to complete (PAR, 2005a). Respondents rate items using a 4-point ordinal scale with choices of false (not at all true), slightly true, mainly true, and very true. Scoring can be completed by hand in 15 to 20 minutes. It can also be scored on a computer or mailed to PAR, Inc., both of which will generate an interpretive report. Profile results provide 4 validity scales, 11 clinical scales, 5 treatment scales, and 2 interpersonal scales. Raw scores are converted to T-scores and percentiles (see Table 9.4), and two standard deviations or greater ($T \geq 70$) are generally used as an indicator of scales requiring clinical attention.

The PAI was normed using three samples: 1,000 adults stratified for gender, race, and age according to U.S. Census statistics; 1,296 patients from 69 clinical locations; and 1,051 college students (PAR, 2005a). Coefficient alphas for the median of the 22 scales were .81, .86, and .83 for the above three samples, respectively (Boyle & Kavan, 1995). Test-retest reliabilities ranged between .68 and .85; however, inconsistency and infrequency validity scores were low, at .31 and .48, respectively. Numerous researchers have analyzed the PAI, in part, to assess its validity. As an example of concurrent validity, researchers examined the ability of the PAI Borderline features scale to assess 58 participants from an outpatient setting (Stein, Pinsker-Aspen, & Hilsenroth, 2007). The PAI was able to correctly classify 73% of the individuals as either having Borderline Personality Disorder or not. In a study of 90 individuals who had been exposed to a trauma, the participants were classified into one of four categories: post-traumatic stress disorder (PTSD), depressive, social phobia, and well-adjusted (McDevitt-Murphy et al., 2007). Both the MMPI-II and PAI were administered to the groups. Results suggested that the PAI anxiety-related disorders scale was more accurate than the MMPI's PTSD scale in identifying and differentiating the four groups.

TABLE 9.4 | PERSONALITY ASSESSMENT INVENTORY SCALES

Validity Scales	• Inconsistency • Infrequency • Negative impression • Positive Impression
Clinical Scales	• Somatic complaints • Anxiety • Anxiety-related disorders • Depression • Mania • Paranoia • Schizophrenia • Borderline features • Antisocial features • Alcohol problems • Drug problems
Treatment Scales	• Aggression • Suicidal ideation • Stress • Nonsupport • Treatment rejection
Interpersonal Scales	• Dominance • Warmth

BDI-II

Quick and easy method to assess depression

BECK DEPRESSION INVENTORY-II   Originally introduced in 1961 by Aaron Beck and his colleagues, the Beck Depression Inventory (BDI) was designed to measure severity of depression (Beck, Steer, & Brown, 2003). The newer version, the BDI-II, was released in 1996, and today the inventory is ranked among the ten most frequently used psychological assessment instruments (Camara et al., 2000).

The BDI-II, which takes only 10 minutes to complete, asks clients to rate 21 questions on a scale from 0 to 3 based on depressive symptoms during the preceding two weeks. Scores are obtained by adding up the total points from the series of answers and are interpreted based on the scales listed in Table 9.5.

TABLE 9.5 | INTERPRETING BECK DEPRESSION INVENTORY SCORES

Score	Level of Depression
0 to 13	No or minimal depression
14 to 19	Mild depression
20 to 28	Moderate depression
29 to 63 (max)	Severe depression
Below 4	Possible faking good

When giving the BDI-II, special attention should be directed to questions 2 (hopelessness), and 9 (suicidal ideation), as scores of 2 or higher may indicate a higher risk of suicide (Beck et al., 2003). The BDI-II is quite useful in identifying and assessing the severity of symptoms of depression; however, as with all tests, it should not be used as a sole criterion for making a diagnosis. Due to its ease of administration, the instrument is also useful as a means of measuring client progress by having the client take the instrument on an ongoing basis (Beck, 1995).

The norm group for the BDI-II included 500 outpatients who had been diagnosed with depression using the DSM-III-R or the DSM-IV. Another smaller sample of 120 Canadian college students was used as a normal comparative group (Beck et al., 2003). Using coefficient alpha, reliability was found to be .92 for outpatients and .93 for college students. As compared to the BDI, the content and criterion validity were increased in the BDI-II by having it more closely conform to the DSM-IV diagnosis criteria. In a study of convergent validity, a correlation of .93 was found for depressed outpatient clients who took both the BDI and BDI-II, and obtained means for the tests were 18.92 and 21.88, respectively (Beck et al., 2003). As was found in this study, scores on the BDI-II are generally about 3 points higher than those on the BDI. Finally, having clients with other disorders take the instrument, and finding scores that were not as high as those of clients with depression, showed discriminant validity.

MBTI

Popular method to assess normal personality; based on Carl Jung's psychological types

MYERS-BRIGGS TYPE INDICATOR®   More than two million people each year take the Myers-Briggs Type Indicator (MBTI)® test, making it the most widely used personality assessment for normal functioning (Quenk, 2000). Although the MBTI® instrument has enjoyed tremendous success and been used in a variety of settings, there has also been a "gap" between scientists' and practitioners' regard for the instrument, which the latest versions have attempted to mend (Mastrangelo, 2001). The MBTI® instrument is based on the original work of Carl Jung (1921/1964) and his book Psychological Types. Through observation, Jung noted that people have basic characteristics along a diametrically opposed continuum regarding several factors, including extroversion or introversion, sensing or intuiting, thinking or feeling.

After reading Jung's book, Katharine Briggs and her daughter Isabel Briggs Myers became fascinated with Jung's typology of people. They ultimately added a fourth dimension to Jung's factors, which they called judging versus perceiving (Fleenor, 2001; Quenk, 2000). Believing this typology could help people with career selection and better understanding of self and others, they created an instrument that eventually became known as the Myers-Briggs Type Indicator® assessment. In 1975 CPP became the exclusive publisher of the MBTI® assessment and has managed and published the assessment since.

Today the MBTI® instrument is used in a wide variety of settings: in therapists' offices to assist clients to develop a deeper understanding of self; in marriage and family counseling sessions and workshops to help couples and families examine differences and similarities of personality; in business and industry to help employees understand why individuals respond the way that they do; and in career counseling to help individuals find careers that match their personality types.

The four dimensions of the MBTI® instrument can be seen in Figure 9.2, and assessment results indicate preferences respondents favor across these four dichotomies. For example, social workers, counselors, and psychologists are often INFP,

Extraversion (E) ----------------------------- **Introversion (I)**
Energy directed   Energy directed inwards
outward to people and   to ideas and concepts
objects

Sensing (S) ------------------------------------ **Intuition (N)**
Perception comes   Perception comes
mainly from the 5   mainly from observing
senses   patterns and hunches

Thinking (T) ----------------------------------- **Feeling (F)**
Processing decisions   Processing decision
based on logic, fact,   based on personal
and rationality   and social values

Judging (J) ------------------------------------ **Perceiving (P)**
Makes decision   Processes decision
quickly based on T or   based on S or N; likes
J; likes organization,   spontaneity, flexibility,
planning, schedules   and diversions

FIGURE 9.2 | THE FOUR MBTI® DICHOTOMIES

INFJ, and ENFJ types, while police officers are often ISTJ or ESTJ types. Although some use the MBTI® assessment as a career selection tool, the manual states that it should not be used as a screening tool for hiring employees (Mastrangelo, 2001).

The latest versions of the MBTI® instrument are forms M and Q. Form M was released in 1998 and contains 93 items with improved accuracy using Item Response Theory (IRT). Form M only takes 15 to 25 minutes to administer, is written at a seventh-grade reading level, and is geared toward individuals 14 and older. It can be hand scored, computer scored, or mailed to the publisher for scoring. A computer-generated profile sheet for form M can be seen in Figure 9.3.

Form Q was released in 2001 and has 144 items, takes 25 to 35 minutes to administer, and is for adults 18 and older. Form Q also uses IRT and the same norm group that form M uses (Consulting Psychologists Press, 2002). The norm group for forms M and Q was a national randomized sample of 3,200 adults. Coefficient alphas for form M are generally .90 or higher for each dichotomous scale. However, another study in the manual using test-retest reliability across all four dichotomies had only 65% of the participants receiving the same score after only four weeks (Mastrangelo, 2001). The MBTI® manual reports several studies providing some evidence of validity. Evidence is sound for the four separate scales, but it is lacking for the synergistic combination of the four scales (Mastrangelo). Another study showing evidence of validity found that 90% of the people taking the test agreed with the results on a self-report best fit. Further evidence of validity was found by comparing the MBTI® assessment with specific scales on the California Psychological Inventory™

Myers-Briggs Type Indicator®
Profile

JANE SAMPLE / ENFP
July 15, 2004

This profile is designed to help you understand your results on the *Myers-Briggs Type Indicator®* (MBTI®) assessment. Based on your individual responses, the MBTI instrument produces results to identify which of sixteen different personality types best describes you. Your personality type represents your preferences in four separate categories, with each category composed of two opposite poles. The four categories describe key areas that combine to form the basis of a person's personality as follows:

- Where you focus your attention — Extraversion (E) or Introversion (I)
- The way you take in information — Sensing (S) or Intuition (N)
- The way you make decisions — Thinking (T) or Feeling (F)
- How you deal with the outer world — Judging (J) or Perceiving (P)

Your MBTI type is indicated by the four letters representing your preferences. Based on your responses to the assessment, your reported MBTI type is ENFP, also described as Extraverted Intuition with Feeling. Your results are highlighted below.

Reported Type: ENFP

Where you focus your attention	**E** Extraversion — People who prefer Extraversion tend to focus their attention on the outer world of people and things.	**I** Introversion — People who prefer Introversion tend to focus their attention on the inner world of ideas and impressions.	
The way you take in information	**S** Sensing — People who prefer Sensing tend to take in information through the five senses and focus on the here and now.	**N** Intuition — People who prefer Intuition tend to take in information from patterns and the big picture and focus on future possibilities.	
The way you make decisions	**T** Thinking — People who prefer Thinking tend to make decisions based primarily on logic and on objective analysis of cause and effect.	**F** Feeling — People who prefer Feeling tend to make decisions based primarily on values and on subjective evaluation of person-centered concerns.	
How you deal with the outer world	**J** Judging — People who prefer Judging tend to like a planned and organized approach to life and prefer to have things settled.	**P** Perceiving — People who prefer Perceiving tend to like a flexible and spontaneous approach to life and prefer to keep their options open.	

Your responses to the MBTI assessment not only indicate your preferences; they also indicate the relative *clarity* of your preferences—that is, how clear you were in expressing your preference for a particular pole over its opposite. This is known as the *preference clarity index*, or pci. The bar graph on the next page charts your pci results. Note that a longer bar suggests you are quite sure about your preference, while a shorter bar suggests you are less sure about that preference.

FIGURE 9.3 | SAMPLE MBTI® PROFILE FOR FORM

Source: Reproduced with permission of the Publisher, CPP, Inc., from the *MBTI® Profile.* Copyright 1998, 2004 by Peter B. Myers and Katharine D. Myers. All rights reserved. MBTI, Myers-Briggs, and Myers-Briggs Type Indicator are trademarks or registered trademarks of the MBTI Trust, Inc.

assessment, a well-known personality instrument that measures basic personality traits somewhat similar to the 16PF discussed in the next section.

16PF

Based on Cattell's 16 bipolar personality traits

SIXTEEN PERSONALITY FACTORS QUESTIONNAIRE (16PF)   The 16 Personality Factors Questionnaire (16PF)®, fifth edition, was developed based on Raymond Cattell's research suggesting 16 primary personality components (Pearson, 2008d; Russell & Karol, 1994). As with the MBTI, the 16PF is not a measure of pathology but rather a method to describe human behavior. The instrument has 185 items written at a fifth-grade level, and it takes about 45 minutes to administer by hand or 30 minutes by computer. Administration can be done individually or in a group, and scoring can be done by hand or computer.

The 16PF profile sheet provides the results in three sections: 16 primary factors, 5 global factors, and 3 validity scales. The 16 primary factors are personality traits along a bipolar continuum. The profile sheet results use sten scores that range from 1 to 10. In Table 9.6, you can see the 16 personality factors and a descriptive summary of the ends of the bipolar continuum.

An "average" sten score will be between 4 and 7, capturing individuals between plus and minus one standard deviation, or the middle 68% of the population. Hence, scores from 1 to 3 or 8 to 10 indicate further deviation from the norm group toward either the left or right end of the bipolar scale and would merit extra attention. As you may remember from chapter 5, a sten score of 1 or 10 indicates a distance greater than two standard deviations from the norm.

The 16PF has five global factors: extraversion, anxiety, tough-mindedness, independence, and self-control. These are a result of factor analysis. As we briefly described in Chapters 3 and 8, factor analysis is a statistical method of determining how individual items or factors correlate (i.e., hold together). For example, if we had written 10 items to capture the construct of sensitivity, we would hope those 10 items would combine (correlate together) to create a factor that is separate from the other items in the test. The 16PF global factors are secondary factors and are a result of how the 16 primary factors hold together. For example, the first global factor, extraversion, is created from combining the primary factors of warmth, liveliness, and social boldness. The global factor of anxiety is created from the primary factors of vigilance, apprehension, and tension. Table 9.7 shows the meaning of the bipolar continuums of the global factors.

The 16PF has three validity scales: Impression management, infrequency, and acquiescence. The impression management scale is a measure of social desirability. An unusually high score may indicate an individual's inability to admit faults or perhaps a desire to "fake good." A low score may indicate a desire to fake bad, or perhaps someone suffering from low self-esteem. The infrequency scale indicates that a respondent answered questions in an unusual way. A high infrequency

TABLE 9.6 | THE 16PF® PRIMARY PERSONALITY FACTORS

Factor	Meaning of left end of scale	Meaning of right end of sale
A: Warmth	Reserved, impersonal, distant	Warm, outgoing, attentive to others
B: Reasoning	Concrete	Abstract
C: Emotional stability	Reactive, emotionally changeable	Emotionally stable, adaptive, mature
E: Dominance	Deferential, cooperative, avoids conflict	Dominant, forceful, assertive
F: Liveliness	Serious, restrained, careful	Lively, animated, spontaneous
G: Rule-consciousness	Expedient, nonconforming	Rule-conscious, dutiful
H: Social boldness	Shy, threat-sensitive, timid	Socially bold, venturesome, thick-skinned
I: Sensitivity	Utilitarian, objective, unsentimental	Sensitive, aesthetic, sentimental
L: Vigilance	Trusting, unsuspecting, accepting	Vigilant, suspicious, skeptical, wary
M: Abstractedness	Grounded, practical, solution-oriented	Abstracted, imaginative, idea-oriented
N: Privateness	Forthright, genuine, artless	Private, discreet, non-disclosing
O: Apprehension	Self-assured, unworried, complacent	Apprehensive, self-doubting, worried
Q1: Openness to change	Traditional, attached to familiar	Open to change, experimenting
Q2: Self-reliance	Group-oriented, affiliative	Self-reliant, solitary, individualistic
Q3: Perfectionism	Tolerates disorder, unexacting, flexible	Perfectionistic, organized, self-disciplined
Q4: Tension	Relaxed, placid, patient	Tense, high energy, impatient, driven

TABLE 9.7 | THE 16PF® GLOBAL FACTORS

Factor	Meaning of left end of scale	Meaning of right end of sale
Extraversion	Introverted, socially inhibited	Extraverted, socially participating
Anxiety	Low anxiety, unperturbed	High anxiety, perturbable
Tough-mindedness	Receptive, open-minded, intuitive	Tough-minded, resolute, unempathic
Independence	Accommodating, agreeable, selfless	Independent, persuasive, willful
Self-control	Unrestrained, follows urges	Self-controlled, inhibits urges

score may represent reading comprehension problems, random responding, or trying to make the right impression. The acquiescence scale measures answering tendencies regardless of content. High acquiescence scores may indicate random responding, misunderstanding item content, or perhaps difficulty evaluating one's self (Russell & Karol, 1994).

The norm group for the 16PF, fifth edition, was taken from a sample of 4,449 people (Russell & Karol, 1994). To stratify the sample to match the U. S. population according to gender, race, age, and education, the norm group was reduced to 2,500. The reliability coefficient alphas for this sample ranged from .64 to .85 for the 16 factors. Two-week test-retest reliabilities from a separate sample of undergraduate students ranged from .69 to .86. Evidence of validity is presented in the administrator's manual in several forms. Factor analysis demonstrates individual items grouped (i.e., factored together) in accordance to the 16 personality factors the test developers had hoped for. Convergent validity was demonstrated through comparing 16PF factors with numerous other personality instruments such as the Myers-Briggs Type Indicator (MBTI), the California Psychological Instrument (CPI), the NEO Personality Inventory – revised (NEO PI-R), and the Personality Research Form (PRF). Criterion-related validity was suggested through comparing 16PF scores with self-esteem (the Coopersmith Self-esteem Inventory), adjustment (Bell's Adjustment Inventory), social skills (the Social Skills Inventory), empathy (CPI), creative potential, and leadership potential.

THE BIG FIVE PERSONALITY TRAITS AND THE NEO PI-R™ & NEO-FFI™   The Big Five personality traits, sometimes referred to as the five-factor model, were first mentioned in the literature by Thurstone (1934). Although Raymond Cattell's research suggested that personality can best be explained through 16 personality traits, numerous independent researchers found that personality variables can be further reduced to five constructs (Raad, 1998). Consequently, and unlike many other instruments, the five-factor model is based on research rather than theory. The five traits are Openness, Conscientiousness, Extraversion, Agreeableness, and Neuroticism ("OCEAN"). The Big Five can be summarized as:

- *Openness* – a willingness or desire to have new experiences, emotions, ideas, and be curious and imaginative; unconventional

- *Conscientiousness* – a sense of duty or self-discipline in one's actions; prefers order and planning; goal driven
- *Extraversion* – having warmth, outgoingness, and a positive attitude; enjoys activity and excitement; high energy
- *Agreeableness* – being cooperative, kind, trusting, and altruistic; believes people are good
- *Neuroticism* – prone toward emotional distress such as anxiety, depression, anger, and impulsivity; emotionally reactive.

NEO PI-R

Uses the Big Five model to assess personality differences

The NEO Personality Inventory – Revised (NEO PI-R)™ is an instrument that measures personality across the five-factor model. NEO in the title is a holdover from an earlier version, when it was called the Neuroticism-Extroversion-Openness Inventory. The current instrument contains 240-items written at a sixth-grade reading level (PAR, 2005b). It can be given to people 17 years or older and takes 35 to 45 minutes to complete. The items are rated using a 5-point Likert-type scale ranging from strongly disagree to strongly agree. Examples of items from the conscientiousness section are "I get chores done right away" and a reversed item, "I leave my belongings around." There are two versions of the test: one is for self-report and the other is for a third-party observer or rater. Each of the Big Five factors consists of six facets or second-order factors that compose the larger constructs (see Table 9.8). Results for the factors and facets are reported using T-Scores which correspond to ranges as follows: below 35 is very low, 35-45 is low, 45-55 is average, 55-65 is high, and 65 and above being very high. In addition, a narrative describing the individual's personality style and 10 personality style graphs that describe 10 broad styles are offered to assist in interpretation of results.

The NEO PI-R is used in numerous countries around the world and is translated into several languages. Reliability alphas from a U.S. sample ranged from .86 to .95 for the Big Five factors and from .56 to .90 for the individual facet scores (PAR, 2005b). Extensive research has been conducted checking the convergent and discriminant validity of the NEO PR-I with other instruments. For example, in a meta-analyses of 24 studies comparing the NEO Big Five factors and Holland's six vocational domains (discussed in Chapter 8), researchers found 5 substantial correlations out of the potential 30 (5 factors × 6 domains) (Larson, Rottinghaus & Borgen, 2002). They were Openness–Artistic, Openness–Investigative, Extraversion–Enterprising, Extraversion–Social, and Agreeableness–Social. In a comparison of the NEO PI and the MBTI, results suggested relationships between the NEO Agreeableness and the MBTI Thinking-Feeling dimensions, the NEO Conscientiousness and MBTI's Thinking-Feeling and Judging-Perceiving constructs, a strong correlation between the NEO Extraversion and MBTI Extroversion-Introversion domains, and no correlation between the NEO Neuroticism scale and any of the MBTI subscales (Furnham, 1996).

Concurrent validity is exemplified in a meta-analyses of 15 samples comparing the NEO PI-R five-factor model and DSM-IV TR personality disorders (Saulsman & Page, 2004). Results indicate neuroticism was associated with high emotional distress personalities such as paranoid, schizotypal, borderline, avoidant, and dependent. Extroversion correlated with gregarious personality qualities such as histrionic and narcissistic, and Lack of Agreeableness related with personalities experiencing interpersonal difficulties like paranoid, schizotypal, antisocial, borderline, and narcicissistic.

Table 9.8 | The NEO PI-R™ Five Factors and 30 Facets

Big Five Factor	Facets
Openness	1. Fantasy 2. Aesthetics 3. Feelings 4. Actions 5. Ideas 6. Values
Conscientiousness	1. Competence 2. Order 3. Dutifulness 4. Achievement striving 5. Self-discipline 6. Deliberation
Extraversion	1. Warmth 2. Gregariousness 3. Assertiveness 4. Activity 5. Excitement seeking 6. Positive emotion
Agreeableness	1. Trust 2. Aesthetics 3. Feelings 4. Actions 5. Ideas 6. Values
Neuroticism	1. Anxiety 2. Hostility 3. Depression 4. Self-consciousness 5. Impulsiveness 6. Vulnerability to stress

A shortened version, called the NEO Five Factor Inventory (NEO-FFI)™ is available for individuals 17 or older. Containing only 60 items, it can be administered individually or in a group in only 10 to 15 minutes (PAR, 2005c). Reliabilities are decreased due to the shorter length with coefficient alphas for the Big Five ranging between .68 and .86 for the self-report version and between .76 to .90 for the observer-rater form. Evidence of validity is suggested through correlations between the shortened NEO-FFI and the full NEO PI-R with the self-report versions correlating between .77 and .92 for the five domains and the observer-rated versions demonstrated relationships from .88 to .94.

COOPERSMITH'S SELF-ESTEEM INVENTORY Coopersmith's Self-Esteem Inventory (SEI) is designed to measure self-esteem of children aged 8 through 15 (Coopersmith,

Coopersmith's SEI

Assesses self-esteem of children in relation to general self, peers, parents, and school

1989). The inventory measures how children regard themselves in relation to four areas: general self (24 items), self in relation to peers (8 items), self in relation to parents (8 items), and self in relation to school (8 items). A total score is obtained by multiplying by 2 the total number of positive self-esteem items chosen by the child. Generally, a total self-esteem score is obtained first, and with individuals showing evidence of low self-esteem, the examiner can go back to the four subscores and determine if one or more areas are particularly low. A lie scale that comprises eight of the items is scored separately, and the authors vaguely state that a "high" lie score can indicate defensiveness. A short form of the test is also available. This form uses 25 of the items and in this case, only a total score is obtained. This form can be used with children and an adapted version of this form has also been used with adults.

Although the manual shows some impressive reliability data, such as internal consistency reliability that ranges from .87 to .90 for grades four through eight, the information is based on some rather dated studies that go back to the early 1970s (Coopersmith, 1989). Similarly, although evidence of construct, concurrent, and predictive validity is given in the manual, the studies are dated and some show meager validity data.

On a positive note, the authors gave the instrument to students in a number of different settings, and thus have broad ethnic comparisons. As a result of differential total scores that are an apparent function of ethnicity, they do not offer one score that is representative of high self-esteem, and instead they leave interpretation of the student's self-esteem score up to the test administrator. They do note that self-esteem should be viewed in broad categories (e.g., low, medium, and high), rather than just one number. Generally speaking, mean scores ranged from the mid-50s to the mid-70s for most of the studies, and the range of standard deviations was between approximately 12 and 20. Finally, due to the dated nature of the instrument, some of the questions may seem a little odd or unclear to some students. Thus, the test is best given one-on-one to assure that students understand the items. This has implications, of course, for group testing, which is desired by some school counselors and others who work with children. Thus, professionals who are interested in examining the self-esteem of children may also want to examine other similar measures, such as the Piers-Harris Children's Self-Concept Scale, the Tennessee Self-Concept Scale, the Multidimensional Self-Esteem Inventory (MSEI), and the Culture-Free Self-Esteem Inventory.

SASSI

A subtle instrument to screen for substance dependence

SUBSTANCE ABUSE SUBTLE SCREENING INVENTORY (SASSI®) The Substance Abuse and Subtle Screening Inventory (SASSI) is a helpful tool for identifying people who have a high probability of a substance-related disorder. There are two versions: the SASSI-3 (Miller, 1999) for adults 18 and older and the SASSI-A2 for adolescents between the ages of 12 and 17 (Miller & Lazowski, 2001). These instruments suggest if an individual has a substance dependency with a 93% and 94% overall accuracy, respectively (Lazowski, Miller, Boye, & Miller, 1998; SASSI, 2001). The adolescent version varies in that it further classifies respondents between substance dependency and substance-abuse disorders. Since both instruments are reasonably similar, we will only discuss the adult version.

The SASSI-3 can be administered in about 30 minutes and scored in 5. The first section, which is the "subtle" component, contains 67 true/false statements, and the second section consists of 26 alcohol- and other drugs-related questions rated on a four-point scale ranging from "never" to "repeatedly." Examples of questions from the first section are "Sometimes I have a hard time sitting still" or "I always feel sure of myself." The second section is overt and asks the frequency of statements such as how often have you "argued with your family or friends because of your drinking?" Scoring generates nine subscales, which are compared against nine rules to determine if there is a low or high probability of a substance-dependence disorder. The instrument has a check for random answering. The subscales can be useful in diagnosis, treatment planning, and interpreting validity. For example, if an individual scores low in the face valid alcohol and other drug scales but scores high in defensiveness and subtle attributes, this indicates that he or she is guarded and may be minimizing his or her substance use. It is important to note that an individual may deny substance abuse, but due to the subtle attributes scale as well as other subscales, the instrument can continue to suggest dependency with high accuracy. If a respondent does not have a dependency but the SASSI suggests he or she does, this is a false positive, as discussed in Chapter 3. A false negative is when a score suggests a low probability of dependency but, in fact, the individual does have an addiction. The SASSI-3 and SASSI-A2 are designed to err towards making false positives rather than false negatives (SASSI, 2001).

Original norming for the SASSI-3 began with a sample of 1,958 participants from clinical settings, prisons, and newspaper advertisements (Lazowski et al., 1998). The sample was reduced to 839 respondents that had full data, such as a DSM-IV diagnosis, and was split in two. One-half of the sample was used to develop the classification rules, and the other half used to test the accuracy of those rules. Reliability coefficient alphas from the larger sample (n = 1,821) were .93 for the overall instrument. Test-retest reliabilities with 40 respondents after a two-week period ranged between .92 and 1.00. Evidence of validity is suggested through comparing the accuracy of the SASSI scores with DSM-IV criteria. As you may recall from Chapter 3, this is criterion-related validity because the developers compared their instrument (SASSI-3) with another criterion (DSM-IV diagnosis) to suggest validity. The comparison between SASSI scores and substance-dependency diagnosis in this sample was accurate 94% of the time (Lazowski et al.).

The SASSI-3 profile sheet provides nine subscales, which can be useful in providing additional information for diagnosis and treatment planning. The nine scales are face valid alcohol, face valid other drugs, symptoms, obvious attributes, subtle attributes, defensiveness, supplemental addiction scale, family vs. controls, and correctional. For example, if an individual has a relatively high face valid alcohol score, symptoms score, attribute scores, and a low defensiveness score, this suggests that he or she is open about using, acknowledges that he or she may have a problem, and is likely ready for treatment. Extremely low SASSI defensiveness scores are often associated with individuals who are experiencing depression (SASSI, 2001). If a profile has a low face valid scores, symptoms scores, and attribute scores, but a high defensiveness score, this suggests that person is likely guarded, resistant, faking good, and precontemplative regarding his or her readiness for change. You would likely approach this individual differently regarding his or her substance use than the previous example.

OTHER COMMON OBJECTIVE PERSONALITY TESTS   Numerous other objective personality tests are available, but we have room to describe just a couple of other personality instruments here. The Taylor-Johnson Temperament Analysis 2002 Edition assesses personality variables that affect social, family, marital, work, and other environments. It is used in counseling emotionally normal adolescents and adults as individuals, couples, families, or in vocational situations (Axford & Boyle, 2005). The Taylor-Johnson Temperament Analysis can be used for relationship assessment; however, other instruments have been created specifically to appraise marriages or partnerships. For instance, the Marital Satisfaction Inventory – Revised (MSI-R) is an instrument to assess the severity and nature of the conflict in a relationship or partnership. The inventory takes only 25 minutes to administer, is inexpensive, and has respectable validity and reliability, making it a nice tool for therapists doing relationship counseling (Bernt & Frank, 2001).

PROJECTIVE TESTING

Projective tests

Responses to stimuli are used to interpret personality factors

In Chapter 1, projective personality testing was defined as a type of personality assessment in which a client is presented a stimulus to which to respond, and subsequently, personality factors are interpreted based on the client's responses. We noted that such testing is often used to identify psychopathology and to assist in treatment planning.

When interpretations about client responses are made, they are often based on normative data. However, with projective testing clients respond in an open-ended manner to vague stimuli that results in a wide-range of responses that often limits norm group comparisons. Thus, with these instruments validity is often called into question. Despite this limitation, projective tests can be quite helpful as one additional tool in the clinical assessment process. Dozens of projective tests exist, and we will explore some of the more prevalent ones.

COMMON PROJECTIVE TESTS

The most popular projective tests include the Thematic Apperception Test (TAT); the Rorschach Inkblot Test; the Bender Visual-Motor Gestalt Test, Second Edition; the House-Tree-Person; the Kinetic House-Tree-Person Test; the Sentence Completion Series; and the EPS Sentence Completion. The following discussion offers a brief overview of these instruments.

TAT

Clients create a story based on cards with vague pictures; TAT is based on Murray's need-press personality theory

THE THEMATIC APPERCEPTION TEST AND RELATED INSTRUMENTS   The Thematic Apperception Test (TAT) was developed by Henry Murray and his colleagues in 1938 and consists of a series of 31 cards with vague pictures on them, although only 8 to 12 cards are generally used during an assessment depending on the age and gender of the client as well as the client's presenting issues. Showing the cards one at a time, the examiner asks the client to create and describe a story that has a beginning, middle, and end. The storytelling process allows great access to the client's inner world and shows how that world is affected by the client's needs and by environmental forces, known as *press*.

The ambiguous pictures on the cards are more structured than inkblot tests such as the Rorschach; consequently, the TAT tends to draw out from the client issues related more to current life situations than deep-seated personality structures (Groth-Marnat, 2003) (see Figure 9.4). The TAT is based on Murray's need-press personality theory, which states that people are driven by their internal desires, such as attitudes, values, goals, etc. (needs), or by external stimuli (press) from the environment. Therefore, individuals are constantly struggling to balance these two opposing forces.

The TAT has been extensively researched; however, it still lacks a level of standardization that most objective personality tests have achieved (Groth-Marnat, 2003). There is no universally agreed upon scoring and interpretation method, although most clinicians use a qualitative process of interpreting responses. Hence there is considerable controversy over reliability and validity of the instrument. When scoring systems have been used in a controlled setting, interscorer reliability has been as high as .82 (Pennebaker & King, 1999); however, if responses were interpreted by clinicians outside of a laboratory setting, this figure would likely drop (Groth-Marnat). Studies to show evidence of validity have been difficult to

FIGURE 9.4 | TAT FIGURE 12F

Source: Reprinted by permission of the publisher from Henry A Murray, Thematic Apperception Test, Plate 12F, Cambridge, MA: Harvard University Press. Copyright © 1943 by the President and Fellows of Harvard College.

perform due to the nature of this projective test, but some argue that objective studies of validity are not as important for this test as for other types of instruments (Karon, 2000). For instance, some suggest that the rich narrative detail developed through the TAT gives the therapist a unique window into the client's psyche. Indeed, the value of the TAT seems to be supported by its widespread use, as it is the sixth most frequently used test by both clinical and counseling psychologists (Camara et al., 2000) (see Table 1 in Section Three of Introduction).

Because the cards are dated, and the fact that the human figures in the cards are almost exclusively white, many of the cards may raise historical and cross-cultural bias. The development of Southern Mississippi's TAT (SM-TAT) and the Apperceptive Personality Test (APT) are two attempts to counter some of these problems. The APT has only eight cards with multicultural pictures and an objective scoring method. Although the SM-TAT and APT are probably superior instruments (more modern, more rigorous methodology, and greater validity), the long tradition of the TAT will probably prevent its replacement (Groth-Marnat, 2003).

In addition to the TAT, the Children's Apperception Test (CAT), designed for children ages 3 to 10, has been developed. Because children have shorter attention spans than adults, the instrument has only 10 cards, and due to the fact that children tend to relate more easily to animals than humans, the pictures depict animals. In addition, a later version of the CAT, the CAT-H, was made that depicts humans. Despite the development of these instruments, the TAT is still frequently used with children, probably due to its familiarity among clinicians.

Rorschach Inkblot Test

Clients are asked to identify what they see in 10 inkblots; the unconscious mind "projects" itself onto the image

RORSCHACH INKBLOT TEST   Herman Rorschach developed his famous inkblot test in 1921 by splattering ink onto pieces of paper and folding them in half to form a symmetrical image (see Figure 9.5). After much experimentation, he chose 10 cards to create the Rorschach Inkblot Test that is still used today. When giving the Rorschach, clinicians show clients the cards, one at a time, and ask them to talk about what they see on the card. A follow-up inquiry with clients addresses issues of what they actually saw, how they saw it, and where on the card it was seen. Ultimately, the clinician wants to see exactly what the client saw on the card.

Rorschach, a student of Carl Jung, believed the ambiguous shapes of the inkblots allowed the test-taker to project his or her unconscious mind onto these images. By 1959 the Rorschach had become the most frequently used instrument in clinical practice (Sundberg, 1961), and it continues to be one of the most frequently used projective personality test (Camara et al., 2000; Hogan, 2005). Although it has had tremendous popularity, it has also been closely scrutinized and criticized. By 1955, more than 3,000 journal articles had been written about it (Exner, 1974), and a recent ERIC and PsychInfo database search shows more than 8500 articles in which the Rorschach is cited. The greatest difficulty with the Rorschach has been providing adequate validity. Another challenge of the Rorschach test is that it requires extensive training and practice to use. However, the authors of the current text believe this instrument still has merit and can be a useful tool in the assessment process (see Box 9.1).

Exner's scoring system examines location, determinants, and content

One of the most popular scoring systems for the Rorschach was developed by Exner (1974). This system uses three components: location, determinants, and content. Location is the portion of the blot to which the response occurred, and the examinee's responses are broken down into categories such as the whole blot (w), common

FIGURE 9.5 | INKBLOT SIMILAR TO THOSE ON THE RORSCHACH

Source: Hulton Archive/Getty Images

details (D), unusual details (Dd), and white space details (S). Determinants are used to describe the manner in which the examinee understood what he or she saw, and these are broken down into (1) form ("that looks just like a bat"), (2) color (e.g., "it's blood, because it's red") (3) shading ("it looks like smoke because it's grayish-white"). Finally, content is scored based on 22 categories such as whole human, human detail, animal, art, blood, clouds, fire, household items, sex, and so on. Specific content can hold

---

BOX 9.1 | RORSCHACH USE IN CLINICAL PRACTICE

Card IV of the Rorschach is known by some as the "father card" because it shows what some see as a hefty, overbearing figure with a large penis. When I was giving the Rorschach to a 17-year-old female high school student, I obtained what is sometimes called a "shock response." I showed her this card and although she had made fairly normal responses to the other cards, when seeing this card she said to me, rather emphatically, "I see nothing there." Upon

inquiry later, I again asked her to give me a response to that card, at which point she firmly put the card face down and said, "I told you I didn't see anything there." When all testing was complete, I looked at the young woman and asked, "Were you molested?" at which point she broke down and started to sob.... This was the beginning of counseling for this young woman who had never shared this secret before.

—Ed Neukrug

meaning; for instance, a goat can be an indication of a person being obstinate, or a number of animal responses by an adult could be an indication of immature psychosexual development (children tend to include lots of animals in their responses). Once all of the data have been recorded, a fairly complex series of calculations are used to create numerical ratios, percentages, and derivations with which to interpret the results. Scoring systems such as Exner's are very complex and are important ways of managing the large amount of interpretive material the client is presenting.

Bender Gestalt II

Assists in identifying developmental, psychological, or neurological deficits

BENDER VISUAL-MOTOR GESTALT TEST, SECOND EDITION   Lauretta Bender originally published the Bender Visual-Motor Gestalt Test in 1938, and after several revisions, it is now called the Bender Gestalt II. A brief test that takes only 5 to 10 minutes to administer, it measures an individual's developmental level and psychological functioning and is also used to assess neurological deficits after a traumatic brain injury. The test asks children aged 4 to 7 and individuals 8 to 85+ to draw the nine figures shown in Figure 9.6. Children 4 to 7 have four additional figures to replicate, and individuals 8 to 85 have three additional figures to copy.

The latest version of the instrument, the Bender Gestalt II, used a norm group of 4,000 individuals who were representative of the 2000 U.S. Census (Riverside Publishing, 2006). This version uses a new, global, 5-point scoring system. A score of 0 represents no resemblance or scribbling, and a score of 4 represents a nearly perfect drawing (Brannigan, Decker, & Madsen, 2004). This version provides standard scores, T-scores, and percentile ranks. As you might suspect, the test can examine psychomotor development of children by comparing a child's response to mean responses of children belonging to the child's age group; personality factors such as compulsivity in completing the drawing accurately (graduate students!); and neurological impairment, such as might be evidenced when an individual cannot accurately place the diamond in drawing 8 (see Figure 9.6).

Accurately interpreting a number of these factors takes advanced training and should not be attempted without such preparation. The original version of the Bender Gestalt showed some evidence that it was measuring the factors it purported to measure, and reliability data showed test-retest reliability at .84 while interrater reliability was shown to be in the low to mid .90s (Naglieri, Obrzut, & Boliek, 1992). The newest version of the test shows even more promise at measuring the educational and psychological constructs it is designed to measure, and the test should continue to evidence high reliability estimates (Brannigan et al., 2004).

Drawing tests

Quick, simple, and effective projective tests

HOUSE-TREE-PERSON AND OTHER DRAWING TESTS   It's not quite clear when the use of drawing tests began, but over the last 50 years they have become some of the most popular, simple, and effective projective devices. By asking clients to draw simple pictures, one can gain tremendous insight into a client's life and perhaps unconscious undertow.

Buck (1948) introduced the original House-Tree-Person (H-T-P) drawing test when he simply asked clients to draw a house, a tree, and a person on three separate pieces of paper. The Kinetic House-Tree-Person Drawing Test is slightly different in that the client is asked to draw all the figures "with some kind of action" on

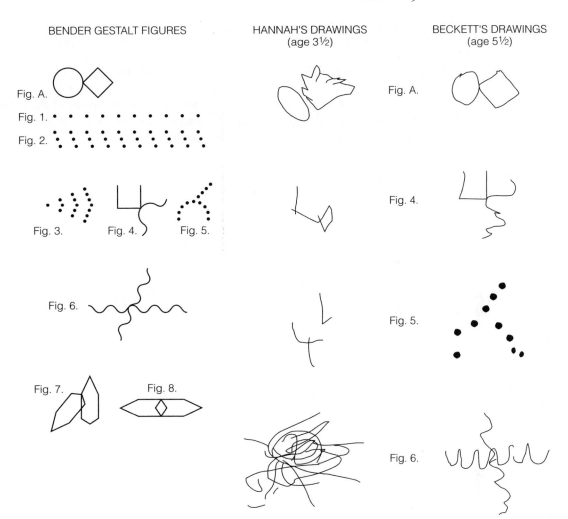

FIGURE 9.6 | **THE BENDER GESTALT FIGURES**

Above are reproductions of four of nine figures of the Bender Visual Motor Gestalt from two children who are developmentally on target. When Hannah couldn't reproduce figure 6, she became very frustrated. Look at how much easier it is for the older child, Beckett, to reproduce the figures.

one sheet of paper (8½ × 11 presented horizontally) (Burns, 1987, p. 5). Burns believes the tree is the universal metaphor for human development as seen in religion, myth, poetry, art, and sacred literature:

> In drawing a tree, the drawer reflects his or her individual transformation process. In creating a person, the drawer reflects the self or ego functions interacting with the tree to create a larger metaphor. The house reflects the physical aspects of the drama. (p. 3)

Numerous books and materials describe how to specifically interpret the H-T-P and K-H-T-P drawings. Table 9.9 provides examples of a few interpretive suggestions (Burns).

Other drawing tests exist, such as the Draw-A-Man, Draw-A-Woman, or the Kinetic Family Drawing, which asks the individual to draw his or her family doing something together. These tests all try to tap into unconscious aspects of the individual's self by focusing on slightly different content. Drawing tests do not require artistic prowess on the part of the client, are quickly administered, and can often produce important interpretive material for the clinician.

Sentence completion tests

Can reveal unconscious issues, but validity and reliability information is unavailable

SENTENCE COMPLETION TESTS   "This book is ——————." Completing a sentence has been used as a projective device since Galton and Jung (see Chapter 1), and although you are not likely to see a sentence stem asking about a specific book, you are likely to see sentence stems that ask you to describe your relationship with your mother, father, spouse, lover, friends, and so on. Two of the more common sentence completion tests are the Sentence Completion Series and the EPS Sentence Completion Technique. In addition, clinicians will sometimes create their own sentence completion tests that can be used when giving a personality battery.

TABLE 9.9 | SAMPLE OF SUGGESTED K-H-T-P INTERPRETATIONS (BURNS, 1987)

Characteristic	Interpretation
General	
Unusually large drawings	Aggressive tendencies; grandiose tendencies; possible hyper or manic conditions
Unusually small drawings	Feelings of inferiority, ineffectiveness or inadequacy; withdrawal tendencies; feelings of insecurity
Very short, circular, sketch strokes	Anxiety, uncertainty, depression, and timidity
House	
Large chimney	Concerns about power, psychological warmth, or sexual masculinity
Very small door	Reluctant accessibility; shyness
Absence of windows	Suggests withdrawal and possible paranoid tendencies
Tree	
Broken or cut-off branches	Feelings of trauma
Upward pointed branches	Reaching for opportunities in the environment
Slender trunk	Precarious adjustment or hold on life
Person	
Unusually large head	Overvaluation of intelligence; dissatisfaction with body; preoccupation with headaches
Hair emphasis on head, chest, or beard	Virility striving; sexual preoccupation
Wide stance	Aggressive defiance and/or insecurity

The Sentence Completion Series is a "semi-projective" series of tests for gathering personality and psychodiagnostic information from adolescents and adults. The series contains eight forms with 50 sentence stems per form. Individual forms address specific issues such as family, marriage, work, aging, and so on. An interpretive manual makes very broad suggestions about how to interpret the responses, such as assessing the examinees general tone and level of defensiveness; however, there is no objective scoring methodology. In addition, there is no reliability, validity, or norm data. It is certainly a useful instrument, but its greatest weakness is the lack of any psychometric data (Moreland & Werner, 2001).

The EPS Sentence Completion Technique, published by Psychological Assessment Resources, is specifically designed for working with clients who are mildly mentally retarded or of borderline intelligence. The publisher defines this range as an IQ between 55 and 83. The instrument contains 40 sentence stems that can be used to elicit responses in one of nine problem themes such as interpersonal relationships, work and school, sexuality, residential living, and so on. An individual can give the test without graduate training in testing; however, interpretation requires graduate level schooling. As with the previous instrument, there is no objective scoring method, norm data, nor validity and reliability information (Peterson & Reinehr, 1998).

Although questions about the validity and reliability of sentence completion tests remain, it is clear that these instruments can provide a quick method of obtaining a client's feelings and unconscious thoughts about important issues in the client's life.

THE ROLE OF HELPERS IN CLINICAL ASSESSMENT

Because clinical assessment can add one more piece of knowledge about a client, it should always be considered as an additional tool to use. Therefore, all helpers can, and perhaps should, be involved in some aspects of clinical assessment. For instance, an elementary school counselor might consider using a self-esteem inventory when working with young children to help identify students who are struggling with self-esteem issues, while a high school counselor might want to use any of a wide range of objective personality measures to help identify concerns and aid in setting goals for students. College counselors, agency clinicians, social workers, and private practice professionals all might use a wide range of clinical assessment tools as part of their repertoire to help identify issues and devise strategies for problem solving. Clinicians should reflect on what kinds of clinical assessment tools would benefit their clients at their particular setting and whether they have sufficient training to give such assessments (e.g., projective tests generally require advanced training).

FINAL THOUGHTS ON CLINICAL ASSESSMENT

The clinical assessment process assists helpers in making decisions that often will affect clients' lives in critical ways. Such decisions can result in persons being labeled, institutionalized, incarcerated, stigmatized, placed on medication, losing or gaining a job, being granted or denied access to their children, and more. Test givers should remember the impact that their decisions will have on clients and monitor the quality of the tests they use, their level of competence to administer tests, and their ability to make accurate interpretations of client material. Acting in any other fashion is practicing incompetence.

SUMMARY

We began this chapter by noting that clinical assessment examines the client through multiple methods, including the clinical interview, the administration of informal assessment techniques, and the administration of objective and projective tests. This process is used (1) as an adjunct to counseling, (2) for case conceptualization and diagnostic formulations, (3) to determine psychotropic medications, (4) for treatment planning, (5) for court decisions, (6) for job placement, (7) to aid in the diagnosis of health-related problem (e.g., Alzheimer's), and (8) to screen for people at risk (e.g., those who might commit suicide).

In the next part of the chapter we examined a number of widely used objective personality tests. First we looked at the MMPI-2 which provides a number of scales, of which the most commonly used are the three validity scales (lie, infrequency, and correction) and the ten basic (clinical) scales: hypochondriasis, depression, conversion hysteria, psychopathic deviant, masculinity-femininity, paranoia, psychasthenia, schizophrenia, hypomania, and social introversion.

In contrast to the MMPI-2, which assesses mostly Axis I disorders, we noted that the Millon assesses DSM-IV-TR Axis II disorders and clinical symptomatology. This test offers six major scales, including Clinical Personality Pattern Scales, Severe Personality Pathology Scales, Clinical Syndrome Scales, Severe Clinical Syndrome Scales, Modifying Indices, and a Validity Index. The Millon sets a Base Rate (BR) to determine responses that indicate a trait's presence.

The PAI is an assessment that offers information regarding both Axis I and II disorders and is growing in popularity. The PAI contains four validity scales, five treatment scales, two interpersonal scales, and 11 clinical scales which include somatic complaints, anxiety, anxiety-related disorders, depression, mania, paranoia, schizophrenia, borderline features, antisocial features, alcohol problems, and drug problems.

The Beck Depression Inventory-II (BDI-II), another very popular objective test, asks 21 questions related to depression, and can be quickly answered and scored. The test is valuable for assessing depression or suicidal ideation, and it can be used on an ongoing basis for the evaluation of positive changes in counseling.

The Myers-Briggs Type Indicator (MBTI)®, which measures normal personality functioning, is based on Jung's six psychological types as well as two additional types identified by the test's creators, Katharine Briggs and Isabel Briggs Myers. The four opposing personality dichotomies are as follows: extroverted (E) versus introverted (I), sensing (S) versus intuiting (N), thinking (T) versus feeling (F), judging (J) versus perceiving (P). Some evidence shows that combinations of the four dichotomies may indicate certain global personality traits.

The 16PF® was developed based on the work of Raymond Cattell and is used to describe the 16 traits of personality that he identified. We learned that similar to the MBTI, the 16 primary scales are bipolar in nature, and scores reflect an individual's personality. The instrument additionally contains five global factors based on a factor analysis of the 16 primary scales, and three validity scales.

The NEO Personality Inventory-Revised (NEO PI-R) TM and NEO Five-Factor Inventory (NEO-FFI) TM use the research based on the Big Five personality model. The Big Five personality traits are Openness, Conscientiousness, Extraversion, Agreeableness, and Neuroticism. Each of the five factors contains an additional six facets or subscales. We discovered that the NEO PI-R is the full-length version of the instrument that takes about 40 minutes to administer. The NEO-FFI is the shortened version, taking 10 to 15 minutes to complete.

Coopersmith's Self-Esteem Inventory (SEI), another objective test we examined, assesses how children aged 8 through 15 regard themselves in relation to four areas: general self, self in relation to peers, self in relation to parents, and self in relation to school. Although the manual shows some impressive validity and reliability data, most of the data are based on studies that go back to the early 1970s. We went on to discuss some other common objective personality tests and relationship inventories.

The Substance Abuse Subtle Screening Inventory (SASSI) has separate versions for adolescents and adults to screen for potential substance dependence. We learned that a portion of the instrument is "subtle" and attempts to capture dependency regardless of whether the examinee is attempting to "fake good" (i.e., minimize or deny substance use). The subscales can be interpreted to evaluate a potential client's readiness for change.

In the last part of the chapter we examined projective tests that are often used to identify psychopathology and to assist in treatment planning. The first projective test we examined was the Thematic Apperception Test (TAT). Developed by Henry Murray in 1938, the TAT consists of 31 cards with vague pictures on them. Showing select cards, the examiner asks the client to tell a story that has a beginning, middle, and end. Client responses are interpreted based on Murray's need-press personality theory, which states that people are driven by their internal desires (needs) or by the external stimuli (press) from their environment. Because some view the TAT pictures as being dated and culturally biased, updated versions of the test have been developed. However, many clinicians continue to prefer the original TAT.

The Rorschach was the next projective test we examined. Developed in 1921 by Herman Rorschach, the examiner asks the client to reveal everything he or she sees on each of 10 inkblots. Interpretation of responses assumes that the client is projecting onto the inkblot his or her unconscious thoughts. One of the most well-known scoring systems for the Rorschach, which was developed by Exner, looks at location, or portion of the blot where the response occurred; determinants, or the manner in which the examinee understood what he or she saw; and content, or what the examinee actually saw.

The Bender Visual-Motor Gestalt Test was originally published in 1938 by Lauretta Bender. Now called the Bender Gestalt II, it is a brief test that asks a client to copy a number of figures. Interpretation of client drawings reveals information about the client's developmental level and psychological functioning, as well as neurological deficits after a traumatic brain injury.

As the chapter continued, we looked at a number of drawing tests, including the House-Tree-Person, the Kinetic House-Tree-Person, Draw-A-Man, Draw-A-Woman, and Kinetic Family Drawing. We pointed out that these drawings symbolize issues and developmental changes in a person's life and that interpretation of such drawings takes a well-trained clinician who understands the multiple meanings of objects.

Sentence completion tests were the final type of projective test we examined in the chapter. We noted that such tests present stems to which the client can respond. We pointed out that such sentence completion tests provide a quick method of accessing a client's feelings and unconscious thoughts about important issues in his or her life.

As the chapter neared its conclusion, we highlighted the fact that clinicians in all settings should consider when it might be appropriate to use a clinical assessment tool. Such tools can add to the clinician's understanding of the client and can aid in treatment planning. We concluded by noting that the clinical assessment process results in making decisions for clients that often will affect their lives in critical ways and that test givers should remember the impact these decisions will have on clients.

CHAPTER REVIEW

1. Describe some of the uses of clinical assessment.
2. Distinguish between objective and projective testing and compare and contrast how each can be used in clinical assessment.
3. For each of the following tests, describe its main purpose, the kinds of scales that are used in test interpretation, and the population for which it is geared.
    a. Minnesota Multiphasic Personality Inventory (MMPI-2)
    b. Millon Clinical Multiaxial Inventory (MCMI-III)
    c. Personality Assessment Inventory (PAI)
    d. Beck Depression Inventory II (BDI-II)
    e. Myers-Briggs Type Indicator (MBTI)
    f. 16 Personality Factors Questionniare (16PF)
    g. NEO Personality Inventory – Revised (NEO PI-R)
    h. Coopersmith Self-Esteem Inventory (SEI)
    i. Substance Abuse Subtle Screening Inventory (SASSI-3)

4. For each of the following tests, briefly describe its main purpose, how it is given, the population for which it is geared, and how test results are interpreted.
    a. Thematic Apperception Test (TAT)
    b. Rorschach Inkblot Test
    c. Bender Visual-Motor Gestalt Test, Second Edition
    d. House-Tree-Person Test
    e. Kinetic House-Tree-Person Test
    f. Sentence Completion Series
    g. EPS Sentence Completion
5. Because many projective tests do not have the level of test worthiness of objective personality tests, some argue that their use should be curtailed. What are your thoughts on this subject?
6. Discuss the role of helpers in objective and projective testing.

REFERENCES

Axford, S., & Boyle, G. (2005). *Review of the Taylor-Johnson Temperament Analysis 2002 Edition. The Sixteenth Mental Measurements Yearbook.* Retrieved from the Mental Measurements Yearbook database.

Beck, A. T., Steer, R. A., & Brown, G. K. (2003). *BDI-II manual.* San Antonio, TX: Psychological Corporation.

Beck, J. (1995). *Cognitive therapy: Basics and beyond.* New York: Guilford Press.

Bernt, F., & Frank, M. L. (2001). *Review of the Marital Satisfaction Inventory* – Revised. In B. S. Plake and J. C. Impara (Eds.), *The Fourteenth Mental Measurements Yearbook* (pp. 710–714). Lincoln, NE: Buros Institute of Mental Measurements.

Boyle, G. J., & Kavan, M. G. (1995). *Review of the Personality Assessment Inventory.* In J. C. Conoley and J. C. Impara (Eds.), *The Twelfth Mental Measurements Yearbook.* Lincoln, NE: Buros Institute of Mental Measurements. Retrieved from Mental Measurements Yearbook database.

Brannigan, G., Decker, S., & Madsen, D. (2004). *Innovative features of the Bender-Gestalt II and expanded guidelines for the use of the global scoring system. Assessment Service Bulletin Number 1.* Retrieved on October 1, 2008, from http://www.riverpub.com/products/bender/pdf/BenderII_ASB1.pdf

Buck, J. (1948). *The H-T-P test. Journal of Clinical Psychology, 4,* 151–159.

Burns, R. (1987). *Kinetic House-Tree-Person drawings (K-H-T-P): An interpretative manual.* New York: Brunner/Mazel.

Butcher, J., Dahlstrom, W., Graham, J., Tellegen, A., & Kaemmer, B. (1989). *Manual for administration and scoring: MMPI-2.* Minneapolis: University of Minnesota Press.

Camara, W., Nathan, J., & Puente, A. (2000). Psychological test usage: Implications in professional psychology. *Professional Psychology: Research and Practice, 31,* 141–154.

Coopersmith, S. (1989). *Self-Esteem Inventory.* Palo Alto, CA: Consulting Psychologists Press.

Consulting Psychologists Press (CPP). (2002). *Comparing the MBTI Form G and Form M.* Retrieved on October 1, 2008, from http://www.cpp.com/products/mbti/FormM_vs_FormG.pdf

Exner, J. (1974). *The Rorschach: A comprehensive system.* New York: Wiley.

Fleenor, J. (2001). Review of the Myers-Briggs Type Indicator Form M. In B. S. Plake and J. C. Impara (Eds.), *The Fourteenth Mental Measurements Yearbook* (pp. 816–818). Lincoln, NE: Buros Institute of Mental Measurements.

Furnham, A. (1996). The big five versus the big four: the relationship between the Myers-Briggs Type Indicator (MBTI) and NEO-PI five factor model of personality. *Personality and Individual Differences, 21,* 303–307.

Graham, J. (2000). *MMPI-2: Assessing personality and psychopathology* (3rd ed.). New York: Oxford University Press.

Groth-Marnat, G. (2003). *Handbook of psychological assessment* (4th ed.). Hoboken, NJ: Wiley.

Hogan, T. P. (2005). Widely used psychological tests. In G. P. Koocher, J. C. Norcross, & S. S. Hill (Eds.), *Psychologists' desk reference (2nd ed.)* (pp. 101–104). New York: Oxford University Press.

Jung, C. (1964). *Psychological types* (Trans. H. G. Baynes). London, England: Pantheon. (Original work published in 1921.)

Karon, B. (2000). The clinical interpretation of the Thematic Apperception Test, Rorschach, and other clinical data: A reexamination of statistical versus clinical prediction. *Professional Psychology: Research and Practice, 31,* 230–233.

Larson, L. M., Rottinghaus, P. J., & Borgen, F. H. (2002). Meta-Analyses of big six interests and big five personality factors. *Journal of Vocational Behavior, 61,* 217–239.

Lazowski, L. E., Miller, F. G., Boye, M. W., & Miller, G. A. (1998). Efficacy of the Substance Abuse Subtle Screening Inventory-3 (SASSI-3) in identifying substance dependence disorders in clinical settings. *Journal of Personality Assessment, 71,* 114–128.

Mastrangelo, P. (2001). Review of the Myers-Briggs Type Indicator Form M. In B. S. Plake and J. C. Impara (Eds.), *The Fourteenth Mental Measurements Yearbook* (pp. 818–819). Lincoln, NE: Buros Institute of Mental Measurements.

McDevitt-Murphy, M. E., Weathers, F. W., Flood, A. M., Eakin, D. E., & Benson, T. A. (2007). The utility of the PAI and the MMPI-2 for discriminating PTSD, depression, and social phobia in trauma-exposed college students. *Assessment, 14,* 181–195.

Miller, G. A. (1999). *The SASSI manual: Substance abuse measures* (2nd ed.). Springville, IN: SASSI Institute.

Miller, G. A., & Lazowski, L. E. (2001). *Adolescent SASSI-A2 manual.* Springville, IN: SASSI Institute.

Moreland, K., & Werner, P. (2001). Review of the Sentence Completion Series. In B. S. Plake and J. C. Impara (Eds.), *The Fourteenth Mental Measurements Yearbook* (pp. 1109–1110). Lincoln, NE: Buros Institute of Mental Measurements.

Naglieri, J., Obrzut, J. E., & Boliek, C. (1992). Review of the Bender Gestalt Test. In J. J. Kramer and J. C. Conoley (Eds.), *The Eleventh Mental Measurements Yearbook* (pp. 101–106). Lincoln, NE: Buros Institute of Mental Measurements.

PAR. (2005a). *Personality Assessment Inventory (PAI)®* by L. C. Morey. Psychological Assessment Resources, Inc. Retrieved on September 27, 2008, from http://www3.parinc.com/products/product.aspx?Productid=PAI

PAR. (2005b). NEO *Personality Inventory – Revised (NEO PI-R)™* by P. T. Costa, Jr., and R. R. McCrae. Psychological Assessment Resources, Inc. Retrieved on September 27, 2008, from http://www3.parinc.com/products/product.aspx?Productid=NEO-PI-R

PAR. (2005c). *NEO Five-Factor Inventory (NEO-FFI)TM* by P. T. Costa, Jr., and R. R. McCrae. Psychological Assessment Resources, Inc. Retrieved on September 27, 2008, from http://www3.parinc.com/products/product.aspx?Productid=NEO_FFI

Pearson. (2008a). *MMPI-2-RF. Assessments for educational, clinical, and psychological use.* Retrieved on September 24, 2008, from http://www.pearson-assessments.com/tests/mmpi-2-rf.htm

Pearson. (2008b). *MCMI-III: Millon Clinical Multiaxial Inventory-III.* Retrieved on October 1, 2008, from http://www.pearsonassessments.com/tests/mcmi_3.htm

Pearson. (2008c). *MACI: Millon Adolescent Clinical Inventory.* Retrieved on October 1, 2008, from http://www.pearsonassessments.com/tests/maci.htm

Pearson. (2008d). *16PF Fifth Edition. Assessments for educational, clinical, and psychological use.* Retrieved on September 24, 2008, from http://www.pearsonassessments.com/tests/sixtpf_5.htm#quickfacts

Pennebaker, J., & King, L. (1999). Linguistic styles: Language use as an individual difference. *Journal of Personality and Social Psychology, 77,* 1296–1312.

Peterson, C., & Reinehr, R. (1998). Review of the EPS Sentence Completion Technique. In J. C. Impara and B. S. Plake (Eds.), *The Thirteenth Mental Measurements Yearbook* (pp. 423–426). Lincoln, NE: Buros Institute of Mental Measurements.

Quenk, N. (2000). *Essentials of Myers-Briggs Type Indicator assessment.* New York: Wiley.

Raad, B. D. (1998). Five big, big five issues: Rationale, content, structure, status, and crosscultural assessment. *European Psychologist, 3,* 113–124.

Riverside Publishing. (2006). *Bender Visual-Motor Gestalt Test, Second Edition: Technical qualities.* Retrieved on October 1, 2008, from http://www.riverpub.com/products/bender/details.html#technical

Russell, M. T., & Karol, D. L. (1994). *The 16PF fifth edition administrator's manual.* Champaign, IL: Institute for Personality and Ability Testing, Inc.

SASSI (Substance Abuse Subtle Screening Inventory). (2001). *Clinical interpretation Training Outline.* Author: Springville, IN.

Saulsman, L. M., & Page, A. C. (2004). The five-factor model and personality disorder empirical literature: A meta-analytic review. *Clinical Psychology Review, 23,* 1055–1085.

Stein, M. B., Pinsker-Aspen, J. H., & Hilsenroth, M. J. (2007). Borderline pathology and the Personality Assessment Inventory (PAI): An evaluation of criterion and concurrent validity. *Journal of Personality Assessment, 88,* 81–89.

Sundberg, N. (1961). The practice of psychological testing in clinical services in the United States. *American Psychologist, 16,* 79–83.

Thurstone, L. L. (1934). The vectors of the mind. *Psychological Review, 41,* 1–32.

White. L. J. (1996). Review of the Personality Assessment Inventory (PAI-™): A new psychological test for clinical and forensic assessment. *Australian Psychologist, 31,* 38–40.

Informal Assessment: Observation, Rating Scales, Classification Methods, Environmental Assessment, Records and Personal Documents, and Performance-Based Assessment

I was teaching a graduate course in testing, and because I knew that some students have trouble understanding basic test statistics, I went out of my way to make sure I was available for them. I gave them my home number and cell phone number, and I met with them individually if they wanted extra help. In addition, I offered two extra classes on the weekend for those who might need additional assistance in understanding some of the more difficult concepts. At the end of the semester, students had an opportunity to rate the class using a 6-point rating scale (1 is low, 6 is high). They rated seven aspects of the class, including such things as the amount they learned, how useful the information was, how helpful and sensitive the instructor was, and so forth. After this particular course was finished, I looked at my ratings, which had a mean of about 5.3. Not bad, I thought to myself. However, to my chagrin, I noticed that the rating for "helpfulness" was only 4.8, the lowest of all the items. I reflected on why this was so, and I couldn't come up with an answer. I must admit it bothered me, especially since I had gone out of my way to offer additional help. The next semester I saw one of the students from the class and asked her about the low rating. She said, "Well, the class was at night (7:10–9:50 PM), and many of the students were upset that you went the whole time." I said, "Well, I was supposed to go the whole time." She said, "Yeah, I know, but a lot of them just wanted to get home." I suddenly real-ized that some of the students may have given me a lower rating for doing what I was sup-posed to be doing—teaching in the allotted time period. "What a drag," I said to myself. Well, I guess that's what happens when you deal with the subjectivity of rating scales!

(Ed Neukrug)

This chapter is about informal assessment procedures. Whether it is an end-of-semester evaluation of faculty or a dream journal of a client, informal assessment techniques can have a huge impact on a person. In this chapter we will start by defining informal assessment and then identify a number of different kinds of informal assessment techni-ques, including observation, rating scales, classification methods, environmental assess-ment techniques, records and personal documents, and performance-based assessment. We will then discuss the test worthiness of these kinds of techniques and talk about how to assess their validity, reliability, cross-cultural fairness, and practicality. Next we will discuss the helper's role in the use of informal procedures. We will conclude the chapter with some final thoughts regarding informal assessment.

DEFINING INFORMAL ASSESSMENT

Informal assessment procedures

"Homegrown" methods devel-oped to meet specific needs

By their very nature, informal assessment techniques are subjective and thus have a unique role in the assessment process. Whereas the kinds of assessment we have ex-amined up to this point in the text were, for the most part, created and produced in association with national publishing companies and used nationally, most of the as-sessments in this chapter are "homegrown"; that is, developed by individuals who have specific assessment needs. Being homegrown, the amount of time, money, and expertise put into their development is generally much less than it is for those nationally developed instruments. Thus, reliability, validity, and cross-cultural issues are generally not formally addressed and often are lacking. Despite this obvious drawback, such instruments can be a practical addition to the assessment process and supply valuable information when assessing an individual.

Although infor-mal assessment procedures lack test worthiness, they have distinct advantages

Although informal assessment techniques are generally not as test worthy as formal assessment procedures, they have some advantages over them:

1. The addition of informal assessment techniques to the total assessment process increases our ability to better understand the whole person.
2. Informal assessment procedures can be designed to assess the exact attribute we are attempting to measure, whereas formal assessment techniques provide a wide net of assessment—sometimes so wide that we do not gain enough infor-mation about the specific attribute being examined.
3. Informal assessment procedures can often be developed or gathered in a rather short amount of time, providing important information in a timely fashion.
4. Some informal assessment procedures are nonintrusive; that is, you are not di-rectly gathering information from the client (e.g., a student's cumulative record file at school). Thus, they provide a nonthreatening mechanism for gathering information about the individual.
5. Informal assessment techniques generally are free or low-cost procedures.
6. Informal assessment procedures tend to be easy to administer and relatively easy to interpret.

TYPES OF INFORMAL ASSESSMENT

Dozens of informal assessment techniques can enhance our understanding of the whole person. In fact, because informal assessment techniques are, by their nature, informal, a creative examiner can often come up with unique procedures never before used. However, several types of informal assessment techniques are frequently used, including observation, rating scales, classification methods, environmental assessment techniques, records and personal documents, and performance-based assessment. Let's take a look at each of these.

OBSERVATION

Observation
Conducted by professionals, significant others, or clients themselves

Observation can be an important assessment tool for understanding the individual being assessed. Observation can be done by professionals who wish to observe the individual (e.g., school counselors observing students in the classroom; social workers observing a family in the home); by significant others who have the opportunity to observe the individual in natural settings (e.g., parents observing a child at home); and even by oneself, such as when a client is asked to observe specific targeted behaviors he or she is working on changing (e.g., eating habits). Often, when observing an individual, the observer conducts an event or a time sample.

Event sampling
Observing a targeted behavior with no regard to time

Event sampling is the viewing and assessment of a targeted behavior without regard for time. Usually, in evaluating the targeted behavior, general comments are made about the behavior or a rating scale is used to evaluate the behavior. For instance, the school counselor who is interested in observing the "acting-out" behavior of a student could view the child for an entire school day and note when the acting-out behavior is exhibited. Of course, "acting out" would have to be clearly defined.

Time sampling
Observing behaviors during a set amount of time

Whereas event sampling is conducted with little concern for time, *time sampling* is when an individual is observed for a predetermined and limited amount of time. For instance, because it would be inconvenient for a school counselor to spend a whole day observing one student, the counselor might choose three 15-minute periods during the day to observe a student. Ideally, this time sample would give the counselor a snapshot of the student's typical kinds of behaviors. The upside is that the counselor does not have to spend his or her whole day observing one student. The downside is that there is a chance the time sample will not be an accurate portrayal of the student's typical ways of being.

Event and time sampling
Observing a targeted behavior for a set amount of time

For the sake of convenience, time and event sampling are often combined. For example, the school counselor mentioned earlier could decide to observe a student's acting-out behaviors (event sample) for three 15-minute segments of time (time sample) during the day. Clearly, scheduling the observation times would free up the counselor to do other important tasks during the day. (see Box 10.1.)

Time and event sampling are often used when an instructor wants to view or listen to recordings of students practicing their clinical skills (e.g., a student working with a client at an internship, a student teacher in a classroom). Instead of listening to or viewing all of the students' work, instructors will often listen to or view targeted responses (e.g., the ability to be empathic, the kinds of questions asked) for a specified number of times (e.g., 3 times) for a designated amount of minutes (e.g., 10 minutes). Listening to all of the recordings of all of the students in an internship would be nearly impossible as it would simply take up too much time.

| BOX 10.1 | DISRUPTIVE OBSERVATION OF A THIRD-GRADE CLASS |

I was once asked to "debrief" a third-grade class that had just finished a trial period in which a young boy, who was paraplegic and severely mentally retarded, had been mainstreamed into their classroom. During this trial period, a stream of observers from a local university had visited the classroom. The observers would sit in the back and take notes about the interactions between the students. This information was to be used at a later date to decide whether it was beneficial to all involved to mainstream the student with the disability.

When I met with the students, they clearly had adapted well to the presence of this young boy who was disabled. Although the students seemed to have difficulty forming any close relationships with him, his presence seemed in no way to detract from their studies or from their other relationships in the classroom. However, almost without exception, the students noted that the constant stream of observers interfering with their daily schedule had been quite annoying. Perhaps if a limited time sample had been used, the students would not have reacted so strongly.

—Ed Neukrug

EXERCISE 10.1   APPLICATION OF OBSERVATIONAL TECHNIQUES

In small groups, devise ways that you might be able to use observational techniques. Try to incorporate the use of event sampling and time sampling in your examples. Share your answers in class.

RATING SCALES

Rating scales
Subjective quantification of an attribute or characteristic

A rating scale is an instrument used by an individual to evaluate or assess attributes or characteristics being presented to the rater. By their very nature, rating scales are subjective because the evaluation or assessment is based on the rater's "inner judgment" and thus can be filled with biases. Thus, the potential for error in ratings is great and although rating scales are easily developed and quick to administer, they should be used carefully.

Halo effect
Overall impression of client causes inaccurate rating

Generosity error
Identification with client causes inaccurate rating

Although a number of sources of error exist for rating scales, two of the most frequently cited are the *halo effect* and *generosity error* (Aiken, 1996). The halo effect, which was first alluded to almost 100 years ago (see Box 10.2), occurs when an overall impression of an individual clouds the rating of that person in one select area, and the generosity error occurs when the individual doing the rating identifies with the person being rated and thus rates the individual inaccurately. An example of the halo effect is the supervisor who mistakenly rates an outstanding supervisee high on being punctual, despite the fact that the supervisee consistently comes to work late. The supervisor's overall favorable impression has caused an error in the rating of this one attribute. An example of a generosity error is the student who ranks a fellow student high on exhibiting effective empathic responses because the first student identifies with the anxiety the second student feels about being under the microscope.

Despite some of the potential problems of error with rating scales, they are easily created and can be completed quite quickly, so they offer a convenient mechanism of

BOX 10.2	A HUMAN TENDENCY?

Edward L Thorndike, one of the early pioneers in modern-day assessment, was one of the first to write of the halo effect way back in 1920, in an article about error in ratings. Our tendency to see people as all one way or another can affect the judgments we make:

> In a study made in 1915 of employees of two large industrial corporations, it appeared that the estimates of the same man in a number of different traits such as intelligence, industry, technical skill, reliability, etc., etc, were very highly correlated and very evenly correlated. It consequently appeared probable that those giving the ratings were unable to analyze out these different aspects of the person's nature and achievement and rate each in independence of the others Their ratings were apparently affected by a marked tendency to think of the person in general as rather good or rather inferior and to color the judgments of the qualities by this general feeling This same constant error toward suffusing ratings of special features with a *halo* belonging to the individual as a whole appeared in the ratings of officers made by their superiors in the army. (Thorndike, 1920, p. 25; italics not in original)

assessing individuals. Commonly used rating scales include numerical scales, Likert-type scales (graphic scales), semantic differential scales, and rank-order scales.

Numerical scale
Statement or question followed by a number line

NUMERICAL SCALES   Numerical scales generally provide a written statement or question that can be rated from high to low on a number line. Numerical scales are commonly used during counseling as a way to prioritize issues or assess progress. For instance, the technique of scaling, commonly used in solution-focused therapy, asks clients to subjectively rate themselves on a scale from 0 to 10 that assesses any of a number of experiences, feelings, or behaviors (De Jong & Berg, 2002). Although clients in solution-focused therapy generally do this verbally, it would be quite easy to have the scale written, which would allow for documentation of progress made in therapy (see Box 10.3)

Similarly, the *Subjective Unit of Discomfort* (SUD) scale is often used in the behavioral therapy technique of systematic desensitization in determining whether to move on to the next level in a hierarchy when imagining anxiety-provoking situations. Using this scale, 0 = the most relaxing experience imagined by a client and 100 = the most anxiety-evoking experience imagined by the client. Clients move up the hierarchy when they experience a 10 or less at their current level (Ferguson, 2003).

Likert-type scale
Items rated on same theme, anchored by numbers and a statement

LIKERT-TYPE SCALES (GRAPHIC SCALES)   Likert-type scales, sometimes called graphic scales, contain a number of items that are being rated on the same theme

BOX 10.3	NUMERICAL SCALE

With 0 being equal to the worst depression you ever had and a 10 being equal to the best you could possibly feel, can you tell me where on a scale of 0–10 your depression is today?

1	2	3	4	5	6	7	8	9	10
Worst Depression									Best I Could Feel

BOX 10.4	LIKERT-TYPE SCALE

Please indicate how strongly you agree or disagree with each of the following statements:

	Strongly disagree	Somewhat disagree	Neither agree nor disagree	Somewhat agree	Strongly agree
It is fine to view a client's personal web page (e.g., MySpace, Facebook, blog) without informing the client.	1	2	3	4	5
It is okay to tell your client you are attracted to him or her.	1	2	3	4	5
I have no problem counseling a terminally ill client about end-of-life decisions, including suicide.	1	2	3	4	5
Self-disclosing to a client is ethical	1	2	3	4	5

and are anchored by both numbers and a statement that correspond to the numbers. Take a look at the items in Box 10.4, which represent a few behaviors drawn from some research currently being conducted on mental health practitioners' perceptions of ethical behaviors (Milliken & Neukrug, 2009).

Semantic differential scale

Number line with opposite traits at each end

SEMANTIC DIFFERENTIAL SCALES   Semantic differential scales provide a statement followed by one or more pairs of words that are across from one another along a line and which reflect opposing traits. The rater is asked to place a mark on the line that is reflective of how much of the quality that rater believes he or she has. A number line may or may not be associated with the dichotomous pairs of words. Box 10.5 shows a semantic differential scale with a number line.

As you can see from the example in see Box 10.5, a Semantic Differential Scale can easily be created if you were interested in quickly assessing the behaviors and/or affect of a client. Such a scale can be helpful in assessing clients' needs and setting treatment goals. Of course, such scales can have many other broad educational and psychological applications.

BOX 10.5	SEMANTIC DIFFERENTIAL SCALE

Place an "X" on the line to represent how much of each quality you possess.

sadness —1— 2 — 3 — 4 — 5 — 6 — 7 —8— happiness
introverted —1— 2 — 3 — 4 — 5 — 6 — 7 —8— extroverted
anxious —1— 2 — 3 — 4 — 5 — 6 — 7 —8— calm

| BOX 10.6 | RANK ORDER SCALE |

Please rank order your preferred method of doing counseling. Place a 1 next to the item that you most prefer, a 2 next to the item you second most prefer, and so on down to a 5 next to the item you prefer least.

_____ I prefer listening to clients and then reflecting back what I hear from them in order to facilitate client self-growth.

_____ I prefer advising clients and suggesting mechanisms for change.

_____ I prefer interpreting client behaviors in the hope that they will gain insight into themselves.

_____ I prefer helping clients identify which behaviors they would like to change.

_____ I prefer helping clients identify which thoughts are causing problematic behaviors and helping them to develop new ways of thinking about the world.

Rank order

A method for clients to order their preferences

RANK-ORDER SCALES Rank-order scales provide a series of statements which the respondent can place in hierarchical order based on his or her preferences. For instance, the rank-order scale in Box 10.6 could be used as part of a larger instrument to determine preference for counseling style.

EXERCISE 10.2 APPLICATION OF RATING SCALES

In small groups, devise ways that you might be able to use rating scales. Try to incorporate the use of the different types of rating scales discussed in the chapter. Share your answers in class.

CLASSIFICATION METHODS

Classification methods

Information regarding presence or absence of attribute or characteristic

In contrast with rating scales that tend to assess a *quantity* of an attribute or characteristic or the *preferences* of attributes or characteristics (e.g., which is liked more than another), classification methods are all or nothing; they provide information about whether an individual has, or does not have, certain attributes or characteristics. Two common classification methods include behavior checklists and feeling word checklists.

Behavior checklists

Type of classification method that assesses behaviors

BEHAVIOR CHECKLISTS Behavior checklists allow an individual to identify those words that best describe typical or atypical behaviors he or she might exhibit. Behavior checklists are easy to develop, simple to give, and can quickly uncover patterns of behavior that are important to look at. Although their usefulness is clearly related to the kinds of behavior being surveyed and whether the client is honest in his or her responses, they should be considered as one more method of client assessment among the many that you might use. The number and types of behavior checklists are only limited by your imagination and what you might be able to find and freely use, for example, from the Internet. Box 10.7 is a behavior checklist that could be used to help identify abusive behaviors.

| BOX 10.7 | BEHAVIOR CHECKLIST OF ABUSIVE BEHAVIORS |

Check those behaviors you have exhibited toward your partner and your partner has exhibited toward you.

	Exhibited by You to Your Partner	Exhibited by Partner to You
1. Hitting	_____	_____
2. Pulling hair	_____	_____
3. Throwing objects	_____	_____
4. Burning	_____	_____
5. Pinching	_____	_____
6. Choking	_____	_____
7. Slapping	_____	_____
8. Biting	_____	_____
9. Tying up	_____	_____
10. Hitting walls or other inanimate objects	_____	_____
11. Throwing objects with intent to break them	_____	_____
12. Restraining or preventing from leaving	_____	_____

Feeling word checklists

Type of classification method that assesses feelings

FEELING WORD CHECKLISTS   Like behavior checklists, feeling word checklists are another simple and practical classification method. By simply checking or circling the feeling on the list, a client can quickly identify a number of feelings which he or she has had, is currently experiencing, or hopes to feel. For instance, school counselors often use such feeling word checklists for younger children to help them begin to discriminate different kinds of feelings they may be having. Identification of feelings is the first step toward being able to effectively communicate one's feelings to others. But identification of feelings is not only important for children. For instance, marital and relationship counselors might want each member of a couple to clearly understand what they are feeling so that each can effectively communicate with their partner. The ability to accurately identify what one is feeling is the first step toward the differentiation of the emotional from the intellectual process, often an important task in couples and family counseling (Guerin & Guerin, 2002). Table 10.1 is an example of a feeling word checklist that can be used in therapy to identify problem feelings. Like the behavior checklist, such lists are only limited by your ability to identify feeling words or find existing checklists.

OTHER CLASSIFICATION METHODS   The kinds of classification methods that one can create are innumerable, and as with behavior checklists, are only limited by your imagination. For instance, one can come up with a classification method that asks clients to examine and choose items which represent their "irrational thoughts"; an individual participating in a career assessment might be asked to check those jobs that look appealing; or an elderly person might be asked to pick,

TABLE 10.1 | FEELING WORD CHECKLIST TO IDENTIFY PROBLEMATIC FEELINGS

Abandoned	Embarrassed	Lying	Stuck-up
Aggravated	Empty	Mean	Stupid
Aggressive	Envious	Miserable	Suppressed
Angry	Exasperated	Misunderstood	Teased
Anxious	Failure	Nauseated	Terrified
Appreciated	Fearful	Neglected	Thoughtless
Apprehensive	Forced	Nervous	Tormented
Argumentative	Forlorn	Obligated	Traumatized
Arrogant	Forsaken	Oppressed	Troubled
Ashamed	Frigid	Overwhelmed	Troubling
Awful	Frustrated	Pained	Unaccepted
Betrayed	Futile	Panicked	Unconcerned
Bitter	Grieving	Paranoid	Undesirable
Blind	Guilty	Pitiful	Uneasy
Bored	Hateful	Powerless	Unfriendly
Broken-hearted	Haughty	Pressured	Unfulfilled
Burdened	Helpless	Provoked	Unhappy
Claustrophobic	Hopeless	Punished	Unhelpful
Concerned	Humiliated	Rejected	Unneeded
Confused	Hurried	Repulsive	Unloved
Criticized	Hurt	Resentful	Unpleasant
Cut off	Impatient	Restless	Unreliable
Deceived	Imposed	Restricted	Unsociable
Defensive	Impossible	Sad	Unsuccessful
Depressed	Inadequate	Scared	Unwanted
Difficult	Incapable	Selfish	Unworthy
Dirty	Indecisive	Shameful	Upset
Disappointed	Insecure	Shattered	Used
Discontented	Intolerant	Shocked	Useless
Discouraged	Irresponsible	Shy	Victimized
Disgusted	Irritated	Skeptical	Vindictive
Disloyal	Jealous	Smug	Wasted
Disrespected	Left out	Spiteful	Weary
Distressed	Let down	Sorrowful	Worthless
Doubtful	Lonely	Sour	Wounded
Drained	Longing	Stifled	Wrong
Egotistical	Lost	Stubborn	

from a long list, any barriers to living fully that he or she faces (difficulty getting out of the bath, problems seeing, etc.).

ENVIRONMENTAL ASSESSMENT

Environmental assessment

Collecting information from a client's home, school, or workplace via observation or self-reports

An often neglected but valuable source of information is an individual's environment. Often called environmental assessment, this kind of assessment includes collecting information from a client's home, school, or workplace, usually through observation or self-reports. This form of appraisal is more systems-oriented and naturalistic than in-office testing and can be eye-opening, because even when clients do not intentionally mislead their therapists, they will often present a distorted view based on their own inaccurate perceptions or because they are embarrassed about revealing some aspect of their lives (e.g., a person living in poverty might not want to reveal an unpleasant home situation). Environmental assessment can be conducted through direct observation, by conducting situational assessment, by applying a sociometric assessment, or by using an environmental assessment instrument.

Direct observation

An environmental assessment through observation

DIRECT OBSERVATION   Visiting a client's home, classroom, workplace, or other setting can yield a plethora of information that might otherwise evade even the most seasoned therapist. For instance, imagine if after administering your in-office assessment procedures and conducting your interview you were to visit your client's home and find that he had old magazines stacked to the ceiling. Or consider the 10-year-old little "angel" in your office who dramatically changes her demeanor when around other girls in her class. Or imagine your surprise when during an assessment of your client's home situation you find his wife to be kind, considerate, and attractive, unlike the "raving, angry, and pathetic" spouse that he had portrayed her to be.

Home visits are almost always profitable, and it is not unusual to discover important information about your client that you would rarely ascertain in therapy (Yalom, 2002; see Box 10.8). Additionally, discussing the home visit with the client beforehand can generate productive conversations. For instance, you might notice that as you discuss an upcoming visit your client suddenly becomes anxious due to some reason not yet discussed. This anxiety can then be processed and explored during the session. Another benefit is the fact that the home visit can be construed by the client as an affirmation of your level of caring and commitment. This can do wonders in building rapport and trust. Visits to the workplace can also generate

---

BOX 10.8 | AN EFFECTIVE HOME VISIT

The master therapist Milton Erickson was known for practicing unusual interventions that were brief and often at the client's home or workplace. For instance, there is the story of how he once spent less than an hour at the home of a woman who was depressed, lonely, and shy. By visiting her home, he realized she was an expert at cultivating African violets and that she was a committed member of her church. He quickly came up with an intervention: every time there was a birth, wedding, or death at the church, she was to send one of her flowers. She did this religiously, which dramatically changed her life as other church members began to get to know and appreciate her. At her death, the newspaper noted that hundreds of people attended the funeral of the "African Violet Lady" (Gordon & Meyers-Anderson, 1981).

useful information; however, caution must be exercised in order to maintain the client's confidentiality.

Finally, school and classroom visits are often useful in making assessments of children and adolescents. The school visit also allows the helping professional to assess other environmental factors such as lighting, seat position, room layout, and distracting noises that may be related to a student's underperformance. Understanding a child's social interactions can often be achieved only by observing the student in the classroom or on the playground.

Situational assessments

Role-play to determine how individuals might act

SITUATIONAL ASSESSMENT   Another type of environmental tool sometimes used to assess a person is the situational assessment. This kind of assessment uses contrived, but natural situations to examine how a person is likely to respond in real-life situations. For instance, when applying to doctoral programs, I (Ed Neukrug) was asked to role-play a counselor with a faculty member. He role-played the same client with every potential student, and the faculty were then able to assess my clinical skills and compare them to those of other potential students in this contrived yet realistic role-play. Today, situational assessments are frequently used in business and industry to determine whether an employee has the skills to be promoted.

Sociometric assessment

Used to assess the social dynamics of a group

SOCIOMETRIC ASSESSMENT   Sociometric assessment is used to determine the relative position and dynamics of individuals within a group, organization, or institution. For instance, if I was interested in knowing how well a group of preschool students liked one another, I could ask each of them to privately tell me the name of the individual who was their best friend. Then I might ask them to tell me the name of their second-best friend. I could then map these rankings (see Figure 10.1).

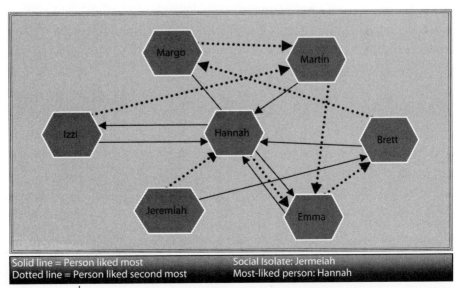

Solid line = Person liked most
Dotted line = Person liked second most

Social Isolate: Jermeiah
Most-liked person: Hannah

FIGURE 10.1 | SOCIOMETRIC MAPPING AT A PRESCHOOL

Solid line = Person liked most
Dotted line = Person liked second most

Social Isolate: Jermeiah
Most-liked person: Hannah

Obviously, the kind of sociometric instrument that is used will vary based on the situation being assessed. For instance, you might want to ask a family: "Who holds the power in this family"; or you might want to ask employees: "Who is most willing to help out at work?"; or if issues of confidentiality and trust were assured, you could ask college students in a residence hall, "Who in your residence hall has most abused drugs and alcohol?"

Environmental assessment instruments

Used with observation and more rigorously constructed than other informal instruments

ENVIRONMENTAL ASSESSMENT INSTRUMENTS   To assist in environmental assessment, a number of instruments have been developed. They are generally used in conjunction with simple observation and usually have more rigorous test construction processes than many of the other techniques examined in this chapter. Below is a very brief list of some of them to give you a sense of how they assess the environment of the client.

- *Comprehensive Assessment of School Environments Information Management System* (CASE-IMS). This instrument is used to assess the entire school environment and climate. It uses self-report surveys of students, parents, teachers, and the principal. The data from the assessment indicate the school's strengths and weaknesses as normed against other schools (Manduchi, 2001).

- *Behavior Rating Inventory of Executive Function—Preschool.* This instrument is a questionnaire that is completed by teachers and parents of preschool children aged two through six years. It is designed to assess a number of cognitive processes important for the management of cognitive, behavioral, and emotional functions. The instrument has 63 items and uses a Likert-type scale to examine a series of behaviors from the past six months (Nellis, 2005).

- *Emotional or Behavior Disorder Scale-Revised.* This instrument is completed by individuals who are "familiar with the student" and helps in the identification of students with emotional and behavioral disorders. There are two broad components that can be assessed through observation, usually by school personnel: a behavioral component that has 64 items and a vocational component that has 54 items (Watson, 2005).

EXERCISE 10.3   SELF-REFLECTION EXERCISE ABOUT ENVIRONMENTAL ASSESSMENT

If you were in therapy and your therapist came to visit your home or work environment, would he or she learn something about you that you had not self-disclosed? In small groups, discuss why you might "neglect" to tell your therapist certain things about your home or work environment and how useful an environmental assessment would be in revealing the "true" you.

RECORDS AND PERSONAL DOCUMENTS

Records and personal documents

Shed light on beliefs, values, and behaviors of the client

Records and personal documents can help the examiner understand the beliefs, values, and behaviors of the person being assessed. Such materials can be obtained directly from the individual, from individuals close to the person (e.g., parents, loved ones), and from just about any institution with which the client has interacted, such as educational institutions, mental health agencies, and clients' places of employment. Some of the more common records and personal documents include biographical inventories, cumulative records, anecdotal information, autobiographies, journals and diaries, and genograms.

Biographical inventories

Provide detailed picture of client's life

BIOGRAPHICAL INVENTORIES   Biographical inventories provide a detailed picture of the individual from birth. They can be the result of an involved, structured interview that is conducted by the examiner, or they can be created by having the client complete a checklist or respond to a series of questions. Biographical inventories will often cover the same kinds of items that are found in a structured interview (see Chapter 12 for a description of the structured interview). The following kinds of information are often gathered in a biographical inventory:

- Demographic information
  - Age
  - Sex
  - Ethnicity
  - Address
  - Date of birth
  - E-mail address
  - Phone number(s) (home and cell)
- Presenting problem
  - Nature of problem
  - Duration of problem
  - Severity of problem
  - Previous treatment of problem
- Family of origin
  - Names and basic descriptions of primary caregivers in family of origin
  - Names and basic descriptions of siblings in family of origin
  - Names and basic descriptions of significant others involved with family of origin
  - Placement in family of origin
  - Quality of relationships in family of origin
  - Traumatic events in family of origin
- Current family
  - Nature of relationship with current domestic partner
  - Length of relationship with current domestic partner
  - Names, ages, and basic descriptions of children, step-children, and foster children
  - Names and basic descriptions of significant others involved with current family
  - Quality of relationships in current family
  - Traumatic events in current family
- Educational history
  - Highest degree attained by each parent and college major, if any
  - Highest degree attained by each spouse and college major, if any
  - Highest or current educational level of children

- Vocational background
  - Detailed work history from adolescence
  - Detailed work history of spouse/significant other
  - Work history of parents
  - Current salary of primary family members
  - Assessment of current job satisfaction of client and spouse or significant other
- Financial history
  - Economic status/social class of family of origin
  - Current economic status/social class
  - History of any financial hardships
- History of counseling and mental illness
  - Detailed counseling/psychiatric history
  - Detailed counseling/psychiatric history of significant other
  - Detailed counseling/psychiatric history of children
  - History of mental illness in family of origin and extended family
  - Use of psychotropic medication in current family and family of origin
- Medical history
  - Significant medical problem
  - Significant medical problems of significant other
  - Significant medical problems of children, stepchildren, foster children
  - Significant medical problems in family of origin
  - Current status of medical problems in immediate family
  - Current use of medication: give names and dosages
- Substance use and abuse history
  - Cigarette smoking
    _____None   Number of years: _____
    Number of cigarettes per day: _____
  - Alcohol use
    _____ None   _____ Occasional   _____ Regular   _____ Heavy   _____ Binge
    Number of years: _____
  - Illegal drugs
    Type of drug(s) (Respond multiple times if more than one drug)
    Usage: _____ None   _____ Occasional   _____ Regular   _____ Heavy
    Number of years: _____
  - Prescription drug abuse
    Type of drug(s) (Respond multiple times if more than one drug)
    Usage: _____ None   _____ Occasional   _____ Regular   _____ Heavy
    Number of years: _____
- History of legal issues
  - Nature of legal issue
  - Effect on self
  - Effect on others

- Check if changes have occurred in any of the following over the last six months:

  _____ Weight   _____ Appetite

  _____ Sleep patterns   _____ Interest in sex

  _____ Sexual activity   _____ General level of activity

  Explain any items checked:

- Sexual orientation

  _____ Heterosexual

  _____ Bisexual

  _____ Homosexual

  _____ Unclear

- History of aggressive behaviors
  - Nature of past acting-out behaviors:
  - Current violent ideation:
  - Likelihood of acting out:
- History of self-injurious behaviors
  - Nature of past behaviors:
  - Current ideation (suicide or other):
  - Likelihood of injuring self:
- Affective and mental state (Check all that apply)

  _____ Depressed   _____ Anxious   _____ Euphoric

  _____ Tearful   _____ Sad   _____ Irritable

  _____ Angry   _____ Passive   _____ Apathetic

  _____ Delusions   _____ Hallucinations   _____ Emotional lability

  _____ Panicky   _____ Compulsions   _____ Obsessive thoughts

  _____ Phobic   _____ Passive   _____ Fearful

  _____ Low self-esteem   _____ Guilt   _____ Memory problems

Explain any items checked (note intensity and duration):

Cumulative records

Collected documentation from a school, employer, or mental health agency

CUMULATIVE RECORDS   Almost assuredly, a cumulative record of significant behaviors we have exhibited has been kept on most of us. For instance, cumulative records are commonplace in schools, where information about a child's test scores, grades, behavioral problems, family issues, relationships with others, and other matters are stored. Also, most workplaces maintain some kind of cumulative record on each employee. These records can add vital information to our understanding of the whole person and can generally be accessed with a written request form signed by the client.

Anecdotal information

Subjective comments or notes in client's records regarding usual patterns or atypical behaviors

ANECDOTAL INFORMATION   Anecdotal information can sometimes be found in an individual's cumulative record and generally includes behaviors of an individual that are consistent (e.g., Jonathan is always punctual) or inconsistent (Samantha, who generally gets along with her co-workers, had an altercation with one today). Anecdotal information can give us insight about the usual manner in which a person behaves or about inconsistent or rarely seen behaviors that may offer glimpses into the inner world of the client.

Autobiography

Asking a client to write his or her life story

AUTOBIOGRAPHY   In contrast to biographical inventories that help us collect in-depth and comprehensive information about a person, asking an individual to write an autobiography allows an examiner to gain subjective historical information that for some reason stands out in an individual's life. In some ways, the information highlighted by an individual in his or her autobiography is a type of projective test in that the individual unconsciously chooses certain information to include—information that has affected the development of the individual's sense of self. For creative and insightful individuals, writing an autobiography can be an enjoyable process that can reveal much about the self-awareness of the client.

Journals and diaries

Having clients log their daily thoughts, actions, or dreams

JOURNALS AND DIARIES   Some individuals enjoy and benefit from keeping an on-going journal or diary. For instance, dream journals can provide valuable insight into self by revealing unconscious drives and desires and by uncovering patterns that indicate issues in a client's life. Clients can often learn how to "get in touch with their dreams" simply by keeping a dream journal next to their beds and writing down their memories of dreams as soon as they awake. In fact, it has been shown that individuals can be taught how to remember their dreams in this fashion (Gordon, 2007; Hill, 2004; Ullman & Zimmerman, 1979). Similarly, diaries can help uncover the inner world of the client and identify important patterns of behavior. By examining themes found in journals and diaries, helpers and clients may focus more attention on behaviors that may have seemed insignificant. Journals and diaries can add an important "inside" perspective to our understanding of the total person.

Genogram

Map of client's family relation-ships and relevant history

GENOGRAMS   A popular and informative assessment tool is the genogram. It can also serve as a focal point or discussion aid during treatment. The genogram is a map of an individual's family tree that may include the family history of illnesses, mental disorders, substance use, expectations, relationships, cultural issues, and other concerns for counseling. Usually the therapist draws the genogram while ask-ing the client questions; however, drawing or completing the genogram can be given as homework. There are numerous symbols and items that can be included on the genogram. Figure 10.2 displays a few of the common or basic symbols. Of course you are always welcome to add more of your own.

Dates or ages are useful on the genogram. Some prefer adding the year born, and if applicable, the year deceased, near each individual's name. Another method is to include the age of the individual inside his box or her circle. Similarly, the year married or the cumulative years married can be placed above the marriage relation-ship line. As noted in Figure 10.3, special symbols identifying substance use or mental illness can be helpful in tracking family genetics, highlighting stressors caused by abuse or illness, and generating discussion with the client. Creating the genogram to at least the level of the client's grandparents is important to fully cap-ture these trends in the family. In Figure 10.3, you can see an abbreviated version of a genogram for Joe Smith.

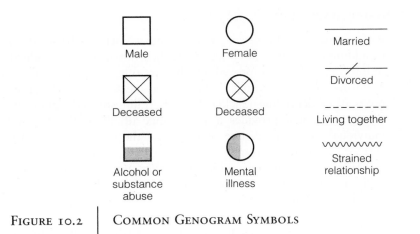

FIGURE 10.2 | COMMON GENOGRAM SYMBOLS

FIGURE 10.3 | ABBREVIATED GENOGRAM FOR JOE SMITH

EXERCISE 10.4 APPLICATION OF RECORDS AND PERSONAL DOCUMENTS

In small groups, devise ways to use records and personal documents. Try to incorporate the various types of records and personal documents discussed in the chapter. Share your answers in class.

PERFORMANCE-BASED ASSESSMENT

Performance-based assessment

Assessment procedures based on real-world responsibilities

Performance-based assessment, which has sometimes been offered as an alternative or addition to standardized testing, is the evaluation of an individual using a variety of informal assessment procedures that are often based on real-world responsibilities. Occuring in many settings, including business, higher education, and for the purposes of credentialing (Sacket, Schmitt, Ellingson, & Kabin, 2001), performance-based assessment provides a wide range of alternative methods of assessing an individual that is predictive of how well the individual will achieve at his or her current or eventual setting.

Standardized testing, which is highly loaded for the assessment of cognitive skills, has been shown to be predictive in a wide range of studies; however, the fact that these tests continue to show race-based differences raises many eyebrows (Sacket, et al., 2001). Some suggest that such differences can be lessened if performance-based assessments that are predictive of desired outcomes are used (e.g., producing a successful counselor). This is particularly the case if the additional measures are based on interpersonal skills, personality measures, and other measures not highly loaded for cognitive skills. The use of additional predictive methods would widen the number of individuals who could demonstrate competency in a specific area and increase the numbers of minorities who could potentially be chosen for a job, obtain a credential, or be admitted into an academic program. One kind of performance-based assessment that has become increasingly popular in recent years is the use of portfolios.

Portfolio assessment

Performance-based assessment often found in higher education

Portfolio assessments have become commonplace in teacher education programs and are increasingly being used in training programs in the helping professions (Cobia, et al., 2005; Studer & Sommers, 2000). Such portfolios ask students to pull together a number of items that demonstrate competencies in a wide range of areas that meet specific standards, such as accreditation standards. Although new materials may be placed in a portfolio, oftentimes student portfolios include major projects that students have already finished and which have been previously evaluated. Sometimes, the projects include comments by teachers or supervisors who may have reviewed the student's work. Students also typically have an opportunity to refine these projects before they are placed in the portfolio.

As an example of what may be placed in a portfolio, a school counseling student might be asked to include any of the following in his or her portfolio: a resumé, videos of the student's work with clients, a supervisor's assessment of the student's work, a paper that highlights the student's view of human nature, examples of how the student helped to build a multicultural school environment, ways that the student shows a commitment to the school counseling profession, a test report written by the student, or a project that shows how the student would build a comprehensive school counseling program. Although portfolios have, in the past, been a "paper" project, today's portfolios are often placed on a CD or online.

The validity of portfolio assessment is based on a number of factors, including ensuring that the content in the portfolio reflects the competencies and/or standards that the portfolio is based upon, a rubric or scoring system that is clear and based on the domains being assessed, the outcomes hoped for (e.g., counselor competency with clients) that should reflect the competencies the portfolio is based upon, and that the portfolio should predict outcomes for what is being assessed as well as related skills (e.g., counselor success with clients) (van der Schaaf, & Stokking, 2008).

Performance-based assessment has become an alternative to traditional ways of assessing an individual and will likely to continue to gain in popularity. As you continue on your career path and become responsible for the assessment of others, you might want to consider using some kinds of performance-based assessment procedures.

TEST WORTHINESS OF INFORMAL ASSESSMENT

As already noted earlier in this chapter, informal assessment techniques tend to be less valid, less reliable, and less cross-culturally sensitive than formal assessment techniques, although they do tend to be quite practical. But let's take a look at what we mean when we talk about these attributes within the context of informal assessment techniques.

VALIDITY

Validity of informal techniques

Based on clearly defining a set of behaviors

Validity of informal assessment techniques has to do with how well the examiner is defining that which is being assessed. For instance, if I am concerned about the acting-out behavior of a middle school child, I need to clearly define the behavior identified as "acting out," and I need to be specific on where acting-out behaviors are being exhibited. For example, does acting out include only inappropriate behaviors in the classroom, or does it also include inappropriate behaviors in the hallway, on the playground, on field trips, and at home? Also, exactly which "inappropriate" behaviors are we talking about? Does acting out include pushing, interrupting, making inappropriate nonverbal gestures, or withdrawing in class? The more clearly one is able to identify the kinds of behaviors and the place the behaviors are exhibited, the easier it will be to collect information about that domain, and consequently, the more valid will be the assessment. Thus, when referring to informal assessment techniques, we are generally not assessing validity in the traditional ways, but are more concerned about how clearly we are defining the domain being measured (see Exercise 10.5).

RELIABILITY

Reliability of informal techniques

Based on inter-rater reliability, which is agreement or consistency among two or more evaluators

With informal assessment, the better we define the behavior being assessed, the more reliable our data collection will be. Thus, with informal assessment there is an intimate relationship between validity and reliability. Ideally, when conducting informal assessment, a minimum of two individuals who are highly trained in understanding the meaning of the data being collected should collect and categorize the data. Practically, this is rarely done. For instance, it would be nearly impossible to have two trained individuals write down the dreams of an individual unless that individual was in a controlled setting, like a sleep clinic. Similarly, it is quite unusual to have two trained raters review and rate the video of a counselor—client role-play by a counselor trainee. Or, consider the earlier example of the acting-out middle school student. In this case, it would be ideal if two individuals observed the child at the same time and knew exactly what acting-out behaviors they were

EXERCISE 10.5   VALIDITY OF INFORMAL ASSESSMENT TECHNIQUES

In small groups, consider the various kinds of informal assessment techniques listed below and demonstrate how you might show evidence that the information being assessed is valid.

Observation
- Event sampling
- Time sampling
- Event and time sampling

Rating Scales
- Numerical scales
- Likert-type scales (graphic scales)
- Semantic differential scales
- Rank-order scales

Classification Systems
- Behavior checklists
- Feeling word checklists

- Other "home-made" classification systems

Environmental Assessment
- Direct observation
- Situational tests
- Sociometric assessment
- Environmental assessment instruments

Records and Personal Documents
- Biographical inventories
- Cumulative records
- Anecdotal information
- Autobiography
- Journals and diaries
- Genograms

Performance-based Assessment
- Portfolio assessment

looking for and in which context to look for them (the classroom, playground, home, etc.). Subsequent to observing the child, they could crosscheck their observations and see if they had collected similar information. If this were possible, when comparing such accuracy statistically, we would be examining the interrater reliability of the observers.

For instance, when I (Ed Neukrug) was in college, I and a friend worked with a psychology professor who was examining how quickly thirsty mice could learn that a drop of water was on a receptacle on the black side of a box. The box had removable sides, one of which was black and the other was white. By randomly moving the sides, but always keeping the water in the receptacle on the black side, the learning curve of thirsty mice could be assessed. My friend and I would place a mouse in the middle of the box and separately rate whether or not the mouse went to the correct side (the black side) and took a drink. However, to increase our validity, and consequently the reliability of our ratings, we had to be clear about what was considered a learned behavior by the mice. For instance, was walking over to the black side and venturing toward the water receptacle, but not touching it, considered a learned response? What if the mouse walked over and looked into the receptacle but did not drink? And what if the mouse walked over to the receptacle, looked in, stuck its tongue out and touched the water, but didn't appear to swallow? Did the mouse exhibit the learned response in this case? A "correct" response had to be clearly defined for us, and the more clearly it was defined, the more similar would be our ratings. In fact, in this case, good interrater reliability was said to have been obtained when the correlation between our ratings reached .80 or higher (see Figure 10.4)

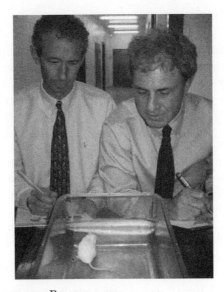

FIGURE 10.4 | INTERRATER RELIABILITY

As Ed and Charlie observe the mouse, they hope that they attain high interrater reliability. But in reality, the mouse is the one observing them.

In another example of interrater reliability, I had two graduate students learn how to rate the empathic responses of dozens of individuals who had responded to a role-play client on an audiotape. These two graduate students were taught how to rate empathy on a five-point scale using increments of .5, from a low of .5 to a high of 5.0. Thus, I had to be clear on what was meant by empathy and how to determine whether a response deserved a .5, 1, 1.5, 2, 2.5, 3, 3.5, 4, 4.5, or 5 rating. In both cases, it took weeks to train the two raters in their understanding of empathy and the use of the scale to the point where they had an interrater reliability of .80. Based on this example, it is easy to see why the attainment of interrater reliability in the use of informal assessment techniques is rarely achieved.

CROSS-CULTURAL FAIRNESS

Cross-cultural fairness

Possibility of bias must be recognized and addressed

The nature of informal assessment procedures makes them particularly vulnerable to cultural bias. This can happen in two ways. First, as a result of unconscious or conscious bias, an examiner, observer, or rater may misinterpret the verbal or nonverbal behaviors of a minority being observed. Second, the examiner, observer, or rater may simply be ignorant about the verbal or nonverbal behaviors of a particular minority group. For instance, an example of unconscious bias affecting one's observation might be an examiner who is asked to observe the behaviors of an Asian student and mistakenly assumes a particular student is bright because Asians as a group tend to do better academically than other ethnic groups. An example of ignorance is when the same observer falsely assumes the student has psychological issues because the Asian student does not readily express feelings. In fact, expression of feelings is valued in many Western cultures but not regarded in the same manner in many Asian countries (Robinson-Wood, 2009).

Despite the fact that informal assessment techniques are easily affected by bias, they still can add much to the assessment of an individual. Because they are uniquely geared toward the particular behavior of an individual, one can pick and choose exactly which behaviors to observe. This can enhance our understanding of the individual. Thus, informal assessment can be a mixed bag when it comes to cross-cultural fairness, and results need to be examined carefully.

PRACTICALITY

Practicality
Informal procedures are inexpensive, easy to administer, and easy to interpret

The practical nature of informal assessments makes them particularly useful. Such assessments are generally low-cost or cost-free, can be devised so they focus on the specific issue at hand, can be created or obtained in a short amount of time, are relatively easy to administer, and with the exception of possible cultural bias, are fairly easy to interpret. Thus, when completing a broad assessment of an individual, informal assessments should often be considered as one additional method of assessment.

THE ROLE OF HELPERS IN THE USE OF INFORMAL ASSESSMENT

The use of informal assessment techniques is only limited by our imaginations. Probably, what is most important is considering whether or not the specific informal technique is adding to our knowledge about what is being assessed. Using a technique that does not add to our body of knowledge about someone is not using it wisely. For instance, if I decided to assess a client's cognitive ability by asking that client to develop a portfolio, and if the portfolio added little because we already had garnered good information about his or her ability from traditional standardized tests, then I would just be wasting my time and the client's time. On the other hand, there are many times when informal techniques can be used wisely and add much.

How do helpers and others use such techniques? School counselors observe children in the classroom and parents can observe their children at home. Teachers and helpers can rate students' and clients' progress. Clinicians can have clients assess their progress by using rating scales, as well as write autobiographies and use journals and diaries to encourage insight. Teachers and school counselors can use anecdotal records and cumulative records in helping to understand the learning style of a student. School social workers can visit the homes of students to better understand them in that important environment. And faculty can use portfolios to help students integrate what they have learned and forgo the traditional end-of-program assessment procedures (e.g., comps). There are an endless number of ways that we can use informal techniques. Can you think of some more?

FINAL THOUGHTS ON INFORMAL ASSESSMENT

Although informal assessment techniques sometimes have questionable reliability, validity, and may not always be cross-culturally fair, they can provide an additional means of understanding a person. Thus, when making decisions about a person, these techniques can be an important addition to a broader assessment battery if they can be shown to accurately measure an important characteristic or quality. Therefore, always consider using an informal assessment technique in combination with other assessment techniques, while keeping in mind the potential impact that such a technique will have on the client.

SUMMARY

This chapter offered an overview of informal assessment. We noted that by their very nature, informal assessment techniques are subjective and are developed by individuals who have specific assessment needs. We pointed out that because they are mostly "homegrown," the amount of time, money, and expertise put into their development is generally much less than for nationally developed instruments. Thus, reliability, validity, and cross-cultural issues are often not formally addressed, and data often are lacking. These techniques do, however, have the following advantages: (1) they offer an additional way of assessing an individual, (2) they can provide a highly specific assessment measure, (3) they can be developed in a short amount of time, (4) they are nonintrusive, (5) they are free or low-cost, and (6) they are easy to administer and interpret.

The first informal assessment technique we discussed was observation. Two types of observation highlighted were event sampling, which is the viewing and assessment of a targeted behavior without regard for time, and time sampling, which takes place when a specific amount of time is set aside for the observation. Sometimes time sampling and event sampling are combined.

Next, we examined rating scales, which are used to assess a quantity of an attribute being presented to the rater. We noted that such scales are subjective and can be filled with bias and errors, including the halo effect and generosity error. Some common types of rating scales included numerical scales, Likert-type (graphic) scales, semantic differential scales, and rank-order scales. We then noted that in contrast to rating scales, classification methods provide information regarding the presence or absence of attribute or characteristic. We specifically discussed two kinds of classification methods, including behavior checklists and feeling word checklists, and also noted that many other classification methods that address additional areas can easily be created.

The next kind of informal assessment instrument we discussed was environmental assessment, which includes the collection of information from a client's home, school, or workplace via observation or self-reports. The four kinds of environmental assessment we discussed were direct observation, situational tests, sociometric assessment, and environmental assessment instruments.

In this chapter we also discussed the use of records and personal documents. These informal assessment tools can help the examiner understand the beliefs, values, and behaviors of the person being assessed and can be obtained from numerous sources including the client, individuals close to the client, institutions, and agencies. Some of the more common records and personal documents include biographical inventories, cumulative records, anecdotal information, autobiographies, journals and diaries, and genograms.

The last kind of informal assessment we presented was performance-based assessment. We noted that performance-based assessment involves the use of a variety of informal assessment procedures, often based on real-world responsibilities, to make decisions about individuals. As an alternative to the use of some tests, such as standardized tests that measure cognitive skills, it is hoped that the use of performance-based assessment procedures will broaden the pool of qualified individuals seeking a job, seeking a credential, or being admitted to school. One kind of performance-based assessment, the portfolio assessment, has become popular in teacher education programs and has increasingly been used in training programs in the helping professions.

We noted that informal assessment techniques tend to be less valid, less reliable, and less cross-culturally sensitive than formal assessment techniques, although they are quite practical. We pointed out that the validity of informal assessment techniques has to do with how well the examiner is defining what is being assessed. We also stressed that the better we define the behavior being assessed (the more valid our definition is), the more reliable will be our data collection. Ideally, informal assessment techniques should be administered by a minimum of two individuals, and the interrater reliability of these two individuals should be at least .80.

Relative to cross-cultural issues, we noted that the examiner may misinterpret the verbal or nonverbal behaviors of a member of a minority group as a result of unconscious or conscious bias. Second, the observer, examiner, or rater may simply be ignorant about the verbal or nonverbal behaviors of a particular minority group. Despite problems with bias, informal procedures are often useful because they are uniquely geared toward the particular behavior of an individual.

Finally, we pointed out that informal assessment techniques are practical in that they are generally low-cost or cost-free, can be created or developed or obtained in a short amount of time, are relatively easy to administer, and are fairly easy to interpret. We stressed that when used wisely, informal assessment techniques provide additional mechanisms for understanding the person.

CHAPTER REVIEW

1. Define informal assessment procedures and describe some of the ways that they can be used.
2. Describe the two types of observation and give some examples of how you might use observation in a clinical setting.
3. Describe and give examples of the following types of rating scales: numerical scales, Likert-type scales, semantic differential scales, and rank-order scales.
4. Many sources of error exist in the application of rating scales. Discuss how the halo effect and generosity error can deleteriously affect the rating of individuals.
5. Give an example of how behavior and feeling word checklists, or other types of classification systems, can be used in a clinical setting.
6. Discuss how the following environmental assessment instruments may be more beneficial than "in office" kinds of instruments: direct observation, situational tests, sociometric assessment, and environmental assessment instruments.
7. Many types of records and personal documents can be useful in the assessment process. For each of the ones listed below, describe how you might use it in a clinical setting:
   a. biographical inventory
   b. cumulative records
   c. anecdotal information
   d. autobiography
   e. journals and diaries
   f. genogram
8. In what ways can performance-based assessment broaden the number of highly qualified applicants for a job or admission to higher education?
9. Discuss how validity is determined with regard to informal assessment procedures.
10. Discuss interrater reliability and its importance to the informal assessment process.
11. Discuss the strengths and weaknesses of informal assessment procedures relative to cross-cultural issues.
12. Because informal assessment procedures can be easily and quickly developed and administered, they are practical to use. However, this very fact means that they often are not developed in a manner that yields good reliability or validity. Discuss the strengths and weaknesses of this aspect of informal assessment procedures.

REFERENCES

Aiken, L. R. (1996) *Rating scales and checklists*. New York: Wiley.

Cobia, C. D., Carney, J. S., Buckhalt, J. A., Middleton, R. A., Shannon, D. M., Trippany, R., & Kunkel, E. (2005). The doctoral portfolio: Centerpiece of a comprehensive system of evaluation. *Counselor Education and Supervision, 44*(4), 242–254

De Jong, P. & Berg, I. K. (2002). *Interviewing for solutions* (2nd ed..). Pacific Grove, CA: Brooks/Cole.

Ferguson, K. E. (2003). Relaxation. In W. O'Donohue, U. J. Fisher, & S. C. Hayes (Eds.), *Cognitive behavior therapy: Applying empirically supported techniques in your practice* (pp. 330–340). Hoboken, NJ: John Wiley & Sons.

Gordon, D. (2007). *Mindful dreaming: A practical guide for emotional healing through transformative mythic journeys*. Franklin Lakes, NJ: New Page Books.

Gordon, D., & Meyers-Anderson, M. (1981). *Phoenix: Therapeutic patterns of Milton H. Erickson*. Cupertino, CA: Meta Publications.

Guerin, P., & Guerin, K. (2002). Bowenian family therapy. In J. Carlson & D. Kjos (Eds.), *Theories and strategies of family therapy* (pp. 126–157). Boston: Allyn & Bacon.

Hill, C. E. (Ed.). (2004). *Dream work in therapy: Facilitating exploration, insight, and action*. Washington, DC: American Psychological Association.

Manduchi, J. R. (2001). Review of the Comprehensive Assessment of School Environments Information Management System. In B.S. Plake and J.C. Impara (Eds.), *The Fourteenth Mental Measurements Yearbook*. Lincoln, NE: Buros Institute of Mental Measurements. Retrieved from Mental Measurements Yearbook database.

Milliken, T., & Neukrug, E. (2009). Perceptions of ethical behaviors of human service professionals. *Human Service Education*. Submitted for publication.

Nellis, L. M. (2005). Review of the Behavior Rating Inventory of Executive Function—Preschool. *The Sixteenth Mental Measurements Yearbook*. Lincoln, NE: Buros Institute of Mental Measurements. Retrieved from Mental Measurements Yearbook database.

RobinsonWood, T. (2009). *The convergence of race, ethnicity, and gender: Multiple identities in counseling* (3rd ed.). Saddle River, NJ: Merrill.

Sackett, P. R., Schmitt, N., Ellingson, J. E., & Kabin, M. B. (2001). High-stakes testing in employment, credentialing, and higher education. Prospects in a post-affirmative-action world. *American Psychologist, 56*(4), 302–318.

Studer, J. R., & Sommers, J. A. (2000). The professional school counselor and accountability. *NASSP Bulletin, 84*(615), 93–99.

Thorndike, E. L. (1920). A constant error on psychological rating. *Journal of Applied Psychology, 4*(1), 25–29.

Ullman, M., & Zimmerman, N. (1979). *Working with dreams*. New York: Delacorte Press.

van der Schaaf, M. F., & Stokking, K. M. (2008). Developing and validating a design for teacher portfolio assessment. *Assessment and evaluation in higher education, 33*(3), 245–262.

Watson, R. S. (2005). Review of the Emotional or Behavior Disorder Scale—Revised. In R.A. Spies and B.S. Plake Eds.). *The Sixteenth Mental Measurements Yearbook*. Lincoln, NE: Buros Institute of Mental Measurements. Retrieved from Mental Measurements Yearbook database.

Yalom, I. (2002). *The gift of therapy: An open letter to a new generation of therapists and their patients*. New York: HarperCollins.

Diagnosis and Writing the Assessment Report

SECTION IV

How to make a diagnosis, which is a type of assessment, and how to write a comprehensive test report are the subjects of this last section of the text and are covered in Chapters 11 and 12, respectively.

In Chapter 11 we begin by discussing the importance of making a diagnosis. We then go on to introduce the *Diagnostic and Statistical Manual, Fourth Edition–Text Revision* (DSM-IV-TR), which is the common diagnostic tool used by just about all clinicians. We offer a brief history of the DSM-IV-TR and then discuss its five axes. Used in making a diagnosis, the five axes include: Axis I: "Clinical Disorders and Other Conditions That May Be a Focus of Clinical Attention," Axis II: "Personality Disorders and Mental Retardation," Axis III: "General Medical Conditions," Axis IV: "Psychosocial and Environmental Problems," and Axis V: "Global Assessment of Functioning." We offer examples of how a five-axes diagnosis is made and present some case studies for practice. We conclude the chapter with a discussion of the importance of diagnosis in the total assessment process.

Chapter 12 is the last chapter in the text, and it is here that we highlight the importance of the assessment report and suggest that the report is the "deliverable" or "end product" of the assessment process. The chapter begins by examining the importance of conducting a good clinical interview and of choosing appropriate assessment techniques. We offer guidelines for conducting an effective interview and distinguish among three kinds of interviews that can be used to gather information: structured, unstructured, and semi-structured interviews. We then offer a brief overview of the different assessment procedures discussed in the text and talk about the importance of choosing appropriate assessment measures that match the client's presenting issues. We stress the importance of considering the breadth and depth of chosen assessment procedures and note that the clinician should choose from a broad array of procedures if he or she is to build a holistic understanding of the individual who is to be assessed.

In the rest of Chapter 12 we suggest ways of writing effective test reports and delineate topics that must be covered to create a thorough assessment of a client. As you read through this chapter, we offer an example of a fictitious client and show how each section of the assessment report would be written. The complete assessment report can be found in Appendix F of the text.

Diagnosis in the Assessment Process

It was 1975, and part of my job as an outpatient therapist at a mental health center entailed answering the crisis counseling phones every ninth night. I would sleep at the center and answer a very loud phone that would ring periodically throughout the night, usually with a person in crisis on the other end. Every once in a while, a former client of the center would call in and start to read aloud from his case notes, which he had stolen from the center. Parts of these notes were a description of his diagnosis from what was then the second edition of the Diagnostic and Statistical Manual *(DSM-II). In a sometimes angry, sometimes funny tone, he would read these clinical terms that were supposed to be describing him. I could understand his frustration when reading these notes over the phone, as in some ways, the diagnosis seemed removed from the person—a label. "Was this really describing the person, and how was it helpful to him?" I would often wonder.*

(Ed Neukrug)

An important aspect of the clinical assessment and appraisal process is skillful diagnosis. Today, the use of diagnosis permeates the mental health professions, and although there continues to be some question as to its helpfulness, it is clear that making diagnoses and using them in treatment planning has become an integral part of what all mental health professionals do. Thus, in this chapter we will examine the use of diagnosis.

We will start the chapter by discussing the importance of making a diagnosis and then describe the *Diagnostic and Statistical Manual, Fourth Edition—Text Revision* (DSM-IV-TR). We will offer a brief history of the DSM-IV-TR and discuss its five axes that are used in making a diagnosis. We will also show how a five-axes diagnosis is made and present some case studies for you to practice on. We will conclude the chapter with a discussion of the importance of diagnosis in the total assessment process.

THE IMPORTANCE OF A DIAGNOSIS

- John is in fifth grade and has been assessed as having a conduct disorder and attention deficit disorder with hyperactivity (ADHD). John's mother has a panic disorder and is taking antianxiety medication. His father is bipolar and taking lithium. Jill is John's school counselor. John's individualized educational plan (IEP) states that he should see Jill for individual counseling and for group counseling. Jill must also periodically consult with John's mother and father.

- Tamara has just started college. After breaking up with her boyfriend, she became severely depressed and unable to concentrate on her schoolwork; her grades have dropped from As to Cs. She comes to the college counseling center and sobs during most of her first session with her counselor. She admits having always struggled with depression but states that "This is worse than ever; I need to get better if I am going to stay in school. Can you give me any medication to help me so I won't have to drop out?"

- Benjamin goes daily to the day treatment center at the local mental health center. He seems fairly coherent and generally in good spirits. He has been hospitalized for schizophrenia on numerous occasions and now takes Haldol and Cogentin to relieve his symptoms. He admits to Jordana, one of his counselors, that when he doesn't take his medication he believes that computers have consciousness and are conspiring through the World Wide Web to take over the world. His insurance company pays for his treatment. He will not receive treatment unless Jordana specifies a diagnosis on the insurance form.

There are many reasons to diagnose

With evidence that a large percentage of Americans have or will experience an emotional disorder (Hersen & Van Hasselt, 2001; Karlin, Duff, & Gleaves, 2008), it is clear that regardless of where you are employed, you will be working with clients who have serious emotional problems. These individuals have been labeled as displaying atypical, unusual, or abnormal behavior and have been given or are in need of a diagnosis for treatment purposes and/or for legal reasons (Galatzer-Levy, 2007; Slovenko, 2002). Recognizing the pervasiveness of mental health problems, and acknowledging that all mental health professionals will be working with individuals with mild to severe problems, most of today's training programs include instruction on diagnosis (Neukrug & Schwitzer, 2006; Schwitzer, 1996). Diagnosis is an important skill for helping professionals, for the following reasons:

1. Federal and state laws (e.g., PL94-142, Individuals with Disabilities Education Improvement Act: IDEIA) now require that students with severe emotional disorders be serviced in the schools. Thus, school counselors, school psychologists, and other school-based mental health professionals often deal with students who have severe emotional problems. The use of diagnosis helps to identify the specific mental disorder with which a student may be struggling and can be useful in deciding treatment strategies.

2. Today, a mental disorder diagnosis is usually mandatory if medical insurance is to reimburse for treatment. In addition, insurance companies will sometimes want to monitor progress as a function of the kind of diagnosis made.

3. With the pervasive use of a diagnostic classification system such as DSM-IV-TR, familiarity with its nomenclature has become critical if clinicians are to effectively communicate with one another.

4. With increasing evidence that many mental health disorders are influenced, if not determined, by biological factors (e.g., genetics, environmental factors such

as lead paint, etc.), a definitive diagnosis that points to a biological influence can be critical for the proper treatment of an individual.

5. Diagnosis has become one additional and critical aspect of the total assessment process and can be helpful in case conceptualization and in treatment planning.

Over the years it has become clear that knowledge of diagnosis is necessary for every mental health professional, and the most well known diagnostic classification system is DSM-IV-TR. But how does this classification system work? Let's take a look.

WHAT IS DSM-IV-TR?

DSM-IV-TR
Accepted diagnostic classification system for mental disorders

Derived from the Greek words dia (apart) and gnosis (to perceive or to know), the term diagnosis refers to the process of making an assessment of an individual from an outside, or objective, viewpoint (Segal & Coolidge, 2001). Although attempts have been made to classify mental disorders since the turn of the 20th century, it was not until 1952 that the American Psychiatric Association published the first comprehensive diagnostic system, called the *Diagnostic and Statistical Manual* (DSM-I). DSM-I had many critics and was indeed a crude effort at a diagnostic system, but it did represent the first modern-day attempt to classify mental disorders. DSM-I was revised numerous times over the years to its current edition, the DSM-IV-TR. This distant cousin of the original DSM-I offers explicit ways of determining a diagnosis and presents a five-part multiaxial diagnostic system (APA, 2000). Although the DSM-IV-TR has its critics (Beutler, & Malik, 2002; Thyer, 2006; Zalaquett, Fuerth, Stein, Ivey, & Ivey, 2008), it has become the most widespread and accepted diagnostic classification system of emotional disorders in the world (Seligman, 1999; 2004).

The DSM-IV-TR offers five axes to assist in diagnosis and treatment of mental disorders. Although many clinicians do not use all five axes, a good number will find two or more of the axes useful. Axis I describes "Clinical Disorders and Other Conditions That May Be a Focus of Clinical Attention," Axis II delineates "Personality Disorders and Mental Retardation," Axis III explains "General Medical Conditions," Axis IV describes "Psychosocial and Environmental Problems," and Axis V offers a "Global Assessment of Functioning."

The use of the five axes underscores one of the most important purposes of the DSM-IV-TR classification system: it allows mental health professionals to accurately describe their clients and communicate with other mental health professionals about them (Neukrug & Schwitzer, 2006). In addition, a diagnosis can help a clinician determine the primary focus of counseling and assist in deciding which interventions might be most useful. Certainly, a focus on a mood problem would be dealt with differently from a focus on somatic complaints. Similarly, a focus on an adjustment problem, which is by its very nature short-term, is handled very differently than a personality disorder, which tends to be problematic throughout a person's life. Although all five axes can be helpful in determining the kind of intervention and in treatment planning, the first two axes focus specifically on helping the clinician determine what kind of disorder an individual may be displaying.

AXES I AND II: THE MENTAL DISORDERS[1]

The first two axes of DSM-IV-TR offer a wealth of information on specific mental disorders. Such information helps clinicians determine which specific disorder a client might be struggling with. The following very brief overview defines the mental disorders included in Axis I and II, highlights cross-cultural issues related to the diagnosis of mental disorders, and summarizes hundreds of pages of information from Axis I and Axis II of DSM-IV-TR. For an in-depth review of the disorders, please go directly to DSM-IV-TR (APA, 2000).

Each item includes features, subtypes, patterns, and differentiation from similar disorders

UNDERSTANDING THE MENTAL DISORDERS   Each mental disorder covered in DSM-IV-TR describes (1) the disorder's main features; (2) subtypes and variations in client presentations; (3) the typical pattern, course, or progression of symptoms; and (4) how to differentiate the disorder from other, similar ones. The DSM-IV-TR also provides findings about predisposing factors, complications, and associated medical and counseling problems when they are known, and it does not hypothesize about etiology of a disorder when information is not known. DSM-IV-TR diagnoses are intended to be theory-neutral descriptions of behavior, thoughts, mood, physiology, functioning, and distress. Thus, using DSM-IV-TR categories and descriptors allows clinicians to describe clients and communicate with mental health colleagues while being able to apply their own theoretical orientation to the treatment planning process (Jongsma & Peterson, 1999; Seligman, 2004). Also, DSM-IV-TR offers a convenient decision tree that can help in distinguishing similar diagnoses from one another.

One misperception beginning clinicians sometimes have is that using clinical diagnoses, like those of the DSM-IV-TR, means that one must view all client concerns from a very clinical, psychopathological viewpoint. In reality, the DSM-IV-TR is used to share information about a subset of human experience—those conditions that meet the "mental disorder" definition. In point of fact, despite the fact that almost all of us have some problems in our lives, most of these struggles do not meet the definition of "mental disorder." However, with as many as 16% of Americans showing signs of a moderate or serious mental disorder every year. (see Kessler, Chiu, Demler, & Walters, 2005), it is probably a good idea to categorize disorders as it helps to discern appropriate treatments. Thus, each DSM-IV-TR mental disorder is constructed to show a distinct pattern of difficulty that is currently causing the client distress (APA, 2000; Schwitzer & Everett, 1997). Finally, it should also be remembered that many of those individuals who meet the definition of having a mental disorder live a rather normal life in many, if not most, ways.

Culturally appropriate responses are not diagnosable

CULTURAL ISSUES AND THE MENTAL DISORDERS   Over the years, the DSM has been criticized as not being cross-culturally sensitive. This has been reinforced by the fact that minorities tend to be misdiagnosed at higher rates than Whites (Atkinson, 2004; Horwitz, 2002). In addition, some argue that the use of a diagnostic criterion tends to minimize the negative influences that external events

---

[1] Parts of this section are paraphrased from DSM-IV-TR (APA, 2000).

(e.g., racism, discrimination) have on clients, particularly minority clients. Others suggest that it may not be the DSM that is the problem, but the fact that it is used by individuals untrained in cross-cultural counseling and in the nuances of DSM-IV-TR.

Whatever your view is concerning the use of diagnoses with clients, it does seem that the developers of DSM-IV-TR made a considerable effort to address cross-cultural issues. For instance, the DSM-IV-TR notes that schizophrenia is sometimes diagnosed instead of bipolar disorder in non-Whites and in younger clients. As another example, the DSM-IV-TR notes that somatic complaints, such as headaches among Latinos and fatigue and weakness among Asians, are symptoms that could be representative of depression more frequently in these cultural groups than in others. In addition, the DSM-IV-TR includes an appendix of culture-specific syndromes not included elsewhere. Although these syndromes would often be problematic in the client's culture of origin, in the United States the syndromes often get misconstrued or exaggerated by an uninformed counselor. For example, *nervios* is included as a common type of stress disorder among Latinos, and includes symptoms of emotional distress, nervousness, tearfulness, and bodily complaints. Also, consider the term *koro*, which is defined as follows in the DSM-IV-TR:

> A term, probably of Malaysian origin, that refers to an episode of sudden and intense anxiety that the penis (or in females, the vulva and nipples) will recede into the body and possibly cause death.... (APA, 2000, p. 900)

The DSM-IV-TR also speaks to expected reactions or culturally appropriate responses to life events and suggests that these are usually not diagnosable as mental disorders, even when they cause distress in the client's life. For example, while counseling a client following the loss of a loved one, a diagnosis of major depression is usually not made even when the person shows signs of what might usually be considered major depression. Similarly, expected developmental experiences are generally not diagnosed regardless of the distress they may cause. For example, identity confusion in adolescence is viewed as a relatively common and somewhat expected reaction to adolescence and therefore not diagnosed as a mental disorder.

The DSM-IV-TR also pays much greater attention to differences in symptom expression as a function of age, gender, socioeconomic status, and culture. For example, the DSM-IV-TR notes that major depression is associated with increased withdrawal in children, over-sleeping in adolescents, and memory loss in older adults. And, relative to gender differences, the clinician is alerted that bipolar disorders are equally common among men and women; major depression is more common among women; and obsessive-compulsive disorder is more common among men.

Axis I disorders are considered treatable and often temporary

AXIS I DISORDERS: CLINICAL DISORDERS AND OTHER CONDITIONS THAT MAY BE A FOCUS OF CLINICAL ATTENTION This axis includes all disorders except those classified as personality disorders or as mental retardation (Axis II disorders). Generally, Axis I disorders are considered treatable in some fashion, and are often reimbursable by insurance companies for mental health or related services. These disorders are described below.

Disorders Usually First Diagnosed in Infancy, Childhood, or Adolescence: The disorders in this section are generally found in childhood; however, at times individuals are not diagnosed with the disorder until they are adults. Particularly important for school counselors, the disorders include learning disorders, motor skills disorders, communication disorders, pervasive developmental disorders, attention-deficit and disruptive behavior disorders, feeding and eating disorders of infancy or early childhood, tic disorders, elimination disorders, and other disorders of infancy, childhood, or adolescence.

Delirium, Dementia, Amnestic, and Other Cognitive Disorders: Delirium, dementia, and amnestic disorders are all cognitive disorders that represent a significant change from past cognitive functioning of the client. All of these disorders are caused by a medical condition or a substance (e.g., drug abuse, medication, or allergic reaction).

Mental Disorders Due to a General Medical Condition: This diagnosis is made when a mental disorder is found to be the result of a medical condition and include personality changes and mental disorders not otherwise specified. Other disorders that may at times be the result of a medical condition are listed under the following specific diagnostic categories: delirium, dementia, amnestic disorder, psychotic disorder, mood disorder, anxiety disorder, sexual dysfunction, and sleep disorder.

Substance-Related Disorders: A substance-related disorder is a direct result of the use of a drug or alcohol, the effects of medication, or exposure to a toxin. These substances include alcohol, amphetamine, caffeine, cannabis, cocaine, hallucinogens, inhalants, nicotine, opioids, phencyclidine (PCP), sedatives, and hypnotics.

Schizophrenia and Other Psychotic Disorders: All disorders classified in this section share one thing in common: psychotic symptomatology is the most distinguishing feature. The disorders include schizophrenia, schizophreniform disorder, schizoaffective disorder, delusional disorder, brief psychotic disorder, shared psychotic disorder, psychotic disorder due to a general medical condition, substance-induced psychotic disorder, and psychotic disorder not otherwise specified.

Mood Disorders: The disorders in this category include mood disturbances of the depressive, manic, or hypomanic type. The mood disorders are divided into five broad categories: depressive disorders, bipolar disorders, mood disorder due to a general medical condition, substance-induced mood disorder, and mood disorder not otherwise specified.

Anxiety Disorders: There are many types of anxiety disorders, each with its own discrete characteristics. They include panic disorder with or without agoraphobia, agoraphobia without history of panic disorder, specific phobia, obsessive-compulsive disorder, posttraumatic stress disorder, acute stress disorder, generalized anxiety disorder, anxiety disorder due to a general medical condition, substance-induced anxiety disorder, and anxiety disorder not otherwise specified.

Somatoform Disorders: Somatoform disorders are characterized by symptoms that would suggest a physical cause. However, no such cause can be found, and there is strong evidence that links the symptoms to psychological causes. Somatoform disorders include somatization disorder, undifferentiated somatoform disorder, conversion disorder, pain disorder, hypochondriasis, body dysmorphic disorder, and somatoform disorder not otherwise specified.

Factitious Disorders: As opposed to somatoform disorders, which describe individuals who believe that their physical symptoms have a physiological etiology, factitious disorders describe individuals who intentionally feign physical or psychological symptoms in order to assume the sick role. Two subtypes include factitious disorder with predominantly psychological signs and symptoms and factitious disorder with predominantly physical signs and symptoms.

Dissociative Disorders: Dissociative disorders occur when there is a disruption of consciousness, memory, identity, or perception of the environment. Dissociative disorders include dissociative amnesia, dissociative fugue, dissociative identity disorder (formerly called multiple personality disorder), depersonalization disorder, and dissociative disorder not otherwise specified.

Sexual and Gender Identity Disorders: This section includes disorders that focus on sexual problems or identity issues related to sexual issues. They include sexual dysfunctions, paraphilias, gender identity disorders, and sexual disorder not otherwise specified.

Eating Disorders: These disorders focus on severe problems with the amount of food intake by the individual that can potentially cause serious health problems or death. They include anorexia nervosa, bulimia nervosa, and eating disorder not otherwise specified.

Sleep Disorders: These disorders have to do with severe sleep-related problems and are broken down into four subcategories: primary sleep disorders, sleep disorder related to another mental condition, sleep disorder due to a general medical condition, and substance-induced sleep disorder.

Impulse Control Disorders Not Elsewhere Classified: Impulse control disorders are highlighted by the individual's inability to stop himself or herself from exhibiting certain behaviors. They include intermittent explosive disorder, kleptomania, pyromania, pathological gambling, trichotillomania, and impulse-control disorder not otherwise specified.

Adjustment Disorders: Probably the most common disorders clinicians see in private practice, adjustment disorders are highlighted by emotional or behavioral symptoms that arise in response to psychosocial stressors. The subtypes of this diagnosis include adjustment disorders with depressed mood, with anxiety, with mixed anxiety and depressed mood, with disturbance of conduct, with mixed disturbance of emotions and conduct, and unspecified adjustment disorder.

EXERCISE 11.1   DIAGNOSING AXIS I DISORDERS

After the class has become familiar with the disorders included in Axis I, your instructor may ask a student to role-play an Axis I diagnosis. Using the criteria listed in the DSM-IV-TR, try to identify the diagnosis (you may also want to use the decision tree located in DSM-IV-TR to guide you). You may want to role-play a series of Axis I diagnoses.

Axis II disorders tend to be lifelong and resistant to treatment

AXIS II DISORDERS: PERSONALITY DISORDERS AND MENTAL RETARDATION   Axis II diagnoses tend to be long-term disorders in which treatment almost always has little or no effect on changing the presenting symptoms of the individual. The two kinds of Axis II disorders are mental retardation and personality disorders.

Mental Retardation: Characterized by intellectual functioning significantly below average (below the second percentile) as well as problems with adaptive skills, mental retardation can have many different etiologies. There are four categories of mental retardation: mild mental retardation (IQ of 50-55 to approximately 70), moderate mental retardation (IQ of 35-40 to 50-55), severe mental retardation (IQ of 20-25 to 35-40), and profound mental retardation (IQ below 20 or 25).

Personality Disorders: Individuals with a personality disorder show deeply ingrained, inflexible, and enduring patterns of relating to the world that lead to distress and impairment in functioning. Such an individual may have difficulty understanding self and others, may be emotionally labile, have difficulty in relationships, and have problems with impulse control. Personality disorders are generally first recognized in adolescence or early adulthood and often remain throughout one's lifetime. There are three clusters of personality disorders, with each cluster representing a general way of relating to the world.

- Cluster A includes paranoid, schizoid, and schizotypal personality disorders. Individuals with these disorders all exhibit characteristics that may be considered odd or eccentric by others.
- Cluster B disorders include the antisocial, borderline, histrionic, and narcissistic personality disorders. Individuals suffering from these disorders are generally dramatic, emotional, overly sensitive, and erratic.
- Cluster C includes the avoidant, dependent, and obsessive-compulsive personality disorders. Common characteristics found within this cluster are anxious and fearful traits.

EXERCISE 11.2   DIAGNOSING AXIS II DISORDERS

After the class has become familiar with the disorders included in Axis II, your instructor may ask a student to role-play one of the personality disorders. Using the criteria listed in the DSM-IV-TR, try to identify the diagnosis. You may want to role-play a few of the personality disorders.

Axis III lists medical conditions that cause disorders or may affect treatment

AXIS III: GENERAL MEDICAL CONDITIONS   Axis III provides the clinician the opportunity to report relevant medical conditions of the client. If the medical condition is clearly related to the cause or worsening of a mental disorder, then a medical condition is noted on Axis I and listed on Axis III. If the medical condition is not a cause of the mental disorder but will affect overall treatment of the individual, then it is listed only on Axis III. An example of an Axis III medical condition that could be a cause of an Axis I diagnosis would be the development of hypothyroidism that causes an anxiety disorder. In this case, on Axis I the anxiety disorder due to a general medical condition is noted, and on Axis III the specific medical condition is listed. The International Classification of Diseases, ninth revision (ICD-9-CM), an abbreviated form of which is found in the DSM-IV-TR, is used to code the Axis III medical condition. Axis I uses the DSM-IV-TR classification and includes a reference to the medical condition, as follows:

Axis I: Anxiety Disorders Due to a General Medical Condition (293.84)

Axis III: Hypothyroidism, acquired (244.9)

On the other hand, if an individual has a sleep disorder and subsequently develops acute prostatitis (infection of the prostate) that worsens, but did not cause, the sleep disorder, the diagnosis would be written as:

Axis I: Narcolepsy (347)

Axis III: Prostatitis (618.9)

If there is no Axis III diagnosis, then "Axis III: None" is included in the diagnosis.

EXERCISE 11.3 DIAGNOSING MEDICAL CONDITIONS

Your instructor may ask one or more of the role-play clients from Exercise 11.1 or 11.2 to role-play a medical condition listed in DSM-IV-TR. Identify the medical condition in DSM-IV-TR and write out the Axis I, Axis II, and Axis III diagnoses. Make sure that the medical condition is referenced on Axis I or II if it is the cause of the diagnosis.

Axis IV lists psychosocial and environmental factors affecting the client

AXIS IV: PSYCHOSOCIAL AND ENVIRONMENTAL PROBLEMS Axis IV includes psychosocial or environmental problems that affect the diagnosis, treatment, and prognosis of mental disorders listed on Axes I and II. Generally, such problems will be listed only on Axis IV, but in those cases where it is believed that such stressors may be a prime cause of the mental disorder, a reference should be made to them on Axis I or II. General categories of psychosocial and environmental problems include problems with one's primary support group, problems related to the social environment, educational problems, occupational problems, housing problems, economic problems, problems with access to health care services, and problems related to interaction with the legal system/crime. An example of an Axis IV diagnosis is:

AXIS IV: JOB LOSS.

EXERCISE 11.4 DIAGNOSING PSYCHOSOCIAL AND ENVIRONMENTAL PROBLEMS

Your instructor may ask the role-play client(s) from Exercise 11.3 to continue to role-play, or start a new role-play, but this time to portray psychosocial and/or environmental problems. Identify the condition in DSM-IV-TR and write out the Axis I, Axis II, Axis III, and Axis IV diagnoses. Make sure that the psychosocial and environmental problem is listed twice if it is a cause of the Axis I or Axis II diagnosis.

Axis V-GAF
Numerical scale (0–100) indicating the client's overall functioning

AXIS V: GLOBAL ASSESSMENT OF FUNCTIONING (GAF) Axis V is a scale used by the clinician to assess the client's overall functioning and is based on an assessment of the client's psychological, social, and occupational functioning. The GAF scale ranges from very severe dysfunction to superior functioning, and a score of 0 means there is inadequate information to make a judgment (see Table 11.1).

TABLE 11.1 | GLOBAL ASSESSMENT OF FUNCTIONING SCALE (GAF)

Code*	
100 | 91	Superior functioning in a wide range of activities, life's problems never seem to get out of hand, is sought out by others because of his or her many positive qualities. No symptoms.
90 | 81	Absent or minimal symptoms (e.g., mild anxiety before an exam), good functioning in all areas, interested and involved in a wide range of activities, socially effective, generally satisfied with life, no more than everyday problems or concerns (e.g., an occasional argument with family members).
80 | 71	If symptoms are present, they are transient and expectable reactions to psychosocial stressors (e.g., difficulty concentrating after family argument); no more than slight impairment in social, occupational, or school functioning (e.g., temporarily falling behind in schoolwork).
70 | 61	Some mild symptoms (e.g., depressed mood and mild insomnia) OR some difficulty in social, occupational, or school functioning (e.g., occasional truancy, or theft within the household), but generally functioning pretty well, has some meaningful inter-personal relationships.
60 | 51	Moderate symptoms (e.g., flat affect and circumstantial speech, occasional panic attacks) OR some difficulty in social, occupational, or school functioning (e.g., few friends, conflicts with peers or co-workers).
50 | 41	Serious symptoms (e.g., suicidal ideation, severe obsessional rituals, frequent shoplifting) OR any serious impairment in social occupational, or school functioning (e.g., no friends, unable to keep a job).
40 | | 31	Some impairment in reality testing or communication (e.g., speech is at times illogical, obscure, or irrelevant) OR major impairment in several areas, such as work or school, family relations, judgment, thinking, or mood (e.g., depressed man avoids friends, neglects family, and is unable to work; child frequently beats up younger children, is defiant at home, and is failing at school).
30 | | 21	Behavior is considerably influenced by delusions or hallucinations OR serious impairment in communication or judgment (e.g., sometimes incoherent, acts grossly inappropriately, suicidal preoccupation) OR inability to function in almost all areas (e.g., stays in bed all day; no job, home, or friends).
20 | 11	Some danger of hurting self or others (e.g., suicide attempts without clear expectation of death: frequently violent; manic excitement) OR occasionally fails to maintain minimal personal hygiene (e.g., smears feces) OR gross impairment in communication (e.g., largely incoherent or mute).
10 | | 1	Persistent danger of severely hurting self or others (e.g., recurrent violence) OR persistent inability to maintain minimal personal hygiene OR serious suicidal act with clear expectation of death.
0	Inadequate information.

*Note: Use intermediate codes when appropriate, e.g., 45, 68, 72.

Source: Used with permission from the Diagnostic and Statistical Manual of Mental Disorders, Fourth Edition—Text Revision, p. 34. Copyright 2000. American Psychiatric Association.

In giving a GAF rating, the clinician can report current functioning, the highest functioning within the past year, or any other relevant GAF ratings based on the uniqueness of the situation.

EXERCISE 11.5 USING THE GAF SCALE

From any of the past role-plays you have done, or from a new one, determine a GAF score for your client(s). In some cases, you may need to probe with the client to make an accurate assessment of the score. The instructor might want to have each student in the class do this exercise independently, and then have the students compare their scores with one another.

MAKING A DIAGNOSIS

When making a diagnosis, list all five axes when possible or appropriate

The DSM-IV-TR offers decision trees to assist the clinician in differential diagnosis. Thus, if one is considering two or more diagnoses that share similar symptoms, the decision tree walks the clinician through a series of steps designed to assist in choosing the most appropriate diagnosis. Making an appropriate diagnosis is critically important because the diagnosis will affect treatment planning and choices of psychotropic medication. It is possible for a client to have more than one Axis I and Axis II diagnosis, and in those cases the additional diagnoses should be reported. A multiaxial assessment may look something like the following:

Axis I	309.0	Adjustment Disorder with Depressed Mood
Axis II	301.82	Avoidant Personality Disorder
Axis III		No Diagnosis
Axis IV		Divorce
Axis V		GAF = 60 (current); 75 (highest in past year)

As you become more familiar with DSM-IV-TR, the process of making a diagnosis will become easier and you will see how helpful such a diagnosis can be in treatment planning. Exercise 11.6 gives you an opportunity to use DSM-IV-TR in making a diagnosis.

FINAL THOUGHTS ON DSM-IV-TR IN THE ASSESSMENT PROCESS

Diagnosis adds clarity to the assessment process

DSM-IV-TR is one additional piece of the total assessment process. Along with the clinical interview, the use of tests, and informal assessment procedures, it can provide a broad understanding of the client and can be a critical piece in the treatment planning process. Consider what it might be like to establish a treatment plan if only one test were used. Then, consider what it would be like if two tests were used, then two tests and an informal assessment procedure, then two tests, an informal assessment procedure, and a clinical interview, and finally, two tests, an informal assessment procedure, a clinical interview, and a diagnosis. Clearly, the more "pieces of evidence" we can gather, the clearer our snapshot of our client becomes and this, in turn, yields better treatment planning.

EXERCISE 11.6 USING THE FIVE AXES OF DSM-IV-TR

Examine the cases that follow, and using this chapter as well as the DSM-IV-TR as your guide, describe each client on the five axes of DSM-IV-TR. The answers can be found at the end of the chapter.

JOSHUA

Joshua is a 10-year-old only child. His parents, Marie, who is 27, and Billy, who is 28, have been married for six years and have commented on what a difficult child Joshua has been since birth. They state that he always had a difficult time in school and could not read until he was in fourth grade. His reading scores have been particularly low, and his teacher has suggested having him tested for a possible reading learning disability. No obvious physical problems have been found to cause his deficiency in reading.

In addition to his reading problems, Joshua seems to cry easily and often "has a fit" when he has to leave home to go to school. He is plagued by nightmares, often revolving around issues of being alone or separated from his parents. He often has stomachaches and has vomited at school on numerous occasions. Joshua's reading problems and his anxiety have interfered with his ability to build friendships, and he has no close friends and few peers he relates to at school. His parents, who are college educated, are worried that their son will not make it through high school, and they are concerned about his social relationships.

TRINA

Trina is a 53-year-old separated female with no children. She presents with moderate depression and states she has had fleeting thoughts of suicide. However, she remarks that she would never kill herself—"that would be just damn stupid." When you inquire about her depression, she notes that her husband just "got up and left me!" Trina goes on to say that her husband left her about two months ago, and she has been feeling depressed ever since. She reports having no past history of depression.

Trina is morbidly obese, weighing about 320 lbs at 5'4" tall. She states, "I have always been

fat, and that's why my husband married me—he loves fat ladies—well, he used to." She states that her life is worthless, and she is worried that she will never find anyone else who will love her like her husband did. She states that her life revolved around her husband because she would be his "cook, errand girl, friend, and everything else." She goes on to note that she has never felt this way before. Although she reports having a few friends, she states that they can hardly fill the hole she has had in her heart since her husband left. Trina has a high school education and has worked intermittently in the food industry. She currently is employed on a part-time basis and states, "At least I don't think about him when I'm at work." She notes that she is relieved that she is in counseling and hopes that she can build a new life, even without him.

HENRY

Henry is 75-years-old and currently lives in a group home for the mentally ill. Until he was in his early 30s, he was married and raising two children. However, when he was about 34 he began to have delusional thoughts, thinking that he had been somehow picked to be the next Czar of the Soviet Empire. At that time, he would often go to the Russian consulate and walk in front of the building carrying a sign that said, "Your Czar is here, I have arrived." A couple of times he tried to run into the consulate, was arrested, and landed in jail overnight. Since his early 30s he has had little or no contact with his children and has alternated between living on the streets, being in state hospitals, and living in group homes. His wife divorced him about forty years ago and he has not heard from her since. Although medication seems to have settled down his delusional thoughts, he has never been the same as he was before he became delusional. For years he has not been able to hold a job and has had no social outlets. He has a flat affect and is often incoherent. Despite his limitations, he seems to be able to function on a minimal level in group homes or on the streets.

SUMMARY

We began this chapter by discussing the importance of a diagnosis and noting that no matter where you work, you will be faced with individuals who have a mental disorder. Specifically, we noted that diagnostic skills are important because there are federal laws pertaining to the schools and the labeling of children, diagnosis is required for insurance reimbursement, having a common system for diagnosis allows us to communicate effectively with colleagues, there is evidence of biological determinants of many mental disorders, and accurate diagnosis is an essential part of the total assessment process.

In the next part of the chapter we gave a brief history of the *Diagnostic and Statistical Manual* and then discussed the five axes of DSM-IV-TR. We noted that Axis I describes "Clinical Disorders and Other Conditions That May Be a Focus of Clinical Attention," Axis II delineates "Personality Disorders and Mental Retardation," Axis III explains "General Medical Conditions," Axis IV describes "Psychosocial and Environmental Problems," and Axis V offers a "Global Assessment of Functioning."

Looking at Axes I and II, we noted that for each mental disorder there is a description of the disorder's main features, subtypes and variations in client presentations, the progression of symptoms, and how to differentiate disorders. We also noted that the DSM-IV-TR provides findings about predisposing factors, complications, and associated medical and counseling problems and does not hypothesize about etiology when information is unknown. We pointed out that DSM-IV-TR diagnoses are intended to be theory-neutral descriptions of disorders, thus allowing clinicians to apply their own theoretical orientation to the treatment planning process.

From a diagnostic standpoint, we noted that the vast majority of human behavior does not meet the definition of "mental disorder."

From a cultural perspective, we noted that expected, culturally appropriate behavior or predictable developmental experiences are not diagnosed as mental disorders. We highlighted the fact that the DSM-IV-TR was constructed with much greater attention to issues of age, gender, socioeconomic status, and culture than were past editions. We also noted that the DSM-IV-TR discusses differences in expression of some disorders as a function of culture and age. Finally, we noted that the DSM-IV-TR includes an appendix of culture-specific client experiences not included elsewhere.

Next we offered a brief overview of the Axis I and Axis II disorders and then went on to describe Axis III Disorders: General Medical Conditions. We noted that when a medical condition is found to somehow cause or be related to an Axis I or Axis II condition, it should be referenced on that axis as well as on Axis III. This, we noted, is similar to how one would list the psychosocial stressors in Axis IV. Finally, we presented the General Assessment of Functioning (GAF) scale and noted how it is used to rate the client's level of functioning on Axis V. We gave examples of how to make a diagnosis using the five axes and offered some case studies as practice.

The chapter concluded with a discussion about the importance of a diagnosis in the total process of assessing a client. We noted that the more "pieces of evidence" we can gather (e.g., tests, informal assessment, clinical interviews, and a diagnosis), the clearer our snapshot of our client becomes and the better our treatment planning will be.

CHAPTER REVIEW

1. Explain why diagnosis is important in the following settings:
   a. schools
   b. mental health agencies
   c. private practice
   d. hospital settings

2. Describe the ways in which diagnosis can be abused.
3. Make an argument for the usefulness of diagnosis.
4. List and describe each of the five axes of DSM-IV-TR and show how it is used.
5. Describe how each mental disorder is explained in DSM-IV-TR (Axis I and Axis II disorders).
6. Relative to the mental disorders, describe how DSM-IV-TR addresses cross-cultural issues.
7. Give examples of how Axis III and Axis IV disorders may or may not be listed on two axes.
8. Describe each of the individuals listed in Exercise 11.6 on the five axes of DSM-IV-TR. If you have already completed Exercise 11.6 or would like additional practice in making diagnoses, use case vignettes from readings or case examples from your classes.

ANSWERS TO EXERCISE 11.6 USING THE FIVE AXES OF DSM-IV-TR

Joshua

Axis I:	315.00	Rule Out Reading Disorder
	309.21	Separation Anxiety Disorder
Axis II:		None
Axis III:		Stomachaches
Axis IV:		Problems relating to peers at school
Axis V:		GAF = 61 (Current)

Trina

Axis I:	309.0	Adjustment Disorder with Depression, Acute
Axis II:		None
Axis III:	278.00	Obesity
Axis IV:		Separation from husband
Axis V:		GAF = 55 (Current) (75 over past year)

Henry

Axis I:	295.60	Schizophrenia, Residual Type
Axis II:		None
Axis III:		None
Axis IV:		Severe psychosocial problems: Intermittent homelessness Problems forming friendships
Axis V:		GAF = 23 (Over past year)

REFERENCES

American Psychiatric Association. (2000). *Diagnostic and statistical manual of mental disorders* (4th ed., text revision). Washington, DC: Author.

Atkinson, D. R. (2004). Addressing the mental health needs of ethnic minorities. In D. R. Atkinson (Ed.), *Counseling American minorities* (pp. 57–80). New York: McGraw-Hill.

Beutler, L. E., & Malik, M. L. (Eds.). (2002). *Rethinking the DSM: A psychobiological perspective.*
Washington, DC: American Psychological Association.

Galatzer-Levy, I.R., & Galatzer-Levy, R. M. (2007). The revolution in psychiatric diagnosis: Problems at the foundations. *Perspectives in Biology and Medicine, 50*(2), 161–180.

Hersen, M., & Van Hasselt, V. B. (2001). (Eds.). *Advanced abnormal psychology* (2nd ed.). New York: Plenum Press.

Horwitz, A. V. (2002). *The social control of mental illness.* Clinton Corners, NY: Percheron.

Jongsma, A. E., Jr., & Peterson, L. M. (1999). *The complete adult psychotherapy treatment planner* (2nd ed.). New York: Wiley. Press.

Karlin, B. E., Duff, M., & Gleaves, D. H. (2008). Patterns and predictors of mental health service use and mental illness. *Psychological Services, 5*(3), 275–294.

Kessler, R. C, Chiu, W. T., Demler, O., & Walters, E. E. (2005). Prevalence, severity, and comorbidity of twelve-month DSM-IV disorders in the National Comorbidity Survey Replication (NCS-R). *Archives of General Psychiatry, 62*(6), 617–627.

Neukrug, E., & Schwitzer, A. (2006). *Skills and tools for today's counselors and psychotherapists: From natural helping to professional counseling.* Pacific Grove, CA: Brooks/Cole.

Schwitzer, A. M. (1996). Using the inverted pyramid heuristic in counselor education and supervision. *Counselor Education and Supervision, 35,* 258–267.

Schwitzer, A. M., & Everett, A. (1997). Reintroducing the *DSM-IV*: Responses to ten counselor reservations about diagnosis. *The Virginia Counselors Journal, 25,* 54–64.

Segal, D. L., & Coolidge, F. L. (2001). Diagnosis and classification. In M. Hersen & V. B. Van Hasselt, (Eds.), *Advanced abnormal psychology* (2nd ed.) (pp. 5–22). New York: Kluwer Academic/Plenum Publishers.

Seligman, L. (1999). Twenty years of diagnosis and the DSM. *Journal of Mental Health Counseling, 21,* 229–239.

Seligman, L. (2004). *Diagnosis and treatment planning in counseling* (3rd ed.). New York: Plenum.

Slovenko, R. (2002). The role of psychiatric diagnosis in the law. *Journal of Psychiatry & Law, 30*(3), 421–444.

Thyer, B. A. (2006). It is time to rename the DSM? *Ethical Human Psychology and Psychiatry, 8*(1), 61–67.

Zalaquett, C. P., Fuerth, K. M. Stein, C. Ivey, A. E. & Ivey, M. B. (2008). *Journal of Counseling & Development, 86*(3), 364–371.

THE ASSESSMENT REPORT PROCESS: INTERVIEWING THE CLIENT AND WRITING THE REPORT

"Increasing numbers of people are writing and reading increasing numbers of mental health records for increasing number of purposes, and that trend is likely to continue"

(Reynolds, Mair, & Fischer, 1995, p. 1).

When I began working with clients in the early 1970s, I was dutiful about writing down my case notes on lined paper. Soon it was the mid-70s, and I got a job as an outpatient therapist at a mental health center. I was compulsive about conducting thorough clinical interviews, and religious about dictating my case notes, my intake summaries, and my quarterly summaries. My dictations were carefully typed out by secretaries and placed in client folders. Ten years later, I was in private practice. I was still compulsive about conducting a thorough interview and about writing up my case notes—again on lined paper. But soon an innovation arrived I hadn't expected—the computer. I started doing my notes on the computer—that was a relief for me, although not everyone felt the same way. Soon after my discovery of the computer, the HMOs and PPOs multiplied and an increasing number of laws were passed that had to do with case note confidentiality, the rights of insurance companies, and the rights of clients. The paperwork was beginning to drive me nutty! Soon, computer programs were devised to help write case reports and Internet connections to the insurance companies to streamline billing became a reality, but it happened a little too late for me. I'm out of here. No more private practice for me—too much paperwork!

(Ed Neukrug)

As you can see from the above quote and vignette, the process of gathering information about clients and writing reports that will affect them has become increasingly complex. Although most practitioners will not respond like I did (I did have another job teaching!), there is little question that paperwork today is a major part of what all practitioners do. In this chapter we will examine this process.

First, we will discuss the purpose of the assessment report and then discuss the process of gathering information for the report, including conducting the interview, and choosing appropriate assessment techniques. Then we will suggest ways to write effective test reports and we will supply an example of such a report.

PURPOSE OF THE ASSESSMENT REPORT

Assessment report

Written summary, synthesis, and recommendations from the assessment

The assessment report is the "deliverable" or "end product" of the assessment process. Its purpose is to synthesize an assortment of assessment techniques so that a deeper understanding of the examinee is made and recommended courses of action are offered (Lichtenberger, Mather, Kaufman, & Kaufman, 2004; Ownby, 1997; Reynolds et al., 1995). Such courses of action can vary dramatically, based on the reason the individual is being assessed. For instance, some of the many purposes of reports include the following:

1. To respond to the referral questions being asked.
2. To provide insight to clients for therapy.
3. To assist in the case-conceptualization process.
4. To develop treatment options in counseling (e.g., type of counseling, use of medications, etc.)
5. To suggest educational services for students with special needs (e.g., for students who are mentally retarded, learning disabled, or gifted).
6. To offer direction when providing vocational rehabilitation services.
7. To offer insight about and treatment options for individuals who have incurred a cognitive impairment (e.g., brain injury, senility).
8. To assist the courts in making difficult decisions (e.g., custody decisions, sanity defenses, determination of guilt or innocence).
9. To providence evidence for placement into schools and jobs.
10. To challenge decisions made by institutions and agencies (social security disability, school IEPs).

Because complex decisions regarding clients' lives are often based on the assessment report, synthesizing the information gathered and placing it in the report is only accomplished after the examiner can conduct interviews successfully, administer assessment procedures proficiently, and write reports skillfully. One of the first steps in this process is to ensure that any information gathered is directly related to the purpose of the assessment and is of high quality.

GATHERING INFORMATION FOR THE REPORT: GARBAGE IN, GARBAGE OUT

Gathering information for the report is as important as writing the report, because your report will reflect the methods you used to obtain your information. If you choose inappropriate instruments or conduct a poor interview ("garbage in"), your report will be filled with error and bias ("garbage out"). To help ensure that the information you are gathering is of high quality, you should always take into account the breadth and depth of your assessment procedures.

Breadth
Covering all important or relevant issues; wide net

The breadth of the assessment has to do with casting a wide enough net to ensure that the examiner has done all that is necessary to adequately assess what he or she is looking for. Breadth should be based upon the purpose of the assessment. For instance, if a middle school student came to see a school counselor to examine career possibilities, the counselor would likely conduct an interview focused on vocational interests and offer a broad-based career interest inventory to gather information from the student about his or her general interests. However, if an adult came to a counseling center as a result of depression, anxiety, and general discontent in life, a very broad assessment might be called for to help establish a diagnosis and determine treatment goals. In this case, it would not be unusual to conduct a clinical interview, administer a number of objective and projective tests, and perhaps interview others to assess the client's relationships at home and at work.

Depth
Extent and seriousness of a concern

The depth of the assessment has to do with ensuring that one is using techniques that reflect the intensity of the issue(s) being examined. As with breadth, depth is also dependent on the purpose for which the client is being assessed. For instance, conducting an in-depth clinical interview and offering a rather complex interest inventory that helps the middle school student *determine* a career would be too involved—too much depth. On the other hand, offering a personality inventory like the Myers-Briggs for the individual suffering from depression, anxiety, and discontentment in life would not entail enough depth. You could simply miss too much because you have not delved more deeply into this client's issues.

In establishing the breadth and depth of the interview, it is important that you are able to establish trust and rapport and assure confidentiality within the limits of the purpose the individual is being assessed. The better the interviewer is able to build trust, the more likely the information obtained will be reliable. With these points in mind, examiners need to determine whether a structured, unstructured, or semi-structured interview would be best when assessing the client.

STRUCTURED, UNSTRUCTURED, AND SEMI-STRUCTURED INTERVIEWS

Clinical interview
Offers ability to obtain reliable information from clients

Determining the kind of interview to conduct is critical to gathering information successfully because the clinical interview accomplishes a number of tasks not possible through the use of other assessment techniques. For instance, the interview

1. sets the tone for the types of information that will be covered during the assessment process,
2. allows the client to become desensitized to information that can be very intimate and personal,
3. allows the examiner to assess the nonverbal signals of the client while he or she is talking about sensitive information, thus giving the examiner a sense of what might be important to focus upon,
4. allows the examiner to learn firsthand the problem areas of the client and place them in perspective, and
5. gives the client and examiner the opportunity to study each other's personality style to assure that they can work together.

Interviewers generally have a choice between three kinds of interviews: structured, unstructured, or semi-structured. With advantages and disadvantages to both, which one to choose is not always easy (Farmer, McGuffin, & Williams, 2002; Lichtenberger et al., 2004; Roth, Van Iddekinge, Huffcutt, Eidson, & Bobko, 2002). For instance, completed verbally or in response to written items, the structured interview has the examiner ask the examinee to respond to pre-established items. This kind of interview can provide the following benefits:

- It offers broad enough areas of content to cover topics a practitioner may otherwise have missed or forgotten to ask (assures breadth of coverage).
- It increases the reliability of results by ensuring that all prescribed items will be covered.
- It ensures that the examiner will cover all of the items because they are listed in detail and there is an expectation that they all will be covered.
- It ensures that items will not be missed due to interviewer or interviewee embarrassment.

Structured interview

Uses pre-established questions to assess broad range of behaviors

On the other hand, the structured interview can have the following drawbacks:

- The examiner may miss information due to the fact that items are pre-determined and the examiner does not feel free to go off on a tangent or a "hunch."
- Clients may experience the interview as dehumanizing.
- Clients, particularly minorities, may misinterpret or be unfamiliar with certain items.
- Follow-up by the examiner to alleviate any confusion on the part of the examinee is less likely as compared to other kinds of interviewing.
- It does not always allow for depth of information to be covered because the interviewer is more concerned with gathering all the information than going into detail about one potentially sensitive area.

Unstructured interview

Examiner asks questions based on client responses

Contrast the structured interview with the unstructured interview, where the examiner does not have a pre-established list of items or questions to which the client can respond. In this case, examinee responses to inquiries will set the direction for follow-up questioning. The unstructured interview offers the following advantages:

- It creates an atmosphere that is more conducive to building rapport.
- It allows the client to feel as if he or she is directing the interview, thus allowing the client to discuss items that he or she deems important.
- It offers the potential for greater depth of information because the clinician can focus upon a potentially sensitive area and possibly uncover underlying issues that the client might otherwise avoid revealing.

On the other hand, the unstructured interview may have the following disadvantages:

- Because it does not allow for breadth of coverage, the interviewer might miss information because he or she is "caught up" in the client's story instead of following a prescribed set of questions.
- The interviewer may end up spending more time on some items than he or she might like.

| BOX 12.1 | MISSING SUBSTANCE ABUSE |

When I first started doing counseling I always used an unstructured interview style. I believed it was critical to let the client take the interview where he or she wanted it to go. However, after a number of years of missing alcohol abuse as well as other "hidden" issues, I slowly began to make the switch to a more semi-structured interview style where I would go through a list of pre-determined items and also have clients complete a genogram. I had learned that clients were often embarrassed about revealing some very important information that sometimes ended up being the focus of treatment. The switch to a semi-structured interview style allowed me to quickly pick up on these issues and more quickly address what in the past had been hidden.

—*Ed Neukrug*

Semi-structured interview

Allows flow between structured and unstructured approaches

Drawing from the advantages of both the structured and unstructured interview, examiners will often conduct a semi-structured interview. This kind of interview uses prescribed items, which allows the examiner to obtain the necessary information within a relatively short amount of time. However, it also gives leeway to the examiner should the client need to "drift" during the interview process. Allowing the client to discuss potentially emotion-filled topics can be cathartic, open up new issues of importance, and be an important tool in the rapport-building process. The skilled examiner can easily flow back and forth between structured and unstructured approaches. If time is not an issue, a semi-structured interview can provide the breadth and depth needed when interviewing clients while still allowing the examiner to focus in on building the relationship (see Box 12.1)

COMPUTER-DRIVEN ASSESSMENT

Computer-driven assessment

Can result in sophisticated assessment and well-written report

Whether you are conducting a structured, unstructured, or semi-structured interview, a number of computer programs can be of assistance. For instance, one such program has the interviewer or the client complete 120 items that requests information about a wide range of personal issues, and the user receives a computer-generated report that describes the client's presenting problems, legal issues, current living situation, tentative diagnosis, emotional state, treatment recommendations, mental status, health and habits, disposition, and behavioral/ physical descriptions (see Schinka, 2003). Computer-assisted questioning is as reliable or perhaps sometimes more reliable than structured interviews and can provide an accurate diagnosis at a minimal cost (Farmer, et al., 2002). Final assessment reports generated by computer-driven programs have become so sophisticated that most well-trained clinicians cannot tell them apart from reports written by seasoned professionals.

In addition to the interviewing process, computers can generate test reports, and oftentimes pieces of these reports can be moved directly into the examiner's written assessment report (Berger, 2006; Michaels, 2006). However, whether it is a computer-generated report that resulted from a client interview or a report that includes aspects of computer-generated tests reports, it is still up to the examiner to make sure that the correct questions are being asked of the client, the correct assessment procedures are being used, and that the material used in the development of the examiner's assessment report is chosen wisely by the examiner.

> While the computer may administer these [tests] and even prepare a report, what the test looks like, how it responds, what it achieves and any reports generated, are predetermined by the author, and it is a person who puts it all together to make the interpretation. (Berger, p. 70)

CHOOSING AN APPROPRIATE ASSESSMENT INSTRUMENT

Only choose assessment technique to match purpose of testing

After the interview, clinicians can consider the purpose of their assessment as well as the breadth and depth of other needed information. Then clinicians can choose from a broad array of assessment instruments, such as those we examined in this text, including assessment of educational ability (Chapter 6), assessment of intellectual and cognitive functioning through intelligence testing and neuropsychological assessment (Chapter 7), career and occupational assessment (Chapter 8), clinical assessment (Chapter 9), and informal assessment (Chapter 10). In this process it is important that clinicians carefully reflect on which are the most appropriate instruments to use, for it is unethical to assess an individual using instruments that are not related to the purpose of the assessment being undertaken (see American Counseling Association, 2005; American Psychological Association, 2002) (see Box 12.2).

> Counselors are responsible for the appropriate application, scoring, interpretation, and use of assessment instruments relevant to the needs of the client, whether they score and interpret such assessments themselves or use technology or other services. (ACA, Section E.2.b)

and

> Psychologists administer, adapt, score, interpret, or use assessment techniques, interviews, tests, or instruments in a manner and for purposes that are appropriate in light of the research on or evidence of the usefulness and proper application of the techniques. (APA, Section 9.01.a)

WRITING THE REPORT

After you have conducted a thorough assessment of your client, you will be ready to write your report. Reports are scrutinized today more than ever before because they are the mechanism used by the interviewer to communicate his or her

| BOX 12.2 | PROPER ASSESSMENT OF A CLIENT |

As mentioned in Chapter 9, I was once hired to write an assessment report for the expressed purpose of challenging the denial of a client's social security disability payments despite the fact that she had been diagnosed as having a multiple personality disorder. Aware of her disorder, and having worked hard to integrate her various personalities in therapy, she was, however, quite depressed and at times would dissociate. Because the task at hand was to assess the client's ability to work rather than to affirm her diagnosis, it was important to choose instruments that would only address the assessment question: Could this client effectively hold down employment?

—*Ed Neukrug*

| BOX 12.3 | 15 SUGGESTIONS FOR WRITING REPORTS |

1. Omit passive verbs.
2. Be nonjudgmental.
3. Reduce the use of jargon.
4. Do not use a patronizing tone.
5. Increase the use of subheadings.
6. Reduce the use of and define acronyms.
7. Minimize the number of difficult words.
8. Try to use shorter rather than longer words.
9. Make sure paragraphs are concise and flow well.
10. Point out strengths and weaknesses of your client.
11. Don't try to dazzle the reader of your report with your brilliance.
12. When possible, describe behaviors that are representative of client issues.
13. Only label when it is necessary and valuable to do so for the client's well-being.
14. Write the report so a non—mental-health professional can understand it (e.g., a teacher).
15. Don't be afraid to take a stand if you feel strongly that the information warrants it (e.g., the information leads you to believe a client is in danger of harming self).

FERPA, HIPAA, Freedom of Information Act

Increase clients' ability to access records

Writing assessment reports

Know "tips" to good report writing

assessment to stakeholders and are often used by funding agencies and supervisors when evaluating a clinician's work. In addition, as a result of laws passed over the years, such as the Family Educational Rights and Privacy Act (FERPA), the Freedom of Information Act, and the Health Insurance Portability and Accountability Act (HIPAA) (see Chapter 2), clients will generally have access to their records if they choose to review them. Keeping all of the above in mind, Box 12.3 offers a summary of a number suggestions concerning how to write a report (Drummond, 2006; Harvey, 1997; Lictenberger et al., 2004; Ownby, 1997; Reynolds et al., 1995).

Although many clinicians these days are asked to write involved reports, the actual format of the report tends to vary from setting to setting. For example, a large mental health clinic may specify a preferred or required format for its therapists. Similarly, a social worker in private practice may be driven to a particular format by insurance provider requirements, while a school counselor may have to use an established format required by his or her guidance supervisor.

Although report formats vary, they will often include the following sections: (1) demographic information, (2) presenting problem or reason for referral, (3) family background, (4) significant medical/counseling history, (5) substance use and abuse, (6) educational and vocational history, (7) other pertinent information, (8) mental status, (9) assessment results, (10) diagnosis, (11) summary and conclusions, and (12) recommendations. Let's take a look at each of these areas in more detail.

DEMOGRAPHIC INFORMATION

In this section we find basic information about the client, including such items as the client's name, address, phone number, e-mail address, date of birth, age, sex, ethnicity, and date of interview. Also, it is in this section that the name of the interviewer is placed. Often, this information is included at the top of the report. The following is an example of the demographic information gathered from a fictitious client, Mr. Unclear.

Name: Eduardo (Ed) Unclear   D.O.B.: 1/8/1961

Address: 223 Confused Lane   Age: 48

       Coconut Creek, Florida   Sex: Male

Phone: 954-969-5555   Ethnicity: Hispanic

E-mail: iunclear@hotmail.net   Date of Interview: 2/22/2009

Name of Interviewer: May I. Assessu

PRESENTING PROBLEM OR REASON FOR REFERRAL

In this section, the person who referred the client is generally noted (e.g., self-referred, physician, counselor) and an explanation is given as to why the individual has come for counseling and/or why the examiner has been asked to do the assessment. For instance, here it might be explained that a social worker has been asked to do a court assessment of a child for a custody hearing; a school psychologist has been asked to assess a child who has been exhibiting severe behavioral problems at school, for a possible diagnosis of emotional disturbance; or a licensed clinician in private practice might suggest to a client an assessment to help sort out a diagnosis and to set treatment goals. Continuing with our example of Mr. Unclear, we might include the following information:

> This 48-year-old married male was self-referred due to high levels of stress. The client reports feeling anxious for the past two years and intermittently depressed for the past seven or eight years. He states that he feels discontent with his marriage and confused about his future. An assessment was conducted to assist in determining diagnosis and course of treatment.

FAMILY BACKGROUND

The family background section of the report is an opportunity to give the reader an understanding of possible factors concerning the client's upbringing that may be related to his or her presenting problem. Trivial bits of information should be left out of this section, and opinions regarding this information should be saved for the summary and conclusions section of the report.

In this section, it is often useful to mention where the individual grew up, sexes and ages of siblings, whether the client came from an intact family, who were the major caretakers, and significant others who may have had an impact on the client's life. The examiner may also want to relay important stories from childhood that have affected how the client defines himself or herself. For adults, one should also include such items as marital status, marital or relationship issues, ages and sexes of any children, and significant others. Using our example, we might include the following information:

> Mr. Unclear was raised in Miami, Florida. His parents were Cuban refugees, and Mr. Unclear notes that when he was 5 years old, his parents fled Cuba on a fishing boat with him and his two brothers, José, who is two years older, and Juan, who is two years younger. Mr. Unclear comes from an intact family. His father died approximately four years ago of a "heart disorder." He states that his parents were "loving but strict" and notes that his father was "in

charge" of the family and would often "take a belt to me." However, he describes both parents as loving and caring and says that they "took care of all my needs." He reports that he and his brothers were always close and that both brothers currently live within 1 mile of his home. He states that his younger brother is married and has two children, and he describes his other brother as single and a "closeted homosexual." His father, he reports, was a bookkeeper and his mother a stay-at-home mom. He and his brothers went to Catholic school, and he states that he tended to be a good student and had the "normal" number of friends.

Mr. Unclear notes that when he was 20 he met his wife Carla in college. They married when he was 21 and quickly had two children, Carlita and Carmen, who are now 27 and 26. Both daughters are college-educated, work in professional jobs, and are married. Carlita has two children aged 3 and 4, while Carmen has one child aged 5. He notes that both daughters and their families live close to him. He states that although his marriage was "good" for the first 20 years, in recent years he has found himself feeling unloved and depressed. He wonders if he should remain in the marriage.

SIGNIFICANT MEDICAL/COUNSELING HISTORY

This section of the report delineates any significant medical history, especially any physical conditions that may be affecting the client's psychological state. In addition, any history of counseling should be noted in this section. Mr. Unclear's medical and counseling history is summarized below:

Mr. Unclear states that approximately four years ago he was in a serious car accident that subsequently left him with chronic back pain. Although he takes prescribed medication intermittently for the pain, he states that he mostly tries to "live without drugs." He notes that he often feels fatigued and has trouble sleeping, often sleeping only four hours a night. However, he reports that his medical exam has revealed no apparent medical reason for his fatigue and sleep difficulties. He notes no other significant medical history, although he reports that in the past two years he has had obsessive worry related to fears of dying of a heart attack.

Mr. Unclear notes that after the birth of his second child, his wife needed surgery to repair vaginal tears. He states that since that time she has complained of pain during sex, and their level of intimacy dropped significantly. He notes that he and his wife went to couples therapy for about two months approximately 15 years ago. He feels that counseling did not help, and he notes that it "particularly did nothing to help our sex life."

SUBSTANCE USE AND ABUSE

This section reports the use and abuse of any legal or illegal substances that may be addictive or potentially harmful to the client. Thus, the interviewer should note the use or abuse of food, cigarettes, alcohol, prescription medication, and illegal drugs. In reference to Mr. Unclear, we include the following information:

Mr. Unclear states that he does not smoke cigarettes and occasionally smokes cigars ("I will never smoke a Cuban cigar," he notes). He describes himself as a moderate drinker and states that he has a couple of beers a day but does not tend to drink "hard liquor." He reports taking prescription medication "intermittently" for chronic back pain and he denies the use of illegal substances. He describes his eating habits as "normal."

EDUCATIONAL AND VOCATIONAL HISTORY

This section describes the client's educational background and delineates his or her job path and career focus. For Mr. Unclear, we include the following information:

Mr. Unclear went to Catholic school in Miami, Florida, and reports that he excelled in math but always had difficulty with reading and spelling. After high school, he went on to college at Miami University, majoring in business administration. After graduating with his bachelor's degree, he obtained a job as an accountant at a major tobacco import company, where he worked for 17 years. During that time he began to work on his master's in business administration but stated he never finished his degree because it was "boring." Approximately eight years ago he changed jobs and obtained employment as an accountant at a local new car company. He states he changed jobs to "make more money."

Mr. Unclear reports that relative to his accounting work, his "books were always perfect," although he went on to note that he was embarrassed by his inability to prepare a well-written report. He reports feeling dissatisfied with his career path and wanting to do something more meaningful with his life. However, he states that "I am probably too old to change careers now."

OTHER PERTINENT INFORMATION

This "catch-all" category addresses any significant information that has not been noted elsewhere. Issues that might be addressed in this section could be related to sexual orientation, changes in sexual desires, or any sexual dysfunction; any current or past legal problems that may be affecting functioning; and any financial problems the client may be having. For Mr. Unclear we include the following information:

Mr. Unclear states that he is unhappy with his sex life and reports having limited intimacy with his wife. He denies having an extramarital affair but states "I would have one if I met the right person." He notes that he is "just making it" financially, and that it was difficult to support his two children through college. He denies any problems with the law.

MENTAL STATUS

Mental status exam

Assesses appearance and behavior, emotional state, thought, and cognitive functioning

A mental status exam is an assessment of the client's appearance and behavior, emotional state, thought components, and cognitive functioning. This assessment is used to assist the interviewer in making a diagnosis and in treatment planning (Polanski & Hinkle, 2000; Aiken, 2003). A short synopsis of each of the four areas of the mental status exam follows.

APPEARANCE AND BEHAVIOR This part of the mental status exam reports the client's observable appearance and behaviors during the clinical interview. Thus, often such items as manner of dress, hygiene, body posture, tics, significant non-verbal behaviors (eye contact or the lack thereof, wringing of hands, swaying), and manner of speech (e.g., stuttering, tone) are reported.

EMOTIONAL STATE When assessing emotional state, the examiner describes the client's affect and mood. The affect is the client's current, prevailing feeling state (e.g., happy, sad, joyful, angry, depressed, etc.), and may also be reported as constricted or full, appropriate or inappropriate to content, labile, flat, blunted, exaggerated, and so forth. The client's mood, on the other hand, represents the long-term, underlying emotional well being of the client and is usually assessed through client self-report. Thus, a client may seem anxious and sad during the session (affect) and report that his or her mood has been depressed.

THOUGHT COMPONENTS The manner in which a client thinks can reveal much about how he or she comes to understand and make meaning of the world. Thought components are generally broken down into the content and the process of thinking. Clinicians will often make statements about thought content by addressing whether the client has delusions, distortions of body image, hallucinations, obsessions, suicidal or homicidal ideation, and so forth. The kinds of thought processes often identified include circumstantiality, coherence, flight of ideas, logical thinking, intact as opposed to loose associations, organization, and tangentiality.

COGNITION Cognition includes a statement as to whether the client is oriented to time, place, and person (knows what time it is, where he or she is, and who he or she is); an assessment of the client's short- and long-term memory; an evaluation of the client's knowledge base and intellectual functioning; and a statement about the client's level of insight and ability to make judgments.

Although much more can be said about each of these four areas, generally, when incorporating a mental status into a report, all four areas are collapsed into a one- or two-paragraph statement about the client's presentation. Usually, a statement about the client's demeanor, orientation, affect, intellectual functioning, judgment, insight, and suicidal or homicidal ideation are included. Other areas are generally reported only if they are deemed significant. A description of Mr. Unclear's mental status follows:

> Mr. Unclear was well groomed for the interview, wearing a tailored suit. He was able to maintain appropriate eye contact and was oriented to time, place, and person. During the interview he appeared anxious, often rubbing his hands together. He stated that he often felt fatigued and that he has difficulty sleeping, often sleeping only four hours a night. He described himself as feeling intermittently depressed over the past seven or eight years. He appeared to be above average intellectually and his memory was intact. His judgment and insight seemed good and he appeared motivated for treatment. He states that he sometimes has suicidal thoughts, but denies he has a plan or would ever kill himself. He notes, "This is against my religion." He denies homicidal ideation.

EXERCISE 12.1   WRITING THE MENTAL STATUS REPORT

Your instructor may ask a student to role-play a client being interviewed. (It might also help if the student chose to reflect a diagnosis in DSM-IV-TR.) After the role-play is complete, all other students in class should write a mental status report. Share your reports with the instructor, and come up with one mental status report for the class. Compare your own report to the final version produced in class. This type of role-play can be repeated in small groups if you would like to gain further practice writing mental status exams.

ASSESSMENT RESULTS

Assessment results

Provide results that will be understandable to reader

It is often helpful to begin this section with a simple list of the assessment procedures that were used. Next, the results of the assessment procedures are generally presented. When presenting test results, it is important to not just give out raw scores. Instead, offering converted or standardized test scores that the reader will understand is usually more helpful (e.g., percentiles, DIQs, etc.). It should be remembered that the client, parents, or some other non-professional may read these results, so it is important to state the results in language that is unbiased and understandable to the reader. An example might be, "Johnny scored a 300 on his SAT, which is 2 standard deviations below the mean and places him at about the 2nd percentile as compared to his peers in the twelfth grade."

The results of the assessment should be concise, yet cover all items that are clearly relevant to the presenting concerns or that clearly stand out as a result of the assessment. Results should be presented objectively, and interpretations should be kept to a minimum if used at all. In the summary and conclusions section, the examiner will have the opportunity to hypothesize about what is happening with the client. The following is an example of the assessment section of the report for Mr. Unclear.

> Tests used: The Beck Depression Inventory; the Sentence Completion Test, the Kinetic Family Drawing (KFD), the MMPI-II, Rorschach Inkblot Test, the Strong Interest Inventory, Thematic Apperception Test, and the Wide Range Achievement Test (WRAT).
>
> Mr. Unclear obtained a BDI-II score of 24, which places him in the moderate range of depression, and his responses showed some evidence of possible suicidal ideation. The MMPI supports this finding, as it shows a man with moderate to severe depression and mild anxiety who is generally "discontent with the world" and feels a lack of intimacy in his life. It suggests assessing for possible suicidal ideation.
>
> The Rorschach and the TAT show an individual who is grounded in reality and open to testing, as was evidenced by his willingness to readily respond to initial inkblots and TAT cards, his ability to complete stories in the TAT, and the fact that many of his responses were "common" responses. Feelings of depression and hopelessness are evident in a number of responses, including not readily seeing color in many of the responses he made to the "color cards"

of the Rorschach and a number of pessimistic stories that generally had depressive endings to them on the TAT.

On the KFD, Mr. Unclear placed his father as an angel in the sky, and included his wife, mother, children, and grandchildren. His mother was standing next to him while his wife was off to the side with the grandchildren. He also placed himself in a chair and when talking about the picture stated, "I'm sitting because my back hurts." The picture showed the client and his family at his mother's house having a Sunday dinner while it rained outside. Rain could be indicative of depressive feelings. A cross was prominent in the background and was larger than most of the people in the picture, which is likely an indication of strong religious beliefs and could also indicate a need to be taken care of.

On the sentence completion test Mr. Unclear made a number of references to missing his father, such as "The thing I think most about is missing my father." He also referenced continual back pain. Finally, he noted discontent with his marriage, such as when he said, "Sex is nonexistent" on the sentence completion.

On the Strong, Mr. Unclear's two highest personality codes were Conventional and Enterprising, respectively. All the other codes were significantly lower. Individuals of the Conventional type are stable, controlled, conservative, sociable, and like to follow instructions. Enterprising individuals are self-confident, adventurous, sociable, have good persuasive skills, and prefer positions of leadership. Careers in business and industry where persuasive skills are important are good choices for these individuals.

On the WRAT4, Mr. Unclear scored at the 86th percentile in math, 75th percentile in reading, 64th percentile in sentence comprehension, and 42nd percentile in spelling. His reading composite score was at the 69th percentile. These results could indicate a possible learning disorder in spelling, although cross-cultural considerations should be taken into account due to the fact that Mr. Unclear was an immigrant to this country at a young age.

DIAGNOSIS

This is the section where a clinical diagnosis is generally made using the criteria from the *Diagnostic and Statistical Manual* (DSM-IV-TR; APA, 2000) (see Chapter 11). The diagnosis is an outgrowth of the whole assessment process and is based on the integration of all of the knowledge gained (Seligman, 2004). As mentioned in Chapter 11, the DSM-IV-TR offers five axes of diagnosis:

Axis I: Clinical Disorders and Other Conditions That May Be a Focus of Clinical Attention. This includes all childhood and adult mental disorders with the exception of personality disorders and mental retardation. It also includes problem areas that are not considered mental disorders, called "other areas that may be a focus of clinical attention."

Axis II: Personality Disorders and Mental Retardation. This is reserved for recording two specific groups of diagnoses: Personality Disorders and Mental Retardation, both of which are long-standing, entrenched, rigid, typically lifelong conditions.

Axis III: General Medical Conditions. This axis provides a place to list medical problems and physical complaints (e.g., chronic pain, thyroid disorder) that might be associated with the client's counseling concerns.

Axis IV: Psychosocial and Environmental Problems. Axis IV provides a place to list external, social, relational, or environmental problems (e.g., poverty, recent divorce) that might be associated with the client's counseling concerns.

Axis V: Global Assessment of Functioning, or GAF Scale. This scale ranges from 1 to 100 and is used by the interviewer to estimate the client's overall functioning in everyday life. Higher numbers represent higher-level functioning.

A fully prepared, formal DSM-IV-TR diagnosis provides complete information about the client's experiences on all five axes. Using our example of Mr. Unclear, we might prepare the following five-axes diagnosis:

Axis I:	296.22	Major Depression, Single Episode, Moderate
	309.28	Rule out: Adjustment Disorder with Mixed Anxiety and Depressed Mood
Axis II:	V71.09	No diagnosis
Axis III:		Chronic back pain
Axis IV:		Discontent with job; Marital discontent
Axis V:		GAF = 45 (Over past year)

In this example, the diagnosis describes a client who is experiencing symptoms of a moderate episode of major depression, including ongoing feelings of depression, fatigue, and sleep problems (Axis I); shows no signs of any long-term personality disorder symptoms (Axis II); has difficulties with chronic back pain—a general medical condition (Axis III); is discontent with his career and marriage—psychosocial stressors (Axis IV); and has several "serious" symptoms such as periodic thoughts about suicide (Axis V).

SUMMARY AND CONCLUSIONS

This section is the examiner's chance to pull together all of the information that has been gathered. Often, this is the only section of the report that is read by others, so it is important that it is accurate and does not leave out any main points. However, it should not be excessively long. Making it accurate, succinct, and relevant is the key to writing a good summary. One major error in writing summaries, we have found, is adding information that has not been included elsewhere. *The* *Report summary* *summary should have no new information.* Although inferences can be made in *should have no* this section, they must be logical, sound, defendable, and based on facts that are *new information* mentioned in your report. We also generally recommend writing a paragraph or two about the strengths of the individual. All too often we have found that this is left out of reports. The following might be a summary and conclusions section based on the information we have gathered from Mr. Unclear:

Mr. Unclear is a 48-year-old married male who was self-referred due to feelings of depression, anxiety, as well as discontent with his job and his marriage.

Mr. Unclear fled from Cuba to Miami, Florida with his parents and two siblings when he was 5 years old. He describes his family as close, and he continues to live near his children, siblings, and mother. His father died approximately four years ago. He married while in college, and he and his wife subsequently raised two girls who are now in their mid-20s, married and have their own children.

Mr. Unclear finished college with a degree in business and has been working as an accountant over the past 25 years. He reports feeling dissatisfied in his career and states that he wants to do something more meaningful with his life. He also reports marital discord, which he attributes partly to medical problems his wife had after the birth of their second child. These problems, he states, resulted in diminishing sexual relations with his wife.

Mr. Unclear was oriented during the session but appeared anxious and talked about feelings of depression. He noted that he often feels fatigued, has difficulty sleeping, and has fleeting thoughts of suicide, which he states he would not act upon. Recently, he has had obsessive worries about having a heart attack, although there is no medical reason to support his concerns. Chronic back pain due to a car accident a few years ago seems to exacerbate his current feelings of depression.

Throughout testing there were consistent themes of depression, isolation, and hopelessness. This was evidenced by high scores on the BDI-II and the MMPI-II depression scale, as well as specific responses to the Rorschach, TAT cards, the KFD, and the sentence completion.

Discontent with his marriage, sadness about the loss of his father, and chronic pain were some major themes that arose during testing. Testing also revealed a person who is in a field that is a good match for his personality. However, he might be more challenged if given a position with additional responsibilities and leadership skills. Such a change should probably not occur unless Mr. Unclear attains a handle on his depression. Finally, testing also shows a possible learning disability in spelling, although cross-cultural issues may have affected his score.

On a positive note, testing and the clinical interview showed a man who was neatly dressed and open to meeting with this examiner. He has worked hard in his life and is proud of the family he has raised. He was grounded in reality, willing to engage interpersonally, and showed good judgment and insight. He seems to be aware of many of his most pressing concerns and showed some willingness to address them.

RECOMMENDATIONS

This last section of the report should be based on all of the information gathered. It should make logical sense to the reader. Although some prefer writing this section in paragraph form, we prefer listing each recommendation, as we believe this format is clearer to the reader. The signature of the examiner generally follows this last section. The following might be some recommendations for Mr. Unclear:

1. Counseling, 1 hour a week for depression, possible anxiety, marital discord, and career dissatisfaction.

2. Possible marital counseling with particular focus on sexual relations of the couple.
3. Referral to a physician/psychiatrist for medication, possibly antidepressants.
4. Possible further assessment for learning problems.
5. Long-term consideration of a career move following alleviation of depressive feelings and addressing possible learning problems.
6. Possible orthopedic re-evaluation of back problems.

_____

Signature of the Examiner

SUMMARIZING THE WRITING OF AN ASSESSMENT REPORT

As you can see, a great deal of information is gathered from the client, and much of it is included in the report. Although one could probably write a short novel about a client after gathering information from an in-depth interview, generally the skilled examiner will keep the report between two and five pages, single-spaced. Box 12.4 summarizes the major points that should be gathered in an assessment report, and in Appendix F you can see Mr. Unclear's report in its entirety.

BOX 12.4 | SUMMARY OF ASSESSMENT REPORT

The following categories are generally assessed in a report:

Demographic Information

Name: D.O.B.:
Address: Age:
Phone: Sex:
Ethnicity: E-mail address:
Date of interview: Name of interviewer:

Presenting Problem or Reason For Referral

1. Who referred the client to the agency?
2. What is the main reason the client contacted the agency?
3. Reason for assessment

Family Background

1. Significant factors from family of origin
2. Significant factors from current family
3. Some specific issues that may be mentioned: where the individual grew up, sexes and ages of siblings, whether the client came from an intact family, who were the major caretakers, important stories from childhood, sexes and ages of current children, significant others, and marital concerns

Significant Medical/Counseling History

1. Significant medical history, particularly anything related to the client's assessment (e.g., psychiatric hospitalization, heart disease leading to depression)
2. Types and dates of previous counseling

Substance Use and Abuse

1. Use or abuse of food, cigarettes, alcohol, prescription medication, or illegal drugs
2. Counseling related to use and abuse

Educational and Vocational History

1. Educational history (e.g., level of education and possibly names of institutions)
2. Vocational history and career path (names and types of jobs)
3. Satisfaction with educational level and career path
4. Significant leisure activities

Other Pertinent Information

1. Legal concerns and history of problems with the law
2. Issues related to sexuality (e.g., sexual orientation, sexual dysfunction)

3. Financial problems
4. Other concerns

The Mental Status Exam

1. Appearance and behavior (e.g., dress, hygiene, posture, tics, nonverbals, manner of speech)
2. Emotional state (e.g., affect and mood)
3. Thought components (e.g., content and process: delusions, distortions of body image, hallucinations, obsessions, suicidal or homicidal ideation, circumstantiality, coherence, flight of ideas, logical thinking, intact as opposed to loose associations, organization, and tangentiality)
4. Cognitive functioning (e.g., orientation to time, place, and person; short- and long-term memory; knowledge base and intellectual functioning; insight and judgments)

Assessment Results

1. List assessment and test instruments used.
2. Summarize results.
3. Avoid raw scores and state results in unbiased manner.
4. Consider using standardized test scores and percentiles.

Diagnosis

1. DSM-IV-TR diagnoses (include other diagnoses, such as medical, rehabilitation, when important)

2. Usually note all five axes of DSM-IV-TR:
   - Axis I: Clinical Disorders and Other Conditions That May Be a Focus of Clinical Attention
   - Axis II: Personality Disorders and Mental Retardation
   - Axis III: General Medical Conditions
   - Axis IV: Psychosocial and Environmental Problems
   - Axis V: Global Assessment of Functioning, or GAF Scale

Summary and Conclusions

1. Integration of all previous information
2. Accurate, succinct, and relevant
3. No new information
4. Inferences that are logical, sound, defendable, and based on facts in the report
5. At least one paragraph that speaks to the client's strengths

Recommendations

1. Based on all the information gathered
2. Should make logical sense to reader
3. In paragraph form or as a listing
4. Usually followed by signature of examiner

SUMMARY

This chapter began by describing some of the purposes of the assessment report, including responding to the referral question, providing insight to clients, developing case conceptualization, developing treatment options, suggesting educational services, providing vocational rehabilitation services, offering insight and treatment options for those with cognitive impairment, assisting courts in decision-making, helping with placement in schools and jobs, and challenging decisions made by institutions and agencies.

We pointed out that putting "garbage" into the assessment report process leads to a flawed report ("garbage out") and that it is important to assure that the breadth and depth of the report is being attended to. Thus, we noted the

importance of providing a wide enough net to appropriately address the breadth of the intended assessment and to provide testing instruments that reflect the intensity or depth of the issue(s) being examined. We also stated that it is critical to establish trust and rapport and assure confidentiality if one is to gather reliable information.

We went on to note that examiners can generally choose from three kinds of interviews: structured, unstructured, or semi-structured. We pointed out that interviews set the tone for the gathering of information process and allows clients to become desensitized to sometimes very personal information, allows the examiner the ability to assess clients nonverbally, allows the examiner to understand the client "firsthand"

and place the client's issues in perspective, and affords the examiner and client the opportunity to see if they can work together.

Distinguishing among the different kinds of interviews, we noted that a structured interview asks the examinee to respond to pre-established items or questions, whereas an unstructured interview is more open-ended. The semi-structured interview, we pointed out, uses prescribed items but also gives leeway to the examiner should the client need to "drift" during the interview process. We pointed out some strengths and weaknesses of each of these approaches, especially as they relate to gathering information that has breadth and depth. We also noted that computer-assisted assessment can often help in the information-gathering process and can be integrated into the examiner's assessment report.

We next examined the process of selecting an appropriate assessment technique, which often will be based on the clinical interview you had with your client. We stressed the importance of considering the breadth and depth of information provided by the chosen instruments and noted that clinicians will often choose from a broad array of instruments, such as the ones examined in this text. We pointed out that clinicians should carefully reflect on which are the most appropriate instruments and that it is unethical to assess an individual using instruments that are not related to the purpose of the assessment being undertaken.

As the chapter continued, we went on to discuss how to write the actual assessment report.

We pointed out that laws such as FERPA, HIPAA and the Freedom of Information Act mean that clients often will have access to their records. We also noted that reports today are scrutinized more than ever before, and we stressed the importance of developing a writing style that is clear, concise, and easy to understand. We suggested an array of points to consider when writing a report, including omitting passive verbs, being nonjudgmental, reducing jargon, not being patronizing, using subheadings, reducing acronyms, minimizing difficult words, using shorter sentences, being concise and having good flow, pointing out client strengths and weaknesses, not dazzling the reader with your brilliance, describing behaviors, avoiding labeling if possible, writing for a non-mental health professional, and being able to take a stand when necessary.

In the last part of the chapter we examined the format of the report. We noted that the areas addressed when gathering information from a client often parallel the areas included in the actual report. They include (1) demographic information, (2) presenting problem or reason for the report, (3) family background, (4) significant medical/counseling history, (5) substance use and abuse, (6) vocational and educational history, (7) other pertinent background information, (8) mental status, (9) assessment or test results, (10) diagnosis, (11) summary and conclusions, and (12) recommendations. We discussed each area and offered a case example.

CHAPTER REVIEW

1. Describe some purposes of the assessment report.
2. Relative to the assessment report process, describe what is meant by "garbage in, garbage out."
3. Describe what it means to choose an assessment instrument with "breadth and depth."
4. Discuss some of the tasks associated with conducting clinical interviews that are not

associated with other kinds of assessment techniques.
5. Compare and contrast structured, semi-structured, and unstructured interview techniques.
6. What place can computer-generated reports take in the assessment report process?
7. Explain the impact of laws such as the Family Educational Rights and Privacy Act (FERPA), the Freedom of Information Act,

and the Health Insurance Portability and Accountability Act (HIPAA) on the preparation of assessment reports.

8. Write down as many of the suggestions for writing a report that you can remember.

9. Make a list of the kinds of information generally obtained in an assessment report.

10. Describe the four components of a mental status exam. Interview a student in class and then write a one- or two-paragraph mental status exam.

11. Conduct an assessment of a client and use the categories listed in this chapter to write an assessment report.

REFERENCES

Aiken, L. R. (2003). *Psychological testing and assessment* (11th ed.). Boston: Allyn and Bacon.

American Counseling Association (ACA). (2005). *Code of ethics.* (Rev.ed.). Alexandria, VA: Author.

American Psychiatric Association. (2000). *Diagnostic and statistical manual of mental disorders* (4th ed., text revision). Washington, DC: Author.

American Psychological Association. (2002). *Ethical principles of psychologists and code of conduct.* Retrieved on October 5, 2008, from http://www.apa.org/ethics/code2002.html

Berger, M. (2006). Computer assisted clinical assessment. *Child and Adolescent Mental Health, 11*(2), 64–75.

Drummond, R. J. (2006). *Appraisal procedures for counselors and helping professionals* (6th ed.). Upper Saddle River, NJ: Pearson.

Farmer, A., McGuffin, P., & Williams, J. (2002). *Measuring psychopathology.* New York: Oxford University Press.

Harvey, V. (1997). Improving readability of psychological reports. *Professional Psychology: Research and Practice, 28,* 271–274.

Lichtenberger, E. O. Mather, N., Kaufman, N. L., & Kaufman, A. L. (2004). *Essentials of assessment report writing.* Hoboken, NJ: John Wiley & Sons.

Michaels, M. H. (2006). Ethical considerations in writing psychological assessment reports. *Journal of Clinical Psychology, 62*(1), 47–58.

Ownby, R. (1997). *Psychological reports: A guide to report writing in professional psychology* (3rd ed.). New York: Wiley.

Polanski, P. J., & Hinkle, J. S. (2000). The mental status examination: Its use by professional counselors. *Journal of Counseling and Development, 78,* 357–364.

Reynolds, J. F., Mair, D. C., & Fischer, P. C. (1995). *Writing and reading mental health records: Issues and analysis* (2nd ed.). Mahwah, NJ: Erlbaum Associates.

Roth, P., Van Iddekinge, C., Huffcutt, A., Eidson, C., & Bobko, P. (2002). Corrections for range restriction in structured interview ethnic group differences: The values may be larger than researchers thought. *Journal of Applied Psychology, 87,* 369–376.

Schinka, J. A. (2003). *Mental status checklist–adult.* Lutz, FL: Psychological Assessment Resources.

Seligman, L. (2004). *Diagnosis and treatment planning in counseling* (3rd ed.). New York: Plenum.

Websites of Codes of Ethics of Select Mental Health Professional Associations

American Counseling Association (ACA)

Main website: http://www.counseling.org
Code of ethics: http://www.counseling.org/Resources/CodeOfEthics/TP/Home/CT2.aspx

American Association of Marriage and Family Therapy (AAMFT)

Main website: http://www.aamft.org
Code of ethics: http://www.aamft.org/resources/LRM_Plan/Ethics/index_nm.asp

American Association of Pastoral Counselors (AAPC)

Main website: http://www.aapc.org
Code of ethics: http://www.aapc.org/content/ethics

American Mental Health Counselors Association (AMHCA)

Main website: http://www.amhca.org
Code of ethics: http://www.amhca.org/code

American Psychiatric Association (APA)

Main website: http://www.psych.org
Code of ethics: http://www.psych.org/MainMenu/PsychiatricPractice/Ethics.aspx

American Psychological Association (APA)

Main website: http://www.apa.org
Code of ethics: http://www.apa.org/ethics

American Psychological Association: Division 5: Evaluation, Measurement, and Statistics

Main website: http://www.apa.org/about/division/div5.html
Code of ethics: Uses APA's (see above)

American School Counselor Association (ASCA)

Main website: http://www.schoolcounselor.org
Code of ethics: http://www.schoolcounselor.org/content.asp?contentid=173

Association for Assessment in Counseling and Education

Main website: http://www.theaaceonline.com/
Code of ethics: Uses ACA's (see above)

Certified Rehabilitation Counselors

Main website: http://www.crccertification.com
Code of ethics: http://www.crccertification.com/pages/30code.html

National Association of Social Workers (NASW)

Main website: http://www.naswdc.org
Code of ethics: http://www.socialworkers.org/pubs/code/code.asp

National Organization of Human Services (NOHS)

Main website: http://www.nationalhumanservices.org/
http://www.nationalhumanservices.org/ethical-standards-of-human-service-professionals

Assessment Sections of ACA's and APA's Codes of Ethics

American Counseling Association's Ethical Code: Section E

Section E: Evaluation, Assessment, and Interpretation

Introduction

Counselors use assessment instruments as one component of the counseling process, taking into account the client personal and cultural context. Counselors promote the well-being of individual clients or groups of clients by developing and using appropriate educational, psychological, and career assessment instruments.

E.1. General

E.1.a. Assessment
The primary purpose of educational, psychological, and career assessment is to provide measurements that are valid and reliable in either comparative or absolute terms. These include, but are not limited to, measurements of ability, personality, interest, intelligence, achievement, and performance. Counselors recognize the need to interpret the statements in this section as applying to both quantitative and qualitative assessments.

E.1.b. Client Welfare
Counselors do not misuse assessment results and interpretations, and they take reasonable steps to prevent others from misusing the information these techniques provide. They respect the client's right to know the results, the interpretations made, and the bases for counselors' conclusions and recommendations.

E.2. Competence to Use and Interpret Assessment Instruments

E.2.a. Limits of Competence
Counselors utilize only those testing and assessment services for which they have been trained and are competent. Counselors using technology-assisted test interpretations are trained in the construct being measured and the specific instrument being used prior to using its technology-based application. Counselors take reasonable measures to ensure the proper use of psychological and career assessment techniques by persons under their supervision. *(See A.12.)*

E.2.b. Appropriate Use

Counselors are responsible for the appropriate application, scoring, interpretation, and use of assessment instruments relevant to the needs of the client, whether they score and interpret such assessments themselves or use technology or other services.

E.2.c. Decisions Based on Results

Counselors responsible for decisions involving individuals or policies that are based on assessment results have a thorough understanding of educational, psychological, and career measurement, including validation criteria, assessment research, and guidelines for assessment development and use.

E.3. Informed Consent in Assessment

E.3.a. Explanation to Clients

Prior to assessment, counselors explain the nature and purposes of assessment and the specific use of results by potential recipients. The explanation will be given in the language of the client (or other legally authorized person on behalf of the client), unless an explicit exception has been agreed upon in advance. Counselors consider the client's personal or cultural context, the level of the client's understanding of the results, and the impact of the results on the client. *(See A.2., A.12.g., F.1.c.)*

E.3.b. Recipients of Results

Counselors consider the examinee's welfare, explicit understandings, and prior agreements in determining who receives the assessment results. Counselors include accurate and appropriate interpretations with any release of individual or group assessment results. *(See B.2.c., B.5.)*

E.4. Release of Data to Qualified Professionals

Counselors release assessment data in which the client is identified only with the consent of the client or the client's legal representative. Such data are released only to persons recognized by counselors as qualified to interpret the data. *(See B.1., B.3., B.6.b.)*

E.5. Diagnosis of Mental Disorders

E.5.a. Proper Diagnosis

Counselors take special care to provide proper diagnosis of mental disorders. Assessment techniques (including personal interview) used to determine client care (e.g., locus of treatment, type of treatment, or recommended follow-up) are carefully selected and appropriately used.

E.5.b. Cultural Sensitivity

Counselors recognize that culture affects the manner in which clients' problems are defined. Clients' socio-economic and cultural experiences are considered when diagnosing mental disorders. *(See A.2.c.)*

E.5.c. Historical and Social Prejudices in the Diagnosis of Pathology

Counselors recognize historical and social prejudices in the misdiagnosis and pathologizing of certain individuals and groups and the role of mental health professionals in perpetuating these prejudices through diagnosis and treatment.

E.5.d. Refraining From Diagnosis

Counselors may refrain from making and/or reporting a diagnosis if they believe it would cause harm to the client or others.

E.6. Instrument Selection

E.6.a. Appropriateness of Instruments

Counselors carefully consider the validity, reliability, psychometric limitations, and appropriateness of instruments when selecting assessments.

E.6.b. Referral Information

If a client is referred to a third party for assessment, the counselor provides specific referral questions and sufficient objective data about the client to ensure that appropriate assessment instruments are utilized. *(See A.9.b., B.3.)*

E.6.c. Culturally Diverse Populations

Counselors are cautious when selecting assessments for culturally diverse populations to avoid the use of instruments that lack appropriate psychometric properties for the client population. *(See A.2.c., E.5.b.)*

E.7. Conditions of Assessment Administration
(See A.12.b, A.12.d.)

E.7.a. Administration Conditions

Counselors administer assessments under the same conditions that were established in their standardization. When assessments are not administered under standard conditions, as may be necessary to accommodate clients with disabilities, or when unusual behavior or irregularities occur during the administration, those conditions are noted in interpretation, and the results may be designated as invalid or of questionable validity.

E.7.b. Technological Administration

Counselors ensure that administration programs function properly and provide clients with accurate results when technological or other electronic methods are used for assessment administration.

E.7.c. Unsupervised Assessments

Unless the assessment instrument is designed, intended, and validated for self-administration and/or scoring, counselors do not permit inadequately supervised use.

E.7.d. Disclosure of Favorable Conditions

Prior to administration of assessments, conditions that produce most favorable assessment results are made known to the examinee.

E.8. Multicultural Issues/Diversity in Assessment

Counselors use with caution assessment techniques that were normed on populations other than that of the client. Counselors recognize the effects of age, color, culture, disability, ethnic group, gender, race, language preference, religion, spirituality, sexual orientation, and socioeconomic status on test administration and interpretation, and place test results in proper perspective with other relevant factors. *(See A.2.c., E.5.b.)*

E.9. Scoring and Interpretation of Assessments

E.9.a. Reporting

In reporting assessment results, counselors indicate reservations that exist regarding validity or reliability due to circumstances of the assessment or the inappropriateness of the norms for the person tested.

E.9.b. Research Instruments

Counselors exercise caution when interpreting the results of research instruments not having sufficient technical data to support respondent results. The specific purposes for the use of such instruments are stated explicitly to the examinee.

E.9.c. Assessment Services

Counselors who provide assessment scoring and interpretation services to support the assessment process confirm the validity of such interpretations. They accurately describe the purpose, norms, validity, reliability, and applications of the procedures and any special qualifications applicable to their use. The public offering of an automated test interpretations service is considered a professional-to-professional consultation. The formal responsibility of the consultant is to the consultee, but the ultimate and overriding responsibility is to the client. *(See D.2.)*

E.10. Assessment Security

Counselors maintain the integrity and security of tests and other assessment techniques consistent with legal and contractual obligations. Counselors do not appropriate, reproduce, or modify published assessments or parts thereof without acknowledgment and permission from the publisher.

E.11. Obsolete Assessments and Outdated Results

Counselors do not use data or results from assessments that are obsolete or outdated for the current purpose. Counselors make every effort to prevent the misuse of obsolete measures and assessment data by others.

E.12. Assessment Construction

Counselors use established scientific procedures, relevant standards, and current professional knowledge for assessment design in the development, publication, and utilization of educational and psychological assessment techniques.

E.13. Forensic Evaluation: Evaluation for Legal Proceedings

E.13.a. Primary Obligations

When providing forensic evaluations, the primary obligation of counselors is to produce objective findings that can be substantiated based on information and techniques appropriate to the evaluation, which may include examination of the individual and/or review of records. Counselors are entitled to form professional opinions based on their professional knowledge and expertise that can be supported by the data gathered in evaluations. Counselors will define the limits of their reports or testimony, especially when an examination of the individual has not been conducted.

E.13.b. Consent for Evaluation

Individuals being evaluated are informed in writing that the relationship is for the purposes of an evaluation and is not counseling in nature, and entities or individuals who will receive the evaluation report are identified. Written consent to be evaluated is obtained from those being evaluated unless a court orders evaluations to be conducted without the written consent of individuals being evaluated. When children or vulnerable adults are being evaluated, informed written consent is obtained from a parent or guardian.

E.13.c. Client Evaluation Prohibited

Counselors do not evaluate individuals for forensic purposes they currently counsel or individuals they have counseled in the past. Counselors do not accept as counseling clients individuals they are evaluating or individuals they have evaluated in the past for forensic purposes.

E.13.d. Avoid Potentially Harmful Relationships
Counselors who provide forensic evaluations avoid potentially harmful professional or personal relationships with family members, romantic partners, and close friends of individuals they are evaluating or have evaluated in the past.

AMERICAN PSYCHOLOGICAL ASSOCIATION
ETHICAL CODE: SECTION 9

Section 9: Assessment

9.01 BASES FOR ASSESSMENTS

(a) Psychologists base the opinions contained in their recommendations, reports, and diagnostic or evaluative statements, including forensic testimony, on information and techniques sufficient to substantiate their findings. (See also Standard 2.04, Bases for Scientific and Professional Judgments.)

(b) Except as noted in 9.01c, psychologists provide opinions of the psychological characteristics of individuals only after they have conducted an examination of the individuals adequate to support their statements or conclusions. When, despite reasonable efforts, such an examination is not practical, psychologists document the efforts they made and the result of those efforts, clarify the probable impact of their limited information on the reliability and validity of their opinions, and appropriately limit the nature and extent of their conclusions or recommendations. (See also Standards 2.01, Boundaries of Competence, and 9.06, Interpreting Assessment Results.)

(c) When psychologists conduct a record review or provide consultation or supervision and an individual examination is not warranted or necessary for the opinion, psychologists explain this and the sources of information on which they based their conclusions and recommendations.

9.02 USE OF ASSESSMENTS

(a) Psychologists administer, adapt, score, interpret, or use assessment techniques, interviews, tests, or instruments in a manner and for purposes that are appropriate in light of the research on or evidence of the usefulness and proper application of the techniques.

(b) Psychologists use assessment instruments whose validity and reliability have been established for use with members of the population tested. When such validity or reliability has not been established, psychologists describe the strengths and limitations of test results and interpretation.

c) Psychologists use assessment methods that are appropriate to an individual's language preference and competence, unless the use of an alternative language is relevant to the assessment issues.

9.03 INFORMED CONSENT IN ASSESSMENTS

(a) Psychologists obtain informed consent for assessments, evaluations, or diagnostic services, as described in Standard 3.10, Informed Consent, except when (1) testing is mandated by law or governmental regulations; (2) informed consent is implied because testing is conducted as a routine educational, institutional, or organizational activity (e.g., when participants voluntarily agree to assessment when applying for a job); or (3) one purpose of the testing is to evaluate decisional capacity. Informed consent includes an explanation of the nature and purpose of the assessment, fees, involvement of third parties, and limits of confidentiality and sufficient opportunity for the client/patient to ask questions and receive answers.

(b) Psychologists inform persons with questionable capacity to consent or for whom testing is mandated by law or governmental regulations about the nature and purpose of the proposed assessment services, using language that is reasonably understandable to the person being assessed.

(c) Psychologists using the services of an interpreter obtain informed consent from the client/patient to use that interpreter, ensure that confidentiality of test results and test security are maintained, and include in their recommendations, reports, and diagnostic or evaluative statements, including forensic testimony, discussion of any limitations on the data obtained. (See also Standards 2.05, Delegation of Work to Others; 4.01, Maintaining Confidentiality; 9.01, Bases for Assess-ments; 9.06, Interpreting Assessment Results; and 9.07, Assessment by Unqualified Persons.)

9.04 RELEASE OF TEST DATA

(a) The term test data refers to raw and scaled scores, client/patient responses to test questions or stimuli, and psychologists' notes and recordings concerning client/patient statements and behavior during an examination. Those portions of test materials that include client/patient responses are included in the definition of test data. Pursuant to a client/patient release, psychologists provide test data to the client/patient or other persons identified in the release. Psychologists may refrain from releasing test data to protect a client/patient or others from substantial harm or misuse or misrepresentation of the data or the test, recognizing that in many instances release of confidential information under these circumstances is regulated by law. (See also Standard 9.11, Maintaining Test Security.)

(b) In the absence of a client/patient release, psychologists provide test data only as required by law or court order.

9.05 TEST CONSTRUCTION

Psychologists who develop tests and other assessment techniques use appropriate psychometric procedures and current scientific or professional knowledge for test design, standardization, validation, reduction or elimination of bias, and recommendations for use.

9.06 INTERPRETING ASSESSMENT RESULTS

When interpreting assessment results, including automated interpretations, psychologists take into account the purpose of the assessment as well as the various test factors, test-taking abilities, and other characteristics of the person being assessed, such as situational, personal, linguistic, and cultural differences, that might affect psychologists' judgments or reduce the accuracy of their interpretations. They indicate any significant limitations of their interpretations. (See also Standards 2.01b and c, Boundaries of Competence, and 3.01, Unfair Discrimination.)

9.07 ASSESSMENT BY UNQUALIFIED PERSONS

Psychologists do not promote the use of psychological assessment techniques by unqualified persons, except when such use is conducted for training purposes with appropriate supervision. (See also Standard 2.05, Delegation of Work to Others.)

9.08 OBSOLETE TESTS AND OUTDATED TEST RESULTS

(a) Psychologists do not base their assessment or intervention decisions or recommendations on data or test results that are outdated for the current purpose.

(b) Psychologists do not base such decisions or recommendations on tests and measures that are obsolete and not useful for the current purpose.

9.09 TEST SCORING AND INTERPRETATION SERVICES

(a) Psychologists who offer assessment or scoring services to other professionals accurately describe the purpose, norms, validity, reliability, and applications of the procedures and any special qualifications applicable to their use.

(b) Psychologists select scoring and interpretation services (including automated services) on the basis of evidence of the validity of the program and procedures as well as on other appropriate considerations. (See also Standard 2.01b and c, Boundaries of Competence.)

(c) Psychologists retain responsibility for the appropriate application, interpretation, and use of assessment instruments, whether they score and interpret such tests themselves or use automated or other services.

9.10 EXPLAINING ASSESSMENT RESULTS

Regardless of whether the scoring and interpretation are done by psychologists, by employees or assistants, or by automated or other outside services, psychologists take reasonable steps to ensure that explanations of results are given to the individual or designated representative unless the nature of the relationship precludes provision of an explanation of results (such as in some organizational consulting, preemployment or security screenings, and forensic evaluations), and this fact has been clearly explained to the person being assessed in advance.

9.11. MAINTAINING TEST SECURITY

The term test materials refers to manuals, instruments, protocols, and test questions or stimuli and does not include test data as defined in Standard 9.04, Release of Test Data. Psychologists make reasonable efforts to maintain the integrity and security of test materials and other assessment techniques consistent with law and contractual obligations, and in a manner that permits adherence to this Ethics Code.

Source: From American Psychologist 57, p. 1060–1073. Copyright © 2002 by the American Psychological Association. Reprinted with permission.

Code of Fair Testing Practices in Education

PREPARED BY THE JOINT COMMITTEE ON TESTING PRACTICES

The Code of Fair Testing Practices in Education (*Code*) is a guide for professionals in fulfilling their obligation to provide and use tests that are fair to all test takers regardless of age, gender, disability, race, ethnicity, national origin, religion, sexual orientation, linguistic background, or other personal characteristics. Fairness is a primary consideration in all aspects of testing. Careful standardization of tests and administration conditions helps to ensure that all test takers are given a comparable opportunity to demonstrate what they know and how they can perform in the area being tested. Fairness implies that every-test taker has the opportunity to prepare for the test and is informed about the general nature and content of the test, as appropriate to the purpose of the test. Fairness also extends to the accurate reporting of individual and group test results. Fairness is not an isolated concept, but must be considered in all aspects of the testing process.

The *Code* applies broadly to testing in education (admissions, educational assessment, educational diagnosis, and student placement) regardless of the mode of presentation, so it is relevant to conventional paper-and-pencil tests, computer-based tests, and performance tests. It is not designed to cover employment testing, licensure or certification testing, or other types of testing outside the field of education. The *Code* is directed primarily at professionally developed tests used in formally administered testing programs. Although the *Code* is not intended to cover tests made by teachers for use in their own classrooms, teachers are encouraged to use the guidelines to help improve their testing practices.

The *Code* addresses the roles of test developers and test users separately. Test developers are people and organizations that construct tests, as well as those that set policies for testing programs. Test users are people and agencies that select tests, administer tests, commission test development services, or make decisions on the basis of test scores. Test developer and test user roles may overlap, for example, when a state or local education agency commissions test development services, sets policies that control the test development process, and makes decisions on the basis of the test scores.

Many of the statements in the *Code* refer to the selection and use of existing tests. When a new test is developed, when an existing test is modified, or when the administration of a test is modified, the *Code* is intended to provide guidance for this process.[1]

The *Code* provides guidance separately for test developers and test users in four critical areas:

1. Developing and Selecting Appropriate Tests
2. Administering and Scoring Tests
3. Reporting and Interpreting Test Results
4. Informing Test Takers

The *Code* is intended to be consistent with the relevant parts of the *Standards for Educational and Psychological Testing* (American Educational Research Association [AERA], American Psychological Association [APA], and National Council on Measurement in Education [NCME], 1999). The *Code* is not meant to add new principles over and above those in the *Standards* or to change their meaning. Rather, the *Code* is intended to represent the spirit of selected portions of the Standards in a way that is relevant and meaningful to developers and users of tests, as well as to test takers and/or their parents or guardians. States, districts, schools, organizations and individual professionals are encouraged to commit themselves to fairness in testing and safeguarding the rights of test takers. The Code is intended to assist in carrying out such commitments.

The *Code* has been prepared by the Joint Committee on Testing Practices, a cooperative effort among several professional organizations. The aim of the Joint Committee is to act, in the public interest, to advance the quality of testing practices. Members of the Joint Committee include the American Counseling Association (ACA), the American Educational Research Association (AERA), the American Psychological Association (APA), the American Speech-Language-Hearing Association (ASHA), the National Association of School Psychologists (NASP), the National Association of Test Directors (NATD), and the National Council on Measurement in Education (NCME).

---

[1] The Code is not intended to be mandatory, exhaustive, or definitive, and may not be applicable to every situation. Instead, the Code is intended to be aspirational, and is not intended to take precedence over the judgment of those who have competence in the subjects addressed.

Index terms: assessment, education.

Reference this material as: *Code of Fair Testing Practices in Education.* (2004). Washington, DC: Joint Committee on Testing Practices.

A. DEVELOPING AND SELECTING APPROPRIATE TESTS

Test Developers	**Test Users**
Test developers should provide the information and supporting evidence that test users need to select appropriate tests.	Test users should select tests that meet the intended purpose and that are appropriate for the intended test takers.
A-1. Provide evidence of what the test measures, the recommended uses, the intended test takers, and the strengths and limitations of the test, including the level of precision of the test scores.	A-1. Define the purpose for testing, the content and skills to be tested, and the intended test takers. Select and use the most appropriate test based on a thorough review of available information.
A-2. Describe how the content and skills to be tested were selected and how the tests were developed.	A-2. Review and select tests based on the appropriateness of test content, skills tested, and content coverage for the intended purpose of testing.
A-3. Communicate information about a test's characteristics at a level of detail appropriate to the intended test users.	A-3. Review materials provided by test developers and select tests for which clear, accurate, and complete information is provided.
A-4. Provide guidance on the levels of skills, knowledge, and training necessary for appropriate review, selection, and administration of tests.	A-4. Select tests through a process that includes persons with appropriate knowledge, skills, and training.
A-5. Provide evidence that the technical quality, including reliability and validity, of the test meets its intended purposes.	A-5. Evaluate evidence of the technical quality of the test provided by the test developer and any independent reviewers.
A-6. Provide to qualified test users representative samples of test questions or practice tests, directions, answer sheets, manuals, and score reports.	A-6. Evaluate representative samples of test questions or practice tests, directions, answer sheets, manuals, and score reports before selecting a test.
A-7. Avoid potentially offensive content or language when developing test questions and related materials.	A-7. Evaluate procedures and materials used by test developers, as well as the resulting test, to ensure that potentially offensive content or language is avoided.
A-8. Make appropriately modified forms of tests or administration procedures available for test takers with disabilities who need special accommodations.	A-8. Select tests with appropriately modified forms or administration procedures for test takers with disabilities who need special accommodations.
A-9. Obtain and provide evidence on the performance of test takers of diverse subgroups, making significant efforts to obtain sample sizes that are adequate for subgroup analyses. Evaluate the evidence to ensure that differences in performance are related to the skills being assessed.	A-9. Evaluate the available evidence on the performance of test takers of diverse subgroups. Determine to the extent feasible which performance differences may have been caused by factors unrelated to the skills being assessed.

B. ADMINISTERING AND SCORING TESTS

Test Developers	**Test Users**
Test developers should explain how to administer and score tests correctly and fairly.	Test users should administer and score tests correctly and fairly.
B-1. Provide clear descriptions of detailed procedures for administering tests in a standardized manner.	B-1. Follow established procedures for administering tests in a standardized manner.
B-2. Provide guidelines on reasonable procedures for assessing persons with disabilities who need special accommodations or those with diverse linguistic backgrounds.	B-2. Provide and document appropriate procedures for test takers with disabilities who need special accommodations or those with diverse linguistic backgrounds. Some accommodations may be required by law or regulation.
B-3. Provide information to test takers or test users on test question formats and procedures for answering test questions, including information on the use of any needed materials and equipment.	B-3. Provide test takers with an opportunity to become familiar with test question formats and any materials or equipment that may be used during testing.
B-4. Establish and implement procedures to ensure the security of testing materials during all phases of test development, administration, scoring, and reporting.	B-4. Protect the security of test materials, including respecting copyrights and eliminating opportunities for test takers to obtain scores by fraudulent means.
B-5. Provide procedures, materials and guidelines for scoring the tests, and for monitoring the accuracy of the scoring process. If scoring the test is the responsibility of the test developer, provide adequate training for scorers.	B-5. If test scoring is the responsibility of the test user, provide adequate training to scorers and ensure and monitor the accuracy of the scoring process.
B-6. Correct errors that affect the interpretation of the scores and communicate the corrected results promptly.	B-6. Correct errors that affect the interpretation of the scores and communicate the corrected results promptly.
B-7. Develop and implement procedures for ensuring the confidentiality of scores.	B-7. Develop and implement procedures for ensuring the confidentiality of scores.

C. REPORTING AND INTERPRETING TEST RESULTS

Test Developers	Test Users
Test developers should report test results accurately and provide information to help test users interpret test results correctly.	Test users should report and interpret test results accurately and clearly.
C-1. Provide information to support recommended interpretations of the results, including the nature of the content, norms or comparison groups, and other technical evidence. Advise test users of the benefits and limitations of test results and their interpretation. Warn against assigning greater precision than is warranted.	C-1. Interpret the meaning of the test results, taking into account the nature of the content, norms or comparison groups, other technical evidence, and benefits and limitations of test results.
C-2. Provide guidance regarding the interpretations of results for tests administered with modifications. Inform test users of potential problems in interpreting test results when tests or test administration procedures are modified.	C-2. Interpret test results from modified test or test administration procedures in view of the impact those modifications may have had on test results.
C-3. Specify appropriate uses of test results and warn test users of potential misuses.	C-3. Avoid using tests for purposes other than those recommended by the test developer unless there is evidence to support the intended use or interpretation.
C-4. When test developers set standards, provide the rationale, procedures, and evidence for setting performance standards or passing scores. Avoid using stigmatizing labels.	C-4. Review the procedures for setting performance standards or passing scores. Avoid using stigmatizing labels.
C-5. Encourage test users to base decisions about test takers on multiple sources of appropriate information, not on a single test score.	C-5. Avoid using a single test score as the sole determinant of decisions about test takers. Interpret test scores in conjunction with other information about individuals.
C-6. Provide information to enable test users to accurately interpret and report test results for groups of test takers, including information about who were and who were not included in the different groups being compared, and information about factors that might influence the interpretation of results.	C-6. State the intended interpretation and use of test results for groups of test takers. Avoid grouping test results for purposes not specifically recommended by the test developer unless evidence is obtained to support the intended use. Report procedures that were followed in determining who were and who were not included in the groups being compared and describe factors that might influence the interpretation of results.
C-7. Provide test results in a timely fashion and in a manner that is understood by the test taker.	C-7. Communicate test results in a timely fashion and in a manner that is understood by the test taker.
C-8. Provide guidance to test users about how to monitor the extent to which the test is fulfilling its intended purposes.	C-8. Develop and implement procedures for monitoring test use, including consistency with the intended purposes of the text.

D. INFORMING TEST TAKERS

Under some circumstances, test developers have direct communication with the test takers and/or control of the tests, testing process, and test results. In other circumstances the test users have these responsibilities.

Test developers or test users should inform test takers about the nature of the test, test taker rights and responsibilities, the appropriate use of scores, and procedures for resolving challenges to scores.

D-1. Inform test takers in advance of the test administration about the coverage of the test, the types of question formats, the directions, and appropriate test-taking strategies. Make such information available to all test takers.

D-2. When a test is optional, provide test takers or their parents/guardians with information to help them judge whether a test should be taken—including indications of any consequences that may result from not taking the test (e.g., not being eligible to compete for a particular scholarship)—and whether there is an available alternative to the test.

D-3. Provide test takers or their parents/guardians with information about rights test takers may have to obtain copies of tests and completed answer sheets, to retake tests, to have tests rescored, or to have scores declared invalid.

D-4. Provide test takers or their parents/guardians with information about responsibilities test takers have, such as being aware of the intended purpose and uses of the test, performing at capacity, following directions, and not disclosing test items or interfering with other test takers.

D-5. Inform test takers or their parents/guardians how long scores will be kept on file and indicate to whom, under what circumstances, and in what manner test scores and related information will or will not be released. Protect test scores from unauthorized release and access.

D-6. Describe procedures for investigating and resolving circumstances that might result in canceling or withholding scores, such as failure to adhere to specified testing procedures.

D-7. Describe procedures that test takers, parents/guardians, and other interested parties may use to obtain more information about the test, register complaints, and have problems resolved.

Note: The membership of the Working Group that developed the *Code of Fair Testing Practices in Education* and of the Joint Committee on Testing Practices that guided the Working Group is as follows:

Peter Behuniak, PhD	Stephanie H. McConaughy, PhD
Lloyd Bond, PhD	Julie P. Noble, PhD
Gwyneth M. Boodoo, PhD	Wayne M. Patience, PhD
Wayne Camara, PhD	Carole L. Perlman, PhD
Ray Fenton, PhD	Douglas K. Smith, PhD (deceased)
John J. Fremer, PhD (Co-Chair)	Janet E. Wall, EdD (Co-Chair)
Sharon M. Goldsmith, PhD	Pat Nellor Wickwire, PhD
Bert F. Green, PhD	Mary Yakimowski, PhD
William G. Harris, PhD	
Janet E. Helms, PhD	Lara Frumkin, PhD, of the APA served as staff liaison.

The Joint Committee intends that the Code be consistent with and supportive of existing codes of conduct and standards of other professional groups who use tests in educational contexts. Of particular note are the Responsibilities of Users of Standardized Tests (Association for Assessment in Counseling and Education, 2003), APA Test User Qualifications (2000), ASHA Code of Ethics (2001), Ethical Principles of Psychologists and Code of Conduct (1992), NASP Professional Conduct Manual (2000), NCME Code of Professional Responsibility (1995), and Rights and Responsibilities of Test Takers: Guidelines and Expectations (Joint Committee on Testing Practices, 2000).

D | SUPPLEMENTAL STATISTICAL EQUATIONS

PEARSON PRODUCT-MOMENT CORRELATION

$$r = \frac{N\Sigma XY - (\Sigma X)(\Sigma Y)}{\sqrt{N\Sigma X^2 - (\Sigma X)^2}\sqrt{N\Sigma Y^2 - (\Sigma Y)^2}}$$

Where: N is the number of scores
X is the first set of test scores
Y is the second set of test scores

KUDER-RICHARDSON

$$KR_{20} = \left[\frac{n}{n-1}\right]\left[\frac{SD^2 - \Sigma pq}{SD^2}\right]$$

Where: n is the number of items on the test
SD is the standard deviation
p is the proportion of correct items
q is the proportion of incorrect items

COEFFICIENT ALPHA

$$r = \left[\frac{n}{n-1}\right]\left[\frac{SD^2 - \Sigma SD_i^2}{SD^2}\right]$$

Where: n is the number of items on the test
SD is the standard deviation
ΣSD_i^2 is the sum of the variances of item scores

STANDARD DEVIATION – ALTERNATIVE FORMULA

$$SD = \sqrt{\frac{\Sigma X^2}{N} - M^2}$$

Where: SD is the standard deviation
X are the test scores
N is the number of scores
M is the mean of the test scores

E | CONVERTING PERCENTILES FROM z-SCORES

The look-up table below can be used to quickly convert a z score to an approximate percentile rank.

z score	Percentile	z score	Percentile	z score	Percentile
−6.0	0.0000001%	−1.1	13.57%	1.1	86.43%
−5.0	0.00003%	**−1.0**	**15.87%**	1.2	88.49%
−4.0	0.0032%	−0.9	18.41%	1.3	90.32%
−3.0	**0.13%**	−0.8	21.19%	1.4	91.92%
−2.9	0.19%	−0.7	24.20%	1.5	93.32%
−2.8	0.26%	−0.6	27.43%	1.6	94.52%
−2.7	0.35%	−0.5	30.85%	1.7	95.54%
−2.6	0.47%	−0.4	34.46%	1.8	96.41%
−2.5	0.62%	−0.3	38.21%	1.9	97.13%
−2.4	0.82%	−0.2	42.07%	**2.0**	**97.72%**
−2.3	1.07%	−0.1	46.02%	2.1	98.21%
−2.2	1.39%	**0.0**	**50.00%**	2.2	98.61%
−2.1	1.79%	0.1	53.98%	2.3	98.93%
−2.0	**2.28%**	0.2	57.93%	2.4	99.18%
−1.9	2.87%	0.3	61.79%	2.5	99.38%
−1.8	3.59%	0.4	65.54%	2.6	99.53%
−1.7	4.46%	0.5	69.15%	2.7	99.65%
−1.6	5.48%	0.6	72.57%	2.8	99.74%
−1.5	6.68%	0.7	75.80%	2.9	99.81%
−1.4	8.08%	0.8	78.81%	**3.0**	**99.87%**
−1.3	9.68%	0.9	81.59%	4.0	99.997%
−1.2	11.51%	**1.0**	**84.13%**	5.0	99.99997%

Due to the fact percentiles are not evenly spaced along the bell curve (by definition), you cannot interpolate between scores on the above table. Consequently, if a more precise percentile is needed that is not listed above, the formula for calculating percentiles can be used.

The formula used to convert a z score to a percentile rank is:

$$f(z) = \frac{1}{\sqrt{2p}} e^{\frac{z^2}{2}}$$

where z is the given z score.

F | ASSESSMENT REPORT

DEMOGRAPHIC INFORMATION

Name: Eduardo (Ed) Unclear

Address: 223 Confused Lane
         Coconut Creek, Florida

Phone: 954-969-5555

E-mail: iunclear@hotmail.net

Name of Interviewer: May I. Assessu

D.O.B.: 1/8/1961

Age: 48

Sex: Male

Ethnicity: Hispanic

Date of Interview: 2/22/2009

PRESENTING PROBLEM OR REASON FOR REFERRAL

This 48-year-old married male was self-referred due to high levels of stress. The client reports feeling anxious for the past two years and intermittently depressed for the past seven or eight years. He states that he feels discontent with his marriage and confused about his future. An assessment was conducted to assist in determining diagnosis and course of treatment.

FAMILY BACKGROUND

Mr. Unclear was raised in Miami, Florida. His parents were Cuban refugees, and Mr. Unclear notes that when he was 5 years old, his parents fled Cuba on a fishing boat with him and his two brothers, José, who is two years older, and Juan, who is two years younger. Mr. Unclear comes from an intact family. His father died approximately four years ago of a "heart disorder." He states that his parents were "loving but strict" and notes that his father was "in charge" of the family and would often "take a belt to me." However, he describes both parents as loving and caring and says that they "took care of all my needs." He reports that he and his brothers were always close and that both brothers currently live within 1 mile of his home. He states that his younger brother is married and has two children, and he describes his other brother as single and a "closeted homosexual." His father, he reports, was a bookkeeper and his mother a stay-at-home mom. He and his brothers went to Catholic school, and he states that he tended to be a good student and had the "normal" number of friends.

Mr. Unclear notes that when he was 20 he met his wife Carla in college. They married when he was 21 and quickly had two children, Carlita and Carmen, who are now 27 and 26. Both daughters are college-educated, work in professional jobs and are married. Carlita has two children aged 3 and 4, while Carmen has one child aged 5. He notes that both daughters and their families live close to him. He states that although his marriage was "good" for the first 20 years, in recent years he has found himself feeling unloved and depressed. He wonders if he should remain in the marriage.

SIGNIFICANT MEDICAL/COUNSELING HISTORY

Mr. Unclear states that approximately four years ago he was in a serious car accident that subsequently left him with chronic back pain. Although he takes prescribed medication intermittently for the pain, he states that he mostly tries to "live without drugs." He notes that he often feels fatigued and has trouble sleeping, often sleeping only four hours a night. However, he reports that his medical exam has revealed no apparent medical reason for his fatigue and sleep difficulties. He notes no other significant medical history, although he reports that in the past two years he has had obsessive worry related to fears of dying of a heart attack.

Mr. Unclear notes that after the birth of his second child, his wife needed surgery to repair vaginal tears. He states that since that time she has complained of pain during sex, and their level of intimacy dropped significantly. He notes that he and his wife went to couples therapy for about two months approximately 15 years ago. He feels that counseling did not help, and he notes that it "particularly did nothing to help our sex life."

SUBSTANCE USE AND ABUSE

Mr. Unclear states that he does not smoke cigarettes and occasionally smokes cigars ("I will never smoke a Cuban cigar," he notes). He describes himself as a moderate drinker and states that he has a couple of beers a day but does not tend to drink "hard liquor." He reports taking prescription medication "intermittently" for chronic back pain and he denies the use of illegal substances. He describes his eating habits as "normal."

EDUCATIONAL AND VOCATIONAL HISTORY

Mr. Unclear went to Catholic school in Miami, Florida, and reports that he excelled in math but always had difficulty with reading and spelling. After high school, he went on to college at Miami University, majoring in business administration. After graduating with his bachelor's degree, he obtained a job as an accountant at a major tobacco import company, where he worked for 17 years. During that time he began to work on his master's in business administration but stated he never finished his degree because it was "boring." Approximately eight years ago he changed jobs and obtained employment as an accountant at a local new car company. He states he changed jobs to "make more money."

Mr. Unclear reports that relative to his accounting work, his "books were always perfect," although he went on to note that he was embarrassed by his inability to prepare a well-written report. He reports feeling dissatisfied with his career path and wanting to do something more meaningful with his life. However, he states that "I am probably too old to change careers now."

OTHER PERTINENT INFORMATION

Mr. Unclear states that he is unhappy with his sex life and reports having limited intimacy with his wife. He denies having an extramarital affair but states "I would have one if I met the right person." He notes that he is "just making it" financially, and that it was difficult to support his two children through college. He denies any problems with the law.

MENTAL STATUS

Mr. Unclear was well groomed for the interview, wearing a tailored suit. He was able to maintain appropriate eye contact and was oriented to time, place, and person. During the interview he appeared anxious, often rubbing his hands together. He stated that he often felt fatigued and that he has difficulty sleeping, often sleeping only four hours a night. He described himself as feeling intermittently depressed over the past seven or eight years. He appeared to be above average intellectually and his memory was intact. His judgment and insight seemed good and he appeared motivated for treatment. He states that he sometimes has suicidal thoughts, but denies he has a plan or would ever kill himself. He notes, "This is against my religion." He denies homicidal ideation.

ASSESSMENT RESULTS

Tests used: The Beck Depression Inventory; the Sentence Completion Test, the Kinetic Family Drawing (KFD), the MMPI-II, Rorschach Inkblot Test, the Strong Interest Inventory, Thematic Apperception Test, and the Wide Range Achievement Test (WRAT).

Mr. Unclear obtained a BDI-II score of 24, which places him in the moderate range of depression, and his responses showed some evidence of possible suicidal ideation. The MMPI supports this finding, as it shows a man with moderate to severe depression and mild anxiety who is generally "discontent with the world" and feels a lack of intimacy in his life. It suggests assessing for possible suicidal ideation.

The Rorschach and the TAT show an individual who is grounded in reality and open to testing, as was evidenced by his willingness to readily respond to initial inkblots and TAT cards, his ability to complete stories in the TAT, and the fact that many of his responses were "common" responses. Feelings of depression and hopelessness are evident in a number of responses, including not readily seeing color in many of the responses he made to the "color cards" of the Rorschach and a number of pessimistic stories that generally had depressive endings to them on the TAT.

On the KFD, Mr. Unclear placed his father as an angel in the sky, and included his wife, mother, children, and grandchildren. His mother was standing next to him while his wife was off to the side with the grandchildren. He also placed himself in a chair and when talking about the picture stated, "I'm sitting because my back hurts." The picture showed the client and his family at his mother's house having a Sunday dinner while it rained outside. Rain could be indicative of depressive feelings. A cross was prominent in the background and was larger than most of the people in the picture, which is likely an indication of strong religious beliefs and could also indicate a need to be taken care of.

On the sentence completion test Mr. Unclear made a number of references to missing his father, such as "The thing I think most about is missing my father." He also referenced continual back pain. Finally, he noted discontent with his marriage, such as when he said, "Sex is nonexistent" on the sentence completion.

On the Strong, Mr. Unclear's two highest personality codes were Conventional and Enterprising, respectively. All the other codes were significantly lower. Individuals of the Conventional type are stable, controlled, conservative, sociable, and like to follow instructions. Enterprising individuals are self-confident, adventurous, sociable, have good persuasive skills, and prefer positions of leadership. Careers in business and industry where persuasive skills are important are good choices for these individuals.

On the WRAT4, Mr. Unclear scored at the 86th percentile in math, 75th percentile in reading, 64th percentile in sentence comprehension, and 42nd percentile in spelling, His reading composite score was at the 69th percentile. These results could indicate a possible learning disorder in spelling, although cross-cultural considerations should be taken into account due to the fact that Mr. Unclear was an immigrant to this country at a young age.

DIAGNOSIS

Axis I: 296.22 Major Depression, Single Episode, Moderate
309.28 Rule out: Adjustment Disorder with Mixed Anxiety and Depressed Mood
Axis II: No diagnosis
Axis III: Chronic back pain
Axis IV: Discontent with job; Marital discontent
Axis V: GAF = 45 (Over past year)

SUMMARY AND CONCLUSIONS

Mr. Unclear is a 48-year-old married male who was self-referred due to feelings of depression, anxiety, as well as discontent with his job and his marriage. Mr. Unclear fled from Cuba to Miami, Florida with his parents and two siblings when he was 5 years old. He describes his family as close, and he continues to live near his children, siblings, and mother. His father died approximately four years ago.

He married while in college, and he and his wife subsequently raised two girls who are now in their mid-20s, married and have their own children.

Mr. Unclear finished college with a degree in business and has been working as an accountant over the past 25 years. He reports feeling dissatisfied in his career and states that he wants to do something more meaningful with his life. He also reports marital discord, which he attributes partly to medical problems his wife had after the birth of their second child. These problems, he states, resulted in diminishing sexual relations with his wife.

Mr. Unclear was oriented during the session but appeared anxious and talked about feelings of depression. He noted that he often feels fatigued, has difficulty sleeping, and has fleeting thoughts of suicide, which he states he would not act upon. Recently, he has had obsessive worries about having a heart attack, although there is no medical reason to support his concerns. Chronic back pain due to a car accident a few years ago seems to exacerbate his current feelings of depression.

Throughout testing there were consistent themes of depression, isolation, and hopelessness. This was evidenced by high scores on the BDI-II and the MMPI-II depression scale, as well as specific responses to the Rorschach, TAT cards, the KFD, and the sentence completion.

Discontent with his marriage, sadness about the loss of his father, and chronic pain were some major themes that arose during testing. Testing also revealed a person who is in a field that is a good match for his personality. However, he might be more challenged if given a position with additional responsibilities and leadership skills. Such a change should probably not occur unless Mr. Unclear attains a handle on his depression. Finally, testing also shows a possible learning disability in spelling, although cross-cultural issues may have affected his score.

On a positive note, testing and the clinical interview showed a man who was neatly dressed and open to meeting with this examiner. He has worked hard in his life and is proud of the family he has raised. He was grounded in reality, willing to engage interpersonally, and showed good judgment and insight. He seems to be aware of many of his most pressing concerns and showed some willingness to address them.

RECOMMENDATIONS

1. Counseling, 1 hour a week for depression, possible anxiety, marital discord, and career dissatisfaction.
2. Possible marital counseling with particular focus on sexual relations of the couple.
3. Referral to a physician/psychiatrist for medication, possibly antidepressants.
4. Possible further assessment for learning problems.
5. Long-term consideration of a career move following alleviation of depressive feelings and addressing possible learning problems.
6. Possible orthopedic re-evaluation of back problems.

Sigmund Freud

GLOSSARY

ability test Test that measures what a person can do in the cognitive realm. Achievement and aptitude tests are types of ability tests.

achievement test A type of ability test that measures what one has learned. Types of achievement tests include survey battery tests, diagnostic tests, and readiness tests.

Accreditation Standards of Professional Associations Professional bodies that oversee graduate schools' curriculum and training regarding therapists to ensure standardization. Examples include the American Psychological Association (APA) and the Council for the Accreditation of Counseling and Related Educational Programs (CACREP).

ACT score Created by converting a raw score to a standard score that generally uses a mean of 21 and a standard deviation of 5 for college-bound students. The mean score for all students, including those who are not college-bound, is 18.

age comparison scoring A type of standard score calculated by comparing an individual score to the average score of others who are the same age.

alternate, parallel, or equivalent forms reliability A method for determining reliability by creating two or more

alternate, parallel, or equivalent forms of the same test. These alternate forms mimic one another yet are different enough to eliminate some of the problems found in test-retest reliability (e.g., looking up an answer). In this case, rather than giving the same test twice, the examiner gives the alternate form the second time.

Americans with Disabilities Act (PL 101-336) Law stating that to assure proper test administration, accommodations must be made for individuals with disabilities who are taking tests for employment and that testing must be shown to be relevant to the job in question.

anecdotal information A record of an individual that generally includes behaviors that are consistent or inconsistent. A type of record and personal document.

aptitude test A type of ability test that measures what one is capable of doing. Include: intelligence tests, neuropsychological assessments cognitive ability tests, special aptitude tests, and multiple aptitude tests.

Army Alpha test An instrument created by Robert Yerkes, Lewis Terman, and others during World War I to screen recruits for the military. Generally considered the first modern group test.

assessment A broad array of evaluative procedures that yield information about a person. An assessment may consist of many procedures, including a clinical interview, personality tests, ability tests, and informal assessment.

assessment report The "deliverable" or "end product" of the assessment process. Its purpose is to synthesize an assortment of assessment techniques so that a deeper understanding of the examinee is obtained and recommended courses of action can be offered.

Association for Assessment in Counseling and Education (AACE) A professional counselors' organization dedicated to the "creation, development, production, and use of assessment and diagnostic techniques."

autobiography A procedure that asks an individual to write subjective information that stands out in his or her life. In some ways, the information highlighted in an individual's autobiography is a type of projective test of his or her unconscious mind. A type of record and personal document.

Axis I Mental disorders of the DSM-IV-TR that are considered treatable and often temporary.

Axis II Mental disorders of the DSM-IV-TR that tend to be life-long and resistant to treatment.

Axis III Lists medical conditions of the DSM-IV-TR that cause disorders or may affect treatment.

Axis IV Lists psychosocial and environmental factors of DSM-IV-TR affecting the client.

Axis V The last axis of DSM-IV-TR. It is used to assess the client's overall functioning and based on the client's psychological, social, and occupational functioning. Ranges from very severe dysfunction to superior functioning (0 to 100).

behavior word checklist A procedure that allows an individual to identify those words that best describe kinds of behaviors an individual might typically or atypically exhibit. A type of classification method.

Binet, Alfred Commissioned by the Ministry of Public Education in Paris in 1904 to develop an intelligence test to assist in the integration of "subnormal" children into the schools. His work led to the development of the first modern-day intelligence test.

biographical inventories Provides a detailed picture of the individual from birth. They can be obtained by conducting an involved, structured interview or by having the client answer a series of items on a checklist or respond to a series of questions.

Boston Process Approach A type of flexible battery approach to neuropsychological assessment.

Carl Perkins Act (PL 98-524) Originally passed in 1984 and subsequently amended, this law assures that adults or special groups in need of job training have access to vocational assessment, counseling, and placement. These groups include (a) individuals with disabilities; (b) individuals from economically disadvantaged families, including foster children; (c) individuals preparing for non-traditional fields; (d) single parents, including single pregnant women; (e) displaced homemakers; and (f) individuals with limited English proficiency.

Cattell, James One of the earliest psychologists to use statistical concepts to understand people. His main emphasis

became testing mental functions, and he is known for coining the term "mental test."

Cattell, Raymond Differentiated fluid (innate) intelligence from crystallized (learned) intelligence and attempted to remove cultural bias from intelligence testing.

Civil Rights Acts (1964 and Amendments) Laws requiring that any test used for employment or promotion be shown to be suitable and valid for the job in question. If this is not done, alternative means of assessment must be provided. Differential test cutoffs are not allowed.

class interval Grouping scores from a frequency distribution within a predetermined range in order to create a histogram or frequency polygon.

classification method A type of informal assessment procedure where information is provided about whether an individual possesses certain attributes or characteristics (asking a person to check off those adjectives that seem to best describe him or her). Includes behavior and feeling word checklists.

clinical assessment The process of assessing the client through multiple methods, including the clinical interview, informal assessment techniques, and objective and projective tests.

clinical interview A critical step in the assessment process. Interviews can be structured, unstructured, or semi-structured.

coefficient of determination (shared variance) The underlying commonality that accounts for the relationship between two sets of variables. It is calculated by squaring the correlation coefficient.

cognitive abilities tests Often based on what one has learned in school, these instruments measure a broad range of cognitive abilities and are useful in making predictions about the future (e.g., whether an individual is likely to succeed in college). A type of aptitude test.

competence in the use of tests In accordance with most professional codes of ethics, examiners are required to have adequate training and knowledge before using a test. Some test publishers have a

tiered system to describe the levels of training required to administer their tests.

computer-driven assessment Allowing a computer program to assist in the assessment process and preparation of reports. Some observers believe computer-assisted questioning is at least as reliable as structured interviews and can provide an accurate diagnosis at a low cost.

Conant, James Bryant Harvard president who conceived the idea of the SAT (formerly Scholastic Aptitude Test), which was developed by the Educational Testing Service after World War II. Conant thought that such tests could identify the ability of individuals and ultimately help to equalize educational opportunities.

concurrent validity Evidence that test scores are related to an external source that can be measured at around the same time the test is being given ("here and now" validity). A type of criterion-related validity.

confidentiality An ethical (not legal) obligation to protect the client's right to privacy. There are some instances in which confidentiality should be broken, such as when clients are in danger of harming themselves or someone else.

construct validity Evidence that a test measures a specific concept or trait. Construct validity includes an analysis of a test through one or more of the following methods: experimental design, factor analysis, convergence with other instruments, and/or discrimination with other measures.

content validity Evidence that the test developer adequately surveyed the domain (field) the test is to cover, that test items match that domain, and that test items are accurately weighted for relative importance.

convergent validity A method of demonstrating construct validity by correlating a test with some other well-known measure or instrument.

Corey, Corey, and Callanan's Ethical Decision-Making Model Eight steps that a practitioner should go through when making complex ethical decisions: identifying the problem, identifying the potential issues involved, reviewing the relevant ethical guidelines, knowing relevant laws and regulations, obtaining consultation, considering possible and probable courses of action, listing the consequences of various decisions, and deciding on what appears to be the best course of action.

correlation coefficient The relationship between two sets of scores. Correlation coefficients range from +1 to −1 and generally are reported in decimals of one-hundredths. A positive correlation shows a tendency for scores to be related in the same direction, while a negative correlation indicates an inverse relationship.

criterion referencing A method of scoring in which test scores are compared to a predetermined value or a set criterion.

criterion-related validity The relationship between a test and a standard (external source) to which the test should be related. The external standard may be in the here-and-now (concurrent validity) or a predictor of future criteria (predictive validity).

Cronbach's coefficient alpha A method of measuring internal consistency by calculating test reliability using all the possible split-half combinations. This is done by correlating the scores for each item on the test with the total score on the test and finding the average correlation for all of the items.

cross-cultural sensitivity Awareness of the potential biases of assessment procedures when selecting, administering, and interpreting such procedures, as well as acknowledging the potential effects of age, cultural background, disability, ethnicity, gender, religion, sexual orientation, and socioeconomic status on test administration and test interpretation.

cumulative distribution A method of converting a frequency distribution of scores into cumulative percentages. A bar graph is often generated by placing the class interval scores along the x-axis and the cumulative percentages along the y-axis.

cumulative records File containing information about a client's test scores, grades, behavioral problems, family issues, relationships with others, and other matters. School and workplace records are examples of cumulative records that can add vital information to our understanding of clients. A type of record and personal document.

derived score Score obtained by comparing an individual's score to the norm group by converting his or her raw score to a percentile or standard score such as z-score, T-score, Deviation IQ, stanine, sten score, normal curve equivalent (NCE), college or graduate school entrance exam score (e.g., SAT, GRE, and ACT), or publisher-type score, or by using developmental norms such as age comparison and grade equivalent.

developmental norms Direct comparison of an individual's score to the average scores of others at the same age or grade level. Examples include age comparison and grade equivalent scoring.

Deviation IQ Standard score with a mean of 100 and a standard deviation of 15. As the name implies, these scores are generally used in intelligence testing.

Diagnostic and Statistical Manual, Fourth Edition – Text Revision (DSM-IV-TR) A comprehensive system published by the American Psychiatric Association that provides five axes to assist mental health professionals in diagnosing and treating mental disorders. (See "Axis I, Axis II, Axis III, Axis IV, and Axis V")

diagnostic test Test that assesses problem areas of learning. Often used to assess learning disabilities. Generally classified as a type of achievement test.

direct observation A type of environmental assessment in which the examiner visits the classroom, workplace, or other setting in an effort to obtain additional information not usually retrieved in the office.

discriminant validity A method of demonstrating construct validity by correlating a test with other dissimilar instruments to ensure lack of a relationship.

Division 5 of the American Psychological Association A professional organization for psychologists that promotes "research and practical application of psychological assessment, evaluation, measurement, and statistics."

environmental assessment A naturalistic and systems approach to assessment in which practitioners collect information about clients from their home, work, or school environments. Includes direct observation, conducting a situational assessment, applying a sociometric assessment, or using an environmental assessment instrument. A type of informal assessment procedure.

environmental assessment instrument A type of environmental assessment in which any of a number of instruments are used in conjunction with simple observation to obtain additional information about a client.

equivalent forms reliability (see "alternate forms")

Esquirol, Jean Used language to identify different levels of intelligence while working in the French mental asylums; his work led to the concept of verbal intelligence.

ethical code Professional guidelines for appropriate behavior and guidance on how to respond under certain conditions. Each professional group has its own ethical code, including guidelines for counselors, psychologists, social workers, marriage and family therapists, psychiatrists, human service professionals, and others.

event and time sampling Observing a targeted behavior for a set amount of time. A type of observation.

event sampling A type of observation in which one is observing a specific behavior with no regard to time.

experimental design validity Using experimentation to show that a test measures a specific concept or construct. A type of construct validity.

feeling word checklist A type of classification method that allows an individual to identify those words that best describe kinds of feelings an individual might typically or atypically exhibit.

face validity Superficial observation that a test appears to cover the correct content or domain. This is not an actual form of validity since the appearance of test items may or may not accurately reflect the domain.

factor analysis This common statistical technique allows researchers to analyze large data sets to determine patterns and calculate which variables have a high degree of commonality. Therefore it is a method of demonstrating construct validity by statistically examining the relationship between subscales and the larger construct. It is also frequently used in multiple aptitude tests to help developers determine differences and similarities between subtests.

false positives and negatives When an instrument incorrectly classifies someone as having an attribute they do not have (false positive) or not having an attribute, which in fact, they do have (false negative).

FERPA Family Educational Rights and Privacy Act of 1974 (also known as the Buckley Amendment), which affirms the right of all individuals to gain access to their school records, including test records.

fixed battery approach to neuropsychological assessment Using a uniform (standard) set of instruments for all clients who require a neuropsychological evaluation.

flexible battery approach to neuropsychological assessment Tailoring the instruments and techniques specific to each client who require a neuropsychological evaluation.

forensic evaluations A specialized type of an assessment to be used in a court of law which often requires the author to testify as an expert witness. The assessing therapist frequently collects information from interviews, specific and specialized testing, and the reviewing of supplemental records. Professional organizations offer particular endorsements for this.

Freedom of Information Act This law assures the right of individuals to access their federal records, including test records. Most states have similar laws that assure access to state records.

frequency distribution A method of understanding test scores by ordering a set of scores from high to low and listing the corresponding frequency of each score across from it.

frequency polygon A method of converting a frequency distribution of scores into a line graph. After combining scores by class interval, the class ntervals are placed along the x-axis and the frequency of scores along the y-axis.

GAF Scale See "Axis V"

Galton, Sir Francis Examined relationship of sensorimotor responses to intelligence. He hypothesized that individuals

who had a quicker reaction time and stronger gripstrength were superior intellectually.

Gardner, Howard Vehemently opposed current constructs of intelligence measurement and developed his own theory of multiple intelligences asserting that there are eight or nine intelligences: verbal-linguistic, mathematical-logical, musical, visual-spatial, bodily-kinesthetic, interpersonal, intrapersonal, naturalist, and existential intelligence.

generosity error Error that occurs when an individual rates another person inaccurately because he or she identifies with the person being rated.

genogram A map of an individual's family tree that may include the family history of illnesses, mental disorders, substance use, expectations, relationships, cultural issues, and other concerns relevant to counseling. Special symbols may be used to assist in creating this map. A type of record and personal document.

grade equivalent scoring A type of standard score calculated by comparing an individual's score to the average score of others at the same grade level.

Griggs v. Duke Power Company Asserted that tests used for hiring and advancement at work must show that they can predict job performance for all groups

Guilford, J. P. Developed a multifactor/multidimensional model of intelligence based on 180 factors. His three-dimensional model can be represented as a cube and involves three kinds of cognitive ability: operation, content, and product.

Hall, G. S. Worked with Wundt and eventually set up his own experimental lab at John Hopkins University. Became a mentor to other great American psychologists and was the founder and first president of the American Psychological Association in 1892.

halo effect Error that occurs when the overall impression of an individual clouds the rating of that person in one or more select areas.

Health Insurance Portability and Accountability Act (HIPAA) Ensures the privacy of client records, including testing records, and the sharing of such information. In general, HIPAA restricts the amount of information that can be

shared without client consent and allows clients to have access to their records, except for process notes used in counseling.

high stakes testing. The term used to describe the pressure placed on examinees, teachers, administrators, and others as a result of the major decisions that are made from the use of tests, usually national standardized tests such as the SATs and those used as the result of No Child Left Behind.

histogram A method of converting a frequency distribution of scores into a bar graph. After combining scores by class interval, the class intervals are placed along the x-axis and the frequency of scores along the y-axis.

item response theory An extension of classical test theory that allows for more detailed analyses of individual test items. Tools such as the item characteristic curve allow in depth examination of an item's discrimination and difficulty.

Individualized Education Plan (IEP) PL94-142 states that children who are identified as having a learning disability will be provided a school team that will create an Individualized Education Plan to assist the student with his or her learning problem(s).

Individuals with Disabilities Education Improvement Act (IDEIA) (Expansion of PL 94-142) This legislative act assures the right of students to be tested, at the school system's expense, if they are suspected of having a disability that interferes with learning. These students must be given accommodations for their disability and taught within the "least restrictive environment," which often is a regular classroom.

informal assessment instruments Assessment instruments that are often developed by the user and are specific to the testing situation. All of these instruments can be used to assess broad areas of ability and personality attributes in a variety of settings. Types of informal assessment instruments include observation, rating scales, classification methods, environmental assessment, records and personal documents, and performance-based assessment.

informed consent Principle that individuals being assessed should give their permission for the assessment after they are given information concerning such items as the nature and purposes of the assessment, fees, involvement by others in the assessment process (e.g., teachers, therapists), and the limits of confidentiality.

intellectual and cognitive functioning Tests that measure a broad range of cognitive functioning in the following domains: general intelligence, mental retardation, giftedness, and changes in overall cognitive functioning. Includes intelligence testing and neuropsychological. Types of aptitude tests.

intelligence quotient Concept developed by Lewis Terman, who divided mental age by chronological age and multiplied the quotient by 100 to derive a score that he called "IQ."

intelligence test, individual tests that assess a broad range of cognitive capabilities that generally results in an "IQ" score. Often used to identify mental retardation, giftedness, learning disabilities, and general cognitive functioning. A type of aptitude test.

interest inventories Tests that measure likes and dislikes as well as one's personality orientation toward the world of work. Generally used in career counseling. A type of personality test.

internal consistency A method of determining reliability of an instrument by looking within the test itself, or not going "outside of the test" to determine a reliability estimate as is done with test-retest or parallel forms reliability. Some types of internal consistency reliability include split-half (or odd-even), Cronbach's Coefficient Alpha, and Kuder-Richardson.

interval scale A scale of measurement in which there are equal distances between measurements but no absolute zero reference point.

invasion of privacy All tests invade one's privacy, but concerns about invasion of privacy are lessened if the client has given informed consent, has the ability to accept or refuse testing, and knows the limits of confidentiality.

Jaffee v. Redmond In this case, the Supreme Court upheld the right of a licensed social worker to keep her case records confidential. Describing the social worker as a "therapist"

and "psychotherapist," the ruling will likely protect all licensed therapists in federal courts and may affect all licensed therapists who have privileged communication.

journals and diaries Procedures that allow individuals to describe themselves and can provide valuable insight into self, or to a clinician, by revealing unconscious drives and desires and by uncovering patterns that highlight issues in a client's life. Types of record and personal documents.

Jung, Carl Developed a list of 156 words (word association) to which subjects were asked to respond as quickly as possible. Depending on the response and the answer time, Jung believed he could identify complexes. He also created the personality type construct that is used in the Myers-Briggs Type Inventory.

Kraeplin, Emil Developed a crude word association test to study schizophrenia in the 1880s.

Kuder-Richardson A method of calculating internal consistency by using all the possible split-half combinations. This is done by correlating the scores for each item on the test with the total score on the test and finding the average correlation for all of the items.

Likert-type scale Sometimes called graphic scales, this kind of rating scale contains a number of items that are being rated on the same theme and are anchored by both numbers and a statement that correspond to the numbers.

mean A measure of central tendency that is calculated by adding all of the scores and dividing by the total number of scores. It is the arithmetic average of the scores.

measures of central tendency Indicators of what is occurring in the midrange or "center" of a group of scores. Three measures of central tendency are the mean, median, and mode.

measures of variability Indicators of how much scores vary in a distribution. Three types of measures of variability are the range, quartile range, and the standard deviation.

median A measure of central tendency which is the middle score, or the score for which 50% of scores fall above and 50% fall below. In a skewed curve or

skewed distribution of test scores, the median is generally the most accurate measure of central tendency since it is not affected by unusually high or low scores.

Mental Measurements Yearbook by **Buros** A sourcebook of reviews of more than 2000 different tests, instruments, or screening devices. Most large universities carry this in hardbound copy and/or online.

mental status exam A portion of the assessment and written report that addresses the client's appearance and behavior, emotional state, thought components, and cognitive functioning.

Miner, J. B. Developed one of first group interest inventories in 1922 to assist large groups of high school students in selecting an occupation.

mode A measure of central tendency which is the score that occurs more often than any other.

moral principles of ethical-decision making model six moral principles often identified as important in making thorny ethical decisions: autonomy, nonmaleficence, beneficence, justice, fidelity, and veracity.

multiple aptitude tests Tests that measure many aspects of ability. Often useful in determining the likelihood of success in a number of vocations. A type of aptitude test.

Murray, Henry Developed the Thematic Apperception Test (TAT), which asks a subject to view a number of standard pictures and create a story to explain the situation as he or she best understands it. This test is based on his needs-press theory.

National Assessment of Educational Progress (NAEP) Sometimes called "the nationas report card," these assessment instruments allows states to compare progress in achievement to other states around the country.

negatively skewed curve A set of test scores where the majority fall at the upper or positive end. It is said to be a negatively skewed curve or distribution because a few "negative" or low-end scores have stretched or skewed the curve to the left.

neuropsychological assessment A specialized form of assessment that evaluates the central nervous system for functioning. It is frequently applied after a traumatic brain injury, illnesses that may have caused brain damage, or with elderly that may be experiencing changes in the brain.

No Child Left Behind (NCLB) Act A federal act that requires all states to have a plan in place to show how, by the year 2014, all students will have obtained proficiency in reading/language arts and math. The act has caused states to create or identify achievement tests whose purpose is to assess all students and ensure they are meeting the minimum standards.

nominal scale A scale of measurement in which numbers are arbitrarily assigned to represent different categories or variables. The only math that can be applied to these numbers is calculation of the mode.

nonverbal intelligence tests Intelligence tests that rely on little or no verbal expression.

norm referencing A method of scoring in which test scores are compared to a group of other scores called the norm group.

normal curve A bell-shaped curve showing the usual frequency distribution of values of measured human traits and other natural phenomena.

normal curve equivalents (NCE) scores Frequently used in the educational community, this is a form of standard scoring that has 99 equal units along a bell-shaped curve, with a mean of 50 and a standard deviation of 21.06.

numerical scale A form of rating in which a statement or question is followed by a choice of numbers arranged from high to low along a number line.

objective personality testing Paper-and-pencil tests, often in multiple-choice or true/false formats, that assess various aspects of personality. Often used to increase client insight, to identify psychopathology, and to assist in treatment planning. A type of personality test.

observation Observing behaviors of an individual in order to develop a deeper understanding of one or more specific behaviors. (e.g., observing a student's acting-out behavior in class or assessing a client's ability to perform eye-hand coordination tasks to determine potential vocational placements). Includes time sampling, event sampling, and time and event sampling. A type of informal assessment.

ordinal scale A scale of measurement in which the magnitude or rank order is implied; however, the distance between measurements is unknown.

parallel forms reliability (see "alternate forms")

Parsons, Frank Leader of the vocational counseling movement.

percentiles A method of comparing raw scores to a norm group by calculating the percentage of people falling below an obtained score, with ranges from 1 to 99, and 50 being the mean.

performance-based assessment. The evaluation of an individual using a variety of informal assessment procedures that are often based on real world responsibilities. This kind of assessment is not highly loaded for cognitive skills, and these procedures are sometimes seen as an alternative to standardized testing (e.g, a portfolio). Type of informal assessment.

personality testing Tests in the affective realm used to assess habits, temperament, likes and dislikes, character, and similar behaviors. Types of personality tests include interest inventories, objective personality tests, and projective personality tests.

Piaget, Jean Approached intelligence from a developmental perspective by observing how children's cognitions were shaped as they grew. He identified four stages of cognitive development: sensorimotor, preoperational, concrete operational, and formal operational. He also believed that cognitive development is adaptive, and he conceived the concepts of assimilation and accommodation.

Portfolio A type of performance-based assessment in which a number of items are collected and eventually shown to such individuals such as potential employer's or potential colleges as an indication of the applicant's ability. Sometimes used in lieu of standardized testing.

positively skewed curve A set of test scores in which the majority fall at the lower or negative end. It is said to be a positively skewed curve or distribution because a few "positive" or high-end scores have stretched or skewed the curve to the right.

practicality When selecting a test, one of the cornerstones of test worthiness is practicality. Practical concerns include time, cost, format, readability, and ease of administration, scoring, and interpretation.

predictive validity Evidence that test scores are able to predict a future criterion or standard. A type of criterion-related validity.

privileged communication The legal right to maintain privacy of a conversation. The privilege belongs to the client, and only the client can waive that privilege.

projective personality tests Tests that present a stimulus to which individuals can respond. Personality factors are interpreted based on the individual's response. Often used to identify psychopathology and to assist in treatment planning. A type of personality test.

proper diagnosis Due to the delicate nature of diagnoses, ethical codes stress that professionals should be particularly careful when deciding which assessment techniques to use in forming a diagnosis for a mental disorder.

publisher-type scores Created by test developers who generate their own unique standard score that employs a mean and standard deviation of the publisher's choice.

quartile range Provides the range of the middle 50% of scores around the median. Because it eliminates the top and bottom quartiles, the quartile range is most useful with skewed curves because it offers a more representative picture of where a large percentage of the scores fall.

quincunx Also known as Galton's board, it is a board with protruding pins or nails whereupon balls dropped will fall along the bell or normal curve.

range The simplest measure of variability is the range, which is calculated by subtracting the lowest score from the highest score and adding 1.

rank order A rating scale providing a series of statements that the respondent is asked to place from highest to lowest based on his or her preferences.

rating scales Scales developed to assess any of a number of attributes of the examinee. Can be rated by the examinee or someone who knows the examinee well. Some commonly used rating scales include numerical scales, Likert-type scales (graphic scales), semantic differential scales, and rank-order scales. A type of informal as sessment.

ratio scale A scale of measurement that has a meaningful zero point and equal intervals and thus can be manipulated by all mathematical principles.

raw score An untreated score before manipulation or processing to make it a standard score, as must be done for all norm-referenced tests. Raw scores alone tell us little, if anything, about how a person has done on a test. We must take an individual's raw score and do something to it to give it meaning.

readiness tests Tests that measure one's readiness for moving ahead in school. Often used to assess readiness to enter kindergarten or first grade. A type of achievement test.

records and personal documents Assessing behaviors, values and beliefs of an individual by examining such items as autobiographies, diaries, personal journals, genograms, or school records. A type of informal assessment.

release of test data Test data should be released to others only if the client has signed a release form. The release of such data is generally granted only to individuals who can adequately interpret the test data, and professionals should assure that those who receive such data do not misuse the information.

reliability The degree to which test scores are free from errors of measurement, also, the capacity of an instrument to provide consistent results. (see test-retest, alternative forms, and internal consistency).

Rorschach, Herman A student of Carl Jung, he created the Rorschach Inkblot test by splattering ink onto sheets of paper and folding them in half. He believed the interpretation of an individual's reactions to these forms could tell volumes about the individual's unconscious life.

SAT-type scores Standard score that has a standard deviation of 100 and a mean of 500 for each section of the exam.

scales of measurement Ways of defining the attributes of numbers and how they can be manipulated. The four types of measurement scales are nominal, ordinal, interval, and ratio.

scatterplot A graph of two sets of test scores used to visually display the relationship or correlation. If the dots are plotted closer together, the correlation is moving toward a positive or negative 1. If the dots are spread out or completely random, the correlation is closer to zero.

Section 504 of the Rehabilitation Act This act applies to all federally funded programs receiving financial assistance and was established to prevent discrimination based on disability.

semantic differential A rating scale that provides a statement followed by one or more pairs of words that reflect opposing traits. A number line may or may not be associated with the dichotomous pairs of words.

semi-structured interview Uses prescribed items and thereby allows the examiner to obtain the necessary information within a relatively short amount of time. However, this kind of interview also gives leeway to the examiner should the client need to "drift" during the interview process.

Sequin, Edouard Worked with mentally retarded persons and developed the form board to increase his patients' motor control and sensory discrimination. This was the forerunner to performance IQ.

single aptitude tests See *special aptitude tests.*

situational tests A type of environmental assessment used to examine how an individual is likely to respond in a contrived but natural situation. An example of this type of procedure is when a potential doctoral student counsels a role-play client.

skewed curve A set of test scores that do not fall along the normal curve.

sociometric instruments A kind of environmental assessment that identifies the relative position of an individual within a group. This type of instrument is often used when one wants to determine the dynamics of individuals within a group, organization, or institution.

Spearman, Charles Edward Believed in a two-factor approach to intelligence that included a general factor (*g*) and a specific factor (*s*), both of which he considered important in understanding intelligence.

Spearman-Brown formula A mathematical formula that can be used with split-half or odd-even reliability estimates to increase the accuracy, which is impaired because of the shortening (splitting in half) of the test.

special aptitude tests Tests that measure one aspect of ability. Often useful in determining the likelihood of success in a vocation (e.g., a mechanical aptitude test to determine success as a mechanic). A type of aptitude test.

split-half or odd-even reliability This method of internal consistency reliability splits the test in half and correlates the scores of one half of the test with the other half. Hence, it requires only one form and one administration of the test.

standard deviation A measure of variability that describes how scores vary around the mean. In all normal curves the percentage of scores between standard deviation units are the same; hence, the standard deviation combined with the mean can tell us a great deal about a set of test scores.

standard error of estimate The range of scores we would expect a person's score to fall on an instrument based on his or her score from a previous known test. The equation allows us to use the score on instrument X to predict a range of scores on instrument Y.

standard error of measurement The range of scores where we would expect a person's score to fall if he or she took the instrument over and over again—in other words, where a "true" score might lie. It is calculated by taking the square root of 1 minus the reliability and multiplying that number by the standard deviation of the desired score.

standards for responsible testing practices Any of a number of standards developed to help guide practitioner's in the proper use of tests and inform test users of their rights (see list of standards, Table 2.1)

standard scores Scores derived by converting an individual's raw score to a new score that has a new mean and new standard deviation. Standard scores are generally used to make test results easier for the examinee to interpret.

stanines Derived from the term "standard nines," this is a standardized score frequently used in schools. Often used with achievement tests, stanines have a mean of 5 and a standard deviation of 2, and range from 1 to 9.

sten scores Derived from the name "standard ten," a standard score that is commonly used on personality inventories and questionnaires. Stens have a mean of 5.5 and a standard deviation of 2.

Strong, Edward Led a team of researchers in the 1920s to develop the Strong Vocational Interest Blank. The test is now known as the Strong Interest Inventory and is still one of the most popular interest inventories ever created.

structured interview An interview in which the examinee is asked to respond to a set of pre-established items. This is often done verbally, although sometimes clients can respond to written items.

survey battery tests Paper-and pencil tests, usually given in school settings, that measure broad content areas. Often used to assess progress in school. A type of achievement test.

T-score A type of standard score that can be easily converted from a z-score. T-scores have a mean of 50 and a standard deviation of 10 and are generally used with personality tests.

Terman, Lewis Professor at Stanford University who analyzed the Binet and Simon scale and made a number of revisions to create the Stanford-Binet intelligence test that is still used today. Terman was the first to incorporate in his test the ratio of chronological age and mental age, calling it the "intelligence quotient" or "IQ."

test administration Tests should be administered appropriately as defined by the way they were established and standardized. Alterations to this process

should be noted and interpretations of test data adjusted if conditions were not ideal.

test scoring and interpretation The process of examining tests and making judgments about test data. Professionals should reflect on how issues of test worthiness, including the reliability, validity, cross-cultural fairness, and practicality of the test, might affect the results.

test security Professionals have the responsibility to make reasonable efforts to assure the integrity of test content and the security of the test itself. Professionals should not duplicate tests or change test material without the permission of the publisher.

test worthiness Determined by an objective analysis of a test in four critical areas: (1) *validity:* whether or not it measures what it is supposed to measure; (2) *reliability:* whether or not the score an individual receives on a test is an accurate measure of his or her true score; (3) *cross-cultural fairness:* whether or not the score the individual obtains is a true reflection of the individual and not a reflection of cultural bias inherent in the test, and (4) *practicality*: whether or not it makes sense to use a test in a particular situation.

test-retest reliability Giving the test twice to the same group of people and then correlating the scores of the first test with those of the second test to determine the reliability of the instrument.

tests A subset of assessment techniques that yield scores based on the gathering of collected data.

Thorndike, Edward Believed that tests could be given in a format that was more reliable than the previous methods. His work culminated with the development of the Stanford Achievement Test in 1923.

Thurstone, Louis Developed a multifactor approach or model of intelligence that included seven primary factors: verbal meaning, number ability, word fluency,

perception speed, spatial ability, reasoning, and memory.

time sampling A form of observation in which behaviors are noted during a set duration of time.

unstructured interview Interview in which the examiner does not have a pre-established list of items or questions to which the client can respond; instead, client responses to examiner inquiries establish the direction for follow-up questioning.

validity The degree to which all of the accumulated evidence supports the intended interpretation of test scores for the intended purpose. Validity is a unitary concept that attempts to answer the question, How well does a test measure what it's supposed to measure? (see content validity; criterion-related validity, and construct validity).

Vernon, Philip Believed that subcomponents of intelligence could be added in a hierarchical manner to get a score for a cumulative (g) factor. Many of today's intelligence tests continue to use this concept.

Woodworth's Personal Data Sheet An instrument with 116 items developed to screen World War I recruits for their susceptibility to mental health problems. It is considered the precursor of all modern-day personality inventories.

Wundt, Wilhelm Developed one of the first psychological laboratories. He also set out to create "a new domain of science" that he called physiological psychology, which later became known as psychology.

Yerkes, Robert President of the American Psychological Association during World War I, he chaired a special committee designed to screen new recruits. The committee developed the Army Alpha test.

z-score The most fundamental standard score, which is created by converting an individual's raw score to a new score that has a mean of 0 and a standard deviation of 1.

INDEX